MW01010257

LOST SOULS

Lost Souls

SOVIET DISPLACED PERSONS AND THE BIRTH OF THE COLD WAR

SHEILA FITZPATRICK

PRINCETON UNIVERSITY PRESS

PRINCETON & OXFORD

Published by Princeton University Press
41 William Street, Princeton, New Jersey 08540
99 Banbury Road, Oxford OX2 6JX

press.princeton.edu

Library of Congress Cataloging-in-Publication Data

Names: Fitzpatrick, Sheila, author.
Title: Lost souls : Soviet displaced persons and the birth of the Cold War / Sheila Fitzpatrick.
Description: Princeton, New Jersey : Princeton University Press, [2024] | Includes bibliographical references and index.
Identifiers: LCCN 2024011739 (print) | LCCN 2024011740 (ebook) | ISBN 9780691230023 (hardback) | ISBN 9780691230030 (ebook)
Subjects: LCSH: United Nations Relief and Rehabilitation Administration. | International Refugee Organization. | World War, 1939–1945—Refugees— Soviet Union. | World War, 1939-1945—Forced repatriation. | Cold War. | Communism and international relations. | United States—Foreign relations— Soviet Union. | Soviet Union—Foreign relations—United States. | BISAC: HISTORY / Russia / General | POLITICAL SCIENCE / Political Ideologies / Communism, Post-Communism & Socialism
Classification: LCC D809.S65 F58 2024 (print) | LCC D809.S65 (ebook) | DDC 940.53/1450947—dc23/eng/20240613
LC record available at https://lccn.loc.gov/2024011739
LC ebook record available at https://lccn.loc.gov/2024011740

British Library Cataloging-in-Publication Data is available

Editorial: Priya Nelson and Emma Wagh
Production Editorial: Kathleen Cioffi
Jacket: Katie Osborne
Production: Danielle Amatucci
Publicity: Alyssa Sanford and Carmen Jimenez

Jacket images: INTERFOTO / Alamy Stock Photo

This book has been composed in Arno

Printed in the United States of America

10 9 8 7 6 5 4 3 2 1

CONTENTS

This is a book about refugees, thus necessarily a story involving suffering and loss. But the "displaced persons" (DPs) from the Soviet Union and elsewhere who found themselves in central Europe at the end of the Second World War score well on any comparative scale of displacement. They were comfortably housed, fed, and clothed by international agencies. Medical and child care was available. No civil war raged around them; no armed men invaded their camps. They could work or not, as they chose. They could go to school and university. Abundant sporting and cultural events were organized in the camps, which were run by administrations elected by the DPs themselves, generally of the same nationality. The DPs' displacement lasted, for the most part, only five to seven years before they were resettled via a process in which they had some choice: Slavic and Baltic DPs mainly settled in First World countries, Zionist Jews in Palestine.

This was in striking contrast to the fate of virtually all other groups of twentieth-century refugees, including Jews fleeing Nazi Germany in the 1930s, who found many doors closed to them, and Palestinians, the DPs' contemporaries in misfortune in the late 1940s.

The contrast is no less striking if we turn to the late twentieth and twenty-first centuries, notable for the millions of refugees in Africa and Asia displaced by decolonization and the accompanying wars of independence and later by war, political turmoil, natural disasters, and climate catastrophe. Every night, TV news programs show us the latest images of desperate people picking through the rubble of their ruined homes, congregating in vast dusty tent cities under the blazing sun, or clinging to small unseaworthy boats shipwrecked as they tried to cross the Mediterranean, the Pacific Ocean, or the English Channel in a vain search for refuge.

As of May 2023, the United Nations refugee authority had 30 million people under its care, but that was less than a third of an estimated 110 million people forcibly displaced. Many countries, including Australia and much of Europe, have turned strongly against "asylum seekers," offering a cold reception to all who try to cross their sovereign borders—with the sole exception of Ukrainians fleeing the country after the Russian attack in 2022.

Back in 1948, when the Palestinians in the Middle East and the DPs in Europe constituted the two refugee groups of most concern to the fledgling United Nations, there were seven hundred thousand Palestinians in the Middle East and a million displaced persons in Europe under the care of international refugee organizations. By 2023, when the DPs and their children and grandchildren had long become Americans, Canadians, Israelis, or Australians, the number of Palestinian refugees had risen to six million (before the Gaza War and a new round of displacement), with no solution to their plight in view after more than seventy years.

The DP history told in this book is an anomaly in the annals of refugee management: a success story. What explains this remarkable success? Was there something about these refugees that made their plight comparatively easy to resolve? Was that resolution the result of luck, or of clever diplomatic and political management? It would be nice to think that, just occasionally, international cooperation can work and good intentions triumph. But outcomes may also flow from unanticipated side effects of intentions that are not particularly benign. This book offers an explanation for the successful resolution of the DP problem after the Second World War. Readers will have to decide for themselves if there is an encouraging moral lesson to be drawn.

Introduction

AS THE WAR ENDED, with Soviet troops occupying east Germany and British and American occupying the western part of the country, one of the most immediate problems was what to do with the hordes of people—a total of up to ten million Allied troops, prisoners of war, German expellees from Eastern Europe, forced laborers and refugees from Eastern Europe, in addition to the normal German population—milling about.[1] The displaced civilians included survivors of Nazi concentration camps and forced laborers brought to Germany during the war, often against their will, from the occupied territories of Eastern and Western Europe. But among them were also Soviet and East European citizens who had retreated westward with the Germans at the end of the war, as well as others who continued to stream out of Eastern Europe after the Allied victory. On the military side, several million Soviet soldiers had ended the war as prisoners in German POW camps. Another substantial group of former Soviet soldiers, recruited from those same camps during the war to fight against the Soviets under German command, found themselves interned after the war, along with the German troops, in Allied camps for enemy POWs.

Sorting all this out was a task of formidable complexity. The short-term solution was to register the civilians, and later the released POWs, as "displaced persons" (quickly shortened to "DPs"—"di-pi" in all languages), delouse and feed them, and put them in camps to await repatriation. But it soon became clear that many DPs, especially from the Soviet Union, were unwilling to repatriate. This created a major diplomatic problem that was to be a bone of contention between the Soviet Union and its wartime Allies, Britain and the United States, in the first years of the Cold War. The Soviets demanded "their" people back; the Western Allies prevaricated, tacitly declining after the first months to cooperate. In 1947, the Allies decided on a solution for the disposal of the unrepatriable "hard core" of about a million DPs from the Soviet Union and Eastern Europe: they were to be resettled outside Europe in whatever countries would take them, which turned out to be primarily in North America, Australasia, South America, and (for Jewish DPs) the new state of Israel. The Soviet Union was outraged at what it regarded as the "theft" of its citizens by labor-hungry capitalists.

In this book, I tell the story of the "DP question" that confronted the Allies at the end of the Second World War and its resolution, primarily through resettlement, in the late 1940s and early '50s. It is, on the one hand, a story of governments and diplomacy, partly fought out in the newly created United Nations, with the Soviet Union and its Eastern European supporters increasingly at odds with the United States, Britain, and the countries of Western Europe. This story starts at the war's end with what seemed to be an unproblematic concerted Allied effort to return all prisoners of war and forced laborers to the countries from which they came; traces the breakdown of the wartime alliance and the emergence of the Cold War; and ends with the successful implementation of a very ambitious, largely American-financed resettlement program, whose budget the US Congress would never have approved had it not seen the DPs in Cold War terms, namely, as victims of communism.

Conflict over displaced persons was a relatively minor issue in the developing antagonisms of the Cold War but one on which Soviet sensitivities and feeling of grievance were particularly pronounced. It was humiliating, in the first place, that so many Soviet DPs refused to repatriate. To be sure, most of the refuseniks came not from the "old" (pre-1939) Soviet Union but from the territories of the Baltic, Western Ukraine, and Belorussia unwillingly incorporated into the Soviet Union in 1939 as a result of the Nazi-Soviet Pact. As Moscow pretended there was no difference between the two groups, however, its spokesmen could scarcely point this out. Like the Marshall Plan for postwar reconstruction of Western Europe, DP resettlement was seen by the Soviets as an example of indecent amounts of capitalist money being thrown around with the intention of damaging the Soviet Union. But the resettlement of Soviet DPs was an even more bitter blow, since in Soviet eyes it involved the illegal appropriation of Soviet property (its citizens).

Running in parallel to the great power story is the story of the displaced persons themselves, from arrival in the camps to departure to various destinations a few years later. DPs have often been described as "pawns of fate," people who had lost control over their destiny and were at the mercy of the vicissitudes of war and then of great power diplomacy. It is a poignant image, and one that appealed to DPs and their children in retrospect, but in fact it is only a partial truth. What happened in the real world is different not only from the story told in institutional archives but also from the story told in memoirs. The closer one looks at DP life in (and out of) the camps, the more striking is the degree of agency, both collective and individual, that the DPs exercised.[2]

Refusing to repatriate was the first great exercise of agency, but that was only the visible tip of the iceberg. DPs were registered by name, age, and nationality—but these were essentially what the DPs themselves said they were: the Allies had no means of checking, any more than they could check an individual DP's claims to be single and not to have collaborated with the Germans during the war. It was collective DP pressure that forced the Allies, against their initial intentions, to allow individual DP camps to assume national identities, and subsequently to accept first "Jewish" and later "Ukrainian" as nationalities. It was individual DPs who decided whether or not to live in the camps (many simply collected their rations there and lived in towns), whether or not to work (it was allowed but not mandated) or continue their education (free tuition at German universities was on offer), or whether, if female, to take advantages of the camps' mini–welfare states and have babies. Once the resettlement program got under way, with different national selection committees open for applications, it was up to the DPs to decide where to try their luck.

Those two parallel stories—great power diplomacy and DP agency—could be told of all the "hard core" DPs left under Western Allied control after the war's end and the large-scale repatriation to various countries that followed in the first months. That would include Poles (the largest group), Jews (mainly from Poland), Yugoslavs, Czechs, and contingents from all the other East European countries, as well as DPs of Soviet origin. But this book is specifically about *Soviet* DPs—or, more precisely, the DPs the Soviet claimed as their own. That group included not only citizens of the pre-1939 Soviet Union—who, by Soviet law, possessed an official nationality such as Russian, Ukrainian, Belorussian, Georgian, Jewish, Tatar, or Kalmyk, in addition to their shared Soviet citizenship—but also residents of the territories incorporated into the Soviet Union under the Nazi-Soviet Pact, namely Latvians, Lithuanians, and Estonians from the previously independent Baltic states; West Ukrainians and West Belorussians who had formerly been citizens of Poland; and even some Bessarabians who had formerly been citizens of Rumania.

The Soviet DPs had several characteristics that make them particularly fruitful objects of study. First, they were the subject of an "ownership" struggle between the Soviet Union and the Allies that was one of the foundational conflicts of the Cold War. Second, individual Soviet DPs often went under false identities (Polish, Yugoslav, stateless Russian, and so on) to avoid discovery and forced repatriation. Deceptive practices, always of interest to social historians, are treated in this book as a significant form of DP agency, tacitly condoned by the Western authorities but initiated by the DPs themselves.

The Allies often used "Russian" as a synonym for "Soviet" in a DP context. But the Soviet Union was a multinational state (though with Russian as the lingua franca), whose inhabitants not only held Soviet citizenship but were also classified by nationality. Among Soviet DPs, Russians-by-nationality were only a minority, although a substantial one. To complicate the matter further, Soviet Russians were not the only Russians in the postwar DP population: there were also "stateless" Russians, émigrés who had left Russia after the 1917 revolution and lived in Paris, Berlin, Prague, or Belgrade ever since. The émigrés initially often had difficulty gaining official acceptance as DPs (not least because of suspicion of collaboration with the Nazis), but these were later smoothed over. For a Soviet Russian, a popular way of avoiding repatriation was to declare oneself a stateless Russian émigré. The Russian émigrés, therefore, have to be a part of our story.

Of the Soviet Union's many nationalities, Ukrainians and Belorussians were overrepresented among DPs, largely because the places they had lived were closest to the West, had come under the longest wartime occupation by the Germans, and consequently had supplied the largest number of wartime forced laborers (in addition to those who departed voluntarily with the retreating Germans at the end of the war.) Many of the Ukrainian DPs were in fact "Polish Ukrainians" or "West Ukrainians," not Soviet citizens before 1939; but, as this was a category that the Western Allies generally regarded as nonrepatriable to the Soviet Union, "Soviet Ukrainians" (Central and East Ukrainians from prewar Soviet Ukrainian republic) also claimed it to avoid repatriation. The Ukrainian theme—including the subcategory of "Cossack" favored by many of the most militant Ukrainian-speaking anti-Soviet groups—is a complex and important part of this book's story.

DPs from the Baltic states (Latvians, Lithuanians, and Estonians) were another large DP group that the Soviets regarded as citizens who should be repatriated. That brings them willy-nilly into my story, which in no way implies that I see them in any real sense as "Soviet." Most of them had fled westward in the autumn of 1944, at the time of the German retreat from occupation of their territories, to avoid living under Soviet occupation for a second time.

Baltic DPs were, in fact, so different in their behavior and reputation from "prewar-Soviet" DPs (mainly Russians and Ukrainians) that I often use the contrast (particularly with the Latvians, the Baltic group I know best) to point out the diversity within the broad category of Soviet-claimed DPs.

Jewish DPs are another group that cannot be left out. For many historians, Jews were the quintessential DPs: their story was one the one that, in 1945–46, first hit the headlines in the United States and set the parameters of understanding for an international public. In fact the majority of DPs were not Jewish but Slavic or from the Baltics. The Jewish DPs did not like the non-Jewish DPs, associating them with their wartime persecution, and Slavic and Baltic DPs often returned this dislike. The Jewish DPs refused repatriation to their countries of origin because those countries had rejected them. In the case of the Slavic and Baltic DPs claimed by the Soviet Union, it was the opposite—it was not that the Soviet Union rejected the DPs but that the DPs rejected the Soviet Union.[3]

It is important to keep the Jewish thread in the story not because it represents all the others but because in important ways it was so different. At the same time, there are intriguing areas of commonality, not least a shared knowledge of Russian. Polish Jews—the largest single Jewish group in the DP camps—had, for the most part, survived the Holocaust by spending the war years in the Soviet Union. This was sometimes a matter of choice, via eastward flight from the Nazis or Soviet evacuation from the newly incorporated West Ukrainian and Western Belorussian territories, and sometimes the result of deportation by Soviet authorities, but the outcome was the same: most (after an amnesty for the deportees) survived, living among Russian speakers during the war and picking up some Russian if they did not already know it. At the end of the war, the Polish Jews (along with ethnic Poles) were allowed to leave the Soviet Union for Poland, from which many quickly moved on to Austria and Germany, becoming late and contested additions to the DP category. As this large group of Polish Jews moved west, a much smaller number of individual Jewish DPs of Soviet origin, some of whose stories will be told in later chapters, were moving east from Germany and Austria as voluntary Soviet repatriates.[4]

———

Lost Souls, the title of this book, refers not only to the DPs' uprooted state and uncertain future but also to the old Russian use of the word "soul" (*dusha*) as a unit of property under serfdom, when a noble landowner's wealth was defined not so much by acreage as by the number of souls (serfs) on his estate. The Russian state, too, was an owner of peasant serfs, and this concept of the workforce as a form of property persisted in subterranean form in the Soviet Union, notably in the Soviet Union's reaction to its loss of almost half a million citizens in the postwar DP camps in Europe.

For the DPs themselves, being "lost" turned out to be only a temporary state, with the great powers offering competitive exit paths, and the DPs themselves weighing the available options. **Repatriation,** the exit path offered by the Soviets, was one of the two major options for DPs. Large-scale involuntary repatriation was a phenomenon only of 1945 and the beginning of 1946, but a small stream of voluntary repatriates continued to flow until the early 1950s. While this was a minority choice, it is an intriguing one—all the more in that Soviet reentry interviews (discovered in Russian archives at an early stage of my research) supply information on DP attitudes and choices not to be found elsewhere. **Resettlement**, the exit path offered by the Western Allies after several years of uncertainty, with the United States, Australia, Israel, and Canada the main destinations, was the option chosen by the majority of those who had not repatriated by the end of 1945. **Remaining** in Germany and Austria, the third and minority outcome, emerged as a last resort at the end of the 1940s, with the closure of the camps after the departure and resettlement of most DPs. For some of those who remained, this was not so much a choice as fate: many were DPs who, because of age, infirmity, security problems, or undesirable (intellectual) professions failed to be selected by any national selection committee for resettlement. Others—including, no doubt, some of the most successful at one of the DPs' basic trades, black marketeering—preferred to stay.

Repatriation was the explicit mission of the first international refugee organization in charge of DPs, the United Nations Relief and Rehabilitation Administration (UNRRA). Set up during the war by the Allies, including the Soviet Union, UNRRA was a wide-ranging reconstruction and relief agency for which repatriation of displaced persons was only one of a number of charges, several of which were considered more urgent. Once the United Nations Organization (UN) was formed in 1945, UNRRA, while remaining a constitutionally independent and separately funded entity, functioned almost as a part of the UN, with major policy issues debated on the floor of the UN's General Assembly. On repatriation, UNRRA acted in association with the military governments of the three Western occupation zones (American, British, and French) in Germany and Austria. (The authorities in the Soviet zone did not recognize the category of DPs, simply repatriating such persons with all possible speed from their zone and dispatching anomalous cases for the Allies to deal with.) A truly international organization in its staffing, UNRRA was initially willing to cooperate with the Soviet Union. This won it a reputation as a do-gooding agency, soft on communism, that lost it the confidence of its main financial backer, the United States. The advent of what British prime minister Winston Churchill famously called an "iron curtain" dividing Europe between East and West made the continuation of UNRRA—and in particular the large part of its funding that came from the US Congress— untenable. It went out of business in 1947.

UNRRA's successor was the International Refugee Organization, IRO, still an international body but more effectively under US control and almost fully funded by the US Congress. IRO took resettlement of DPs as its central mission, to the outrage of the Soviet Union, which had declined to join the organization. This institutional switch coincided with the onset of the Cold War, and resettlement was one of the period's early signature policies. While IRO's Cold War orientation was not absolute—it inherited many of UNRRA's staffers, including a contingent of Americans whose prior experience was in President Roosevelt's "New Deal" agencies—it was much more clearly than UNRRA a Western institution implicitly at odds with the Soviet Union. In the latter years of IRO's resettlement program, which ran from 1947 to the early 1950s, the occupation governments of the British, French, and US zones withdrew, handing over authority to the new US-supported Federal Republic of Germany—the western portion of a now divided Germany whose other (smaller and weaker) portion, formerly the Soviet occupation zone, became the German Democratic Republic.[5]

It was during IRO's tenure that the conventional understanding of the meaning of "displaced person" underwent a significant change to fit the new Cold War environment. Initially, "displaced persons"—most of them from Eastern Europe and the Soviet Union—had been officially defined by UNRRA as victims of Nazism and war. From around 1947, without any formal change in definition, DPs began to be seen in a different light as victims of communism, whose unwillingness to repatriate to their native lands, now under varying degrees of pro-Soviet communist control, was the essential cause of their displacement. One consequence of this shift was that collaboration with the Nazis, previously a major impediment to the acquisition of DP status (a prerequisite for IRO resettlement), ceased to be much of a problem. Even wartime military service under German command by Russians, Ukrainians, and Latvians was now represented as indicative of a desire to fight Soviet communism rather than of any positive sympathy for the Nazi cause.[^]

Sources

The handling of the DP issue by the great powers and the international relief organizations is recorded in their respective archives, which, as usual with state and organizational archives, are particularly illuminating when it comes to bureaucratic conflicts. I have tried to tell the diplomatic story not just from the more familiar Western side but also from the Soviet side, using Russian-language as well as English-, French- and German-language sources, published and archival. Among the resettlement countries, the one whose archives I have used most extensively is Australia (second only to the United States in the number of DP migrants accepted), a necessary strategy for a historian living in Australia during the COVID-19 pandemic, when most of this book was written, but one that has the advantage of putting the United States, whose resettlement history is the most familiar, in a comparative perspective.

Archives are generally much better at informing historians about political and diplomatic developments than about individual experience. For the DP experience, in all its variety, historians are bound to rely mainly on memoirs (an immensely valuable source, even though the way people see things fifty years after the event is likely to be different from the way they saw it at the time), supplemented by bureaucratic material such as reports made by UNRRA and IRO officials on conditions in the DP camps. In the West, nobody systematically interviewed arriving DP migrants, although some material from the selection committees is available in the archives of resettlement countries. The Soviet authorities, however, did conduct loosely structured interviews with repatriates that turn out to be surprisingly illuminating about DP attitudes and choices more generally. Another rich source of individual DP lives—which, to my knowledge, has no counterpart elsewhere in the diaspora—is the Australian Russian-language journal *Avstraliada*, which for two decades published memoirs and biographies of Russian DPs resettled after the war in Australia.[6]

Finally, there is a source that has particular significance for me: the papers of my husband, Michael Danos (Misha to me; Mischka to those who knew him in the German years), and his mother, Olga Danos, both DPs from Riga in Germany in the postwar years. When Misha died in 1999 I inherited these very rich papers, including diaries and regular letters between the two over the years 1944–51 (fortunately for the historian, they almost always lived in different German cities and DP camps); these are now in Special Collections at the University of Chicago. The letters of the resourceful and entrepreneurial Olga taught me a great deal about DP agency and options that does not show up in other types of documentation. I also learned much from interviews after Misha's death with his Latvian friends and DP contemporaries, who told their parallel stories (along with their reactions to Misha's version!) from their individual perspectives.[7]

As for Misha, it is not only from papers or interviews that I have his story but from intimacy with the man himself at a time, forty years on, when he was finally ready to think about this episode of his youth. Misha is always a presence when I am working on DPs, providing not only the case study I know best but also a kind of running commentary, audible only to me, on the events and circumstances I am writing about. From time to time in this book, I throw in a small quotation from that commentary, to remind the reader that, however detached my style as a professional historian, I have a personal stake in the subject matter of this book.

PART I

The Great Power Story

1

UNRRA and Its Mandate

IF YOUR INTEREST is in displaced persons, it is easy to assume that the question of their fate was foremost among the concerns of the great powers at the end of the Second World War. In fact, the DP issue was only one of a host of acute problems confronting the victorious Allies, and not at the top of the list. As British foreign minister Ernest Bevin noted distractedly to the House of Commons in November 1945, "All the world is in trouble and I have to deal with all the troubles at once." Repatriation was certainly a sticky issue. But for the great powers involved—Britain, the United States, and the Soviet Union— it was not as existentially important as the problems of governing occupied Germany, repairing the European nations' war-scarred economies, setting and extracting reparations from Germany, demobilizing forces and getting soldiers home, and handling relations between the Soviet Union and the Western Allies in light of the Soviet Army's de facto control of Eastern Europe.

When General Lucius Clay arrived in Germany in May 1945 to serve as Eisenhower's deputy at Supreme Headquarters, Allied Expeditionary Forces (SHAEF), he found a dismal situation. "All central and state government had collapsed; county and city government no longer existed. Mail service had stopped; communications were taken over completely for security and for the use of the invading armies," the American forces alone numbering about three million. Seven million German prisoners of war who had surrendered to the Allies had to be coped with, in addition to the millions of German refugees expelled from Eastern European states who were pouring into Germany, and similarly large numbers of non-Germans displaced by the war and now in Germany. "The scenes on highway and railway were indescribable as these huge mass migrations took place."

In the six years that followed before the last of the unplaceable "hard core" of DPs would be subsumed in the German population as "homeless foreigners" (*heimatlöser Ausländer*), displaced persons remained a constantly vexing problem for and between the Allies, but a problem that was nevertheless always secondary. This applied even to the Soviet Union, for whom, unlike the Western Allies, the question of repatriation of Soviet DPs "seemed to touch a central nerve regarding . . . self-image and sense of justice." For the Western Allies, the most difficult aspect of the DP problem was not its Soviet dimension but its Jewish one—a matter of great concern to the United States on which US and British interests and policy diverged. In the newly formed United Nations, the displaced persons problem became part of the nascent discussion of human rights, featuring verbal contests between US representative Eleanor Roosevelt and Soviet representative Andrei Vyshinsky. But this too was essentially a sideshow: a debate on principles, not a negotiation about action.[1]

Allied interactions, so unexpectedly well-functioning in the wartime meetings of Winston Churchill, Franklin D. Roosevelt, and Joseph Stalin were completely knocked out of kilter by two events: the death of Roosevelt in April 1945, a month before Victory Day, and the defeat of Churchill and the Tories in the British general elections on July 28. How disruptive and disconcerting the latter event proved may be seen from the fact that at the Allies' conference in Potsdam from July to August 1945—the Allied leaders' first meeting since victory—the United Kingdom's initial representatives, Prime Minister Churchill and his foreign secretary Anthony Eden, had to be replaced in midsession as a result of their electoral defeat by the new Labour prime minister Clement Attlee and his foreign secretary Ernest Bevin. Soviet foreign minister Vyacheslav Molotov couldn't understand how the British could have dumped their "organizer of victory" so unceremoniously ("Evidently one needs to understand English life better"). There were other shocks to come at Potsdam, since Truman took the occasion of his first and only personal meeting with Stalin to let him know that the United States had "a new weapon of unusual destructive force"—the atomic bomb, dropped on Hiroshima on August 6, 1945, just a few days after the conference ended.

The United States, rich and relatively unscarred by the war, was essentially calling the shots in 1945, and its wartime Allies just had to get used to it. Britain—on the verge of bankruptcy, with the United States the only possible (but not yet convinced) rescuer, in the process of losing its empire and the top power status that went with it—still had to maintain its occupation zones in Germany and Austria. British-US relations were rocky for the first postwar years, before the Americans agreed to bail out the British with the Marshall Plan. The Soviet Union was in bad economic straits, too, though with less reason to hope that the United States would come to its rescue. But it had at least the comfort of being an up-and-coming great power, no longer an outcast as it had been in the prewar decades, rather than a declining one.

The formal situation established in Germany was one of quadripartite government, the French having been added to the occupying powers along with the British, Americans, and Soviets. The British zone was the most industrialized and populous part of Germany (the northwest), but industry was at standstill and there was no agreement on how to restart it. The US zone in the south, which included Bavaria, was the largest and the best funded. The Soviets had the eastern part of the country, while the French, included as a concession to General de Gaulle, had a small zone squashed in between the Soviet and Western occupation zones. The former capital, Berlin, was divided between the powers.

Even at the height of wartime goodwill, the Soviets never forgot that their allies were capitalists. Their analysis of the postwar situation led them to expect that competition for the spoils would lead to conflict between Britain, the declining power, and the United States, the rising one; that contradictions in capitalism would show themselves; and that there would probably be another Great Depression in the West. This was an encouraging prognosis from the Soviet standpoint, especially if the United States quickly withdrew from Europe, as it had done at the end of the First World War. In the short run, it did not suggest a need for a confrontational stance towards the Western powers on the Soviet part, and indeed, in the early days after the end of the war, the Soviet intention was to cooperate in order to secure economic reconstruction assistance in whatever forms it might be available, from German reparations to American loans, while "allow[ing] time for British-American differences to surface." But the Soviets also had a strong sense of what was due to them as (in their understanding) the victors in the war against Germany, namely "a just distribution of the spoils of war, a war won by great sacrifice from the Soviet people," and recognition of their nation "as a legitimate great power." Hitler had tricked them in 1939–41, but this was not going to happen again. "My task as Minister of Foreign Affairs was to ensure that they didn't make dupes of us," Molotov later remembered.[2]

That tough approach on the Soviet part quickly started causing problems with the Western Allies. In December, Sir Archibald Clark Kerr, the British ambassador to Moscow since 1942, offered a rather sympathetic summary of Soviet hang-ups in a cable to his masters in Whitehall, noting

> their obsession with security ever since the Revolution; their belief that the rest of the world was against them; the immense relief they felt when the Germans were driven back; the shock of discovering that the old nightmare of insecurity was still there with the West's invention of the A-bomb the disappointment of their hopes that the secret would be shared with them; the humiliation to their pride and the revival of all their distrust of the West when it was not.

Clark Kerr was on unexpectedly cordial terms with Stalin as well as with former foreign minister Maxim Litvinov (whose views he probably summarized in the passage above). But his opinion of Molotov, Litvinov's successor as foreign minister, was much less favorable: in the same cable, commenting on the proposal to hold a foreign ministers' meeting in Moscow, he remarked that Molotov had "set his malevolent heart" on it. The view of Molotov as an ungracious, hostile non-negotiator with whom nobody, not even the genial Clark Kerr, could establish a personal relationship was widespread in the diplomatic world; and it did damage to Allied postwar relations as well as setting an unfortunate style for Soviet diplomacy. Molotov, as he himself recognized, was not a diplomat. His stubborn, nonempathetic style had actually worked quite well in his first diplomatic encounters (with Hitler and Ribbentrop, over the Nazi-Stalin pact of 1939 just after he took over as foreign minister), and Stalin was clearly encouraging him to continue in the same vein in dealing with the Allies after the war.

It should have been an advantage as far as postwar diplomacy was concerned that Molotov was still ostensibly number two in the Soviet political hierarchy, something much more than a mere career diplomat. Unfortunately, Stalin liked to keep even very senior subordinates on their toes; and, back in the Soviet Union, within the closed circle of the inner leadership and unknown to the outside world, he had just delivered a tremendous snub to Molotov. To make things worse, the ostensible grounds of his slap-down were that "old Stone Face," as he was irreverently known, was being too liberal dealing with Westerners. Under these circumstances, Molotov was both severely constrained with regard to independent initiative and in political danger. No wonder his dealings with the West became ever harsher and more unpleasant in tone.[3]

Molotov's two offsiders as Soviet representatives abroad were his deputy (and, in 1949, successor as foreign minister) Andrei Vyshinsky and Andrei

Gromyko. Vyshinsky was a jurist of no independent political standing who had made his name with "shoot the mad dogs" rhetoric in the show trials of the 1930s and enjoyed demonstrating the same skills in a diplomatic forum. The much younger Andrei Gromyko, thrust to the top with minimal training and experience in the post-Purge shake-up of Soviet diplomacy, was less rhetorically vicious but by temperament dry, cautious, and detached. Before the war, two eminent Soviet diplomats—Maxim Litvinov, Molotov's precursor as foreign minister, and Ivan Maisky, Soviet ambassador to Britain—had established good rapport with their Western counterparts, but both were now removed from high office and on the way to being completely sidelined.

The deterioration of Soviet relations with its erstwhile allies after the war was exacerbated by the fact that Stalin and other Soviet leaders, mourning Roosevelt's loss, thought Truman was a nonentity and loathed Ernest Bevin, the British foreign secretary, with a passion. It might have been thought that Bevin, an old Labour man from way back, could have found a common language with the Soviets, but in fact the opposite was true: as a right-wing Labour trade unionist who had cut his teeth fighting British communists, he extended the old belligerence to Soviet communists, while the Soviets disliked him as a representative of the spirit of the Second International who exemplified everything they despised about the nonrevolutionary British working class. Remarkably for egalitarian socialists, both Stalin and Molotov sneered at Bevin, even sometimes publicly, for not being a "gentleman."

The obverse was, of course, also true: Dean Acheson—not a hardline anticommunist in US domestic terms—was repelled by the Soviet style of "cultivat[ing] boorishness as a method of showing their contempt for the capitalist world." In all his years of dealing with various Soviet diplomats, he recalled, he never felt a sense of rapport with any of them, and neither did any of his colleagues. Eleanor Roosevelt, widow of the late US president, whose views had generally been further to the left than his, at first bent over backward to understand and allow for the insecurity of Soviet diplomats in her stint as US delegate to the United Nations General Assembly. But she was consistently rebuffed in her efforts to establish anything like a personal relationship with them. By 1948, after repeated clashes with Vyshinsky over human rights, she had given up, writing that in dealing with the Russians, "sweetness and light" didn't get you anywhere; you had to be tough.

To be sure, relations between US and Soviet military leaders were much more cordial, to the point that General Clay felt hurt and disappointed when, circa 1947 and presumably under political pressure, his Soviet counterpart,

General Vasily Sokolovsky, lost "his former warmth" in personal interactions. UNRRA troubleshooter Commander Robert A. Jackson, personal assistant to the director-general of European operations, also had good relations with many of the Soviet officials he dealt with during and after the war, especially the trade personnel he encountered in the wartime Middle East—but not when the topic was displaced persons, where disagreements with Moscow were "total and fundamental." As he told an interviewer in the 1980s, "It was over the displaced persons that we fought Stalin."[4]

UNRRA's Establishment

The Allies had thought in advance about the mess that would be left at the end of the war. In 1943, they set up UNRRA with a mandate to relieve suffering, prevent pestilence, help restore essential services, and "return prisoners and exiles to their homes." This grew out of a Soviet suggestion the previous year that an international relief organization be created for Europe when the war ended (although at this point there was no mention of a repatriation function). Organizationally the basis was the Middle East Relief and Refugee Administration—formed by the United Kingdom in mid-1942, where a number of future UNRRA leaders cut their teeth on relief problems and had their first encounters with displaced persons, as well as with each other—and the US Office of Foreign Relief and Rehabilitation Operations, created in the Department of State during the war and headed by New York governor Herbert Lehman. As plans moved forward, with the Soviet Union a full partner along with the United States and the United Kingdom, and in addition a potential beneficiary of relief, a Soviet representative hailed "the mutual understanding and spirit of collaboration" that had marked discussion and hoped it would continue.

The new organization was launched in November 1943, President Roosevelt welcoming the delegates from forty-four countries at the White House before they proceeded to Atlantic City for their meeting. With a prior agreement in place that an American would head the new organization, it was starting to feel like an American enterprise. Governor Lehman, who had previously served as director of the US State Department's Foreign Relief and Rehabilitation Operations, was elected UNRRA's first director. "Close to Roosevelt and acceptable to the US Army, the British and the Russians," he was chosen over other more dynamic potential candidates like Fiorello La Guardia, mayor of New York, and ex-president Herbert Hoover, who had organized a massive

American relief effort in Europe after the First World War. Lehman's unassertive style led him to accept without serious objection an UNRRA budget of £450 million that one historian estimates "was at least less than half of what it actually needed."[5]

In financial terms, UNRRA was largely an American enterprise, and this circumstance was to shape its history in a number of ways. Member countries were supposed to contribute 1 percent of their national income, a very substantial burden, particularly for the United Kingdom, which would have made the US contribution 40 percent of the total and the UK contribution 15 percent. But in the event the US contribution was about three-quarters of the total, with Britain and Canada the next largest donors. The Soviet offering—only 0.1 percent of the total, according to UNRRA's official statistics—was miserable, a fact that, in a context of substantial UNRRA help in postwar relief in Ukraine and Belorussia, exacerbated Western irritation at the characteristic Soviet combination of arrogance (as a great power) and self-righteousness (as a major war victim). The only Soviet offer of funds— from Stalin in response to La Guardia's request in Moscow August 1946—came too late and contained no dollar figure.

Another pragmatic problem of UNRRA's largely American funding was that it had to be approved annually by a suspicious and insular Congress, so that every year was a struggle, and the ability of the institution to continue operating was often in doubt. UNRRA and its supporters, ranging from the Vatican to Representative Ed ("Boss") Crump from Tennessee, lobbied energetically every time and claimed that US public opinion was behind them, but the poor relations between the State Department and Congress were a constant problem. As a result, UNRRA had scarcely started postwar operation when discussion began about when it would be closed down (as it turned out, less than two years after the end of the war). At the fifth meeting of UNRRA's council in August 1946, Fiorello La Guardia (appointed director-general in March 1946) opened his address with the statement that, while UNRRA's activities remained necessary, its work was slowing down because "no provision has been made for UNRRA for 1947," that is, the US Congress had pulled the plug. For its final six months (January–June 1947), UNRRA operated essentially without funding.

Criticism of UNRRA's organization and recruitment policies was unrelenting. "UNRRA the unready" was its moniker, and for its first fifteen months, according to Robert Jackson, it did virtually nothing except take people who did little or no useful work onto the payroll. Sir Raphael Cilento, arriving from

Australia via the Middle East to work in UNRRA, was struck by "the doubtful ability and, sometimes, the plain dishonesty of many UNRRA employees." Marvin Klemmé, coming from the United States, had similar criticisms and aimed his fire particularly at the "continental" (that is, not British or American) employees, whom he characterized as "grafters and black marketeers who were out to get everything that they could in any way that they could." The organization was functioning so poorly that in the spring of 1945 Jackson was sent on an emergency mission from New York to rescue "a sinking ship." It might not have survived at all had it not been for its relationship to the United Nations. UNRRA, originally a free-standing international institution, had just been coopted into the new body, and its collapse on the eve of the triumphant inaugural meeting of the United Nations Organizations in San Francisco would have been a bad look.[6]

UNRRA was an international institution, in staffing policy as in other respects, with headquarters in Washington and European operations, including DP matters, run out of its European Region Office in London (11 Portland Place). Before the Jackson reforms, the European office was jointly headed by a British, an American, and a Soviet appointee, each of whom had full power to countermand any order of another. Jackson corrected that obvious malfunction, but the different administrative cultures of its senior officers remained a problem. UNRRA's staff came from a total of thirty-three countries, with Americans and British predominating. English was the institution's working language. The United States was the source not only of most of its funding but also of most of its procurement, which came through various agencies in Washington.

Given its London location, it was perhaps not surprising that the European office had a markedly British (including Commonwealth) character. Jackson, who conducted the 1945 reorganization as an emissary of the American Governor Lehman, was an Australian seconded to the British Navy during the war, one of those, including Australian Raphael Cilento and Canadian Marshall MacDuffie, who had bonded while working together in the Middle East during the war. Lieutenant General Sir Frederick Morgan, a British Army officer with a background in India as well as active service in both world wars, was both chief of operations at the European office and deputy chief of staff at Allied forces. The army background was typical of the British seconded to UNRRA. The military were the ones "that knew what they were doing," in Morgan's opinion; in the Australian Cilento's perhaps jaundiced view they were usually "middle-aged officers at the retirement level, who maintain their military rank" (UNRRA counted as active service) but otherwise "had no further prospects in the Army and certainly not civilian life." On the ground in the British occupation zone, according to the American Klemmé, UNRRA was practically a part of the army. It annoyed both Cilento and Klemmé that the British insisted on wearing their army uniforms and badges of rank and being addressed by their military titles and that they tended to commandeer German castles for their personal residences.[7]

As for the top American officers in UNRRA, the typical political affiliation was with the Democrats (the party of President Roosevelt and of UNRRA first director, Herbert Lehman); and a number came from Roosevelt's New Deal agencies, founded to fight poverty and often inspired by a radical idealism not too far removed from socialism. In the British General Morgan's acid formulation, UNRRA was "a place for all the New Dealers now out of work in US to shelter." Myer Cohen, the head of UNRRA's displaced persons division, formerly assistant director in charge of migratory camps, Farm Security Administration, San Francisco, was one of the ex-New Dealers in the UNRRA bureaucracy. It was Americans that brought the mysterious word "rehabilitation" into UNRRA's title, incomprehensible to many (especially in the military), but a key concept to those who felt that UNRRA must "not only relieve, it must revivify" by helping people, as one might train children, to look after themselves. President Roosevelt himself had used the term in his speech of November 9, 1943, describing the newly created UNRRA's task as offering "relief and rehabilitation for the victims of German and Japanese barbarism." The American social workers, "trained in the Depression era and formerly employed by US Federal Agencies, aggressively promoted 'active' welfare over 'passive' charity." Their assumption was that in the modern world, governments and not private philanthropists should take responsibility for welfare.

It was the Americans, above all, who brought a liberal internationalist spirit to UNRRA, not least the eager young women, often with a social work background, who flooded into junior ranks. Susan Pettiss, a young American who worked with DPs under UNRRA for three years, recalled an atmosphere of "pervasive idealism" among her peers: "All hoped to see established a true world community with new social systems and international relations." This was in sync with the United Nations, with which UNRRA was closely associated in ethos and activities, although it was not necessarily congenial to those of its members who came from the military. UNRRA's fifth council meeting was the first international assembly to meet (in August 1946) at the Palais des Nations in Geneva, built to house the League of Nations and now beginning a "new life under the United Nations." Most of UNRRA's American idealists were not socialists, but they could often see virtues in the socialist approach to social organization, including the Soviet version. This was particularly evident in UNRRA's field missions but also present in its repatriation departments in Germany and Austria.[8]

As Cold War attitudes started to take root, this internal culture naturally exposed UNRRA as an institution to charges of being pro-Soviet and soft on communism. In fact, that had been a view that many of the old-style British army officers and American opponents of the New Deal had held from the beginning. When Marvin Klemmé arrived from the United States in 1945 to work in UNRRA, he noted that "one of the most common charges against the organization, . . . that it was overstaffed with Communists, aliens [foreign-born] and Jews, . . . [was] at least partially justified." For Klemmé, "a grass-roots sage" from Oregon with a prejudice against big-city eastern liberals, it was not surprising that the State Department—"known to be thoroughly infested with Communists or Communist-sympathizers"—would be sending to UNRRA the type of person for whom "Soviet Russia was always right and the United States always wrong." Such views were particularly prevalent among "the alien, foreign-born" among them, in other words, the Jews. Everybody privately agreed that there were too many Jews in UNRRA, Klemmé wrote. Both the British and the Canadians were wary of the organization on those grounds, and when General Frederick Morgan ran into trouble for antisemitism, there was particular outrage when the man who replaced this towering figure was "an American Jew by the name of Myer Cohen whom [sic] I believe had held the rank of Staff Sergeant in the U. S. Army." This insult "was something that the British will not get over in a long, long time."

There was no reconciling the sharply opposed views of UNRRA held by its idealist staffers and those like Klemmé who despised them. Morgan himself characterized the institution of which he had been a leader as a "frightful racket," an "adventitious assembly of silver-tongued ineffectuals, professional do-gooders, crooks and crackpots." Even Judge Simon Rifkind, Army adviser on Jewish affairs in Germany, dismissed the UNRRA idealists as "a bunch of social workers." But UNRRA also inspired great loyalty among many of those who worked for it. Commander Jackson described himself as "broken hearted at the blow to the practical application of the international United Nations concept of humanitarian operations" when UNRRA went under in 1947. He and many others envisaged a postwar world in which the internationalist principle would grow, and the United States and other Western governments would continue to cooperate with the Soviet Union. This was looking increasingly unlikely by mid-1947, when UNRRA finally went out of business and was replaced by IRO. Moreover, such attitudes would, within just a few years, put those who held them—including a number who had worked for UNRRA—at risk of being tarred as communists.[9]

Getting Started

UNRRA's mandate of relief and rehabilitation was primarily aimed at the countries emerging from occupation and war damage and their populations in situ. Displaced persons came under the mandate too, but they were not conceived as the central task. UNRRA's official historian—who had himself worked in UNRRA's European office and Lendlease administration—expressed his frustration that what he saw as the secondary issues of repatriation and DP care became so prominent and damaging to the institution's reputation:

> No questions were to take up so much time in successive Council meetings and to cause so much controversy as these two. No operations of the Administration were to get so much publicity—good and bad—as those arising from the answers supplied by the member governments. No other field operations were to require the employment of so many people. Yet in no operation was so small a portion of the funds of the Administration used. No operation was so misunderstood within the Administration, by member governments, and by the public. In no operation was the early organizational control of the administration so unsatisfactory.

The trouble was that repatriation emerged very early as a problem, long before some of UNRRA's most successful operations, such as the field missions in Ukraine and Belorussia, got started. Two enormous substantive and reputational issues emerged within a few months of the end of the war: one was the fact that many Soviet displaced persons and others from Eastern Europe did not want to go home, and the other was the particular plight of Jewish displaced persons, coming out of concentration camps and hiding, who absolutely rejected the idea of return to their former countries.

The forced repatriation of Soviet prisoners of war and laborers that took place in the summer of 1945 occurred under the watch of Allied forces, before UNRRA was really in the picture. Public outcry led to the Western Allies withdrawing cooperation with Soviet repatriation (discussed in chapter 2). It was at this point that the Allies had to formulate an attitude on a question to which they had previously given little thought, namely whether repatriation was a question for individual decision; and UNRRA had to reassess its original assumption that its job was to offer only temporary protection for displaced persons until the mechanics of repatriation could be organized. As Woodbridge puts it, the "real role—the care of displaced persons, mostly in enemy territory, who either did not wish to return home or did not wish immediately to do so—was not foreseen."

Repatriation of prisoners of war and forced laborers was originally dealt with by the military, first by SHAEF under General Eisenhower, then (after SHAEF went out of business in July 1945) by the military governments set up in the British, US, and French zones. Often, in the initial stages, the camps were organized like standard army camps whose residents did not have freedom to come and go at will. In the opinion of General Patton, commander of the Third Army in Bavaria, "the DPs should be treated as prisoners and put behind barbed wire" to stop their looting and pillaging.[10]

The military had had no particular wish for an organization of UNRRA's type to be involved, as they were used to dealing with the International Red Cross or relief organizations like the Quakers associated with particular religious or ethnic groups. These, in contrast to previous practice, were now sidelined, allowed to operate only under UNRRA's direct supervision and with proper authorization (the exception to this, the Jewish Joint Distribution Committee [JDC], is discussed later in this chapter). American military men, like many back in the States, tended to think it would have been better to have a purely American organization in charge, along the lines of Herbert Hoover's relief mission to Europe after the First World War. Even some people within UNRRA thought that "with less than half the money that UNRRA was spending," the British and American Armies could have done a much better job.

It took months before Eisenhower, the Supreme Allied Commander, acknowledged UNRRA's existence in November 1944; and it was not until almost a year later, in October 1945, that the American and British military governments agreed, without any particular enthusiasm, to hand over responsibility for day-to-day running of the camps to UNRRA—and even then it took the US zonal authorities four months to sign a formal agreement. In the division of responsibility agreed, military governments paid for the DP camps, providing security, food, clothing, medical supplies and transport, and did political screening, while UNRRA managed the camps (known as "assembly centers" to avoid awkward associations with the Nazi concentration camps), having responsibility for their internal administration and providing medical services, recreational facilities, and vocational guidance. It had only consultative authority on repatriation, with the military in charge of "executive action in connection with the movement of displaced persons" as well as providing transport, accommodation, supplies, and rations ("displaced persons will have priority over the German population")—essentially covering most costs apart from payment of UNRRA staff.[11]

The Soviet Union was not involved in these negotiations, since it did not acknowledge the existence of a "displaced persons" problem: such people located in their zone were simply directly repatriated to the Soviet Union and East European countries, or, if there were complications, trucked over into the American or British zone for the Allies to deal with. From the beginning, Soviet representatives insisted that they wanted their potential repatriates in the Western zones to be "segregated and put in special centers to be run by Soviet officials . . . regardless of their individual wishes," and SHAEF directed accordingly. The Soviet Union did not welcome the mediation of an international organization in the disposition of displaced persons, considering such matters properly the subject of "bilateral agreement between the two countries concerned—the country of origin and the country of refuge."

From the beginning, the Soviet Union made clear that it regarded the automatic repatriation of its nationals who found themselves outside the state's borders at the end of the war to be a nonnegotiable matter of national rights. Since there was no room for individual repatriates' decisions on this, there was no need for UNRRA or the military governments in the Western zones to provide facilities for looking after those who did not wish to be repatriated: "non-repatriable" was a noncategory as far as the Soviet Union was concerned. The Western powers, by contrast, were willing to accept that some people might not wish to repatriate for legitimate reasons (other than being war criminals and/or collaborators seeking to avoid punishment) and that, while they remained outside their countries of origin, they deserved support. These deep differences, which emerged clearly for the first time at UNRRA's third council session in August 1945, soured relations between the wartime Allies, while at the same time creating new problems in the Western zones about how to deal with non-repatriable DPs.[12]

The Problem of Jewish DPs

The other issue that had quickly become an international political football, although for different reasons, was that of Jewish displaced persons. The Allied military forces first encountered them as they emerged from the concentration camps, initially barely alive and then angry and uncooperative, and were at a loss how to handle them. As Klemmé remarked, "These people [the Jewish DPs] were a source of embarrassment to the [US] army." A few, like General Patton, reacted with disgust: in his view, those who thought DPs in general were human were wrong, "and this applies particularly to the Jews who are lower than animals." But for many others, to whom the full horror of the Nazi campaign to eliminate the Jews had only just become apparent, the state of the newly liberated Jews aroused feelings of distress and confusion. Back home, the press coverage left American readers shocked, and it was President Truman's own personal concern that prompted him to send a mission to Europe in July 1945 to investigate.

Led by Earl Harrison, a Methodist lawyer from the Midwest who had been US commissioner of immigration and naturalization during the war, the mission included Dr. Joseph Schwartz, head of the main American-based but international Jewish relief organization, the Joint Distribution Committee. In short order, it issued a scathing report condemning the US military's treatment of the Jews, calling on them to be housed in separate camps and recommending that they should be given the opportunity to resettle in Palestine. The sharpness of its criticism, as well as the substance of the report, caused a great stir. As Israeli historian Yehuda Bauer notes, it left an indelible mark on the US Army in Europe, which was not used to such direct rebukes from the civilian side, and "in the future ... would handle all Jewish problems very gingerly." The report also had an immediate impact on US immigration policy: in December, President Truman issued an executive order of December 1945 facilitating, on a one-off basis, the entry of displaced persons from the American zone. This resulted in the speedy issue of about twenty-three thousand visas, about two-thirds of which went to Jewish DPs in Germany.[13]

The presence in Germany of large numbers of Jewish DPs who, understandably, refused to return to their countries of prewar residence (mainly Poland and other East European countries) required a solution. This was one of the rare issues on which the line-up of great powers differed from the one soon to be enshrined in the Cold War, that is, the United States and Britain against the Soviet Union. In this instance, the United States and the Soviet Union had basically similar positions (albeit without acknowledging each other as allies on the issue), which were opposed by the British. The solution preferred by the United States and the Soviet Union was that the Jewish DPs should be helped to resettle in Palestine, still under British mandate but moving (with US and Soviet encouragement) toward independence as the Jewish state of Israel.

Had the British accepted this solution, the Jewish DPs in Germany would have been the first group of DPs to be resettled. But since the British, still holding administrative control in Palestine, staunchly resisted its opening for unrestricted Jewish immigration, the situation remained unresolved for several years, with the bulk of the Jewish DPs remaining in camps in Germany and Austria.

The beginning of a large-scale influx of Jewish refugees from Eastern Europe in the winter of 1945–46 exacerbated the problem. Many of these were from prewar Poland but had survived the Holocaust by escaping or being deported to the Soviet Union during the war. After the war, the Soviet government sent them back to Poland, but when they saw the devastation of their old life and encountered antisemitism from the local population, many decided to move on. The goal of the Zionists among them was Palestine, but in the meantime they sought to join the earlier cohorts of displaced persons under Allied care in Europe. Included in the category of "persecutees" by the Americans, they found a comparatively warm welcome in the US zone, despite being illegal border-crossers. The Soviets also did nothing to impede their progress, as long as they moved on to the Western zones and the financial support of the Americans and the international organizations. The British, however, were furious, calling them "infiltrees" and doing their best to keep them out of the British zone. The British had already had some painful clashes with Jewish DPs over their handling of Bergen-Belsen, a former concentration camp in the British zone that became a Jewish DP camp. According to Klemmé's perhaps exaggerated report, "friction between the Jewish D.P.s and the British military authorities increased from month to month until by the spring of 1947 it was quite evident that many of the British hated the Jews more than the German people ever did."

The new Jewish arrivals were "infiltrees" for UNRRA as well, that is, an unlooked-for extension of its mandate to provide care and maintenance for persons directly displaced by the Second World War. The conflicts over Bergen-Belsen extended to UNRRA (staffed, in the British Zone where the camp was located, mainly by British army officers), which in October 1946 withdrew its team from the camp following objections by Jewish inmates to the fact that the team included non-Jews. In general, UNRRA tacitly accepted the extension of its mandate, albeit under American pressure. The European office had to be reminded by UNRRA's head office in Washington of the delicacy of any issue involving Jews in terms of American public opinion: there was essentially no choice about accepting postwar refugees, since such a policy would require expelling Jewish "infiltrees" who had already been accepted, "a policy exceedingly difficult to carry out for administrative as well as humanitarian reasons."[14]

Central to the handling of all issues involving Jews was the JDC, which was the "notable exception" to the general rule of sidelining voluntary organizations under the UNRRA regime. The head of its European operations was Joseph Schwartz, already mentioned as a member of the Harrison mission, an exceptional resourceful and energetic officer who had been in Europe (based in Lisbon during the war) since 1940. Unlike the JDC's conservative German-Jewish leadership in the States, Schwartz was a European cosmopolitan, a rabbi with a PhD in Oriental studies born in Ukraine and brought up in the United States. It was undoubtedly a tribute to the JDC's organizational prowess in Europe that the DP intake following the Truman Statement contained such a large proportion of Jews.

The JDC's influence was particularly strong in the American occupation zone, which was where the majority of Jewish DPs congregated; according to one historian, "for all practical purposes" the JDC "was put in charge of the Jews in the United States zones," despite the fact that formal responsibility lay with the American occupation authorities and UNRRA. The accuracy of this assessment is indicated by the fact that, when UNRRA was handing over the reins to IRO in 1947, General Joseph McNarney, commander of the American zone, actually suggested to Schwartz that the JDC might assume "full administrative control of the Jewish DP camps." While this did not happen, the distinction between US military forces and JDC personnel may not always have been apparent to DPs on the ground, given that the JDC people, who required military clearance for appointment, wore US army uniform (with the addition of the JDC's blue and white chevrons and the letters "AJDC" on the sleeve), had military ranks, and operated with military permits.

In the British zone, relations were less happy. To be sure, UNRRA officials in the zone (mainly British themselves) worked with the JDC, but Jewish DPs complained that this amounted to an offloading of responsibility by people whose attitude to the Jews was "unfriendly and unsympathetic." The culmination of ongoing tensions with the British came with a scandal provoked by the comments of Lieutenant General Sir Frederick Morgan, director of occupation forces in the British zone, that the Jewish "infiltrees" were not refugees fleeing persecution but part of a Zionist plot to smuggle Jewish DPs into Palestine; that there were no pogroms in Poland; and that these refugees appeared "rosy-cheeked and with their pockets stuffed with money." All hell broke loose in the American media when Morgan's comments were published, and the affair culminated some months later in his withdrawal from UNRRA by the British War Office. This well-publicized episode was one of the milestones in the destruction of UNRRA's reputation in the eyes of its major funder, the United States.[15]

Which Displaced Persons Fell under UNRRA's Mandate?

The original November 1943 agreement for the creation of UNRRA made no statement as to who exactly qualified to receive its relief and rehabilitation, referring only to "the population" of areas liberated from enemy occupation, along with "prisoners and exiles" who needed to be returned to their homes. This did not specify whether the population of Germany, when liberated from Nazi control, would qualify for UNRRA care, but on the conclusion of the war it was decided without much discussion that it did not. Thus the non-German "displaced persons" living in Germany, as beneficiaries of UNRRA relief, were set apart from (and in terms of supply, above) the German population.

Although the November 1943 agreement included "prisoners" in its scope, the same UNRRA Council session at which it was issued decided that UNRRA "should not normally have any responsibility for the repatriation of prisoners of war," which would presumably be handled by the military authorities. (At this point it was not envisaged that significant numbers of POWs would successfully refuse repatriation. When this happened, the nonrepatriating POWs generally found their way into UNRRA's DP camps, although often after a period in Allied military camps.) UNRRA's responsibility would cover those "who have been obliged to leave their homes by reason of the war and are found in liberated or conquered territory"; those "displaced within their own (liberated) countries"; those who are "exiles as a result of the war"; and "stateless persons who have been driven as a result of the war from their places of settled residence." The last provision meant that prewar Russian émigrés qualified for UNRRA care only if the war had displaced them from their previous countries of residence. With regard to the Russian émigrés, as well as those from the Baltics who had voluntarily left with the Germans, the possibility of collaboration was likely to be an issue, but this would be a matter from the military authorities, which would be responsible for the identification of collaborators and their removal from UNRRA camps: "UNRRA is not, repeat not, authorised to make any determination on collaboration."

According to the agreements signed by UNRRA with the military commanders of the zones between November 1945 and February 1946, the "displaced persons" for whom UNRRA was responsible comprised Allied ("United Nations") nationals; persons of "undetermined nationality and stateless persons"; and enemy and ex-enemy nationals who were forced to leave their place of origin "because of race, religion or activities in favour of the United Nations." While the agreement signed with the British military authorities (though not the one signed with the American) stated that UNRRA had the right to decide whom to admit to its camps, common sense dictated that its criteria should correspond to those of the military, "as UNRRA was dependent upon Army for accommodations, supplies, and so forth."[16]

There were Germans in the general mass of the displaced, some ten million of them pouring out of East European countries in which they were no longer welcome. But it was soon decided that these Volksdeutsche were not eligible for UNRRA care, since their nationality—that of the wartime enemy—implied collaboration. This applied in principle to Volksdeutsche from the Baltic states who had answered the Führer's call for repatriation to Germany in 1939–41 (a group that included several of Mischka Danos's schoolfriends from Riga), although in practice it was hard for UNRRA and the military authorities to distinguish them from other Baltic refugees. Thus, the primary group for which UNRRA was responsible were citizens of Allied nations who were not German (or Austrian) by nationality.

It was recognized that the situation of Jews was exceptional. Regardless of their citizenship of origin, they were clearly "victims of war and fascism," which emerged as UNRRA's working definition of the group for which it had responsibility. The issue was raised as early as September 1944 by the US delegate to UNRRA's second council, as well as Jewish international organizations concerned about the possible exclusion of Jews whose original citizenship was German, Austrian, or that of other countries in the Axis orbit. UNRRA's mandate was accordingly extended to care for "a group of people who came to be known as 'persecutees,' whatever their nationality, if found in enemy, ex-enemy, or liberated territories." Implementation of this was apparently patchy in the British zone, where as late as October 1946 it was reported that, contrary to instructions from UNRRA headquarters, German Jews were "not regarded by the British Military as displaced persons and are not receiving UNRRA's assistance." As of November of that year, a British zonal directive was in place confirming that "German Jews are eligible for UNRRA care"—although in practice most of them lived outside UNRRA's camps and were looked after primarily by the JDC and other Jewish voluntary societies.[17]

The Allied forces initially tried to classify DPs by their country of origin to expedite efficient repatriation. But this immediately became a problem with regard to Jews, who were generally hostile to their countries of origin, notably Poland, and were unwilling to live in camps with non-Jewish DPs from those countries whom they regarded as the next thing to fascists. An UNRRA directive of January 1946 gave Jews the option of declaring their nationality to be either "Jewish" or the nationality of their prewar citizenship. First the Americans and then, reluctantly, the British, conceded the principle of Jewish as a nationality and of separate Jewish camps, or at least (in the British case) enclaves within camps.

From the beginning, nationality was a key marker of DP identity, inscribed on the individual's DP care along with name and age. It was something the British and Americans would have thought of as self-evident until they found out how complicated it was in practice. Along with Jewish nationality, Soviet nationality was a very vexed problem. In the Soviet view, everyone who held Soviet citizenship was "theirs" and ought to be repatriated. This included residents of the Baltic States, the parts of Ukraine and Rumania incorporated into the Soviet Union after the Nazi-Soviet Pact of 1939, whose citizenship was acquired by fiat from above and who often regarded the Soviet Union not as a homeland but as an enemy occupying power. But the West did not share this view of the legitimacy of the 1939 acquisitions, although the strength and consistency of its rejection was greater with regard to the Baltic States (Latvia, Lithuania, and Estonia) than with the West Ukrainian and Belorussian territories.

To further complicate matters, the anglophone use of the term "nationality" differed from that of the Soviet Union and East European countries. For the Americans and British, nationality was the same thing as citizenship. For the Poles, it might be the same thing or it might be different: that is, you might be a Polish citizen of Polish nationality (ethnicity), but you might also be a Polish citizen whose nationality was Ukrainian or Jewish. For the Soviets, it was always different, for there was no "Soviet" nationality, only Russian, Ukrainian, Georgian, Uzbek, Jewish, and other nationalities, all of whom shared Soviet citizenship.

The Western Allies, with the exception of the French, had relatively little difficulty in accepting Latvian, Lithuanian, and Estonian nationality as acceptable national identifications, invoking both their own nonacceptance of the 1939 pact and the prewar existence of independent Latvian, Lithuanian, and Estonian states. "The category of USSR includes all Soviet Republics," the military government in the US zone noted in November 1945, but "the incorporation of Estonia, Latvia and Lithuania into the Soviet Union as republics has not been recognized by the US Government," meaning that the nationality of displaced persons from the Baltic would be recognized as Estonian, Latvian, and Lithuanian. There was a minor difficulty about their eligibility for DP status, namely that, if one subtracted the Baltic states from the Soviet Union, they ceased to be part of the "United Nations" that had fought the war, which on the face of it made them ineligible. This, however, was brushed aside by the British and Americans. The French dissented, recognizing the DPs from the Baltic States as Soviet citizens and allowing the Soviet military to treat them as such in the period of forced repatriation. But there had never been many DPs from the Baltic states in the French zone anyway.[18]

The British and American position was not just an abstract legal judgement but a political one about the appropriateness of Soviet repatriation. In General Morgan's summation of the British view, there was "no question of [the Balts'] return to their home countries which, since 1939, had been systematically depopulated and destroyed by the Russians." Of course there was the problem of Balts who had supported the Germans and were therefore war criminals—but that was one for the military authorities to fight out with the Soviets. Certainly it was not a question that bothered Colonel Mickelson, director of civil affairs in the US zone, as a disapproving UNRRA staffer complained: Mickelson's "unofficial advisor" on Baltic affairs was the Alfred Valdmanis, minister of finance in the prewar Ulmanis government in Latvia and well-known as a Nazi collaborator during the war. On the other hand, opinion in UNRRA was not uniform, as the disapproving comment attests. Indeed, Klemmé thought UNRRA was full of "pro-communist" officials who assumed all Baltic DPs were collaborators: "I have heard a number of them say that if they could have had their way, none of the Baltic peoples would ever have been admitted to a D. P. Camp at all." *New York Times* correspondent Drew Middleton, a star wartime reporter from London, however, could not be called "pro-communist," and his reports on Baltic DPs also noted the Baltic collaboration problem. "At least one-third of the Balts in the DP camps had been collaborators," he wrote in October 1945, but they tended to make a good impression on American military government personnel, not just because most of them spoke English but because the US officers were often "only too willing to believe [the Baltic DPs'] . . . anti-Russian propaganda.[19]

Ukrainians were next on the list of DPs aspiring to be considered an independent nationality. This was complicated by a number of factors. In the first place, Ukrainians, unlike the citizens of the Baltic states, could not point to an actually existing prewar sovereign state to legitimate their nationality claim. To be sure, this was also the case of Jewish DPs, whose insistent claim to be allowed to identify themselves as Jewish by nationality was in process of being accepted. In the second place, the people likely to identify as Ukrainians had mainly, up to the Nazi-Soviet Pact of 1939, been divided between West Ukrainians, living in Poland with Polish citizenship, and East Ukrainians, living in the Soviet Ukrainian republic and Soviet citizens. With the pact, they all became "Soviet," in the Soviet view, and this was initially not contested by the Western Allies. "HMG does not recognize Ukrainian as a nationality" was firmly stated as British policy, and people claiming this identity under the heading of nationality on their DP cards should, in that view, be classified by their country of origin / prewar citizenship, that is, as either Polish or Soviet. However, the new Polish government, while recognizing "Ukrainian" as the nationality of some of its former citizens, indicated that it did not want such people repatriated and considered them now to be Soviet citizens.

Regardless of the stance taken by the various diplomatic players, substantial numbers of DPs persisted in calling themselves Ukrainians, mainly to lessen the possibility of forcible repatriation to the Soviet Union. When they were put in camps with Poles there were clashes and resentment on both sides. Their placement in separate camps in the US zone began as early as the summer of 1945, and by the fall of 1946 the practice was given official sanction. But the issue of principle on Ukrainian as a nationality took time to resolve. The British, unwilling to concede it, were under pressure from US and Canadian lobbyists upholding the Ukrainian national cause. Finally, never quite conceding the question on principle, UNRRA started to accept "Ukrainian" as a nationality entry on DP cards, thus generating statistics on numbers of "Ukrainians" that (however inaccurate) were much valued by Ukrainian nationalists. While for the West the illegitimacy of the Soviet acquisition of Western Ukraine and Belorussia in 1939 was not quite so clear-cut as in the case of the Baltic states, it nevertheless had widespread acceptance. Even within UNRRA, which tried not to be pushed into explicitly anti-Soviet positions, there were undoubtedly many officers who privately shared Morgan's view that this was all hair-splitting and that Ukrainian was a nationality of people who had been mistreated by the Soviets.[20]

Belorussians tried to push the same case as Ukrainians, since their situation (an existing Soviet "Belorussian" republic, into which West Belorussians, formerly Polish citizens, were automatically incorporated with the Nazi-Soviet Pact of 1939) was analogous. But they were a much smaller group, and their claims were confused by the proliferation of labels that they used in their claims for separate nationality (Ruthenian, Krivich, Belorussian, White Russian). The

Allies, moreover, frequently got confused about whether the label "White Russian" was a political one, applying to prewar Russian émigrés labeled "Whites" in the Russian Civil War to distinguish them from the Bolshevik "Reds," or simply a geographical one, applying to persons from the lands on the borderlands between Russia and Poland known as Belorussia (which in Russian means "white Russia"). Whatever their name, they never got separate recognition as a nationality.

Russian, too, was never a recognized nationality for the purpose of DP status, although readers of contemporary UNRRA and zonal documents might be forgiven for thinking it was, so often was it used as a synonym for "Soviet." Russians from the Soviet Union, like other Soviet citizens, were formally ineligible for anything but transitory UNRRA care before being handed over to Soviet authorities for repatriation. There were, however, a few camps in the UNRRA system conventionally referred to as "Russian" (Mönchehof the best known), run by Russians who were prewar émigrés. Officially, the only prewar émigrés who qualified for DP status were those who had been displaced during the war from their habitual residence, that is, those taken by the Germans from East European cities with substantial Russian émigré communities like Belgrade and Prague to Germany, not those who had settled before the war in Paris or Berlin and stayed there during the war; in practice, such fine distinctions were not easy to draw. But the majority of the Mönchehof camp's residents—as opposed to its self-appointed leaders—were actually Soviet Russians, going under false papers as "stateless" to avoid repatriation.[21]

UNRRA under La Guardia

By the time of the fourth council of UNRRA met in March 1946, the situation in Europe looked worse than ever, as UNRRA confronted food supply and financial crises plus the problem—completely unanticipated a year earlier—of millions of DPs under UNRRA care who didn't want to go home. Prospects for the future looked bleak: it was not only that the US Congress was unhappy about continuing funding but that the US military leaders—fed up with having to keep GIs in Europe—wanted to close the DP camps for all but Jewish DPs. Secretary of State Byrnes agreed in principle, and there was sympathy for the idea of closing the DP camps in the British Foreign Office as well.

With all these signs that UNRRA was a sinking ship, senior staffers started thinking about their next career moves—either lobbying for jobs in its prospective successor (IRO), or in the new United Nations institutions like the

World Health Organization that were currently hiring. Lehman, who "assumed, as did many delegates, that the end of UNRRA was in sight," and who also had his eye on a new political opportunity (in his case, the US Senate), offered his resignation in March 1946. His successor, appointed on March 29, 1946, was Italian American Republican Fiorello La Guardia, an energetic former mayor of New York, "a good tough little fighter" as well as "a showman to his fingertips," in Commander Jackson's assessment, though others said the British viewed him as a "New York gangster."

La Guardia's task was basically to close down an institution that, in American eyes, had outlived its usefulness. But once in office, his characteristic energy came to the fore, and he plunged UNRRA into a flurry activity that, on the face of it, contradicted his mandate for closure. Used to seeing Jews as an important constituency from his New York days (where he had even picked up some Yiddish), he was eager to help the Jewish DPs resettle in Palestine and appeared to accept his personal emissary Ira Hirschmann's assessment that the non-Jewish DPs were likely to be collaborators and antisemites. According to General Morgan, an early casualty of the La Guardia reign, La Guardia's "chief interest [in the DPs] lay with the Jewish camps. For the rest, among Poles, Balts and others there was thinly disguised impatience with these people who were not gladly hurrying back to their fatherlands," and he dismissed the DPs' apprehensions about return as "imagination based on propaganda stories." A purge of other UNRRA staffers considered antisemitic followed Morgan's departure.[22]

La Guardia's major undertaking as director was a campaign for mass repatriation of Poles known as "Operation Carrot" for the blatantly materialist incentives offered. Poles were the largest single national group in the camps and their hesitancy to return home was influenced both by anti-communist propaganda from the London Poles and by anxiety about economic conditions and stability back in Poland. Operation Carrot was a plan—opposed by many in the British and American military, as well as by General Morgan before his removal—for expedited repatriation, according to which Polish DPs who repatriated before the end of 1946 would receive two months food rations from UNRRA when they crossed the border. Kathryn Hulme, an UNRRA officer in the Polish Wildflecken camp, has described the effect on hungry DPs of a mock-up of the rations on offer—"flour, dried peas, rolled oats, salt, evaporated milk, canned fish and a small mountain of lard"—displayed in the canteen, at which Polish DPs "stood in awe, star[ing] at the terrible fascination of the bait, thrashing, twisting and turning before they took the hook." But in spite of a large take-up in Wildflecken, the overall results were disappointing. Almost 124,000 Polish DPs were repatriated from the three Western zones of Germany in the period from September to December 1946, but about 200,000 DPs identifying as Poles were still in UNRRA care at the beginning of 1947. Moreover, criticism of the campaign by nationalist Poles stimulated an anti-communist backlash in the United States, with Charles Rozmarek, president of the Polish American Congress, claiming before an audience of eight thousand in Chicago that UNRRA was "under communist domination, being used as an instrument of political persecution and coercion."[23]

Polish repatriation was not the only issue on which La Guardia offended US anticommunists in the United States. One of his first acts after arrival in Europe in the summer of 1946 was to embark on a seven-week inspection tour of UNRRA's field missions in Soviet Ukraine and Belorussia, Yugoslavia, Czechoslovakia, and Poland, a perennial object of anticommunist disapproval in the States. In the course of the trip, he took the opportunity to make a side trip to Moscow, set up by Commander Jackson, using his good Soviet contacts. This included a personal meeting with Stalin on August 29.[24]

It could have been a watershed moment for UNRRA, and Allied relations more broadly; and no doubt that was what La Guardia, a man of political ambitions beyond UNRRA, hoped. His plan, apparently, was to extract a financial contribution to UNRRA from the Soviet Union (which had so far paid almost nothing to UNRRA) and thereby impress the US Congress sufficiently for it to continue its own funding. Stalin played along at their meeting, speaking effusively about UNRRA (whose help in postwar reconstruction of Ukraine and Belorussia he greatly appreciated) and about La Guardia personally, and letting UNRRA off the hook by restricting his criticism of noncooperation on Soviet repatriation to the British and American occupation regimes. La Guardia did some boasting about his success with Stalin in the United States (though attributing to Stalin a suggestion on repatriation he is most unlikely to have made) and received some favorable publicity there. But his hopes of a diplomatic coup resetting Allied relations with the Soviet Union were disappointed. Despite Gromyko's public repetition of the promise to contribute financially to UNRRA in at the United Nations on November 26, 1946, and Jackson's energetic lobbying with Foreign Minister Bevin and Stafford Cripps, chancellor of the Exchequer, to get the British on side with their own promise to keep paying, it all came to nought. As Jackson explained it in retrospect, the United States had decided that UNRRA's activity was "strengthening Eastern Europe," that is, the other side in the emerging Cold War, and the best way to stop this was to close the institution down. La Guardia did not wait for UNRRA's final demise but resigned on December 13, 1946.[25]

Cold War and the End of UNRRA

By the time of La Guardia's resignation, the growing antipathy between the Soviet Union and Western allies was hardening into the settled state of competitive hostility and suspicion that would become known as the "Cold War." Some of the big questions of the immediate postwar period had already been answered. The United States was *not* contemplating a swift postwar withdrawal from Europe, in contrast to what had happened after the First World War. Contrary to Soviet hopes, the British and the Americans were not going to split, but rather to unite in opposition to the Soviet Union in a bipolar world. The cooperation over postwar reconstruction epitomized by UNRRA's field missions was not going to be the model in the future.

In the United States, the popular and political mood had swung sharply in an anti-communist and anti-Soviet direction. Even someone as pragmatic and nonideological as Dean Acheson succumbed to this mood, criticizing UNRRA for using US-funded relief to allow "governments bitterly hostile to us to entrench themselves" in Eastern Europe. La Guardia's strategy for UNRRA was foiled by the new mood. Relations between Allied and Soviet representatives became cool, even when—as in the case of Generals Clay and Sokolovsky—they had previously been cordial.

Churchill had supplied a metaphor for the new situation in his address in Fulton, Missouri, on March 5, 1946, speaking of an "iron curtain" that had descended on Eastern Europe. Deploring the Sovietization of Eastern Europe, he called on the United States and United Kingdom to join hands with the rest of democratic Europe to stand up for their values.[26] While Churchill was now a private person, having failed to win reelection as prime minister in the British elections, his successors had encouraged him to make the trip to the United States, and his speech had been approved in advance by President Truman and his secretary of state. For the Soviets, and Stalin in particular, with his complex attitude to Churchill—the old anti-Bolshevik of the Russian Civil War whom Stalin had charmed into wartime cooperation—there could not have been a messenger more likely to catch them on the raw. "Churchill's speech was blackmail," Stalin told Polish communist leaders. "Its aim was to frighten us." The Soviet response was as rude as they could make it, to show they were not frightened.[27]

As anti-Soviet feeling grew in the West, anti-UNRRA sentiment grew along with it. A particular source of grievance stemmed from the UNRRA field missions providing aid to Soviet Ukraine and Belorussia, which congressional critics held allowed the Soviet Union to divert its own funds for military purposes. But corruption and left-wing penetration of the institution were also issues. The US ambassador to Warsaw thought that UNRRA people were too tolerant of communist-dominated regimes and inclined to "whitewash" them. Frederick Morgan, former UNRRA head in Germany, claimed that the organization was "honey combed with spies," a process facilitated by the "infiltration" of Jewish refugees from Eastern Europe. As McCarthyite fervor increased in the United States, specific UNRRA officials found themselves accused of being Soviet spies.[28]

The death knell was sounded at the Geneva council of UNRRA in August 1946, when William L. Clayton, representing the United States, announced that "UNRRA had fulfilled its two purposes: to furnish supplies to those liberated countries which themselves lacked the foreign exchange to pay for basic necessities, and to establish an organization to procure, to ship and to deliver such supplies." While the Soviet Union and a number of other countries spoke in favor of UNRRA's continuance, Britain supported the United States on closure—and, since they (especially the States) contributed the great bulk of the funding, their voices were decisive. Few tears were shed for UNRRA, despite its substantial achievements in the delivery of supplies to war-damaged countries ("three times the total amount of American aid following the First World War," according to one scholar). As for the displaced persons under UNRRA's care, they were living in comparative comfort in well-functioning camps—but about a million of them had rejected repatriation, and UNRRA had no clear long-term alternative to offer.

UNRRA missions and offices were serially closed down from January to June 1947, with a new displaced persons headquarters for Germany, Austria, Italy, and the Middle East being set up in Paris in February. In July, the International Refugee Organization (IRO) took over UNRRA's functions with regard to displaced persons, but with a different mandate. From now on, resettlement, not repatriation, would be the mission.[29]

2

Repatriation to the Soviet Union
and Allied Conflict

AT YALTA, the Allies had agreed to repatriate all nationals outside their home territory at the end of the war. It was anticipated that there would be some resistance, since those slated for repatriation included persons captured in German uniform, deserters from the Soviet Army, and Vlasov Army fighters and other collaborators. As all these categories implied punishment on return, it was explicitly stated that such persons "will be repatriated without regard to their personal wishes and by force if necessary." As for other categories— persons who, although not clearly liable to punishment, nevertheless preferred not to return—no explicit statement was made on the question of forcible repatriation, but there was certainly no positive affirmation of any individual right to opt out. Yet it was obvious that here, too, there might be problems. Of the million or so displaced persons claimed by the Soviet Union who remained in Europe after the big forced repatriations of 1945, perhaps three quarters were not prewar Soviet citizens but had involuntarily acquired Soviet citizenship as a result of annexation—or, in the perspective of many of them, illegal occupation—according to the terms of the Nazi-Soviet Pact of 1939. These people included West Ukrainians and West Belorussians, citizens of Poland before 1939 who were often highly nationalistic and anticommunist, and for-mer citizens of the Baltic states of Latvia, Lithuania, and Estonia that had been independent between the wars. According to Soviet definition, they were all as much Soviet citizens, subject to repatriation, as those who had grown up as its citizens since the establishment of the Soviet Union. With this definition, trouble over repatriation was inevitable, for the majority of those DPs the Soviet Union claimed as its citizens did not so regard themselves.

UNRRA was only marginally involved in the forced repatriations, as it had barely started effective operation with DPs at the time they occurred; the mechanics of repatriation were handled by the military. But UNRRA officers had given possible repatriation problems at least some thought before the end of the war, judging by a report of a meeting in Washington between Director Lehman and a Czech delegation at which "it was made clear that UNRRA could not oblige a displaced person to return to his country if he himself did not want to do so and that UNRRA could not oblige a Government to take a national back whom it did not wish to readmit." But here the specific issue under consideration—the question of repatriation of a Czech national who had acquired German citizenship—was part of a different East European repatriation problem, that of whether citizens not of the majority (titular) nationality would be welcome back after the war. A number of East European countries would, in fact, decline to receive such persons. But the Soviet Union was not among the countries that wished to discriminate against particular ethnicities in the context of repatriation.[1]

In an age that Rogers Brubaker has called that of the "unmixing" of nationalities, the Soviet Union was notable for sticking to its old endorsement of mixing. It was probably unique among the East European nations pursuing repatriation in being willing to take everybody who could prove citizenship (while at the same time basically closing the door on anyone without citizenship, notably foreigners who had married Soviet citizens during or after the war). It did not discriminate on the basis of ethnicity (known as "nationality" in the Soviet bloc): Armenians, Soviet Germans, Tatars, and Kalmyks were as welcome as Russians to return, as long as they had held Soviet citizenship on the outbreak of war. Indeed, the Soviet Union repatriation welcome was truly eclectic: it embraced criminals and people with TB, venereal diseases, or psychiatric disorders, as long as they were Soviet citizens. The Soviet Union did not even attempt to prevent persons regarded as "class" or political enemies from returning, as it had done after the First World War, when Russian émigrés were stripped of their citizenship. It was willing, even eager, to take people it regarded as "war criminals." No distinction was drawn between prewar Soviet citizens and those in the Baltics and western regions who had acquired their Soviet citizenship involuntarily as the result of the Nazi-Soviet Pact of 1939. The Soviet approach after the Second World War was to accept everyone, regardless of class, ethnicity, politics, religion, health, or criminal record, and put them to work on their return—but to sort out the undesirables at the border in a process called "filtration" and send them to labor camps to work as convicts.

This was a sharply different approach from that of Poland, Yugoslavia, and Czechoslovakia (all more or less in the Soviet bloc by 1948), since those countries were eager to repatriate their titular citizens but not others, for example, ethnic Ukrainians and Belorussians who before the war had been Polish citizens. The unwillingness to accept nontitular citizens as repatriates was a counterpart to these same countries' expulsion of citizens of German nationality at the end of the war, even if their citizenship was of long standing, and both formed part of a general push toward ethnic homogeneity within states. Jews were not overtly excluded from UNRRA-organized repatriations to Poland. In practice, however, there is no indication that Polish Jewish DPs either sought to join the UNRRA efforts or were in fact repatriated by that route. From the spring of 1946, news of antisemitism in Poland brought by "infiltrees" leaving the country after repatriation from the Soviet Union would have constituted a powerful discouragement.[2]

Forcible Repatriation and Resistance

At the end of the war, the Soviets estimated that about five million of their citizens were in Europe, three million of them in territories under control of the Western Allies and the other two million in those under Soviet control (the Soviet zones of Germany and Austria, plus East European countries liberated by the Soviet Army). The majority of these were forced laborers taken from the Soviet Union during the war, together with about 1.7 million who had been prisoners of war. The British and US military set out to cooperate with the Soviets on repatriation. Not only did it seem natural, after cessation of hostilities, that all POWs, forced laborers, and others displaced by the war should be returned home as soon as possible, there was also the reciprocal angle—British and US citizens who had ended up the war in parts of the Reich occupied by Soviet forces needed to be sent home too.

At Yalta in February 1945, Stalin had warned Churchill that, among the Soviet citizens who would need repatriating after the war, there were both people "whom the Germans forced to work" and people "who voluntarily raised arms against the Allies," stressing that the Soviet Union considered both categories to be Soviet citizens subject to repatriation. Churchill's response was that the British government "wants to return both categories of people as soon as possible to their native land." But very quickly, problems surfaced with the repatriation of those who feared they were liable for punishment on return. The Americans encountered these when attempting to move a small group of

Russian Liberation Army (Vlasovite) prisoners from Fort Dix back to Germany on June 29, 1945. The POWs barricaded themselves in and set fire to the building, and three of them hanged themselves—all of which was widely publicized in the US press. The British in Austria, trying to hand over Cossacks—officers and soldiers of military units, some of which had fought with the Germans, along with their huge entourages of family, civilians, and animals—encountered fierce resistance at Lienz in May–June 1945, which subsequently became an iconic place of martyrdom for anti-Soviet resisters. The Cossack officers were lured to a meeting, and when they failed to return a crowd of perhaps four thousand gathered in protest at an open-air service. Twenty thousand Cossacks were handed over to the Soviets, while those that escaped and ran away to hide were hunted down by Soviet troops for a month, with over a thousand recaptured. As in the United States, the Allied troops involved were distressed and public opinion shocked at the news of suicides and scenes of desperation.

There were reasons for the Cossacks' and POWs' alarm. A much-quoted Soviet wartime order of August 16, 1941, had declared POWs to be traitors, regardless of the circumstances in which they were taken prisoner, and made their families liable to punishment. Punishment was mandated around the same time for persons who had "voluntarily retreat[ed] with the fascist forces." These directives were never officially cancelled, and the Soviets (unlike the Poles) failed to declare an amnesty in the early postwar period.[3]

The mood in the American and British military was turning against forced repatriation (especially the lower ranks that actually had to execute it) and the same was true in the US State Department. The British Foreign Office, however, remained very uneasy about any policy change that would overtly break the Yalta Agreement. In early September, General Eisenhower ordered US troops in Germany to suspend participation in forced repatriation and called on the State Department to reexamine its policy in this respect. A month later, he went public with this suspension, perhaps to force the State Department's hand, but also without consulting the British, who were furious when they read about it in the *New York Times* on October 5, 1945. The initial British reaction was irritated reaffirmation that British policy remained unchanged—namely that force might be exercised by Soviet troops invited into the zone to carry out repatriation of their nationals, although British troops would use force only as a last resort. Anxious about the effect of a violation of Yalta on the Soviets, they advised the Americans to take a similar line. But in fact, rather than Eisenhower reconsidering his position to stay on side with the British, it seems to have been British commander-in-chief Montgomery who blinked, since a confidential British memo noted that he had stated on October 19 that he was "no longer prepared use for force for the repatriation of Soviet nationals," but that this should not be publicized.

Behind-the-scenes argument continued, along with some contradictory behavior by the military. The Allies' attitude was itself somewhat schizoid, as a practical desire to clear the refugees out of Central Europe as quickly as possible coexisted with growing anti-Communism and distrust of the Soviet Union. Maverick General Patton managed to flout the evolving consensus in both directions, first releasing five thousand Soviet POWs against orders in June 1945, and then in November ordering that all identified Soviet citizens in UNRRA DP camps or working in German farms and factories be declared ineligible for UNRRA care and handed over to the Soviets for repatriation. Others were less precipitate, but in any case, "identified" turned out to be the key word. There had always been an escape clause with regard to individual repatriations, though probably it took time for this to sink in, namely that Allied personnel were meant to accept that a DP's citizenship was whatever he said it was, "regardless of its plausibility or supporting documentation."

The official position of the British War Office was that, as of the winter of 1945–46, "there are no Soviet nationals, British interpretation, left in prisoner of war camps in this country." So that was a problem solved, and if some Soviet POWs had managed to assume another identity, it was no business of the British. The US position more or less stabilized with the McNarney-Clark directive of December 20, 1945, which "limited the use of force to individuals captured in German uniforms, Red Army soldiers that had not been demobilised and those charged with assisting the enemy." This essentially covered all POWs, but with emphasis on those who had fought with the Germans. It did not, however, cover forced laborers. From early in 1946, the Allies in practice stopped cooperating with Soviet mass repatriation—but this had, in any case, been largely accomplished, except for those who remained hidden in UNRRA's DP camps and German towns and villages. As of March 1, 1946, 4.4 million Soviet citizens had been repatriated, about two-thirds of them from the Western zones of Germany and Austria and the rest from the Soviet zone. Of these, 1.6 million had been POWs and the rest former forced laborers and other civilians. According to Soviet estimates, that left close to about seven hundred thousand Soviet citizens, including those from the Baltic states, on the wrong side of the Soviet border a year after the war's end.[4]

Filtration

The Allied objection to forced repatriation was based not only on resistance among the DPs but also on the assumption that those who were repatriated were all bound for punishment—Gulag or even execution. This was the universal assumption in the DP camps and also in the Allied command. As already indicated, it was known that during the war Stalin had declared that all POWs, regardless of the circumstances of their capture, were traitors. Probably the Western Allies, like the DPs, had heard stories of Soviet prisoners taken during the Russo-Finnish war in 1940 who, on being returned to the Soviet Union at the end of that war, were reportedly sent to Gulag and the officers executed. They also heard from fierce DP resisters to repatriation their conviction that harsh punishment awaited them.

Building on the Finnish War experience, the Soviets started setting up a regular procedure for checking returnees who had been in German hands to uncover traitors, spies, and deserters as early as December 1941, and by early 1945 it was fully regularized under the heading of "filtration," with a network of filtration check points under the NKVD set up in the border zone just inside the (now reclaimed) Soviet borders. "Filtration" did not mean stopping some people entering and letting others through, but rather—given that everyone was let through except noncitizens—sorting them into categories. The two basic categories of repatriates were the harmless ones, who should be sent home, and the dangerous ones, who should be sent to the Gulag. Women, who made up half the forced labor contingent at the end of the war (1.25 to 1.5 million), as well as children and the elderly, went more or less automatically into the harmless category. The Gulag group, much smaller, consisted mainly of former POWs who had served under German command. In between were the men of working age who should be drafted back into the Soviet Army (if former soldiers) or into labor units (former forced laborers). Given the drastic shortage of labor in the Soviet Union in the immediate postwar years, it is not surprising that the filtration process, initially conceived as a purely security one, quickly acquired an additional and crucial function of manpower distribution.

Initially, as the first contingents came through filtration points at the end of 1944, almost half (45 percent) were consigned to Gulag, while 15 percent were drafted back into the army and 40 percent sent home. The Soviets, of course, did not announce this, but no doubt the news trickled back across the border (there were always some successful escapees from the repatriation/

filtration process) and confirmed the DPs' and the Allies' fears. As we now know, though the Allies probably did not, the distribution changed quite sharply in 1945, when the numbers were much larger and the rate of arrest much lower. Of more than four million former POWs and forced laborers who had gone through filtration as of March 1946 (including the 1944 contingent), less than 7 percent were assigned to Gulag, with 19 percent being redrafted into the army, 14 percent drafted for labor as civilians, and the remaining 60 percent sent back to their homes. Perhaps another 1 to 3 percent passed through filtration successfully but were arrested on arrival. From the standpoint of the Allies, however, repatriation to the Soviet Union continued to mean Gulag or death for the repatriates.

The aggregate figures hide significant differences in outcomes for POWs and "civilians" (mainly forced laborers), as well as for men and women. Gulag was the outcome for 15 percent of returning POWs, while of the civilians, 81 percent of the men and over 99 percent of women were sent home. A detailed breakdown of 11,609 repatriates arrested at filtration as of October 1945 shows that 8,466 were identified as having fought under German command against the Allies, divided about evenly between volunteers for the Wehrmacht, on the one hand, and members of military formations that fought under German command (the Vlasov Army, the various national legions from the Baltic, and White emigrant units), on the other. The other substantial group consisted of people who had held police and other offices under German occupation (2,297).[5]

Running Conflicts over Repatriation

The Soviets were not reconciled to leaving seven hundred thousand of their citizens in Europe to form a new anti-Soviet emigration and deprive the Soviet Union of much-needed labor for postwar reconstruction. They continued to try to persuade Soviet DPs to repatriate voluntarily, while at the same time keeping up the hunt for persons they regarded as war criminals who would need to be repatriated by force. The Western Allies had to pretend to cooperate with both these tasks, while in fact often impeding them. It became a bitter issue in relations between the wartime Allies and in the United Nations. UNRRA, in whose camps many of the DPs lived, was caught in the middle, basically going along with the American and British military governments (which, given the institution's dependence on them could scarcely be avoided), despite the fact that some UNRRA staffers had sympathy for the USSR's wish to repatriate its citizens and were concerned by the thought that, by sheltering the nonrepatriating, they might be protecting war criminals.

A number of Soviet institutions with different styles and missions were involved in repatriation. The Soviet armed forces had carried out the forcible mass repatriation of 1945, with NKVD support on the filtration aspect. Subsequently, voluntary repatriation (with much smaller numbers involved) was handled by the Soviet Military Administration in Germany (SVAG, the counterpart in the Soviet zone of the American and British zonal occupation governments) in association with a special Repatriation Agency established in Moscow in 1944 under the Soviet Council of Ministers in 1944. For the SVAG, which was responsible for running the Soviet zone of Germany, setting up a civilian administration, directing the Soviet forces stationed there, handling reparations, and a host of other urgent tasks, repatriation was a relatively minor concern. For the Moscow-based Repatriation Agency, it was the only concern; and this was the Soviet agency that knew most about DPs and was most likely to understand—sometimes even to sympathize with—their problems. But the agency's clout within the Soviet government was limited. Its head, General Filipp Golikov, previously of military intelligence (GRU), was not admitted to the top counsels of government and party (where, for all the Soviet leaders' oft-expressed concern for repatriating Soviet DPs, the issue was rarely discussed). He was unlikely to prevail in any conflict with the Soviet military or, despite his intelligence background, with the security forces. Such conflicts were particularly frequent with SMERSH (an acronym for "Death to Spies"), whose job was the capture of Soviet war criminals, some of whom had found shelter in DP camps. The possibility of kidnapping by SMERSH was one of the nightmares of Soviet DPs.

In November 1944, shortly after taking office, General Golikov gave a promise, published in *Pravda* and broadcast on the radio, that repatriates would not be punished:

> The Soviet nation remembers and cares about its citizens who fell into German slavery. They will be received at home like sons of the motherland. Soviet circles consider that even those Soviet citizens who under German pressure and terror committed actions against the interests of the USSR will not be brought to responsibility if they will honestly fulfil their duty of returning to the USSR.

This, however, rang a bit hollow in light of the Soviet government's failure to issue any formal amnesty. Soviet repatriation offices, jointly subordinate to the

SVAG in Berlin and the Golikov agency in Moscow, were set up in the American, British, and French zones of Germany and Austria. As of February 1946, the Soviet Union had sixty-four liaison officers working there, mainly in the American and British zones (the second largest contingent after the Poles), plus a smaller group in Austria. The British and American military often regarded them as spies, or feared disturbances if they admitted them to camps, while the Soviets, at least judging by a later memoir by one of their number, were indignant at their treatment and saw themselves as carrying out a noble mission of recovering lost Soviet souls. UNRRA hovered uneasily in the middle. Even UNRRA's top officials were not authorized to meet Soviet liaison officers except in the presence of a representative of the military government of the zone in which they were working. No wonder that, as UNRRA's historian wrote, "liaison officers . . . were a cause of irritation." The Western military authorities were frequently skeptical of granting free access to their zones to army officers of the Eastern powers. They particularly disliked admitting Soviet officers to camps of Baltic DPs, even under UNRRA sponsorship, since unpleasant incidents often resulted. UNRRA, for its part, felt bound by its own council's resolutions to fight for the free movement of the liaison officers, even though such action "troubled relations with the very authorities on whom the whole enterprise depended."

In addition to dealing with the Soviets, which was no picnic, UNRRA had to negotiate the complexities of relations with the military occupation authorities, British and US, and the governments behind them. Increasing hostility and distrust between the Soviets and the Western powers complicated the situation, as did the existence of different opinions on repatriation and the Soviet Union within UNRRA's own ranks, and the diplomatic need on the part of UNRRA's leadership to avoid looking too leftwing or pro-Soviet.[6]

Some officers in UNRRA sympathized with the Soviet stand on repatriation, distrusted the Balts as likely collaborators, and were inclined to the view that DPs unwilling to repatriate were likely to be hiding a collaborationist wartime record. Ralph Price, chief of repatriation in the US zone in Germany in 1947, was one such, penning a long, fierce memo criticizing UNRRA for failing to implement any real repatriation program, and in effect offering only a welfare service. This, he implied, was in large part the result of intimidation, since any visible initiative on repatriation met an automatic negative response from the military authorities, the camp administrations, the Catholic welfare organizations, and a section of the US press (notably the *Chicago Tribune* and the *New York Daily News*).

The US military were generally suspicious of any UNRRA personnel involved in repatriation, Price wrote, especially if they spoke Russian or any other East European language, and still more suspicious of any UNRRA officer responsible for distribution of Soviet publications in the DP camps. They put their trust in East European DPs who had probably been Nazi collaborators, and allowed them to sabotage repatriation operations, as anticommunist Poles tried to do in Wildflecken. "A DP who elected to repatriate was allowed to be ridiculed as a sucker or a fool. He was laughed out of camp, without clothing, without medical assistance, and without food—while UNRRA Welfare officers administered to every need of those who called the repatriate a sucker and a fool and who elected to remain in Germany." UNRRA, though formally an international organization, was effectively hostage to the national interests of its chief sponsors, Price concluded.

The "Edwards incident" in May 1947 was a complicated imbroglio arising from statements made by Paul Edwards, UNRRA director in the US zone, emphasizing UNRRA's commitment to repatriation and its continuing view that this was a better outcome than resettlement. Edwards had urged the removal from the camps of anti-Soviet, anti-repatriation agitators who "are not the product of democratic processes but are rather the remnants of prewar regimes that reflect Nazi and Fascist concepts." This had produced an angry rebuttal published in the *New York Herald Tribune* by an official in the Intergovernmental Committee on Refugees, a body active on a small scale in resettlement, as well as a critical write-up in the US forces newspaper, *Stars and Stripes*. Myer Cohen stood by his embattled subordinate, however, and Edwards not only kept his position but successfully made the transfer from UNRRA to IRO a few months later.

These attitudes were not unique to Price and Edwards. Cohen himself, one of UNRRA's most senior officials, shared them at least to a degree. Margaret Bond, an UNRRA repatriation officer in Austria, strongly urged that "nonrepatriable" persons, notably émigrés and Nazi collaborators, be removed from the camps because, apart from the fact that they should not be in UNRRA camps to begin with, they exert "political pressure . . . to influence repatriable persons against returning to their countries." She noted, however, that some UNRRA team directors were "sheltering" such people.[7]

The anti-repatriation view (which was more or less coterminous with a broader anti-Soviet political orientation) was indeed well represented in UNRRA, including by top British UNRRA leaders such as Generals Frederick Morgan and Evelyn Fanshawe. UNRRA's fifth council meeting in Geneva in

August 1946 had reiterated the organization's primary commitment to repatriation and moreover resolved "that the Administration shall remove all UNRRA personnel who discourage repatriation," as well as banning from the DP camps voluntary agency personnel working against repatriation of their nationals. But there is little evidence that any significant purge was undertaken. Raphael Cilento, himself no lover of the Soviet bloc, had had to move one UNRRA team director in the British zone, a US citizen of Polish origin, who boasted of the *low* repatriation figures in his region—but Cilento simply transferred the man "to a camp of non-repatriable Balts whose expressed views are more compatible with his own." As for the pro-repatriation faction in UNRRA, its members were always at risk of suspicion that their support for repatriation was actually a mask for support of the Soviet Union. General Fanshawe reported to his counterpart in the military government of the British zone that someone—presumably one of these "sympathizers"—seemed to be leaking cables between UNRRA's Washington and European offices and the military government to Soviet liaison officers.

Relations between Soviet missions and the military governments were often tense, and UNRRA leaders, too, were chary of getting close to the Soviet mission. General Alexander Davidov, first head of the Soviet Mission, complained that Lieutenant-General Frederick Morgan, head of UNRRA operations in Germany, was never available to see him, and that when he requested a meeting with Fiorello La Guardia, UNRRA's director-general, he was put off. His efforts to establish closer ties with UNRRA leaders received the evasive response that as a chief repatriation officer, most of his work should be with the Army. His plaintive concluding remark at one meeting that "finally, I want UNRRA not to forget that there is a Soviet Representative with UNRRA" evidently fell on deaf ears.

The missions' problems seem initially to have been worst with the British. In September 1946, there was a mini-scandal when General Davidov, based in the US zone, was forced by British military authorities to leave the British zone without accomplishing a planned meeting with Major-General Evelyn Fanshawe, head of UNRRA in the British zone (he had travel permission from the US military command, but, despite Fanshawe supporting his request, had not received advance clearance from the British military government). Miss Hansi Pollak, an UNRRA repatriation officer in the British zone, called around trying to sort this out, but to no avail. When Davidov complained to senior UNRRA official Myer Cohen and others, Cohen offered a personal apology for what had happened. (The opinion that "the military authorities have no respect for an international organization at this point" was attributed to Cohen in UNRRA's original transcript, although this was later changed to make the criticism come from Davidov.)[8]

Fanshawe—who claimed that while serving in the British Army during the war he had enjoyed "the most friendly, cordial and close relationships with members of the Soviet forces"—started off on a reasonable footing with Colonel Alexei Brukhanov (Davidov's successor as head of the Soviet mission) in October 1946, even going out of his way to thank Brukhanov for his cooperation and remarking on the "friendly atmosphere" of their meeting. But the two soon found out that they couldn't stand each other. Brukhanov was rude, verbose, and belligerent, in Fanshawe's view. He complained privately to Myer Cohen that "Col. Brukhanov, as usual, grilled me as though I had been a criminal in the dock. It seems to me almost impossible to work on our democratic ideas of freedom of the individual with Col Brukhanov's outlook on life." Brukhanov returned the compliment, naming Fanshawe as one of the worst of many obstructors he encountered, in the end refusing meet Soviet representatives at all, on the pretext that he needed the permission of the British government ("that's a representative of an international organization for you!").

From Brukhanov's standpoint, UNRRA was a potentially valuable organization hijacked by reactionaries.

> UNRRA took quite a few good resolutions on the speedy return home of displaced persons. But these resolutions were not implemented. Placing reliable emissaries at the head of the UNRRA's zone departments, the influential reactionary circles of USA, England and France distorted the sense of this international organization and turned it into a weapon of mass detention of citizens of the Soviet Union in capitalist countries.

These abstract sentiments covered a keen sense of humiliation at the runaround he personally had encountered from UNRRA and Western military authorities. When La Guardia, as new head of UNRRA, made his first and only official visit to Europe, Brukhanov was so desperate to see him that he actually went to his hotel and waited around until La Guardia returned at 1 a.m. At least La Guardia gave him a hearing, but relations with his subordinates only got worse in subsequent months.

At successive meetings between Soviet liaison officers and military and UNRRA representatives in the American zone in November 1946 and February 1947, the Soviet reiterated the same grievances: limited access to camps to talk to DPs, insults and difficulties on their camp visit, concealment of Soviet

DPs, and general deception and evasion. They wanted lists of DPs from UNRRA, as well as permission to participate in an advisory category in screening of DPs; and they urged UNRRA to take action against anti-Soviet camp committees and prevent circulation of anti-Soviet and anti-repatriation propaganda in the camps. They never wavered in their insistence that Balts and West Ukrainians were Soviet citizens, subject to repatriation just like prewar Soviet citizens. By early 1947, Brukhanov's complaints had become even more vehement. "My officers have been subject to terrorist attacks when visiting camps," he alleged.[9]

Soviet Efforts to Locate and Contact DPs

Since repatriation was now voluntary and on an individual basis, the first task was to locate Soviet DPs and try to persuade them to come home. This was not easy, given that most former Soviet citizens who did not want to repatriate had assumed other national identities and were living in camps, or out of them, as Poles, Yugoslavs, and West Ukrainians. This evasion strategy occurred with the connivance of the military governments and UNRRA, since all persons identified as Soviet were supposed to be handed over to the Soviets for repatriation. Have them register as pre-1939 citizens of Poland and the Baltic States was the advice that the head of the Russian Mönchehof camp, Konstantin Boldyrev, reported receiving when he visited General Eisenhower's headquarters in Frankfurt in 1945 to discuss his request that the Allies set up special camps for nonrepatriating Russians.

Finding Soviet DPs in the Western zones would, in principle, have been greatly facilitated if the Soviets had had access to lists of the DPs in UNRRA's camps. But this happened only rarely, despite repeated Soviet requests; and in fact the utility of such lists would have been limited, given the prevalence of false statement of nationality in DP registration. As time passed, Soviet requests became increasingly testy and included suggestions (justified, but very annoying to the Western side) that the military authorities were hiding Soviet citizens and condoning the false statements of nationality.

On the untypical occasions when lists were given, and the Soviet citizens in question gathered, the results were not always happy. Early in 1946, an officer of the US Third Army made up a nominal list of Soviet DPs in the Geisenfeld camp in Bavaria and advised the DPs that a Soviet liaison officer would be there to interview them the next day. During the night "all these Soviet citizens disappeared from camp of their own volition," leading the angry and humiliated Soviet representatives to conclude that UNRRA had hidden the DPs and to complain of "the mockery of the Soviet Liaison Officer and the Sabotage in carring [*sic*] out of the agreements about the repatriation of Soviet citizens."

The Western stance was not only contradictory in practice but also, to a degree, in principle, since the institutions involved did not always agree or act in concert. The British military authorities had always forbidden "handing over registration documents and lists of Soviet citizens living in UNRRA camps" to Soviet liaison officers. UNRRA's position, similarly, was that lists of DPs should *not* be given to Soviet representatives, as this would be incompatible with its duty of care to the DPs. At most, UNRRA officers might provide Soviet representatives with the names of individual DPs who had stated a desire to return. In the American zone, however, the military authorities were authorized to provide lists of Soviet citizens living in UNRRA camps to the Soviets—until UNRRA's acting chief of operations, Cyrus Greenslade, noticed this and made such a fuss that the Americans backed off, rescinding the Third Army's order on providing lists of Soviet DPs to the Soviet repatriation officers in January 1947. That left the Western authorities united, but the Soviets aggrieved.

Even if UNRRA had been more forthcoming, its lists might not have helped. As one Soviet representative complained acidly, according to UNRRA's lists (he did not explain how he had seen them), there were no Soviet citizens registered in its camps anyway. Indeed, how many Soviet citizens were in fact in the DP camps was the subject of an acrimonious running dispute between the Soviet Union and the Western powers. At a meeting in October 1946, General Fanshawe said there were 341 Soviet nationals registered in UNRRA camps in the British zone, while General Lenclud said there were 75 in French zone. Brukhanov, however, claimed that the real number in the British zone was more like 113,000.[10]

There was even less clarity on the issue of Soviet DPs living *outside* the camps. This was a question on which UNRRA and the zone authorities genuinely had very poor information, not just on nationality but on everything. UNRRA, at least in the US zone, had apparently agreed in principle to provide names and addresses of such people, while at the same time stating with dubious accuracy that there were "very few people receiving UNRRA care living outside the camps." In the British zone, General Fanshawe simply told Soviet representatives that UNRRA was not authorized to register DPs living outside the camps, which was probably true. General Davidov was of the opinion that there were probably five thousand Soviet citizens (including those from the Baltic states and West Ukrainians) living outside camps in the American zone alone. This had to be a guess, since the Soviets had no firm data to go on. They were explicitly forbidden, at least in the British zone, from trying to get lists of "free-living" Soviet DPs (those residing outside the camps) from local German officials ("It is a matter between the German authorities and Military Govern-ment, and direct intervention by a Soviet L[iaison] O[fficer] with Burgermeis-ters [sic] in this matter will not be tolerated"). As of mid-1948, the Soviet estimate of the total number of "Soviet" DPs in Germany and Austria, inside and outside camps, was 233,928, of whom 9,292 were Russians, 63,238 Ukrai-nians, and 149,575 from the three Baltic states.

The task of tracking down Soviet citizens not desiring repatriation who lived outside camps in the Western zone, in rented accommodation in Ger-man towns and villages, was formidable, but the Soviet liaison officers did their best. As SMERSH, looking for war criminals, was doing the same, and stories of kidnapping were rife among the DPs, the efforts of the Soviet liai-son officers caused great alarm. "Free-living" DPs would run away or abruptly change residences if a Soviet officer was spotted in the neighborhood. When cornered, the DPs often said they were agreeable in principle to the idea of repatriation, but their current circumstances—marriage to or cohabitation with a foreigner, health problems and the like—prevented them doing so in the short term. One DP woman contacted by repatriation officers, living with an American serviceman and the mother of a toddler, said she was willing to repatriate, but not until her child grew up.[11]

Visits to DP camps were allowed, provided that the visit was scheduled in advance and the Soviet liaison officer was accompanied by Allied and UNRRA personnel, but the Soviets regarded such visits in practice as "a farce." In the British zone, Soviet liaison officers properly accompanied would be "granted permission to address willing audiences" only "providing the camp authorities consider that no violence will ensue as a result." It was the Soviet officers, not the DPs, who were at risk of violent attack. There were very few specifically Russian camps in the UNRRA system, and those that existed were generally run by fiercely anti-Soviet émigrés. If Soviet representatives attempted to visit these to persuade DPs to return, it is not evident from the record. The camps they usually went to were Baltic or Ukrainian, dominated by anti-Soviet nation-alists and populated by DPs who had become Soviet citizens only inadver-tently, by virtue of the 1939 Nazi-Soviet Pact, and did not consider the Soviet Union their homeland. In these camps, the response to the visit of a Soviet liaison officer was usually one of hostility, organized and directed by the elected camp administrations, and the visits themselves tumultuous. In one Baltic camp, the DPs hung flags of independent (prewar) Estonia, Latvia, and Lithuania in the interview room and asked hostile questions about repression in the Soviet Union. At another camp, Soviet liaison officers were shut out of the administration building by the DPs and reduced to poking Soviet newspapers through the window—to which the DPs inside responded by setting the papers on fire. Mud, rocks, and catcalls often greeted the Soviet liaison officers' arrival and accompanied their departure. At the NTS-dominated Russian Mönchehof, the insults to a visiting Soviet repatriation officer were more subtle: as the officer left the camp club, accompanied by his American protectors, he noticed a Russian (I. N. Rostovtsev, of distinguished noble origin) standing by the exit and asked if he had a question, to which Rostovtsev's answer was "I am waiting for you to leave, so that I can lock the door."

"It is not a normal condition, when a Soviet representative has to enter a camp in company with Military Police," said General Davidov at a meeting with the US military in July, complaining that when they visited the camps "groups of DPs stand around and mock us. Three Soviet officers have been beaten . . . DPs sometimes throw rocks into our cars." Brukhanov, while expressing gratitude for the provision of "a group of British riflemen" to protect him on his proposed visit to one camp, noted that "the state of affairs when a Soviet officer cannot visit a camp without being assaulted is not as conditions should be." He cited the case of one Soviet officer, stabbed in the back with a dagger, who survived only by "a fortunate accident." An independent report to the United Nations General Assembly commissioned by Secretary-General Trygve Lie confirmed that Soviet, as well as Yugoslav, repatriation officers had suffered "embarrassment, humiliation or injury" on some occasions while visiting DP camps.[12]

Distribution of Soviet newspapers in the camps was another way of making contact with Soviet DPs, but on this issue, too, there was perennial conflict. Soviet representatives repeatedly complained of obstacles put in the way of distribution and of the Allies giving evasive answers to their justified protests. As of September 1946, no agreement had been reached on free interchange of newspapers and published material between the Soviet and Western zones. UNRRA strictly forbade Soviet repatriation officers to provide newspapers and information on repatriation in person to DP camps, while agreeing that "Soviet newspapers and other literature suitable for informing Soviet DPs of conditions in the USSR and the conditions of repatriation" might be handed over to Allied authorities for distribution. How diligent the Allies were in this task is open to question, but even when that hurdle was overcome, camp administrations—free to make their own decisions on such matters—often banned Soviet publications from their camps. The French, as usual more inclined to cooperate with the Soviets than were the British or Americans, allowed the distribution of newspapers of the DPs' country of origin in DP camps in the French zone. Radio was another means of communication: the Soviet station "Volga" was set up in mid-1947 to broadcast throughout the Western zones in Ukrainian, Estonian, Lithuanian, and Latvian languages on the weekend—and presumably in Russian at other times—in mid-1947. But repatriating Soviet DPs regularly reported difficulties obtaining access to Soviet newspapers or Soviet broadcasts in the camps.[13]

Frustrated by the failure to get usable lists of names from military authorities or UNRRA, the Soviets developed their own methods of locating "their" DPs, one of which was via correspondence with family members back in the Soviet Union. In October 1946, the Soviet liaison officer asked an UNRRA representative in the American zone to publish advertisements in the zonal newspapers telling Soviet citizens that they could send and receive letters through the UNRRA camps letters by bringing them directly to the Soviet mission in Heidelberg. Postal service was operating again in Germany, so such letters could have been sent by regular mail. But the advantage of routing them through the mission was that it would enable Soviet liaison officers first to obtain the addresses of DPs and then to use their delivery as a pretext for making personal contact. A Soviet source gives the total volume of letters for the eighteen months from mid-1948 to 1950 as forty-two hundred letters from the Soviet Union to DPs for the period from the middle of 1948 to 1950, with eighteen hundred letters sent from DPs to the Soviet Union.

The Soviets were concerned that too many of the letters going through the regular mail contained anti-repatriation content, including warnings from relatives not to come back to the Soviet Union and over-favorable accounts of life in the West from the DPs. It was decided in 1947 that all letters between DPs and their Soviet relatives should go through "control" by the repatriation agency, in addition to the regular Soviet censorship. This seems to have amounted to selection of the most suitable letters, mainly those from DPs who had repatriated that praised their warm welcome on return, and suppression of the rest.

By 1950, Moscow was often sending only the addresses of letters received to the missions in Europe, not the letters themselves, requiring the recipients,

once contacted by a Soviet representative, to specifically request their letters—
a practice that, as one of those Soviet representatives abroad protested, was
unhelpful in the effort of convincing DPs of the Soviets' good faith. DPs
tended to respond very "warily" to Soviet liaison officers seeking to deliver
letters from home, much preferring to receive them by mail. It was only rarely
possible to persuade the mission to send their letter on through the mail rather
than hand-delivering it, although one Jewish woman DP, located in an
UNRRA camp that Soviet liaison officers were unable to visit, brought it off
after repeatedly rebuffing the mission's invitation for her to come and pick it
up herself. It was a really bad idea to involve the Soviet mission in the delivery
of letters, one returning DP, a lawyer, told his interviewer: "It arouses suspicion
among the recipients that these letters are inspired by the Soviet authorities,
that they are written under pressure."[14]

Some letters from home were genuinely initiated by Soviet families in search
of missing relatives, while others were written after official solicitation, and yet
others probably dictated by the authorities. The preparatory work that often
went into the production of a "letter from home" is evident from the Repatriation Agency's files. Having located a free-living Lithuanian DP in the British
zone, repatriation officers urgently requested Moscow to "get letters from her
husband" to encourage her to return. When a similar request came in from
Argentina, Moscow responded regretfully that it had proved impossible to
"organize" letters from relatives to persuade a resettled DP to repatriate. How
the letters were used in practice is illustrated by the case of DP Anisimova in
1948: tracked down by Soviet liaison officers and found to be living with a German man and disinclined to repatriate, she had been given letters from relatives
to persuade her to change her mind, so far to no avail, but members of the team
"are continuing work to persuade Anisimova to return."

One of the talents that DP life had sharpened was that of practical criticism
of Soviet texts. When the Danos family received a letter from Mischka's elder
brother, back in Riga, in 1948, they subjected it to stringent stylistic and content analysis, concluding, on the basis of the handwriting, that it had indeed
been written by him, but, on the basis of untypical official language and content, that it had probably been composed under duress. The Repatriation
Agency itself noted that the letters arriving through its Ukrainian department
tended to be suspiciously standard and clichéd. Some family letters actually
did help to convince DPs to repatriate, or so they told interviewers on reentry.
But others were received only with silence, or even mockery, like the response
from a Russian landlord in Australia (evidently a prewar émigré) stating that

the addressee, his former tenant, had departed for parts unknown, and concluding impudently with the Orthodox salutation "God preserve you."

Another way of getting the names of Soviet DPs in the camps was to encourage repatriating DPs to provide lists of names from the camps they had been living in. Some responded willingly; many others either provided names of DPs who had already left the camps for resettlement destinations or simply failed to comply, saying they could not remember the names of any of their fellow residents. But even the minority of helpful repatriates could rarely identify DPs in their camps likely to respond positively to contact from a repatriation officer. It seems doubtful that, as an American-sponsored German-language newspaper in the US zone claimed, the Soviets were so desperate to get their DPs to return that they were secretly offering them money (allegedly 200 DM per family), but they certainly had their backs to the wall in their efforts to popularize repatriation.[15]

Rhetorical Framing of the Repatriation Debate

The international agreements on the conduct of war (the Hague Convention of 1907 and the Geneva Convention of 1929) mandated the return of prisoners of war as quickly as possible after the conclusion of peace. The focus was entirely on states' obligations, with no discussion of the possibility of individual unwillingness to return. The problem, First World War experience suggested, was that states with large numbers of enemy prisoners of war might retain them for their own labor needs in postwar reconstruction, as the French and others had done for some years at the end of the war. In any case, states were used to negotiating prisoner of war returns on a bilateral basis, leaving room for mutual reprisals. None of these rules and precedents adequately covered the situation at the end of the Second World War, when there was no formal conclusion of a peace treaty and the main defeated state, Germany, was under quadripartite occupation by four military governments whose prisoners of war, alas, were not conveniently congregated in the appropriate zones. Nor did it provide any guidance about the return of civilians moved out of occupied countries to Germany during the war for use as forced labor.

The Soviet Union was not a signatory to the Geneva Convention, but its thinking on the need for immediate return of prisoners was fully aligned with it. When difficulties arose (because of resistance to return among POWs and the Allies' embarrassment about it), the Soviet Union's first and gut response was outrage at any talk of delays or individual choice, on the basis of a strong sense of entitlement (as was also the case with reparations). As Vyshinsky told the UN, "We refuse to accept this tolerance. We paid a high price for it, with too much blood and too many lives."

Remembering the First World War, the Soviets assumed that, once again, economic motives lay behind slowness of the European Allies to repatriate POWS and forced laborers—and even found this confirmed, by occasional off-the-record comments along the same lines by sympathetic Western officials. Initially, their concern was to recover tens of thousands of Soviet citizens brought to Germany as forced labor who were still, a few months after cessation of hostilities, employed in German farms and factories. But then their focus shifted to Allied employment of these individuals. Brukhanov reported in his memoirs that a cynical British Army officer had remarked to one of the Soviet liaison officers, Major Safonov, that "while Safonov, as a patriot, wanted his people back to work on restoration of their national economy, he as an English patriot, wanted them working on restoration of his." In 1946, when the British launched their *Westward Ho!* scheme to recruit workers for particular labor areas experiencing scarcity from among DPs in the German camps who were unwilling to repatriate, the London *Times* would make its own wry comment that the resettlement of displaced persons smacked of slave labor.

Another theory that the Soviet Union developed about the Western Allies' retention of the DPs was that they planned to use them for ideological and even military subversion (more on this in chapter 4). This idea could also have had roots in the First World War experience, when one of the reasons the nascent Soviet state was not eager to return the German and Austrian POWs it held from the war was an interest in recruiting them for international revolution, and, more specifically, as volunteers for the Red Army.[16]

The Soviet view of UNRRA's task vis-à-vis displaced persons was that it was temporarily taking care of them pending their repatriation—a short-term, finite task. Those who did not wish to repatriate should not be considered bona fide political refugees but rather as war criminals and collaborators, afraid to return and face the consequences of their actions. UNRRA and the UN should not allow "influential reactionary circles of USA, England and France" to impede this via "mass detention of citizens of the Soviet Union in capitalist countries."

In fact, however, the Soviet Union did not consider that all the DPs were war criminals and collaborators. Their spies, infiltrated into a Ukrainian camp in the British zone run by a strongly anti-Soviet and nationalist Ukrainian émigré who they believed to have been brought over from Canada by the British, told them otherwise. The spies observed a passive majority of Soviet DPs in the camps who had been brainwashed and coerced by an activist minority of anti-Soviet émigrés who had been enabled by the complicity of the Western Allies to gain dominance in the DP camps. "The DPs stayed in the West not of their own will but as a result of psychological pressure put on them, sometimes accompanied by physical force," Vyshinsky told the United Nations.

When the issue was raised at the United Nations General Assembly early in 1946, Andrei Vyshinsky conceded the principle that "the people who refuse to return to their country are not forced to do so." But the quid pro quo was that anti-repatriation propaganda should be prohibited in the DP camps, and it should be clearly stated that "no help and no assistance shall be given to quislings, traitors and war criminals, that these gentlemen shall be handed over to their respective Governments for trial and punishment and that they shall be sent back to their countries to undergo hard labour, whereby they might make amends for their crimes, which inflicted so much suffering upon the peoples of the United Nations." In other words, they should be kicked out of UNRRA camps.

The Western counterargument, developed in the context of human rights discussions at the United Nations, focused on individual rights, namely the right of individual adults to live, or not, in the country of their birth. It was Eleanor Roosevelt, US representative to the United Nations commission on human rights, who was as much as anyone responsible for this argument. Her attention had been drawn to the plight of Jewish DPs by a visit to the Jewish Zeilsheim DP camp: she sympathized with the determination of these Jews not to return to their country of origin; and to some extent she probably extrapolated to all DPs on this basis. Her argument on principle, based on a liberal understanding of individual rights, was that any individual had the right to decide his/her place of residence, and that states had no right either to demand that citizens remain there or to forbid it. As US representative—and somewhat ironically, given her own left-of-center position, her disinclination to join the anti-Soviet camp, and her late husband's stellar reputation in the Soviet Union—she found herself as Vyshinsky's main rhetorical opponent, and she stepped up to the task. On liberal grounds, she wouldn't go along with Vyshinsky's demands to a prohibition on propaganda in the camps and made this impromptu rejoinder:

Are we so weak in the United Nations, are we as individual nations so weak, that we are going to forbid human beings to say what they think and to fear whatever their friends with their particular type of mind happen to believe in . . . It is their right to say [things] and it is the right of men and women in refugee camps to hear them and to make their own decision.[17]

Lost Children

A popular Soviet radio program of the 1960s and '70s featured a Soviet woman poet, Agniya Barto, tracing lost children, mainly from the Second World War, with the help of information from listeners, and reuniting them with their families. The emotional appeal of this was huge. It fitted into a whole genre of Soviet propaganda whereby children became the vehicle for a broader Soviet message and the moral virtue of Soviet policies was revealed by putting them in the context of children. *I Want to Go Home*, a 1950 film based on the play by Sergei Mikhalkov (author of the words to the Soviet national anthem) described the travails of a Soviet orphan trapped in Europe by Western occupation authorities who finally manages to escape to the Soviet zone and get home. Of course, in Soviet propaganda adult repatriation was essentially an act of rescue too—but in the case of adults there was the problem of filtration and selective arrests to complicate the picture, and an awareness that what in Soviet eyes was rescue might be seen by others as forcible removal. Repatriation of children was repatriation without that embarrassing complication. It showed the moral issue in its simplest and, from the Soviet standpoint, truest form.

For years after the war, as the Soviets liked to emphasize to their Western counterparts, Soviet agencies continued to receive heart-wrenching enquiries from parents about their lost children. It was a sore issue for the Soviet public: "Parents were petitioning Marshal Stalin for the return of their children," as the Soviet mission plaintively informed the British. One such petition came from Anastasia Belova, who was still searching in October 1952 for her son Mikhail, taken from her in the Salaspils concentration camp near Riga in 1943 and sent to Austria. "A gypsy by ethnicity, he has straight dark hair, eyes black and open, color of skin swarthy; as a child, he loved to dance." Perhaps moved by this image of the lost dancing boy, acting director of the Repatriation Agency Filatov wrote personally asking the head of the DP department of Soviet military forces in Austria to look for him.

Of course, in real life, the issues were always more complicated. In the unlikely event he had survived the Nazis, the gypsy boy was no longer a child but a twenty-three-year-old man who might or might not have wished to return to the Soviet Union. One of the many problems surrounding the return of children to their native lands was that the "children" (a term formally covering anyone under eighteen) had developed minds of their own. Those who had been adopted by German families often wanted to remain with them. Many who had spent the war years in Germany had become linguistically and culturally Germanized. In some cases, their names had been changed, so that "considerable interviewing skill and language facility are necessary to extract the pertinent information which will re-establish the [national] identity of the child." While with the passage of time the military governments were increasingly inclined to leave East European children in the German families they had grown up in, UNRRA and IRO favored removal.

Soviet repatriation officials discovered these problems painfully for themselves when, having identified a group of orphaned Ukrainian "children" (actually, teenagers) in a school in Bavaria, they went out at the end of 1946 to interview them. Only a third of the children showed up for interview, the others mysteriously "disappearing" for the day; and those who showed up "all said that they did not wish to return, giving as their reason that 'their parents were dead and there was no-one there [in the Soviet Union] belonging to them.'" Afterward, the accompanying UNRRA official tried to console the baffled Soviet representative (perhaps a new arrival, as he seems to have been genuinely surprised and upset at his reception) by assuring him that it wasn't just a Soviet problem: during the war "the children had been Germanized so entirely and taught anti-Ally propaganda so thoroughly that none of them wish to return to their native lands." This particular repatriation official accepted UNRRA's good faith, expressing confidence that UNRRA would somehow be able to counteract the German influence and "bring the children to a position where they would accept repatriation." (This was actually very unlikely, as the children were currently pupils in a Ukrainian school, almost certainly taught by anti-repatriation Ukrainian nationalists.)[18]

There was also the complication of competing national claims on the children, seen as a form of "national property," a phenomenon first noted by Tara Zahra. "Overzealous" attempts on the part of various countries to recover children, even to the point of kidnapping them, were a perennial problem for UNRRA, with the Soviet Union, for once, not always the prime offender, as so many other nations were actively participating. At another Bavarian children's center, Soviet and Polish repatriation officers were initially in competition for the "Ukrainian" children until the Polish government (now being rapidly Sovietized) agreed to accept that the children in questions were Soviet nationals.

Predictably, the Soviets suspected the British and Americans of "hiding" Soviet children from them. Brukhanov wrote that "at the end of 1947 we discovered as a result of stubborn searches that there were more than 30 orphanages in the British zone in which 4,000 children, the majority of them Soviet, were living." Most of these children were probably Ukrainian, thus open to definition either as "Polish" or "Soviet" Ukrainians, but in Brukhanov's interpretation, the capitalists "needed these little Soviet citizens for some kind of bad purpose." American inhumanity was illustrated by the behavior of US authorities in Germany in the case of teenager Daria Kavchak, taken to Germany as a child with her mother but later separated from her. The mother had repatriated, but when the girl was found by the Soviet mission in the US zone, the Americans refused to hand her over to the Soviets for repatriation.[19]

The Soviet charges of lack of Allied goodwill were no doubt overblown but not without foundation. The Allies' working assumption was that all DPs, adults or children, would be better off not wearing a Soviet label and not repatriating to that country. And there was indeed an international market for the children, as witnessed by the couple who turned up at IRO's office in Lima, Peru, seeking to adopt a girl of up to six years of age, "Christian. preferably blonde. In perfect health (physically, mentally, morally). From any West European country plus Estonia, Lithuania, White Russia plus Eastern Europe."

Nobody knew exactly how many lost "Soviet" children (by any definition) there were in Germany and Austria. As of March 1, 1947, UNRRA had registered almost 12,000 unaccompanied children in the American, British and French zones of Germany, of whom 2,316 were identified as "Russian" and 82 "Ukrainian" (Soviet Ukrainian, since "Ukrainian-Polish" children were listed separately). But of more than two and a half thousand children repatriated from the US zone in the period November 1946 through March 1947, only 124 (43 "Russians" and 81 "Ukrainians") had gone to the Soviet Union. A few more children were repatriated to the Soviet Union in subsequent years, but the numbers were so small that each one was hailed as a triumph. A Russian father stationed in Azerbaijan was one of the lucky ones, informed by telegram in 1948 "that your son Evgenii was sent with an echelon to Kaliningrad education department where you should collect him." The boy, seven years old, had somehow ended up in an orphanage in the British zone along with 120 others, all of whom had evidently been returned to the USSR. A nine-year-old, born out of wedlock to a well-off Riga German woman and a Russian father and taken by the mother to Germany, was miraculously recovered from his mother's cousin in Germany in 1948 and returned to his father in the Soviet Union.

One of the problems, as always, was lack of coordination between different authorities on the Western side. The Allied military, according to UNRRA's Cyrus Greenslade in November 1946, were preparing to announce as policy that "a child of unknown parents born either in Germany or outside Germany in an undetermined country will be assumed to possess German nationality," in other words that any lost child in Germany would henceforth be assumed to be German and thus the responsibility of German authorities. UNRRA feared that this "will result in the loss of some United Nations' children to the Germans" and recommended that "once it has been established that a child is not of enemy or ex-enemy origin he should be recognized as a United Nations' child and removed from German care, even though it is not possible to determine his true nationality." "United Nations children" included those from the Soviet Union, and Greenslade (acting chief of UNRRA operations) felt sufficiently strongly about this, and sufficiently sympathetic to the Soviet point of view on lost children, to tip off the Soviet military mission in Berlin about what was happening.

By 1950, the shift into Cold War mode meant that this kind of behind-the-scenes communication would have been highly unlikely. From the standpoint of US authorities, the return of children to the Soviet bloc was only rarely deemed to be in "the best interests of the child." But there were occasional exceptions. When the case of eight-year-old Johanna Bobrowitsch, child of a West Ukrainian single mother, came before the courts in the US zone of Germany in 1951, the Soviets pulled out all the stops, with the Soviet consul-general in Berlin accusing IRO of being in the business of "selling children." The mother, Sinaida Bobrowitsch, had given birth to Johanna in German-occupied Krakow in 1943, and Johanna was then placed in a German nursery home that toward the end of the war was evacuated to Germany. Johanna came under UNRRA's charge after the war, her nationality being given as Polish. Sinaida, meanwhile, had been repatriated to the Soviet Union and was living in Lvov [now Lviv] and searching for her child. Finally in September 1950 she made contact with IRO and Johanna was found in the US zone—but the question was whether the US zonal authorities would allow her to be sent to the Soviet Union. The case came before an American judge of the District Court, who ruled, untypically, that after such a tumultuous start to life it was in the child's best interest to be reunited with her mother and grow up in a family.[20]

War Criminals

It had been clear even before the war's end that war crimes were likely to be a thorny topic. A United Nations War Crimes Commission had been set up in 1943, but it could never agree on a definition of "war crimes," the Soviets dillydallied about joining, and the British Foreign Office was unenthusiastic. Soviet foreign minister Molotov had already emphasized his country's expectation that when the war ended all states would cooperate "in searching for, turning over to the authorities, bringing to trial and severely punishing the Hitlerites and their accomplices guilty of organizing, abetting or committing crimes on occupied territories." The Soviets wanted public war crimes trials at all levels and started organizing them on liberated territory even before the war's end. This was viewed with suspicion in the West as reminiscent of the prewar Soviet "show trials," and the British feared the Soviets were likely to use such trials to settle scores with political opponents.

Under American and Soviet pressure, the British agreed to hold the Nuremberg Trials of Nazi leaders in 1945 and 1946, although British prime minister Winston Churchill thought it would be simpler just to shoot them. But this was not meant to set a precedent for war crimes trials in the West, or imply Western cooperation with prosecutions of Soviet citizens who had worked for the Germans during the war and committed war crimes against the Soviet population in the occupied territories. Since most of these crimes had been committed in Ukraine, Belorussia, and the Baltic states, most of the perpetrators were of those nationalities, with relatively few ethnic Russians among them. As of 1945–46, many of the "war criminals" the Soviets wished to find, return to the Soviet Union, and put on trial were currently DPs in Germany and Austria, sheltered—however uneasily—by UNRRA and protected by the disinclination of the Western Allies to cooperate in forced repatriation.

In principle, the Western Allies more or less accepted that they should hand over Soviet DPs against whom there was convincing evidence of war crimes to the Soviet Union. But practice was very different, in part because of British and US sensitivity on the repatriation question, and in part because of disagreements about exactly who merited the label of war criminal. The situation was further complicated by the fact that the Soviets, frustrated by lack of cooperation from the Allies but also probably doing what came naturally, had starting kidnapping and sometimes assassinating "war criminals," as well as others identified as enemies, in Europe. As far as can be ascertained, their targets were generally people who had actually led military or subversive movements allied with the Germans, like the Banderites, or were prominent in anti-Soviet political organizations, but the perception among DPs as well as the authorities was that any former Soviet citizen might be at risk. Reports of apparently random "removal by force" of young women by Soviet officers, backed up German policemen, led the head of UNRRA in the French zone to reaffirm the principle that forced repatriation would not be tolerated, and if the Soviets had lists of wanted persons, as they claimed, they must communicate them to zonal authorities for appropriate measures rather than taking unilateral action.

It was UNRRA policy not to admit war criminals to its DP camps, but this was obviously very difficult to enforce, in the first place because such individuals were unlikely to declare themselves as such and were probably going under false names and nationalities, and in the second because Allied military leaders sometimes pressured UNRRA to admit people who had probably been collaborators. This happened in the spring of 1946, when the Allied military were looking for somewhere to offload Soviet POWs who had served under German command, up to now under their charge in special camps. Deputy chief of operations Brigadier W. A. Stawell wrote urgently from UNRRA headquarters to zone directors telling them to "resist . . . all attempt by the military to declare eligible for UNRRA care any ex-Wehrmacht Balt, Pole"; and if, "over your strongest objections," the Army should persist, insist that they provide a written attestation that the individual in question is not a war criminal, traitor, or collaborator. (Good luck with that one, his zone directors must have thought.)

Protesting against UNRRA's de facto tolerance of collaborators in its DP camps, UNRRA's chief repatriation officer in Austria, Margaret Bond, noted that "their presence in our camps is highly undesirable because of the political pressure they exert to influence repatriable persons against returning to their countries." This was exactly what the Soviets were always complaining about. The DP camps were full of Soviet citizens "afraid to return to their homeland because of the crimes they have committed," Brukhanov reiterated to Western officials in the fall of 1946, adding that "in some instances, they are being concealed by the UNRRA workers themselves." That was undoubtedly true, although it was also true that not all UNRRA workers, or for that matter Allied military personnel, were of that persuasion. In his memoirs, Brukhanov himself claimed that he had sympathizers on the war criminals issue even in the British military government in Germany, one of whose officers said in private conversation in January 1947 that the screenings of DPs conducted in the

Western zones to detect war criminals and collaborators were perfunctory, and "if the camps were cleansed of war criminals, people [the DPs] would go home."

The Soviets tried to give lists of the war criminals they sought to the Allies, but these offers were generally ignored. The British Foreign Office view was that the Allies had their own list of "Wanted War Criminals," compiled according to the United Nations War Crimes Commission's criteria. Unless the name was on the UNWCC list, "policy is that no person not so listed may be extradited to another zone on 'War Crimes' grounds."

The archives show that the Soviets' belief that the Allies were intentionally failing to hand over war criminals had some justification. A Soviet national who, during the war, had worked for Organisation Todt (the big German engineering organization using forced labor to build concentration camps), ended up after the war in the British zone, but the British War Office advised that handing him over to the Soviets was not necessary. "We would be very reluctant to have him arrested by the Police, which step, due to his connections with certain British families in this country, would cause unhealthy publicity." In a later case of two Azerbaijanis sought as war criminals by the Soviets, a discussion occurred behind the scenes, with some officials thinking they probably were war criminals and others indifferent to that issue, but all in favor of dragging their feet. Chancery suggested that they were probably in the DP camps, and perhaps efforts should be made to locate them, but "we would, of course, not disclose their whereabouts to the Soviet Government."

In response to a Soviet request to trace six persons who allegedly worked for the Gestapo, General Staff Intelligence informed the Displaced Persons division of the military government in the British zone that "it is regretted that no trace of them has been found." As for the others requested by the Soviet mission, it was not worth "employment of F[oreign] S[ervice] personnel," who were already fully extended. The British high commissioner in Vienna was blunter in a private memo in 1948 commenting on the regular Soviet demands for Soviet war criminals. Britain actually had two of them in detention, he said, although the Soviets only knew about one of them. With regard to the one the Soviets didn't know about, the commissioner conceded that "the Director of Legal Division is of the opinion that there is a prima facie case against him but he does not consider he would be condemned to death in a British court on the evidence available. In consequence, provided you have no objection I . . . propose to release this man to displaced person status."[21]

From time to time the Allies did actually hand over war criminals, for example in the case of groups of POWs held in Italy who had fought with the Germans, transferred to the Soviets in Operation Keelhaul in August 1946 and Operation Eastwind in May 1947 (both were joint British-American operations). But news of such transfers always produced a flood of hostile questions in Parliament, so that the British government became very leery of cooperating, even with regard to people it conceded were war criminals: "I agree we should regard our Yalta obligations as no longer obliging us to repatriate these . . . men forcibly," wrote Minister of State C. P. Mayhew to the parliamentary undersecretary on July 6, 1948, in response to the latest Soviet demand, although he anticipated that "it will be difficult to explain this to the Russians; and equally difficult to explain to the House why we could not apply this interpretation of Yalta earlier, before we forcibly repatriated numbers of Ukrainians."

Mayhew acknowledged that different rules now applied ("I recognise that in the changed atmosphere to-day we should not continue to apply our previous policy"). That change was also observed by a former Soviet citizen, sometime chaplain in the German-controlled Vlasov Army, who had been arrested by the Americans in the spring of 1946 and kept in prison until the autumn. He was interrogated, and his initial understanding was that he would been handed over after interrogation to the Soviets for repatriation. But somehow this didn't happen, and in the end the Americans let him go—with the suggestion that he should think of emigrating (he went to Argentina).[22]

———

Within the Soviet repatriation bureaucracy, there was a fairly realistic understanding of why Soviet DPs in the Allied zones were disinclined to return. According to a 1948 report from the SVAG, some of the DPs were war criminals and collaborators fearful of punishment. Others were working for the Allies for good pay, or had married foreigners and looked forward to a better life in the West. Neither of these two groups was open to persuasion about repatriation. Any hopes of success must lie with the third group: DPs frightened by anti-Soviet propaganda that emanated primarily from their own elected leaders in the DP camps. How to combat the nationalist, anti-Soviet, and anti-repatriation views of these leaders was discussed at length, but without any clear solution emerging.

It is interesting that, for internal purposes, the Soviets put the blame on the DP camp leaders rather than the machinations of the Allies. They pointed out correctly that some of these leaders were prewar émigrés but stopped short of noting that (with the exception of a few Russian camps like Mönchehof) the majority came from West Ukrainian and Baltic territories, involuntarily incorporated into the Soviet Union in 1939, and regarded the Soviet Union not as a motherland but as an occupying power.

The fact that the rank-and-file Soviet DPs in the camps accepted this leadership, and the political views that went with it, remained a bit of a mystery to the report's authors. Presumably they were aware of, but rejected, the view increasingly accepted by the Allies that life in the Soviet Union was so repressive and antidemocratic that anyone who had the chance to leave would take it. But the Allied view itself was somewhat simplistic. Soviet DPs stayed in the West for a variety of reasons, including the assumption that having been in the West, voluntarily or not, would be a permanent black mark against them in the Soviet Union. This did not necessarily imply a principled hatred of communism or repudiation of the Soviet system. Once these DPs had decided not to repatriate, however, an inexorable logic clicked in: since they did not want to repatriate, they were necessarily refugees from communism. It was from this logic, and from within the DP camps themselves, that the new understanding of DP identity emerged that was to have great significance for the future. A DP was no longer the victim of war and fascism as in UNRRA's original definition, but a victim of communism.

To be sure, there were other factors at play that neither the Soviet authorities nor the Western ones cared to examine, notably economic ones. The immediate economic discouragement to returning, especially for DPs from Ukraine, was fear of dying of hunger. The ending of mass (forced) repatriation in the spring of 1946 was followed within a few months by the onset of famine in the Soviet Union in which Ukraine, home of a large proportion of the Soviet DPs, was particularly badly hit. The crisis continued in acute form until after the next harvest in the autumn of 1947. DPs knew about the famine via the DP grapevine, and it is not surprising that they should prefer not to repatriate to a hungry country when they were being adequately fed in UNRRA camps in Europe. Arguably, by the time the famine crisis lifted, the pattern of nonreturn had already been set. The SVAG obviously knew about the famine, but it was a more or less undiscussable topic even in Soviet internal communications. It also went virtually unmentioned in UNRRA's internal discussions about problems of repatriation to the Soviet Union.

The other likely contributing factor in Soviet DPs' decision not to repatriate was that the standard of living was substantially higher in the West than in the Soviet Union, and this was evident even in war-damaged Germany. DPs may have landed in the West by accident, but once they were there, many must have looked around and seen the potential for a better life. But nobody on either side wanted to see nonrepatriating Soviet DPs as in any sense economic migrants. Later, when the Allies switched to a resettlement policy, the Soviets developed their own geopolitical economic argument, which was that the West was "stealing" Soviet DPs for cheap labor. But such a materialist Marxist lens was never applied to the DPs themselves, whose choices were seen by both sides, then and later, as purely political.[23]

PART II

The DP Story

3

Organization of DP Life

THE METAPHOR OF "pawns of fate" emphasizes the DPs' powerlessness and status as victims and calls on the listeners' compassion. UNRRA officials sometimes used such imagery in appealing for support in their efforts to save these refugees, who were in danger of becoming a "barrack race, . . . a demoralized, hopeless mass of stranded humanity." The *New Yorker*'s Janet Flanner, perhaps with a similar implicit agenda, described the DPs as "living a simulacrum of life that has no connection with the world outside except through the world's callousness and charity." Of course there must be trauma where there has been displacement and loss of home, and uncertainty about the future remains. Yet the DPs' situation, especially after the first chaotic months, was one that most twentieth-century refugees would have envied: comfortably housed, fed, clothed, allowed to run their own affairs in the camps, and provided with a variety of occupational options (including study at university) and entertainments. The term "pawns of fate" ignores the many way in which DPs could and did collectively and individually influence what happened to them.

Varieties of DP Agency

Refugees on the roads of Germany and Austria in 1945 might look like anonymous swarms, tramping with no clear destination, but this was to some extent an illusion. Even at this early stage of displacement, some of those trampers had plans and preferred destinations, and many would make choices along the way. There is no way of knowing how many within those "swarms" were headed for particular towns in Germany, with addresses of contacts, friends, and family committed to memory as well as written on scraps of paper, and prior arrangements with other family members about where to meet up. But

Mischka Danos and his mother Olga, heading northwestward from Czechoslovakia and Dresden respectively, had made detailed plans for communication and meeting: they were headed for Flensburg in Schleswig-Holstein in the hope of getting over the border into Denmark. Some adventures occurred on the way, including Mischka's coming down with diphtheria and having to spend weeks in an infectious diseases hospital unable to write to the agreed poste restante addresses, but they did indeed meet in Flensburg in April 1945. Mischka's friend Andrejs Bicevskis, having deserted from the German unit with which he had left Latvia in May 1945, knew that his in-laws, the Jerums family, had found refuge in a small North German town, Verden, and was making his way there; his grandmother, moving quite independently out of Latvia, was doing the same.

Others made decisions about destinations as they went along, on the basis of information picked up on the road. A young Latvian, Stanislavs Zmuidins, was headed to Coburg in the late summer of 1944 when Latvian former cabinet minister Valdmanis (sought by the Soviets as a war criminal, but protected by the Allies) came by, also fleeing but in a chauffeur-driven car, and suggested that Fulda was a more promising destination. No doubt Latvians were a better-informed group than Soviet POWs and Ostarbeiters, but the road was as full of information (not necessarily accurate) as it was of trampers—here you can sleep overnight in the church, there the Allies have opened up a camp with good housing, further on you will find many fellow Ukrainians/Russians/Jews/Poles gathered—and, of course, key information on the location of the borders between Allied and Soviet zones.

The way official records tell the story, refugees became DPs through a bureaucratic process through which, after being interviewed to establish their credentials, UNRRA issued them with a numbered card attesting to their status as a DP and recording their name and nationality, and then assigned to an "assembly center" (bureaucratese for camp). But even the process of obtaining an identity document from UNRRA provided considerable space for agency. The names, ages, marital status, places of origin, and nationalities provided by the DPs were essentially whatever the DPs chose them to be, since documentation was rarely available, and British or American officials were rarely in a position to know whether someone who claimed to be, for example, Polish was, in fact, a native speaker of that language. Fear of forcible repatriation was the main, but not the only, reason why DPs would choose to misstate their nationality and country of origin; other prudential considerations on the DPs part led to frequent misstatement of age and marital status. Soviet Ukrainians became West Ukrainians by self-identification; Soviet Russians became state-less émigrés; middle-aged women took years off their age (Olga Danos lost two years on her original registration in the British zone; and another six years for resettlement purposes after she later moved to the US zone); men with wives and children back home became bachelors, single women with children became war widows.

There was considerable spontaneous movement into and out of camps, uncontrolled by UNRRA and only weakly supervised by the occupation au-thorities. It was stimulated and directed by information on the DP grapevine, described by Flanner as "the best and most alert underground communication system in Western Europe today." Once in the camps, DPs could decide to become active in their self-government, to seek employment or education in-side or outside the camp in which they lived, and to engage or not in the black market (selling off UNRRA supplies to the local German population that was on lower rations; stealing animals from local farmers and slaughtering them for sale). Or they could do nothing in particular. For Flanner of the *New Yorker*, this was part of the bleakness of camp life. But some, especially women, em-braced it. Their choice of idleness and dependency was despised by more active DPs—"free-living" DPs were said to have "all but looked down on those who seemed to them (fairly or not) content to wallow there [in the camps]"—but that choice itself was an exercise of agency. Women's "idleness," as we shall see in a later chapter, often meant in practice bearing and bringing up children.[1]

These were acts of individual, or sometimes family, agency that might be interpreted as taking place within a framework laid down by the occupation governments, international organizations, and diplomatic negotiations be-tween the great powers, something over which the DPs had no control. But on a closer look, this generalization, too, needs qualification. The DPs did not have any formal mechanisms of collective agency above the level of the camp. Yet it was essentially the dramatic public refusal of many DPs to repatriate to the Soviet Union in 1945, and the bad publicity it generated in the West, that forced the Western Allies to change their policies of cooperation with the So-viet Union on this question. Later, determined resistance to Soviet repatria-tion on the part of Latvian, Lithuanian, and Estonian DPs, supported and publicized by North American diasporas, was a factor in the decisions of Britain and the United States that citizens of the Baltic states were not to be repatriated to the Soviet Union, unless by their own individual choice. Resistance on the part of Ukrainian DPs pushed the Western Allies toward a de facto decision that West Ukrainians and Western Belorussians, who had become involuntary Soviet citizens as a result of the Nazi-Soviet Pact of 1939, were similarly not liable to Soviet repatriation. At the level of individual agency, Soviet Russians and Ukrainians falsified their nationalities and places of birth to put them in these desirable "non-repatriable categories." When Soviet spokesmen complained that the Allies were frustrating their efforts to repatriate their citizens by condoning such practices, they were correct—but the Allies' behavior was only a secondary effect of the primary cause, DP resistance.

It was not originally Allied policy to put DPs into camps specific to their nationality. This was a practice that emerged, despite some reservations in principle on the part of the Allies, because that was the way the DPs wanted it. Jewish DPs were at the forefront of this effort, refusing to live in camps with their former oppressors (Poles, Ukrainians, or whoever); and they also scored an important early victory with the acceptance first by the United States and later, uneasily, by Britain of the idea that their nationality should be registered as "Jewish," regardless of their country of origin. At local level, Jewish DPs also declined housing and clothing they considered inferior and later, when the refugee organizations tried to get DPs to work, refused to comply. They were the first, but by no means the last, ethnic group of DPs to organize and forge contacts with the appropriate lobby groups in the United States who could act as spokesmen for their collective demands. As mentioned earlier, following the Jewish example, and also against the Allies' initial judgement, Ukrainians successfully insisted on having "Ukrainian" accepted as a nationality for DP registration, despite the fact that no sovereign Ukrainian state existed.

It was certainly not UNRRA policy to define DPs as anti-communists, yet, as we have seen, this was a spontaneous redefinition, based on the logic of nonrepatriation, that quickly emerged from the Slavic and Baltic DPs themselves. This logic did not apply to Jewish DPs, however, since their unwillingness to go back to their countries of origin had quite different roots. For them, anti-communism and anti-Sovietism were more or less irrelevant— an important distinction between different DP communities that is generally overlooked.

DP agency was also exercised in the resettlement process that began in 1947, since individual DPs had to decide where they wanted to go and apply accordingly. True, in order to go to the destination of their preference, they had to be accepted by the national selection committees and immigration authorities, and some people found themselves with effectively no choice. But certain categories of DPs, such as healthy young single Latvian men, were likely to be acceptable everywhere, so their choice was real. The same applied to Jewish

DPs, who from 1948 had the automatic (nonselective) option of going to Israel, but could also try their luck with selection for an alternative destination such as the United States, Australia or Canada. The DP grapevine became frenetically active passing as information on different destinations was exchanged and the first reports from resettled DPs passed on. Olga and Mischka Danos deployed a wealth of such personal information, as well as the results of their close reading of the press on the progress of amendments to the US Displaced Persons Act, in their arguments about the best place for them to go. Every DP was making mental lists of relatives and contacts from Chile to New Zealand, comparing the different contractual arrangements in different countries; some of the more savvy were reading the employment ads in local newspapers. There were contacts to be cultivated in Germany, too, for example with IRO staffers who might say a good word or US government employees who could provide recommendations for US immigration.[2]

Life in the Camps

DP camps of a variety of sizes and configurations were set up in German villages and towns, or sometimes out in the countryside, wherever there was appropriate housing available—army barracks, former concentration camps, schools, asylums, sanatoria, monasteries. UNRRA's official historian divided camp housing in Germany into three main types: caserne camps, usually former German Army centers, consisting of permanent buildings of three or four stories built of brick, stucco, or stone; barracks, single-story wooden buildings that had generally been used during the war as concentration camps or forced labor centers; and camps based on ordinary houses formerly occupied by Germans. A two-story house that had formerly held two German families was likely to take six DP families, each with one room, with a kitchen on each floor, one toilet between floors, and no bath or shower. The Ukrainian Lysenko camp was a caserne, as was Bettenhausen and the Polish Wildflecken; Schleissheim, where many Russians lived, and the Latvian Esslingen were barracks camps. The Jewish Zeilsheim camp was simply part of a town, with houses occupied by DPs mixed in with shops also used by Germans.

The early days were chaotic, with accounts of fighting, looting, and disorder on the one hand and strict military discipline, including barbed wire, on the other. But the barbed wire soon disappeared, leaving the DPs free to come and go. In relation to the occupying armies and other international personnel, the DPs were inferior beings, scarcely visible as people: British officers, in particular, behaved with "arrogance, aloofness," as Mischka Danos remembered, still resentfully, half a century later: "They did not see the person standing in front of them; be that a German (the ex-enemy) or a DP, the so-to-say person liberated by them." Nevertheless, in relation to the surrounding German population, the DPs were privileged, receiving higher rations from the Allies than the Germans, being to a fair extent outside the jurisdiction of German courts, and being under Allied protection.

The authorities' preference for the term "assembly centers" rather than "camps" was related to the sinister connotations that the latter had acquired during the war, with the advent of Konzentrationslagers (concentration camps), and Stalags (prisoner-of-war camps), together with the awkward fact that immediately after the war some occupation Army personnel thought it natural (before being ordered to do otherwise) to lock up the displaced persons who came into their hands behind barbed wire, like POWs and internees. There were bad connotations in a Soviet context, too, since the Russians had borrowed the German word *Lager* and used it for the labor camps run by Gulag (Glavnoe Upravlenie Lagerei). But there were also good Soviet connotations: the same word (*lager'*) was used for the holiday camps such as Artek in the Crimea where lucky Soviet children might be sent for a summer month in the sun. Ultimately, whatever associations they attached to the word, DPs spurned the term "assembly centers" and called the places where they received housing and sustenance "camps."

The sociologist Erving Goffman developed the concept of "total institution" to cover the peculiarities of social interaction in closed settings like asylums, prisons, concentration camps, and boarding schools, where the inmates are dependent on warders/teachers/medical personnel for all the necessities of life and subject to their diktat. This concept has been applied to DP camps by historian Tomas Balkelis, and it catches some aspects of the DP camps: the "them" and "us" attitudes of inmates, the strategies of scrounging ("organizing") needed goods, the advantages of becoming a "trustie," the prevalence of denunciation or tale-telling on fellow inmates, and the option of sinking into passivity. "Denunciations became a general psychical sickness of DPs," an IRO staffer recorded sadly, seeing this as "a consequence of camp life." But DPs from the Soviet Union had known about denunciation and how to "organize" the necessities of life before they ever arrived in UNRRA camps—knowledge that probably stood them in good stead in DP-land.

In any case, the camps were not really "total institutions." DPs, unlike prisoners or boarding school pupils, could pick up and move to another camp, or move out of the camps altogether to rent a room from a German landlady in town. Their institutions had two sets of bosses, UNRRA/IRO and the military occupation authorities, creating the possibility of playing one off against the other. In addition, there were a host of supporting players, foreign charitable and ethnic organizations of various kinds, that could be included in the political game. Above all, the camp was an institution whose everyday life was run by the inmates. Its undoubted coercive powers were mainly exerted by the dominant inmates who had got control of its administration and the subordinate inmates who were under their control.[3]

An unusual feature of the DP camps was that from the beginning of UNRRA's rule they were encouraged to develop self-government. For pragmatic reasons, the Allied military command instructed early on that "displaced persons should be encouraged to organize themselves as much as is administratively possible" because of a shortage of supervisory personnel. But for UNRRA, it was also a question of principle and idealism: "While anxious for efficiency, [UNRRA] also wanted to rehabilitate the individuals in the camps; it wanted . . . to help people to help themselves; it did not want to run the camps, it wanted the residents to run them." This was part of UNRRA's progressive American strain, a counterpart to the efforts of the US military government to instill democratic values and practices in the German population. At first, the pattern was for the local Army commander to appoint a camp leader from among the dominant ethnic group in the camp; later, elections of camp leaders and committees, to be held every six months, were introduced. From the summer of 1945, the Baltic camps—with a population universally regarded by the Allies as the most disciplined and cultured—led the way, holding their first elections in the summer of 1945, and the Jewish camps followed. Self-government never worked as well in the Polish or mixed-nationality camps, and, as of August 1947, 10–15 percent of all camps had not achieved it.

The camp administrations could set up their own DP police forces and reward their supporters with privileges and paid positions. They could introduce local rules about inmates' behavior, including sexual, and even issue—or refuse to issue—marriage licenses. According to Janet Flanner's observations in Bavaria in 1948, "Like a well-functioning imitation of a town, each camp has its D.P. mayor, police chief, rival political leaders, teachers, and garbage collectors." Flanner also noted that there was likely to be also "one socially superior barracks, where the bourgeois remnants maintain the familiar notion of a select neighborhood, and where they cling together among fewer odors and try to keep up their French." A similar report of Lithuanian camps noted that they frequently reproduced the social structure of prewar Lithuania, so that "having just arrived in the camp, people soon became divided according to their former jobs and rank."

The camp administrations, an UNRRA report noted, were often headed by "an aggressive individual . . . who seemed to have ability to enforce discipline among the Displaced Persons of his nationality." That usually meant an individual or group with militantly nationalist views, in touch with broader nationalist organizations operating in the Western zones. The seven Aschaffenburg camps "comprised five distinct national groups [including Ukrainians, Estonians, and White Russians], all organized like little Tammany Halls, all bristling with national antagonisms"; the police in the Ukrainian camp were "organized like a paramilitary outfit." In the Baltic, Ukrainian, and émigré Russian camps, in particular, the elected leaderships tended to come from anticommunist, nationalist cliques, often drawn from émigré groups or wartime (anti-Soviet) partisans, strongly opposed to repatriation and actively discouraging less-politicized "rank-and-file" DPs from considering it. "London Poles" (that is, representatives of the London-based Polish government in exile) were influential in the Polish camps, Banderites (followers of the wartime Ukrainian anti-Soviet partisan leader Stepan Bandera) in the Ukrainian, and Latvian nationalists opposed to Soviet occupation of their country in the Latvian. The Jewish camps developed similarly, with strongly Zionist leadership, except that here anti-communism was not part of the nationalist mix and repatriation was not an issue.[4]

There was substantial evolution in the first postwar years from the chaotic situation of 1945. The Junkers Camp at Bettenhausen near Kassel provides a good illustration. When the Germans fled before the advancing US Army in April 1945, the Ostarbeiter (foreign laborers from the East) who had been working at Junkers Aircraft and Motor Works were left to fend for themselves. Order was remarkably restored when Mrs. Anni Shepe, an English nurse married to a Pole, who had been working in the Ostarbeiters' hospital, "took over command on her own initiative" and managed to get some food rations from the local German authorities. When the Americans arrived a few days later, they appointed her camp commander; and when UNRRA finally made it into the area some months later, they took her on their payroll. Mrs. Shepe's original group was predominantly Russians, and in the first weeks of liberation they went completely out of control:

> Practically no one wanted to work, DP and German schnapps was plentiful and consumed in large quantities with the usual results, many DPs slept

most of the day and spent the nights dancing, drinking, fighting and frolick-
ing, especially the latter. Black marketing was rampant, and vandalism was
widespread. Practically every wardrobe in the camp was broken up and
used as firewood by DPs too lazy to cut their own wood or steal it from the
Germans, and the Russians are said to have broken up all the mirrors with
which every washroom in camp was equipped and to have sold the frag-
ments to the Germans.

Mrs. Shepe lost patience with the Russians and had them removed to another camp, which they also trashed before being repatriated. Then, on May 26,
a group of twenty-nine Latvians "scouting around for a good location" arrived
and were admitted by Mrs. Shepe. Soon there were 300 of them, and they had
already elected a committee. By July 1945, there were 765 in the camp (mainly
Latvians, but also Estonians and Poles), each national group having its own
leader—elected in the Latvian case, appointed in the case of some of the
smaller nationalities, and Bettenhausen was on its way to becoming a show-
piece DP camp. In its mature form it would boast an elementary school and a
high school (set up in two dwelling houses outside the camp), the Latvian
People's University, a hospital, workshops, room for meetings and movies, and
sports facilities.

Wildflecken, immortalized by Kathryn Hulme, was out in the boondocks
in the American zone: in its underpopulated area on the border of northwest-
ern Bavaria and Hesse there were no nearby towns and almost no work opportunities. The camp which at its peak held up to twenty thousand DPs, had
formerly been a German Army training ground. "Vast . . . wild and unpredict-
able," according to Hulme, its large Polish population was undisciplined and
poorly led. For all the efforts of Hulme and her colleagues, UNRRA's historian
considered it one of the organization's failures, compared with camps like
Hanau, a Latvian and Lithuanian center, "with its excellent workshops and
vocational training schools, its well-equipped, self-created hospital, its extremely high employment level."[5]

The best situation for DPs was to be in a camp of their own nationality, run
by a committee of fellow nationals. There were often minority nationalities in
camps, but they tended to feel themselves to be second-class citizens, subject
to the dictates of the "titular" nationality. This was a problem for Soviet DPs
since—as UNRRA and the military authorities generally denied their existence
and the Soviets were bent on repatriating them—they could scarcely be the
titular nationality in a camp. They often found themselves in Ukrainian or Polish camps, either passing as the titular nationality or constituting an informal

"Russian" minority. Stateless White (émigré) Russians, however, were in a different situation, since they were not liable to repatriation and UNRRA was not under the same pressure to deny their presence in the camps.

Mönchehof: A Russian Camp

Mönchehof was unique in being set up as much as a construction enterprise as a DP camp in the first months after the war. The engineering firm Erbauer, staffed mainly by (Soviet) Russians, had operated during the war first in German-occupied Brest and later Nordhausen, helping the Germans build V2 rockets during the war. As the war ended, its senior personnel headed west, looking for a safe location to continue business. Along the way, they encountered Konstantin Boldyrev, a Russian émigré from Yugoslavia with excellent German and good English, and a member of the anti-Soviet organization NTS (narodno-trudovoi soiuz, or People's Labor Union). "Born to lead," with "extraordinary diplomatic and organisational skills as well as adaptability," Boldyrev scouted around Germany for a site, at first establishing a camp in Niedersachswerfen in Thuringia, but, when that become part of the Soviet occupation zone, moving on to a new site near Kassel. He persuaded the American commandant to let him settle his group there and was soon taken on the payroll of the American military government, with responsibility for registration of DPs in sixteen camps in the area.

One of Boldyrev's assets was that he had transport, generally a monopoly of the military governments. Apparently some of his trucks were "trophies" acquired from the Germans in Nordhausen; during the group's Thuringia residence, they were used—labeled "Typhus"   not only to bring typhus victims to hospital but also to collect NTS members and officers of the Vlasov Army and bring them to safety in the camp. Other transport was supplied by the American military government (briefly in charge of Thuringia before it was allocated to the Soviet zone); and when the Boldyrev/Erbauer group evacuated Thuringia, they did so in nineteen trucks and eight cars, taking with them some hundreds of Soviet DPs who preferred to try their luck in the American zone.

Several thousand DPs were accommodated under Boldyrev's leadership in Mönchehof camp and three other satellite camps in the Kassel region. The leaders were prewar émigrés with collaborationist pasts and NTS connections, but the majority of camp residents (65 percent) were nonrepatriating Soviet citizens, accepting the leadership of the émigrés, who helped them both literally and metaphorically shed their Soviet identities. This program was so successful that between political screenings by the Allies, the proportion of residents with documents showing them to be stateless Russian émigrés who had spent the interwar years in Poland, Czechoslovakia, Yugoslavia, and elsewhere in Europe rose from 35 percent to 83 percent. Georgy S. Okolovich, the head of NTS operational staff in Germany, who also gave lectures at Mönchehof on history, was the chief organizer of production of these false documents. Some of the Soviet DPs were former Russian, Ukrainian, and Belorussian Ostarbeiter from camps in Thuringia who, in a typhus epidemic after the end of the war, were helped by Erbauer's two doctors. But the camp also became a mecca for Russians with the appropriate political sympathies, who made their way to it from other camps. Almost two thousand DPs who tried to join the Mönchehof camp were turned away, the majority for space reasons, but some on grounds of political uncongeniality and suspicion of being Soviet agents.

Mönchehof did not provide the most luxurious living available to DPs. When one family moved from it to a camp in suburban Regensburg, they noted a rise in their standard of living: in the new camp, DPs lived in houses formerly occupied by German aviation workers (now evicted) employed by Messerschmidt, and the family was given a room in a "clean two-room apartment with its own kitchen and conveniences." But the scale of the camp's economic activities and amenities was impressive. The camp had seven workshops, including automotive, carpenter, shoemaking, and children's toys, mainly for sale outside the camp. Moonshine was also produced for sale and internal consumption. At a subsidiary camp near the airfield, two hundred DPs repaired hangars and runways for the US Army.

Mönchehof's cultural life was particularly fondly remembered by its inhabitants. The camp built a church (Orthodox, of course) with a cupola and bell-tower, and a flourishing church choir was established. The camp also had a theater and good symphony orchestra, as well as a clubhouse offering lectures, trade courses and English lessons, and even a publishing house (for an NTS journal). There was a Scouts group, a pharmacy, and a dentist as well as a hospital. The camp established a primary school in the camp and an eight-year German-accredited high school (gymnasium) and hospital for residents in a nearby village.

Education was of paramount importance at Mönchehof, not just in the schools but in the Scouts groups, where a nationalist, anticommunist ideology was inculcated. Svetlana Schlüsser, teenage daughter of a right-wing

Russian family that had come to Germany in the 1920s, joined the Russian Scouts troop in Mönchehof (though the family was living in Frankfurt), where she not only "sang Russian songs, recited poems, learned survival skills and undertook extended hikes through the countryside" but also received training "for guerilla warfare if war came between the Soviet Union and the West."

The émigré intellectuals had a strong sense of their civilizing mission with regard to their students, many of whom had been Soviet blue-collar workers or peasants back in the Soviet Union. Resentful "kolkhozniks" with a "kulak" mentality, was how Belgrade-educated Irina Halafoff remembered them (mixing her Soviet metaphors, since "kolkhozniks" meant workers on the Soviet collective farms while "kulaks" were the allegedly avaricious exploiting peasants expelled from the village during collectivization). What she meant, in any case, was that they were peasants, and "forcing them to work for the common good was very difficult." Other DP residents needing civilization were Soviet "frontline soldiers aged 17–19, orphans from broken homes, girls taken off the streets by the American military police and normal children of various levels of literacy. All had to be sorted out, disciplined, trained and educated."[6]

Boldyrev was the camp's boss and ran it as a kind of dictatorship, both personal and on behalf of NTS; there was some implicit pressure on its residents to join the association, and those who opposed it politically were liable to be expelled from the camp by the Boldyrev administration. But what remained in his followers' memory above all was the richness of the camp's spiritual-political life, "the life of people free of Communism," and the sense of its independence, protected from interference from UNRRA and the Americans by its official characterization as a labor camp of old, prewar Russian emigrants.

The camp's independence from the control of UNRRA and the American military was indeed remarkable, a tribute to Boldyrev's political skills and determination, but even he could not avoid friction forever. Mönchehof was actually registered with the German authorities as a normal business, making its status vis-à-vis UNRRA, which established a presence in the area in late summer of 1945, something of a puzzle. Boldyrev's good connections in the American occupation forces were a counterweight to any attempt on UNRRA's part to establish its own authority, but such attempts were nevertheless made when the local branch acquired a new head, Philippe Balmelle, a tough Frenchman with a Resistance background. Balmelle saw the camp administration as exploiting the labor of the rank-and-file members for their own profit and tried to cut back the camp's business activities outside the camp by limiting their access to gasoline (as noted above, Boldyrev had secured his own transport). Boldyrev shot back by accusing the French UNRRA officials of corruption and black-marketeering.

There were problems even with Boldyrev's protectors, the Americans, that led briefly in July 1945 to Boldyrev's arrest by US counterintelligence on charges of wartime collaboration, after allegations were made by the Soviets against him to Eisenhower (the charges were later dropped). By early 1946, Boldyrev's relations with the Americans had again deteriorated to the point that he and three other camp leaders were ordered to leave Mönchehof, making way for a democratic elections of new camp leaders, presumably less tainted by collaboration. His actual departure was effected only after his arrest by the German police in May and subsequent removal by the Americans to Bavaria (a lakeside hotel in Hopfen am See). With Boldyrev's departure, pre-war émigré S. P. Rozhdestvensky—like Boldyrev, a member of NTS—was elected camp chairman. This was the point at which UNRRA finally got control of the camp, but it was also the beginning of the end.

Early in 1947 a new political screening by the US authorities deprived NTS chairman Baidalakov and ninety-nine other Mönchehof residents of their status as DPs, and by March more than half of camp's population—including "a large percent of the intelligentsia, almost all from the 'old' emigration, a substantial number of NTS members and almost all the NTS leadership"— had lost their DP status and been expelled from the camp. The camp struggled on for a few years, riven with political dissension. In April 1949 most of remaining residents were moved by IRO to the Schleissheim DP camp near Munich, and a few months later Mönchehof DP camp was closed.

There was, however, a postscript to the Mönchehof story. Off-stage, Boldyrev was pulling strings with friend in high places in France to arrange the removal of the entire NTS group to Morocco—a remarkable exercise, given that scarcely any resettlement of DPs was taking place at that point—and a number of Mönchehof residents did in fact make the journey. Morocco's appeal, as Boldyrev saw it, was that it was geographically well placed to serve as a base in the event of World War III between the United States and the Soviet Union. Freed from the "mouse trap" of Europe but "close to European shores," where the crucial battles would presumably be fought, "a cohesive Russian group . . . with sensible political support from the USA, could form the seed for the creation of a Russian army of liberation."[7]

Esslingen: A Latvian Camp

Baltic DPs were everyone's favorites—"splendid people" whose camps were "clean, bright, and civilized," according to a British comment. "Clean, neat, non-violent and undemanding," they were "by far the best we have got," an American commandant later remembered. "They give much less trouble and behave better than any of the other categories," probably because over a third of them were white-collar professionals and many came in families. Latvian DPs' later memories of camp life tended to be equally rosy, especially if they were young in the camps. "Life was good in [the DP camp in] Fulda," Stanislavs Zmuidins recalled. "There was plenty of food . . . I started to play volleyball." The Blomberg camp had own broadcasting station, while the Insula camp boasted an internal telephone service set up by DPs.

Esslingen, the largest Latvian DP camp, on the Neckar River in the American occupation zone, was remembered particularly fondly. UNRRA had a team in the area from June 1945, trying to deal with about ten thousand DPs of various nationalities, housed in seventeen camps spread over three administrative districts. In September UNRRA and the US military government started consolidating nationality-based camps and shuttling the DPs around to attain this end. Esslingen, which already had over a thousand Latvians, received another couple of thousand via this process. They formed the nucleus of a primarily Latvian camp, which also included some "stateless" (presumably Russian émigré) DPs living in the area in private houses, many of whom were employed by UNRRA, the US Army, or German factories. Like the Latvians, the stateless Russians had their own elected leader and committee, working under UNRRA supervision.

Among the 5,692 residents in 1947, a tenth had higher education. There were 37 surgeons among the DPs, 27 musicians, 41 actors, 24 painters, and 150 teachers, according to a list compiled by UNRRA in February 1947. But the list does not entirely do justice to the Esslingen camp's concentration of artistic luminaries, which as of 1949 included dozens of singers from Riga and what looks like the entire ballet corps of the Riga opera. The camp had its own elementary school, academic high school, and technical school, not to mention the 123 registered residents who were off attending universities in Stuttgart, Heidelberg, Göttingen, Tübingen, Munich, and elsewhere. It published its own Latvian newspaper and journal and had a ballet school with 120 pupils and a choir. A song festival held at Esslingen in the spring of 1946 was attended by 3,000 DPs from camps throughout Germany, and its Latvian Theater toured other

DP camps. An exhibition of painting organized by the camps art studio in 1947 was covered by the UNRRA *DP News.*

In addition to all this cultural activity, a variety of trades were practiced in the camp—watchmaking, tailoring, and dressmaking and so on—and there was also a camp pharmacist and dispensary, mechanics vulcanizing tires for UNRRA and other local institutions. Of the breadwinners among the DPs (about half the total), most were working for UNRRA or the US Army. There were also DP clergymen representing "23 different confessions" (!) serving the camp population, which was predominantly Lutheran Protestant, with Catholic and Orthodox minorities (mirroring the situation in Riga, the Latvian capital, from which many of these DPs had come). Those adults not formally employed busied themselves with voluntary work improving camp amenities, for example, turning garbage dumps into a sports field. "All the refugees were employed taking care of each other," the daughter of a camp doctor remembered. "There were nurses, teachers, street sweepers. I mean, they were all doing something."[8]

Half a century later, in 2004, a nostalgic musical (*Eslinga: A Musical*) written by two former residents of the camp premiered in Toronto and went on to play in Chicago, Indianapolis, and finally Riga. It was a great hit with the Latvian diaspora, making its audiences cry but also laugh as they remembered happy days. One of the authors, who had spent six years from age eleven to seventeen in Esslingen, noted that "some say that I have shaped the production by looking through rose-colored glasses, but that can't be helped—that's how I remember the time . . . My memories of the camp are light, happy." Equally striking was the degree to which the musical emphasized DP agency in describing camp life: "School children protest overzealous school marms who harp upon the minutia of Latvian history . . . , speculators provide scarce provisions through traditional shenanigans (hiding a pig in a baby carriage), a volunteer crew of 'academic elites' marches off to cut wood, audiences frantically rush from one cultural and social event to another, friends socialize in a corner tavern while young girls flirtatiously jitter-bug with American soldiers." Home brew is made and hidden from the "eyes of prying officials." The camps' variegated inhabitants—"boastful, affluent city dwellers, single mothers and small children, teenagers, frail elders, former soldiers, widows, speculators, professionals"—mingle with and hold their own against "flirtatious American soldiers, visiting American generals, angry German civilians, soviet repatriation officers, German nightclub divas, UNRRA screening officials."

To be sure, not everybody liked Esslingen. Rasma Prande, a young Latvian woman in her twenties from a family of Riga's artistic elite, was reunited with her parents there after a period of wartime separation, married one of the camp's priests, and worked as a nurse for UNRRA while at the same time studying at the camp's art studio. But she divorced the husband after finding out that he had a family back in Riga, and quarreled bitterly with her own family. Running away secretly to repatriate to the Soviet Union, she left a bitter note for her parents ("You did a lot of bad things to me; you won't see me again"); gave her Soviet interviewer a scathing report of the anti-communism of her fellow DPs (though by her own account she herself had previously had no communist sympathies); and took her revenge on the whole bunch at Esslingen by handing over a maliciously annotated list of 470 DPs in the camp known to her—who, as it happened, included Mischka Danos's aunt Mary's former husband, singing professor Paul Sakss, who was working in the camp theater, and his new wife, Irma Kalniņs-Sakss, also a singer, said by Prande to be "actively conducting anti-Soviet propaganda."[9]

DP Choices

DPs were people in difficult situations who constantly had to make choices to maximize their chances. The first choice, when they registered as DPs, was who they wanted to say they were—name, birthplace, age, nationality, marital status. Forgetting about a wife and children back home, as Rasma Prande's husband had done, was standard. Dropping some years off your age (in case of being caught by age cutoffs in resettlement programs) was also a prudent act. But of all acts of self-reinvention, probably the most common and important to outcomes was nationality (country of former citizenship)—also the most immediately salient, at least for Soviet citizens, because of the question of repatriation.

Citizens of the Baltic states had no reason to hide their nationality because the Western Allies did not consider them Soviet citizens subject to repatriation. To be sure, there were some complications that it was best not to puzzle the Westerners with: Riga, for example, had long consisted of parallel societies (with a range of specific social and cultural institutions, from schools to opera) of Riga Germans, Riga Russians, Riga Poles, and Riga Jews as well as just plain Latvians—but just plain Latvian was what everyone was going to have written on their DP cards. It was a "good" nationality, offering maximum options for resettlement. Hyphenated Russian-Latvians and German-Latvians, who might otherwise have encountered problems in selection for resettlement, happily qualified and abandoned the hyphen. Mischka Danos's complicated origins—son of a Hungarian Jewish father, passing in Latvia as a Catholic, and Latvian mother—largely disappeared: the nationality on his DP card was simply "Latvian."

Soviet citizens (other than those from the Baltic or former Polish Ukraine and Belorussia, acquiring Soviet citizenship involuntarily in 1939) were the ones with the greatest incentive to disguise their origins because of the fear of forced repatriation. We have seen in the case of the Mönchehof camp how Soviet Russians could be transformed en masse, with the help of the camp leaders, into "stateless" (that is, prewar Russian émigrés). Other Soviet DPs became West Ukrainians, Poles, and Yugoslavs. When this involved living in the appropriate national camp, say Ukrainian, it often put the Soviet DPs in a disadvantaged situation vis-à-vis the dominant Ukrainians, since other camp residents knew that they were flying under a false flag, even if they had no intention of telling UNRRA or the occupation authorities so. As DPs in Germany, two opera singers from St. Petersburg—Eleonora Bogdanova (actually of Polish origin, but Orthodox) and the Russian Ivan Kornilov (whom the Germans had taken to Riga)—called themselves Latvian as safer option. The Russian Maria Samoilenko, taken to Germany as a nineteen-year-old during the war, lived in a Polish camp (Rotenburg am Tauber) in Germany.

It should not be assumed, however, that all such choices of nationality were fraudulent. Ethnic life was complex in the Soviet Union and Eastern Europe, and many people quite legitimately had multiple identities to choose from. Evgeny Zubrin, born in Poland in 1933 in a Russian family, lived in a Ukrainian DP camp in American zone in the immediate postwar years. After his resettlement in Australia in 1949, he at first moved in Ukrainian circles but then tired of "the unending Russophobia of the Ukrainians" and, "being drawn to Russian culture, . . . joined Russian society." Two Russian-Ukrainians who met and married as DPs and lived before resettlement in a Ukrainian DP camp could quite reasonably identify themselves both as Ukrainian (as they did as DPs, living in a Ukrainian camp) and Russian (as they did after resettlement in Australia). Ivan Nikolajuk, brought up in Brest, could plausibly claim Russian, Ukrainian, and Belorussian nationality, and at different times did claim all three.[10]

There was movement between DP camps, although the authorities disapproved; and after a while there was movement between zones as well. Many DP memoirs report shifting from one camp to another to find a more congenial environment. The American zone was a magnet because the living conditions were better than in the British zone: the camps there acquired "a mythical reputation" for abundance because of the so-called PX stores (which provided provisions to US soldiers) and the Americans' generosity. But there was also the consideration, from 1947 on, of which country you hoped to be resettled in. The British *Westward Ho!* scheme took only DPs from the British zone. The assumption was that the Americans were more likely to select you if you were living in the American zone. There were also other considerations: for example, Leonid Vertsinsky, a first-wave émigré, went to French zone after the war because he could speak French.

Some moves were modest and involved petitions to the authorities for better conditions. Modris Eckstein's middle-class Latvian family was placed in the Meesen barracks in Lübeck, "first in a small room with another family, whose raucous behavior my parents found unbearable, and then in a larger room with ten other people. After many entreaties we were moved again, on January 1946, to a new camp in Artillerie Kaserne, all Baltic, where they got their own room—two beds, a stove and a window." Moves from mixed nationality camps to a camp of the DP's own nationality were common. The Mönchehof camp attracted Russians, particularly those sympathetic to NTS's anti-communist orientation; Esslingen attracted Latvians, particularly those in the cultural professions. Viktor Istomin, a doctor from Dnepropetrovsk (in Soviet Ukraine) who had been called up into the Soviet Army and became a POW, was initially in a Polish camp but then moved to the largely Russian Fischbek camp in Hamburg in 1946. Georgy Nekrasov, schoolboy son of a White officer from Yugoslavia, also landed in Fischbek after an odyssey that took him and his family to Austria, Silesia, and South Bavaria and graduated from the Russian high school there.

Mischka Danos arrived in Flensburg from Dresden in the spring of 1945, hoping to meet up with his mother (coming from Sudetenland) so that, when the war ended, they could cross the border into Denmark. This plan was thwarted because Mischka caught diphtheria on the trip, which resulted in several weeks in the hospital. By the time he got out, the border was closed, and Olga had registered with the British occupying forces as a displaced person. The two of them were put in a hotel (serving as temporary DP accommodation) in Glücksburg, a resort on the fjord near Flensburg; and when Olga's sister Mary was released from Ravensbrück concentration camp, she joined them there. That meant that they were all in the British Zone, but that was not a positive choice, rather a consequence of Mischka's wish to get across the border to Denmark in order to study physics with Niels Bohr. They were, however, intent on being displaced in one of the Western zones, not the Soviet one.

As soon as German universities reopened, Mischka was off on the road (or, literally, on the railway) looking over the options for continuing his interrupted studies in electrical engineering. He was already registered as a DP in the British zone under the name of Mikelis Danos, Latvian (Mikelis being the Latvian version of his first name). En route, however, he paused to register as a DP at the Jewish Zeilsheim camp, on the outskirts of Frankfurt in the American zone. Here he used the name "Michael Danos," Latvian, with his actual birth date (January 10, 1922) but claimed to have been born in Pleskau (Pskov, since 1940 part of the Soviet Union) rather than his actual birthplace, Riga, and identified himself as a university student with a Frankfurt city address, registered as a DP at Zeilsheim. Presumably this double registration was a form of insurance in case he decided to enroll in a university in the American zone.

For a while, Mischka and his friend Andrejs Bicevskis thought they would be able to register at Brunswick Technical University, so Mischka changed his DP registration to the Rosalie Kaserne barracks in Brunswick where Andrejs and his family were already living. That didn't work out, and Mischka and Andrejs both moved to Hanover (still in the British zone), where they were able to register at the Hanover Technical University. The two of them found separate lodgings in Hanover, but their official DP registration throughout their student days as DPs was a former cadet flying school in a suburb of Hanover, serving as a DP camp, Fliegerschule-Herrenhausen. After graduation, following the physics professor who was his academic mentor, Mischka moved to the American zone to do his PhD at the University of Heidelberg. Olga, meanwhile, shuttled around between various camps and noncamp addresses within the British zone, ending up establishing a business in Fulda. Mary stayed in Geestacht (one of Olga's camps) in the British zone for a while before moving to the Black Forest in the French zone; she later came back to the British zone to join Olga in Fulda.

The Danoses may have been atypical in the frequency of their movements— including interzonal ones—but it may also be that this is a rare case where detailed personal records happen to be available from contemporary correspondence. In retrospect, it is likely that former DPs often simplified their stories. It was possible for DPs legally to enter the American zone, with permission, from the British and French zones if one could make an argument such as the presence of relatives; and it was also possible to enter it illegally. From the Soviet zone, a steady stream of DPs entered the American zone illegally. Some people came to avoid security problems in their original zone. The Latvian Robert Klanners, aka Larnieks, moved to the French zone after running into problems in the British zone. Others, especially from the French zone, came in search of better living conditions. Indeed, the French seem to have encouraged such movement, perhaps to reduce the strain on their own resources, by freely handing out passes to enter the American zone.[11]

"Free-Living" DPs

Foreign observers often wrote as if all the DPs lived in camps, but this was far from the truth. Lots of DPs were living outside camps—"free-living," as it was officially known or living *privat*, as the DPs themselves described it— but no official body had accurate information on where and how many. A Harvard team in Germany seeking to locate Soviet DPs for an interview project concluded that so many of them were living outside camps, their real whereabouts unknown to UNRRA, IRO, the military authorities, and the international voluntary organizations, that they were impossible to find except by DP word of mouth. UNRRA and IRO occasionally offered statistics on free-living DPs, ranging from 20 to 40 percent of the total number of DPs, but these must be approached with great skepticism. For one thing, none of the statisticians allowed for what was evidently a common phenomenon: living part of the time in camps, where the DP maintained registration, and part of the time outside.

It was not difficult for DPs to afford living outside the camps in private lodging, since they could barter UNRRA cigarette rations and their labor (as help around the house) to pay their way with landladies. There were a number of reasons for preferring to live outside the camps. Fear of being identified as a wartime collaborator was one often cited for Soviet DPs, as was the fear of being discovered by the Soviets and forcibly repatriated. All Mischka's DP student friends lived *privat,* as he did, partly for convenience but perhaps partly also to emphasize the "student" aspect of their mixed identity rather than the "DP" one. A former Vlasovite POW gave a different reason for avoiding the camps—his intense desire for independence. "The camp atmosphere sucks you in and makes you change," he told an American interviewer a few years after the war. "The herd instinct develops, your interests become petty." Mischka Danos remembered similar feelings; and he also noted that living with DPs in camp corrupted his previously impeccable German. Linguistic ability was surely an important variable in the decision to live inside or outside camps. With good German, living outside was a natural choice; without it, the camps offered a safer haven.

Some female DPs lived in the city with a spouse or protector, often German or from the occupation forces. Most of the Soviet women DPs who ended up marrying foreigners (Belgians, Dutchmen, Italians) had lived with them outside the camps before moving to the spouses' home countries. Students often lived *privat* in the city of their place of study, even when registered at a camp that might be in quite a different part of Germany, as we saw in the case of the Esslingen camp. Mischka and his Hanover University friends dropped in on their Fliegerschule-Herrenhausen camp every week or so to pick up rations (and in Mischka's case also to play the piano and use the billiard table).

It was possible, and even quite common, to combine maintaining a residence in a camp and living *privat*, or to move between the two. Robert Klanners, whose move from the British zone to the French has already been reported, lived in a camp from a while, combining this with work as a porter in an American restaurant, but then after being fired from his job he moved into an apartment and tried to get by working in private business in leather goods.

In 1945–46, Olga Danos was renting a room in Hamburg, thinking of starting a business there, while commuting between Hamburg and her camp residence in Geestacht. It seems that Mischka and his Latvian student friends in Hanover probably actually had beds allocated to them in the four-beds-a-room dormitory of the Fliegerschule (formerly used by German aviation cadets), despite lodging in the town. One of those friends, Andrejs Bičevskis, who had lived in lodging throughout his student life in Hanover, moved back into a Hamburg camp after graduation and worked for a while as camp quartermaster while awaiting departure from Germany.[12]

Of course UNRRA and IRO were not happy with this Liberty Hall approach to their facilities. In May 1946, an internal UNRRA memo in the British zone noted that many registered DPs were not living in the camps and recommended that this led to "irregularities and abuses" and should be restricted, once UNRRA had worked out how to do this. As a first step, those living outside because they were working for the military government should be required to receive written authority for their living arrangements. At a later point, DPs living outside camps who refused to move back in would lose their DP status and rations.

But this was all very difficult to enforce, and UNRRA had other more urgent concerns. In the case of a Yugoslav DP who was officially in residence in the Luitpold Kaserne while at the same time renting a private room in town, IRO recommended eviction from the camp, noting that "it is felt that DP's who receive full IRO Care (billets and food in an IRO installation) should not in addition be permitted to occupy a private room in town, or then they should choose to live on the Germany economy." But the very language of this recommendation ("it is felt") conveys a sense that systematic enforcement was an unwinnable battle. Some conscientious DPs like Michael and Olga Danos did in fact apply to move into the German economy once their positions in it (as PhD student and businesswoman, both with decent housing available) were sufficiently assured, although to be sure this was after several years of frequent movement in and out of camps. But others continued to move in and out—some, like Russian "stateless" or Vlasovite DPs under suspicion of wartime collaboration, actually moving *into* camps for the first time at the end of the 1940s, once they felt safer from retribution or forced repatriation to the Soviet Union and to facilitate their participation in IRO-organized resettlement.[13]

DP Politics

Political activity in the camps was theoretically prohibited for DPs by the occupation authorities, UNRRA, and IRO. But in fact it flourished, partly because of the democratic election principle the authorities supported, which tended to put strongly nationalist leaders with connections to political movements in charge. As one historian writes, "Various elite groups vied for the political and ideological backing of the refugees. These self-appointed camp authorities spoke on behalf of the rank and file," often developing "political or cultural agendas based on their pre-war political or religious affiliations." Combined with the isolated and regimented life of the camps, this made them "almost an ideal setting for political indoctrination."

In the Slavic and Baltic camps, the overwhelmingly dominant strain of politics was nationalist, anti-Soviet, and anti-communist. In the Jewish camps, a variety of nationalism—Zionism—was dominant too, but the anti-Soviet and anti-communist strains were largely absent. This was partly because the Soviet Union was not the perpetrator of the Holocaust but had in fact provided shelter, albeit ungraciously, for many Polish Jews during the war; moreover, in the years immediately leading up to the creation of the state of Israel in 1948, the Soviet Union was one of the main proponents of the project (somewhat ironically, given the Bolsheviks' historical opposition to Zionism). While immediately after the war enthusiasm for Zionism swamped all other political attitudes among Jewish DPs, before the war socialism had had substantial support among

European Jews, with the socialist Bund offering real ideological competition to the Zionists. Given the wave of Zionist enthusiasm in the DP camps, Bundists were scarcely visible, but that did not mean they had totally disappeared. The suspicion of US senators (and, later, some resettlement countries) that Jews tended to be left-wing was not wholly without foundation. At any rate, theirs were the only DP camps where socialism was a part of the political spectrum. At the Jewish camp at Leipheim Airport in the US zone, the UNRRA director, Miss E. Robertson, reported in 1947 that "you have all shades of colour—from deepest blue to brightest pink. Socialists, conservatives, nationalists, Zionists— you will find them all there in Leipheim," though the divergent groups were united by an unbreakable bond forged by common suffering and the determination to survive and build a new home in Palestine.

Miss Robertson evidently approved of a diversity that included socialists, an attitude not uncommon in UNRRA. Formally, however, UNRRA tried to prohibit overt political organization and activity on the part of the DPs, and the occupation authorities took a similar line, at least early on. In Hamburg, for example, the British authorities not only closed down the Ukrainian National Committee in Hamburg for violating its ban on political activities but even sentenced the committee's president to a year in prison. But enforcement was difficult for the Western Allies, all the more since it involved conflict with democratically elected camp administrations.

Soviet representatives were keenly aware of the anti-communism of the DPs. They complained ad nauseam (as the British and Americans felt) about anti-Soviet and anti-repatriation activism on the part of the DPs. Again and again in their meetings with the Western powers, they pointed out that the camps were run by anti-Soviet nationalists who did their best to block the Soviet repatriation effort, whether presented in person by liaison officers or in newspapers or on radio. They said the camp administrators were "as a rule war criminals," that is, collaborators, who ruled with an iron fist. Would-be repatriates, treated as Soviet spies, were liable to be arrested and beaten up by camp police; when Soviet representatives visited, camp leaders would warn that "if anyone talks to the Russian officer, he'll get a knife in the ribs tonight." Soviet officials also claimed their nationals had been given false documents of statelessness so that they could evade repatriation.

All of this was, broadly speaking, true, and known to UNRRA, but despite their repeated complaints, the Soviets got little concrete satisfaction. It was not that they found no sympathy from individual UNRRA officials, but this was usually expressed privately. In addition, for all that the Soviets often claimed that that the DPs' fierce anti-communism was the result of Allied coaching, they knew quite well that, regardless of any occasional coaching, the intense resistance to repatriation and hostility to the Soviet Union came from the DPs themselves. Admittedly, it came mainly from DPs from the Baltic and Western Ukraine who did not recognize themselves as "Soviet" in the first place. Had the Soviets been willing to admit that important distinction between "old" and "new" Soviet citizens, it might have been easier for them to deal with the issue of DP anti-Sovietism. As it was, they were in the humiliating position of begging the Allies to prevent "Soviet" DPs from expressing their aversion to the Soviet Union.

In line with their prohibition on DP political activity, the US and British occupation authorities ruled that self-styled national committees could act only as "local refugee relief agencies," not as central organs of a national DP movement. This was extremely difficult to enforce in practice. "Avoid[ing] conferring undue status on the self-styled DP leaders" was a constant preoccupation. But it was impossible to avoid dealing with them to some extent— even overlooking the fact that the United States Forces European Theater (USFET) was using people like the dubious Latvian political figure Alfred Valdmanis as advisor on DP matters—since the camps were increasingly organized on a national basis, with emphasis on the principle of self-administration, which made it difficult to defend a refusal to deal with national DP organizations on questions of DP welfare.[14]

Two parallel sets of national organizations emerged in postwar DP-land: the ones whose immediate rationale was to lobby UNRRA and the occupation authorities, ostensibly only on matters of DP welfare and without an overt ideological position, and the others, actively political in a nationalist and anti-communist direction, that less visibly sought to influence and recruit DPs, to oppose repatriation of DPs, and ultimately to further the cause of "liberation" from the yoke of the Soviet and other communist governments. The relations between these two sets were opaque, intentionally so, and shifting. A national organization that was looking too political to UNRRA, like the Ukrainian National Committee, might morph into the harmless looking "Ukrainian Red Cross." Soviet representatives at Allied meetings knew that anti-communist political groups were getting round UNRRA's prohibitions on political activity by rebranding themselves in this way and complained about it, as usual with little effect.

The list of such organizations claiming to represent DPs in the camps was seemingly endless. Central councils, central committees, national councils, coordinating centers, and national representations proliferated in lobbying letters to UNRRA on behalf of national groups of DPs. All were factious and mutually competitive, many led by prewar émigrés, some with prewar and wartime intelligence contacts. Overlapping of membership and moving from one association to another were commonplace: one has the impression of a relatively small number of activists wearing a number of different hats to suit different occasions. A number of the associations had their origins in organizations set up under and by the Nazis that, in the postwar period, they strove to slough off. Almost all represented one national group only, and co-operation between different organizations in approaches to UNRRA was comparatively rare. All feared Soviet spies and periodically denounced them within their ranks.[15]

It was the Ukrainians whose nationalist political activity among the DPs first alarmed the British, who, as already noted, closed down the Ukrainian National Committee and forbade the display of national flags and the playing of national anthems. But, trained in wartime conspiratorial activity, the Ukrainians easily outwitted Western officials, rebranding their organizations as charitable, religious, and cultural. They even managed to fly the Ukrainian flag under the Union Jack in the Ukrainian Heidenau camp. UNRRA did its best, but ignorance of Slavic languages and culture was a major hindrance. When UNRRA officials visited camps prominently featuring portraits of nationalist leaders in the administration building, the DPs told them they were famous Ukrainian poets—and how was UNRRA to know the contrary?

High culture and a civilizational heritage linking them to the West, fundamentally different from the Asiatic barbarism represented by the Soviets, was a centerpiece of Ukrainian DP self-presentation to the Allies. A Ukrainian pamphlet opposing repatriation of Ukrainian DPs to the Soviet Union argued that

> the Ukrainians, a highly cultured civilized people, belong to the nations of the world whose way of life is based on human freedom and Christianity. Their whole history bears out their obhorrence [sic] of slavery and barbarity. They seek only the human rights and justice due to a civilized Christian people. Shall they seek in vain? Shall they be hunted mercilessly for destruction by the atheistic, anti-Christian, despotic and aggressive enemy without the subvention [sic] of the Democracies?

Civilized or not, Ukrainian nationalism as represented in the camps had a strong paramilitary aspect. The most influential of the Ukrainian nationalist organizations was the Bandera faction of the Organization of Ukrainian Nationalists (OUN), the Nazi collaborationist aspects of its wartime history overshadowed for many Ukrainians by the successes of its partisans fighting the Soviets. Russophobia was a characteristic of the movement, in which West Ukrainians dominated, with Ukrainians from the old Soviet Union, often suspected as being "tainted by communism" as well as "insufficiently nationalistic," playing a secondary role.

The Ukrainian nationalists had some major successes to their credit. They managed to get Ukrainian recognized as a nationality, despite the initial resistance of the Allies, especially the British. In addition, they were the inspiration behind the most durable and influential of all émigré anticommunist movements, the Anti-Bolshevik Bloc of Nations (ABN). This was founded at a conference in Munich in April 1946 on the initiative of the Bandera faction of OUN, its leader being the Ukrainian Iaroslav Stetsko, a close associate of Stepan Bandera, who managed to put together an organization that united most of the disparate national anti-communist movements of the postwar diasporas, a feat that nobody else had accomplished. ABN claimed to represent more than thirty-two nationalities, including Belorussians, Estonians, Latvians, Lithuanians, Cossacks, Georgians, Armenians, and Azerbaijanis as well as East Europeans. But Russians were not among them: they were as much hated as Soviets in the ABN book, seen as by nature violent aggressors, essentially Asiatic and incompatible with the Western principle with which ABN associated itself.

Some in UNRRA were deeply uneasy about the activity of the "Banderites" in Ukrainian camps and complained that US military authorities allowed them into the camps under the guise of relief organizations. The Soviets disliked it even more strongly, *Pravda* denouncing the Bandera OUN groups in Regensburg and Munich as fascist collaborators.

Belorussian groups—specifically the White Russian Committee in Regensburg—received the same treatment from *Pravda*. Anti-communist nationalists though they were, however, their biggest concern was establishing exactly what the relevant nation was: Belorussian, White Ruthenian, or Krivich. A Belorussian Council, White Ruthenian National Committee, and Belorussia (Kryvian) Committee all existed, and their lobbying to UNRRA was mainly for recognition of their nationality's existence and of their own status as its legitimate representative. There was a big quarrel in the Rosenheim camp in 1949, with complaints and countercomplaints to IRO, between supporters of Belorussian Central Administration and the smaller Belorussia

(Kryvian) Committee, both seeking recognition from the American occupation authorities of their superior claim to represent their people.[16]

For nationalist groups from the Baltic, suspicion of collaboration with the Nazis was an even bigger problem than for the West Ukrainians. The Latvians came out of the war with two lines of national association, one of which had official recognition under the Nazis, the other representing Latvia's wartime resistance. The former, known as the Latvian National Committee, included the controversial figure of Alfred Valdmanis, a minister in the prewar Ulmanis government and leading collaborator. The latter, the Latvian Central Council, included some prewar social-democratic parliamentarians. Both lobbied the Allies for recognition and support, and both were represented in the umbrella group, the Latvian National Council, created in April 1948.

The immediate aim of the Latvian association at the war's end, to secure Allied recognition that citizens of Latvia and the other Baltic states were not liable for repatriation to the Soviet Union, was quickly realized. Subsequently, the Latvian Legion became a central issue, Latvian organizations arguing that its members should be eligible for DP status and not regarded as war criminals. The legionnaires had their own organization, Daugavas Vanagi (Hawks of the River Daugava), which took a particularly militant anti-Soviet stand but also joined the umbrella group in 1948. This issue took longer to resolve, but by the end of the 1940s the Western powers had decided to accept both the Latvian Legion and, tacitly, Daugavas Vanagi. Within the Latvian émigré community, the issue of wartime collaboration remained a rancorous one.

In addition, Latvian DPs had created their own association, the Latvian Central Committee. Latvian camp administrations were, as usual with the Latvians, exemplary in their avowed commitment to democratic principles and free elections, which implied not only pro-Westernism and anti-communism but also a critical view of the Ulmanis government in Latvia in the 1930s, which had been a dictatorship. Nevertheless, they shared the emerging consensus in the Latvian diaspora that the Soviet Union and Russia were the enemy; that Soviet occupation of Latvia had been "a project of genocide"; and that Latvia was part of Western democratic mainstream that had become an "innocent victim of totalitarianism." It was also part of this consensus that Latvia was ethnically homogeneous: both the National Council and the National Committee used the adjective "Latviešu" in their titles, meaning Latvian in the ethnic sense, as opposed to "Latvijas," referring to a geographical concept.

While there was a Baltic Central Council that made occasional representations to UNRRA, most of the political organization and lobbying was focused on the three separate Baltic nations, Latvians, Lithuanians, and Estonians. Lithuanians DPs, like their Latvian counterparts, had their choice of nationalist anti-communist organizations. These included a strongly anti-Soviet and Catholic Lithuanian Exile Committee, in a line of descent from the former Christian Democratic Party of Lithuania; a Lithuanian Central Executive Committee; and a Supreme Committee for the Liberation of Lithuania. The Estonians had a Central Council, an Estonian Committee in Germany, and an Estonian Central Committee. All three Baltic nations were represented in the ABN.[17]

As already indicated, Russians were the one group of anti-communist Slavs not admitted to the ABN, which regarded Russia, no less than the Soviet Union, as historically a dangerous aggressive power with expansionism as well as Asiatic despotism and violence built into its DNA. Russians' anti-communism in the camps was thus a parallel phenomenon to that of the other Slavic and Baltic national groups rather than a part of it. Another peculiarity was that it came from an entrenched prewar emigration, anti-communist but also with intellectual and aristocratic pretensions, that assumed leadership in the camps over the larger but less cultured group of Soviet DPs.

When former Soviet POW and Vlasov Army recruit Sigizmund Dichbalis looked around at the Russian émigré political scene as manifest in Erlangen at the war's end, he found no shortage of choice of nationalist, monarchist, Orthodox, and anti-communist groups to join: the Committee for Affairs of Orthodox Refugees, the NTS, the Russian National Committee, the Committee of Emigrants, the Committee of Stateless People, and the Union of the Andreev Flag, which was the one he joined. But even this impressive array was not comprehensive. For a Soviet DP looking for a Russian émigré organization to join, a wide range of "Liberation Movements," "Anti-Bolshevik Centers," "Unions of Struggle," and the like were available, all anti-communist, representing a spectrum of positions from passively disapproving of the Soviet Union to actively seeking to overthrow it, from backward-looking monarchist to Vlasovite democratic ("Soviets without Bolsheviks") and quasi-fascist (the NTS).

Soviet POWs recruited from the POW camps to serve in the Vlasov Army were a quantitatively significant group among the DPs, but hampered by a lack of leadership (Vlasov himself having been handed over to the Soviets at the end of the war and executed) and ideological dissension. These were people who, despite having taken up arms against the Allies—often, undoubtedly, to stay alive, given the terrible conditions in the German prison camps— nevertheless retained a substantial "Soviet" component in their thinking and behavior. The old émigrés, generally better educated and of higher social standing, tended to look down on them, and often outmaneuvered them in factional struggles. If, as historian Anna Holian estimates on the basis of her work on the politics of Russian DPs in the Munich area, they were the most popular of the competing groups in the DP camps, this did not translate into dominance and setting the agenda. Nor did the monarchist and officers' associations with appeal to an older generation of "Whites" win much sway among the mainly young DPs.

It was NTS (the National Labor Union) that filled that role. Influenced in its prewar days by fascist corporatist ideology, dedicated to active subversion of Soviet communism by all available means, it had an aura of modernity and determination that appealed to the young, and its leaders were first-rate political in-fighters and propagandists. In addition to running the Mönchehof camp, which gave those leaders a safe haven in the first postwar years, it managed to get hold of printing presses early on and publish an influential weekly, *Posev*, whose first number came out on February 10, 1946. It had to go through UNRRA censorship, which supposedly removed anything political, but the savvy NTS journalists knew about Aesopian language and "succeeded in running an anti-communist line in *Posev* without breaking the elementary censorship limitations of the American military administration." Even after many of the NTS activists were expelled from the camps, and therefore lost their DP status and the right to publish a DP newspaper, one who kept the DP accreditation stepped in to keep *Posev* going.[18]

In general, the Western authorities' censorship of political content in DP publications was becoming progressively weaker, until by 1948–49, as an NTS editor remembered, his newspaper was able "to become fully anti-communist." This was part of a broader shift accompanying the development of the Cold War. If in the immediate postwar years US occupation officials had "little sympathy" for nationalist anti-communist groups and made "significant efforts to control [DP] anticommunist activities," there was always a contradictory impulse coming from US intelligence assistance to refugee liberation groups; and that contradictory impulse consistently gained strength. In October 1947, the US military authorities abandoned strict neutrality with regard to political groups and adopted a new policy of favoring those inclining to anticommunism while asserting the right to take action against the "undemocratic" ones. By mid-1948, the military authorities and IRO had recognized the Central Representation of the Ukrainian Emigration, formerly regarded as too overtly political to deal with.

US intelligence agencies had already plunged deeply into the world of Russian émigré organizations, particularly favoring the NTS, and in 1948 the CIA received formal permission to conduct covert operations against the Soviet Union, including assistance to "refugee liberation groups." That meant a major increase in funding possibilities. The ABN also picked up funding from the new German government's Ministry for Expellees, Refugees, and War Victims. By early 1949, Cold War anti-communism was so much in vogue that even overt DP anti-communist demonstrations—like the one organized by Ukrainians affiliated with the ABN against the sentencing of Joszef Cardinal Mindszenty, to life in prison in Hungary—were tolerated by the US authorities in Germany on the grounds that they were not political but concerned with religious persecution. By 1951, it became acceptable for US officials not only to tolerate but also to participate in such events, as a way to "give appropriate concrete evidence of our sympathy and support for non-Communist groups in exile."

The world was now definitively divided into two camps, with the displaced persons firmly attached to the Western one. It no longer mattered that some of the DPs had collaborated with the Nazis. What was important was that they were passionate opponents of communism who had shown their hatred of the Soviet Union by leaving it to find freedom in the West.[19]

4

Occupations

CONGRESSMEN AND other critics of UNRRA often expressed concern that the DPs were being maintained in idleness on the US taxpayer's dollar. It was a touchy question, made the more difficult by the issue of Jewish "persecutees," who often refused to work on principle and whose refusal was respected by UNRRA and the Americans. UNRRA's mission included rehabilitation as well as relief, and presumably a fully rehabilitated person was occupied. On the other hand, UNRRA's central task as far as the DPs were concerned was repatriation, which could potentially be undermined by too deep an involvement in work or study in Germany.

By the middle of 1946, all the zones had introduced some kind of work requirement, without enforcing it: that was the compromise reached with one eye on international public relations. Many of those working were employed by UNRRA itself or the military governments; and of the latter, a proportion wore US Army uniform and had weapons in their hands, regardless of Soviet objections. Those not working for the Allies were mainly working in paid or unpaid positions in the camps—"taking care of each other" by administering, policing, teaching, fixing things, making things, cleaning, and so on.

After the first year or so, manual jobs outside Germany were available on a contract, notably for work in Britain and in the Belgian and French mines. These were initiated outside the UNRRA framework, because of the urgent need of former belligerent countries for labor, and UNRRA viewed them with some suspicion. Normally, dependent family members were not welcome in these foreign contract jobs, and it was unclear how they would affect the DPs' prospects for permanent resettlement.

Not mentioned in any formal list of DP occupations, but omnipresent, were black market activities, facilitated not only by the fact that DP rations were better than those of the German population but also because employment with UNRRA and the military governments gave many DPs close access to the main sources of goods coming into the economy. Moonshine was another basic DP activity. All this annoyed the German authorities, especially the German police, but their power to deal with the DPs was limited.

Black Market

Any kind of rationing system produces a black market, but the one that sprang into being in postwar Germany and Austria was particularly extensive and complex. There were four occupation zones, each with its own rationing system and range of available goods. A wide range of equipment and manufactured goods of all kinds came in to support the occupation forces, and some of this trickled down to DPs. The DPs' rations (mainly dried and canned foods and cigarettes) were larger than those allocated to Germans, but it was German farmers who were, not always willingly, the source of fresh food—meat, milk, fruit, and vegetables, bartered for DP dried rations. More serious black marketeers smuggled in desirable products not easily available in Germany from neighboring countries like Italy and France. There were also desperate Germans who, for whatever reason, had valuable goods they wanted to offload without publicity.

Probably all DPs had some connection with the black market at some time, if only by buying milk from a local farmer or paying for urban lodgings in cigarettes. DPs were issued cigarettes in their rations, and "the cigarette became the most popular medium of exchange, a veritable alternate currency." In Brunswick in the British zone, six hundred cigarettes could get you a bicycle. For some, the black market was essentially a full-time occupation. "The standard DP scam was the 'dead souls' racket, whereby block leaders claimed rations for inflated numbers of people in the camps and then used the surplus for trading. Whether the proceeds thus generated were distributed round the camp or converted by individuals into 'portable wealth' such as cameras, watches, diamonds and hard currency was down to local circumstances." In 1947, "67 Latvians and Lithuanians received prison sentences after a police raid on the Artillerie Kaserne camp in Lübeck . . . uncovered 109 mature live pigs and a huge stash of other footstuffs." Leather and gramophone needles were the main commodities in another DP camp raided around the same time.

Detailed personal accounts of such activities are understandably rare, but some DPs who later repatriated to the Soviet Union told colorful stories on their return of the degraded life they had led under capitalism. A young Soviet Moldavian fell in with a group selling cigarettes on the black market in a Jewish camp in Austria. He worked with them until the rest of the group emigrated to Palestine, at the end of 1949. A young Ukrainian woman, taken to Germany as forced labor during the war, made the acquaintance of an Italian woman, probably also a DP, and went into black market business with her. They would cross the border to Italy illegally and bring back cognac, stockings, mandarins, lard, and butter for sale in Innsbruck; later they added Swiss watches to their trade. But the bottom fell out of this activity with the currency reform of 1947, so the Ukrainian gave up the black market and went back to her previous work in a hotel.[1]

Sometimes UNRRA and IRO personnel were involved in the black market too, to the chagrin of their respective institutions. A confidential UNRRA internal memo of August 1946 noted "recent grave irregularities in black market and currency dealings" evidently involving UNRRA personnel in the Schleswig-Holstein region. American soldiers engaged in it as individuals, "receiving a generous monthly cigarette allowance which could easily be exchanged on the black market for items such as cameras or jewellery that starving Germans were prepared to sell." It was no different in the British zone, where reportedly "it was possible to buy anything from British soldiers on the black market."

The occupation forces evidently made their own use of black-market channels for provisioning. A Soviet DP working as a driver for the US Army had the official task of moving foodstuffs from the Army warehouse to the city of Nuremberg, but his actual duties were broader. "Once a week, or sometimes more often, I set off in a 6-ton truck with orders for the warehouse. The people working there were Russians or Russian-speaking Ukrainians," that is, men with whom he could strike up an easy rapport. "They loaded my truck with all the goods. I signed for it and took it to the base." But, since the Americans had everything but fresh food, an unofficial part of his job was "exchange of cigarettes and chocolates for fresh eggs. Receiving a few cartons of 'Lucky Strike' and 'Camel' and a box or two of chocolate, I went the nearby villages and exchanged them all (or practically all—after all I had my own acquaintances and girlfriends!) for boxes of eggs, prepared earlier for me to pick up." In other words, the DP driver dealt himself into his American employers' black marketeering, in one instance securing from his mates at the warehouse half a dozen twenty-liter cylinders of ice-cream off the books to impress his German girlfriend.

Bartering was not actually illegal, at least in the British zone, but speculation in goods and currency as a means of accumulating capital obviously caused concern. Periodically, steps were taken to control DP black-marketeering. In November 1946, UNRRA's director ordered that "any person trafficking in goods or currency in the black market—seller as well as buyer—shall immediately lose his status as a displaced person and be instantly expelled from our camps." But this seemed largely to be honored in the breach. The US Army also launched a big "search-and-seizure" raid, labeled "Tally-ho!," in the US zone on December 27, 1945, "when, simultaneously, every DP camp was surrounded and house to house searches made"—resulting in the Wildflecken camp in a monumental snafu when the soldiers seized Red Cross parcels given to the DPs at Christmas.

Enforcing anti–black market rules was fraught with complications. Some contemporary observers thought that Jewish DPs were the biggest black market operators. Zionist leader Nahum Goldmann called the Belsen DP camp (Jewish; on the site of the former Nazi concentration camp) "the centre of one of the great black market rings in Europe," from which the Belsen DPs' leader, Josef Rosenhaft, became rich. But when Western authorities staged a raid on a Jewish DP camp nearby that was also a center of black market operations, "the [US] Under-Secretary of State [in Washington] received a call in the middle of the night," probably from a staffer at one of the Jewish voluntary organizations alerted by DPs at the camp, complaining that "a pogrom was being carried out." A number of such incidents were reported in the US press and caused more trouble. In Stuttgart, on March 29, 1946, about 180 German uniformed police plus 8 American military police "attempted to raid the Jewish DP camp located on Reinsburgstrasse" looking for black market activity, but "a mob formed and drove the German police from the camp." Shots were fired, one camp inhabitant was killed and three injured; twenty-eight German police were injured. Protest demonstrations and memorial services for the DP victim were held in many Jewish centers, and the US military command ordered that "German police were not to be used in raids on Jewish Camps."

Many DPs ended up serving prison sentences, usually short, in British or American jails for black-marketeering. But German police, revived a year or so after the war, might also come to DP camps searching for black marketeers. "DP criminality" was a running cause of German indignation and conflict with German police and courts, exacerbating the existing hostility between DPs and the surrounding German population.[2]

Jobs in Germany

Work, in particular the requirement to work, was a sensitive topic with DPs. Many of them, after all, were former forced laborers, brought to Germany against their will, so for the Allies to push the DPs to work immediately after the war could have seemed simply a change of masters—an argument often put by the Soviets. While some DPs did continue working for their former employers after the war, especially on the farms, this was not encouraged (and sometimes formally banned) by the Allies, partly because of the administrative problems involved in getting employers to change their status to normally remunerated workers. The Soviets strongly opposed it, claiming that it amounted to a continuation of "servitude to German kulak farmers."

UNRRA initially expected that virtually all the DPs would be quickly repatriated, which meant that it did not at first focus on the question of work. The DPs were always allowed to work (for pay), but there was initially no sense of a requirement. It was not until the middle of 1946 that all zones introduced instructions that able-bodied DPs were expected to work—although this was softened in the US zone by the exemption of Jewish persecutees from the requirement and a broader concern on the part of UNRRA that DPs' labor might be exploited. "The basic policy, according to UNRRA's official historian, was that employment should be voluntary but that it should be encouraged by every possible means, provided, of course, that it did not interfere with repatriation."

The Allied military had originally favored a more straightforward policy "that refugees who did not repatriate must register for work." But according to Raphael Cilento's jaundiced summary, "this was attacked as intimidation and so varied a sheaf of arguments raised for 'exemptions', 'special cases' and so forth, that this, too, became farcical . . . It was a cumulative defeat: we were all rebuffed. The Army and the Control Commission for Germany shrugged themselves into a more distant detachment—if that was the way UNRRA wanted it, very well, then!"[3]

In any case, there "wasn't much work, and Jews and most Balts wouldn't do it anyway." Jewish DPs often refused outright. An unsympathetic UNRRA report summarized their attitude as being that they had to work in the concentration camps and "deserve a rest and it is the world's duty to work for them." A report from representatives of Jewish voluntary organizations made the same point less censoriously but also noted that Jewish DPs might be more willing to work if offered money rather than privileges like extra food. It was not surprising, the Jewish report continued, that many of them "fear 'tomorrow'—that is are afraid of arriving in a new country with empty pockets. This desire to accumulate savings is turned into undesirable channels [that is, black market operations] because arrangements have not been made to exploit those normal instincts in a healthy way." Other DP groups made specific demands as well. Latvians objected to being expected to do manual work and to working for German employers. "It should be declared that Latvians are the victims of the last war and that they should be treated as such . . . Latvians are willing to do work, but they prefer to do it for the Allies," a meeting of Latvian DPs in Kassel resolved in February 1947. The many professionals among them wanted to be offered jobs in their specialties.[4]

While UNRRA did its best to boost the numbers, only a minority of DPs were employed, and employment was often sporadic and short-term. Opportunities to work, in any case, were unevenly distributed. Ukrainians in the Ellswangen camp east of Stuttgart were eager to work as laborers for local farmers, but there were far more potential workers than jobs available, while Poles at the Wildflecken camp had basically no work opportunities because of its geographical location. In the US zone as of August 1946, 38 percent of male DPs of working age and 18 percent of females were registered as being in fulltime employment. In the Baltic Scheinfeld camp in the American zone in the first year after the war, only 112 residents were employed (a tenth of the total DP population), of whom 43 worked in the camp administration and 17 were members of the camp police. Camps like the mixed-nationality Seedorf camp in the British zone, where most of the male DPs were employed in forestry, were "the exception rather than the rule." "Russians" (former Soviet citizens) were the keenest to work, perhaps surprisingly in view of their reputation for being undisciplined, with two-thirds of men and women employed, in contrast to a quarter of the Latvians and Poles. In the Soviet Russian group, women had about the same high employment rate as men (presumably a reflection of the high rate of women's employment in the prewar Soviet Union), whereas for Russian émigrés it was much lower. Jewish DPs in the working-age group, with under 2 percent of women and only 31 percent of men employed, were at the bottom of the list.[5]

As time passed, it became evident that large numbers of DPs were not going to repatriate but might be in Europe for the long haul; consequently, the equation changed and much larger numbers of DPs found employment. About 70 percent of employable DPs in all three Western zones of Germany were working by mid-1947. The British zone lagged behind, with not quite 60 percent employed—but that included even the recalcitrant Baltic DPs, many of whom now had jobs in construction in Hamburg (a city in ruins after wartime Allied bombing).

If these employment figures look impressive, this must be qualified by the fact that the great majority of working DPs were employed by UNRRA itself. In the US zone in August 1946, more than three-quarters of the relatively small numbers in employment were working for UNRRA in some capacity. As of the summer of 1947, almost 60 percent of working DPs in all zones were employed by UNRRA's successor, IRO, and another 31 percent by the Western military governments. Thus UNRRA/IRO employment was the norm in DP-land. The majority of these UNRRA/IRO jobs involved work in the DP camps themselves as "internal police, firemen and janitors, as well as teachers in camp schools and doctors and nurses in camp hospitals," although some DPs worked in UNRRA/IRO offices. Smaller groups had white-collar jobs in the UNRRA/IRO administrations and short-term manual jobs working on construction projects. These camp jobs existed, by definition, only as long as the UNRRA/IRO camp regime lasted; and their allocation within a camp was one of the perks of office for the elected camp leaders.[6]

The corollary of the Allies' near-monopoly of DP employment was that very few DPs were either working for Germans or running their own (legal) businesses within the German economy. In fact, running a business was not even one of the varieties of DP employment listed in UNRRA's statistics, and there is virtually no discussion of the possibility in the scholarly literature. This is probably because all such activity on the part of DPs was assumed to be on the black market. When a Jewish DP at the Hohne camp near Bergen-Belsen— one of the camps raided by German police on suspicion of black market activities—applied to UNRRA for a permit for the German assistant in his "trade as a furrier" to be allowed to enter the camp, an UNRRA official's response was that this indication that "he is not without means of livelihood" merited an inquiry "as to whether his present status as DP is justifiable." This strikingly unhelpful reaction reflected a reluctance on the part of the Allied authorities to give business licenses to Jews, including German Jews (part of UNRRA's remit) who were trying to reopen their prewar businesses.

It is interesting to compare the Jewish furrier's experience with that of (non-Jewish) Olga Danos, who not only engaged energetically in business activities without adverse consequences but even received UNRRA support for her enterprises. (It is worth noting that Olga's activities, though apparently legal, are known only through surviving private papers, not from documents to be found in archives; this may be another instance of documentary invisibility.) Olga had had some business experience in Riga before the war, when Danos family fortunes were at a low ebb; after she registered as a DP in Geestacht in the British zone in March 1946, she told Mischka that she was planning to set up a tailoring business in Hamburg, evidently employing other DPs as labor. The UNRRA director in Geestacht, who supported her initiative, had provided her with two sewing machines. Olga had no capital to invest, but as she remarked to Mischka, that had never stopped her. By April, with her Geestacht workshop functioning, she was talking of opening a workshop in Flensburg as well.

Still, despite the benevolence of the Geestacht director, it seems to have been UNRRA's general (though unarticulated) expectation that if DPs established a business or gained permanent employment in their specialty, they should discharge themselves from UNRRA care ("go onto the German economy") while retaining DP status with regard to resettlement opportunities. Mischka discharged himself when he moved to Heidelberg to do a PhD, Olga when she moved to Fulda to establish a new one-woman business as a sculptor of religious figurines for Germany's many bombed-out churches. She maintained her tailoring business, however, which by mid-1949 had been upgraded to Olga Danos Fashion Salon, Bespoke Clothing to Your Own Pattern, Florengasse 53, Fulda.[7]

Working for the Amis

Working for the Americans does not show up as a major DP employment option in UNRRA and IRO documents. Yet, if one goes by DP interviews and memoirs written after resettlement in anglophone countries, a completely different impression is given: almost every DP with mechanical, engineering, or linguistic skills seems to have worked for the American military at some point. This suggests that the statistics are unreliable and/or that working for the military increased a DP's chances of resettlement in North America and Australasia. DPs worked for the "Amis" in a variety of capacities, from translators and mechanics to warehousemen and guards. Many DPs worked for the occupation forces as drivers. Alexei Kisliakoff, who had served as a translator for the Germans during the war, found similar employment with the Americans after it. Paul Schlüsser, an émigré Russian DP, possibly with Western intelligence connections, had a job teaching Russian night classes to members of the US forces at the Frankfurt Army Education Center. Several repatriating Soviet DPs told their Soviet interviewers that they had worked at some point for the Americans, even though this was information they might have been expected to suppress. This work was not necessarily better paid than jobs with UNRRA/IRO in the camps, but it brought connections that could be useful in resettlement selection, and the same was true of the equivalent work for the British. Mischka Danos worked as a radio repair man for the British military in Flensburg, and he and his engineering-student friends seem to have assumed throughout their DP lives that such work would always be available on a casual basis when needed.[8]

One likely reason for the statistical confusion was that the British and Americans were both semi-covertly employing DPs in military and paramilitary units. This started spontaneously at the end of the war with the ad hoc use of DPs for guard duties by the military occupation forces. Senior UNRRA official Sir Raphael Cilento, reporting in July 1945 on the chaotic situation in the occupation zones, noted in passing that in the British zone "the Army has recruited some thousands of Poles to act as guards." As the US and British occupation forces found their strength dwindling with demobilization in 1945–46, it was natural to think of supplementing their ranks with former POWs and other DPs, available "at minimal wages to provide security for displaced persons, expellee and German POWs camps, the prisons where German war criminals were held, American military installations, warehouses, offices, and airports, and the towns, villages, and cities adjacent to these sites." The British led the way, but the United States soon followed. As of January 1946, it was claimed that 37,500 Poles were employed by the US Army in guard units, wearing "dyed American uniforms" and issued with arms. Yugoslavs were also used, receiving uniforms, enhanced rations, decent wages, and PX privileges. Latvian and Estonian platoons of men with military experience (presumably often acquired under German command) were formed for guard duties.

Allied use of DPs in military and paramilitary units was the subject of frequent complaint from the Soviet Union, although the Allies generally denied that such complaints had any basis. From the Soviet standpoint, the employment of DPs, wearing British or American Army uniforms and bearing weapons in units commanded by the British and American military, was sinister, an indication of the Western Allies' intentions to use the DPs for their own Cold War purposes, namely as the nucleus of military forces that might be used against the Soviet Union in the future. At a meeting of the Third UN

Committee on Social, Humanitarian, and Cultural Issues late in 1946, the Soviet Union proposed a ban on the employment of DPs in military and semi-military formations in the occupation zones. Although nobody spoke against the Soviet proposal, and the US delegate, Eleanor Roosevelt, even agreed that DP military formations should be disbanded, it was voted down. This odd result suggests that there were indeed "semi-military formations" of DPs around, if not "military formations" as well, and that the Western Allies intended to retain them.

Allegations made by Soviet representatives to the Third UN Committee focused on military units like the Ukrainian Petliura Division, detachments of the Royal Yugoslav Army, various Cossack detachments, and the Russian émigré Rogozhin unit that had all fought under German command during the war and were now under Western control, but, according to the Soviets, were not yet disbanded. The response of the British representative was that these were all prisoner-of-war groups whose disposition was a purely military affair, nothing to do with UNRRA and IRO. This must be regarded as somewhat disingenuous, however, given that the slowness of the British government in disbanding such units was related to behind-the-scenes discussions of how they might be useful. Proposals had been made to the British Foreign Office (though not adopted) to recruit Ukrainians from the Waffen-SS Galician Division into the British Army or even to form them into a British foreign legion.[9]

As in Britain, ideas of formalizing this use of DPs were in circulation in Washington. The US War Department considered the possibility of creating its own foreign legion in Germany, to supplement German police and carry out guard duties. But the main impetus came from Henry Cabot Lodge Jr., a Republican senator from Massachusetts who in 1953 would become a member of President Eisenhower's cabinet and ambassador to the United Nations. He succeeded in securing passage of the Lodge Act in June 1950, authorizing the employment of foreigners in the US military. But the larger goal—the formation of a Volunteer Freedom Corps of Eastern European refugees in Europe, to be stationed in Germany and constituting a front line in the Cold War, with US citizenship down the road as a recruitment incentive—proved elusive.

There was sympathy in the US Department of War for Lodge's plan, although General Clay, the man on the ground in Germany, thought any such initiative undesirable. "During the past year," Clay wrote early in 1947, "we have used civilian guard companies composed of displaced persons to some advantage," although they posed discipline problems and exhibited a tendency to get involved in black market. "Our experience does not indicate that a Foreign

Legion would be desirable. It would have to be composed largely of displaced persons who have refused to be repatriated. Its formation would be regarded by the countries from which its personnel was recruited as an unfriendly act on our part." It would also be inconsistent with "our objective in trying to create a democratic and peace-loving Germany." Germans would be outraged by the creation of a DP foreign legion, and any such enterprise would jeopardize the relations of American troops with the German population.

There were advantages to the military in Germany of using DPs to fill the gaps, particularly for maintenance and support duties, all the same. As the wartime Army demobilized, manpower shortages in the US occupation forces made themselves felt. When the US draft law expired on April 1, 1947, the US Army's personnel and administration (P&A) director proposed "that an efficient and effective way to at least partially alleviate the personnel shortage [in the] next fiscal year" would be to recruit foreign nationals to serve "with the occupation forces in Germany." Specifically, it was proposed to recruit Polish former POWs for the task. Army intelligence in Frankfurt responded that "the Polish Guard Corps, composed of displaced persons with military training, was already providing all the supplementary 'foreign' manpower the military required." But Army P&A persevered, proposing to recruit an additional twenty-five thousand Polish DPs and eighteen thousand from Baltics for "guard and service duty." Cabot Lodge put a bill to that effect before the US Congress. It was voted down, but the terms of the debate made clear that the practice was well established and continuing.

The State Department strongly objected to the Army's proposal. Secretary of State James Byrnes wrote to Secretary of War Robert P. Patterson to "point out that the use of these Polish nationals as para-military units in the American occupation zone in Germany may have serious political repercussions . . . The Polish Government may allege that . . . we are encouraging them to remain in our zone instead of returning to Poland." A month later, the *New York Times* ran a front-page story criticizing US involvement in the creation of "armies of mercenaries . . . dominated by anti-Semitic and anti-Soviet sympathizers . . . This concentration is regarded in Polish, Russian and Yugoslav eyes as the nucleus of a counter-revolutionary force in central Europe" that could potentially be used in an action comparable to Western intervention in support of the Whites during the Russian Civil War.[10]

The Soviets believed that some of these DPs had been handpicked for special training in anti-communism and policing for later use in the camps. The US discussion focused mainly on recruitment of Polish and Yugoslav DPs. But

Soviet citizens were involved as well, and that was a cause of particular Soviet alarm. In the first year after the war, Soviet repatriation officer Aleksei Brukhanov had believed that the Allies were seeking out DPs, especially former Nazi collaborators, for training in anti-communism and police duties in the camps. At a meeting with the Western Allies in 1949, he claimed that the Soviets had "evidence that Soviet nationals in the British Zone are being recruited into the American Army, the French Foreign Legion and the British police, and are being taken out of the Zone" and that "during the last nine months 10,000 Soviet citizens have disappeared without trace." No doubt many of these disappearances were related to resettlement, but some individuals had undoubtedly found their way into military units, and the Soviets knew about it, inter alia from repatriation interviews.

Soviet suspicions that the Western Allies proposed to use DPs as a Cold War weapon were not just paranoia. In 1953, when he joined Eisenhower's cabinet, Henry Cabot Lodge pushed energetically once again for a Volunteer Freedom Corps—"250,000 stateless, single, anti-Communist young men from countries behind the iron curtain," who were to be offered US citizenship at the end of their term of service—and won Eisenhower's support. But the project foundered in the face of strong opposition from European allies, notably the Austrians and Germans, no lovers of the DPs, on whose territories the corps would be stationed.[11]

Jobs outside Germany

The French Foreign Legion was, as the Soviets claimed, a recruiter of Soviet DPs, although this was in theory prohibited and the Western Allies always denied it. The legion was famous for enlisting anyone for service in the colonies without demanding identification documents and was thus traditionally attractive to adventurers and those with pasts they wanted to bury. Formally speaking, the legion was not supposed to take either DPs or Soviet citizens, but given that the legion did not demand identity documents, it is hard to see how this could have been enforced, even though some Soviet DPs reported signing up as Poles as a precaution. One repatriate told Soviet interviewers that the legion recruited men aged eighteen to thirty-five in Italian DP camps, sent them off to induction in Ventimiglia on the French border, and then shipped them out from Marseilles "for service to the French colonies," usually in North Africa. Vietnam (still a French colony) was sometimes on offer as well. The initial contract was for five years; after fifteen years of service, legionnaires were eligible for French citizenship and a pension.

Of the cases reported in Soviet repatriation files, several were recruited to the French Foreign Legion in 1946, immediately after their release from Allied POW camps. There were also cases where the recruits appear to have been much younger: one claimed to have been sent to Germany from a Soviet orphanage as a child and recruited to the French legion during the war at the age twelve, serving five years in Algeria until the expiration of his contract in 1947; another, taken to Germany with his parents during the war, somehow found himself in Africa at the end of the war and claimed to have been "sent" to the legion (not clear by whom) at the age of about fifteen.[12]

Recruitment to the French Foreign Legion was done surreptitiously. But there was also some small-scale public recruitment of DPs for other jobs outside Germany in the first postwar years that UNRRA and the occupation authorities permitted, albeit at arm's length. Some European nations, experiencing a shortage of labor, were interested in taking DPs for work under contract, perhaps with the possibility of future settlement, perhaps not. The British, although hesitant at the prospect of landing themselves with DPs as migrants, began tentatively in October–November 1946 by taking one thousand single women aged twenty-one to forty from the Baltics to work mainly in British hospitals. But it was actually the Belgians who got in first with a major DP-employment scheme, signing an agreement with the occupation authorities on January 23, 1947, to take twenty thousand male DPs (without dependents) as coal miners on two-year contracts. This was to be administered not by UNRRA but by the Intergovernmental Committee on Refugees (IGCR), a prewar institution maintaining a vestigial presence in the first postwar years, which had previously staked out an interest in resettling "nonrepatriable" stateless persons. The Belgians made no stipulations with regard to nationality. At the Polish Wildflecken camp, as Kathryn Hulme remembered, "it was the first door to open to our displaced, the only hopeful sign in that desolate spring." When recruiters from the Belgian mission showed up in early May, six hundred DPs packed a hall to listen to a pitch that included the possibility (though not guarantee) of renewal of the original contract or transfer to other employment in Belgium and eligibility after five years work in Belgium to apply for citizenship.[13]

With worsening labor shortages and the fear of losing the best DP worker prospects to others, the British took the plunge in March 1947, launching an ambitious scheme under the dashing name *Westward Ho!* to bring one hundred thousand DPs to Britain to work in the cotton and coal industries and agriculture. This was specifically a British government initiative, although organized in consultation with the IGCR, and initially recruiting only in the

British zone. In addition to its labor problems, Britain perceived itself in postwar years as facing a long-term population problem because of declining birthrate, which required correction by eugenically based immigration. UNRRA was not keen on *Westward Ho!* on the grounds that it would interfere with repatriation, still its major objective, and in addition was not a resettlement program, but rather a labor-recruitment employment scheme to meet immediate British needs. The Soviet Union was even more critical, wanting the scheme halted altogether until DP repatriation was completed. IRO became involved in a secondary role only in the summer of 1947, when recruitment was extended to the American zone.

Westward Ho! was restricted to men between the age of eighteen to fifty and women under forty. Those chosen, known in Britain as European Volunteer Workers (EVW), were allocated jobs by the Ministry of Labour and National Service, and, at least initially, could change jobs only with the ministry's consent. Because of housing shortages in Britain, the British did not encourage bringing dependents, and those who did come were put up in separate hostels from the breadwinners. This made the scheme less appealing to DPs. The British also reserved the right to return recruits who proved undesirable, including those suffering from TB, venereal diseases, or mental illness and women who turned out to be pregnant.

The British at first "took only DPs from the Baltic states and Ukrainians, but the net was eventually widened to include Poles, Yugoslavs, Hungarians, Bulgarians, Czechs, and Slovaks." Russians (Soviet or émigré), Jews, and Armenians were formally excluded (although in the event, a few hundred Russian émigrés made it in). More than seventy-seven thousand DPs ultimately migrated to Britain under this scheme between 1946 and 1949, the largest contingents being Latvians, Poles, and Ukrainians, of whom three thousand returned to Europe (most of their own volition, but some deported).

Although in the end *Westward Ho!* became a resettlement scheme, with the possibility of applying for naturalization after five years' residence, there was a degree of uncertainty about the recruits' long-term status that was only fully dissipated in 1951, when restrictions were formally lifted on changes of employment for those who had been in Britain for three years. The DPs found themselves facing an unenthusiastic welcome in Britain. Under the headline "Let Them Be Displaced," the London *Daily Mirror* suggested in 1948 that Britain had recruited "most of the scum" from the camps and that these people were responsible for "swelling the crime wave and black-market rackets." There were other disadvantages too, notably that recruitment by *Westward Ho!* queered

the DP's pitch for later resettlement by IRO. In the British view, such recruitment "should not prejudice the refugee's further resettlement opportunities."
But IRO (which had recognized *Westward Ho!* as a resettlement as well as
temporary employment scheme in 1948) took the position that, once a DP
had taken employment in a country in which he could settle, "no further resettlement opportunities could be offered by the IRO."[14]

Meanwhile, the Belgian scheme was running in competition, with thirty-
two thousand DPs (admittedly below the target of thirty-five thousand)
signed up by 1949. While Janet Flanner of the *New Yorker* gave it high marks—
"only Belgium has put into practice a humane scheme," she wrote in 1948—
this opinion was not widely shared by participants. "Disappointment" is the
main response of DP recruits reported by a Belgian historian. This was partly
because the work was hard and there was a lack of housing for the men, and
particularly for their families, but there were other problems. First, their relations with other workers and Belgians in general was soured by the fact that the
local Communist Party launched a campaign against them as collaborators.
Second, there was an ambiguity, similar to the British case, about whether they
were refugees being offered a new home or labor on short-term recruitment.
"Despite the fact that they were recognized as refugees by the international
Refugee Organization, the Belgian actors—both government and mining
boards (and trade unions)—tried to fit them into the traditional guest workers' system. In other words, whereas the Refugee Organization considered the
recruitments as a resettlement operation, the Belgian actors saw the whole
project as a (strictly) economic labour recruitment." Although the original
contracts had promised the possibility of working elsewhere in the Belgian
economy after the two-year contract, an economic downturn in 1949 meant
that many simply had their mining contracts renewed for a year.

As with *Westward Ho!*, the eligibility of those who had taken a Belgian contract for subsequent resettlement was disputed. Not wanting them to pour
back into Germany, IRO encouraged DPs to continue working in the mines
while promising them support with visa applications and ship reservations
(although, unlike other DPs, they would have to pay for their passage). This
was already much resented by the Belgian contingent, and then things got
worse with the US Displaced Persons Act, which in its initial form specified
admission of DPs still living in DP camps. There were public protests by DPs
in Belgium demanding readmission to Germany and full eligibility for resettlement. As a result, fifty were accepted back to the US zone legally in 1949 and
another three hundred in the spring of 1950, with others making their own way

back as best they could. There were few DP experiences less popular than work in the Belgian mines—one of the factors most likely to produce a subsequent decision to repatriate, judging by reentry interviews to the Soviet Union. Repatriates complained both that the work was unbearably hard and that when their contracts expired in 1949, Belgium was in economic crisis and work was very hard to find.

The French were also potentially in the market for DP labor, but not with huge urgency, since they still had 450,000 German POWs in the country providing cheap labor. There were reservations, too, from the powerful French communist party, which suspected the DPs, particularly Balts and Poles, of fascism (ironically, Volksdeutsche were preferred). The French selection teams, which included communists, reportedly asked candidates about their politics, leading to the rumor in the DP camps "that one must be a communist sympathizer in order to immigrate to France." Starting their DP recruitment in the spring of 1947, and holding out hopes of future resettlement, the French recruited thirty-eight thousand workers.

At the end of the day, the total number of DPs recruited for work, and possible future residence, in various countries of Western Europe was around 150,000, with about two-thirds of that number settling in England and most of the rest in France and Belgium.[15]

Studying

Education was one approved exemption from the formal work requirement, and in Raphael Cilento's jaundiced contemporary assessment, thousands of DPs "enrolled in every sort of study-category, some utterly absurd" simply to take advantage of that loophole. Seen in historical retrospect, however, tuition-free study in universities, technical schools, and high schools was one of the great perks of DP life, as well as one of UNRRA's notable achievements.

Displaced persons in Germany after the war had lost many things, but not the opportunity for an education. Often, given the excellence of the German educational system, it was a better one than they would have received at home. Some DP children attended primary and secondary schools in the camps and were taught in their native language: in many of these—the Latvian camps, for example, and the Russian Mönchehof—the quality of the academic instruction must have been first-rate, given the professional credentials of the DP teachers available, even if for some tastes the patriotic motif was overstressed. Ukrainian DPs, under strongly nationalist leadership, had managed to set up a network of twenty-nine high schools and eighty primary schools for DP children in Germany and Austria. At the high school level, German gymnasia were also available for the academically gifted.

UNRRA and later IRO, in association with various international voluntary societies such as AJDC and YMCA, provided free vocational and technical courses for adult DPs who wished to learn sewing, machine-shop work, and carpentry or more specialized trades like watchmaking, typewriter repair, or radio mechanics. As of September 1, 1947, over thirty thousand DPs in Germany, Austria, and Italy were registered in such courses. These included Jewish students being trained in agricultural and industrial skills by the international voluntary society ORT (Organisation Reconstruction Travail/Organization for Rehabilitation through Training). Other nationalities set up their own vocational training courses for DPs, the Ukrainians alone running over three hundred such courses in Germany and Austria.[16]

The most remarkable educational opportunity available was study in German universities. UNRRA and the occupation authorities were originally strongly supportive of the DPs' right to higher education, if they were qualified for it. In November 1945, UNRRA in the British sector obliged German authorities to make 10 percent of all student places available for DPs, tuition-free, with students receiving a stipend as well as rations. By mid-1946, a total of 3,326 DP students were enrolled in German higher educational institutions in the British, American, and French zones—and these included some of the best universities not just in Germany but in the world at the time, including the University of Tübingen in the French zone, the University of Göttingen in the British zone, and the University of Heidelberg in the American zone. As of July 1946, medicine and engineering were the fields that most DPs wanted to study in, but the largest enrolments were actually in medical schools, with the numbers accepted for engineering (including Mischka and his Latvian friends at Hannover) lower than those for medicine, natural science, philosophy, and economics. As a DP student commentator rightly remarked, the DP students "might very well be considered a privileged group as compared with thousands of starving students in many other countries today."[17]

The first enrolment of DP students early in 1946 was predictably chaotic. UNRRA had no systematic plan worked out for vetting student qualifications and matching student with university, and staffers wrote of "utter confusion," with would-be students arriving with "pseudo-authorization" from various national DP committees. It was not until March that UNRRA even decided which department was responsible for taking applications and allocating DPs to different universities—and that department's first step was to send out a questionnaire asking DPs where they had actually enrolled. In other words, as so often happened, the DPs themselves had taken the initiative, with UNRRA and other institutions scrambling in their wake.

This was certainly the case with Mischka Danos and his Latvian friends, former engineering students from the University of Riga. Munich, in the American zone, was on Mischka's itinerary in November 1945, when he did his extensive (unauthorized) tour out of the British zone by train, and he wrote to his mother that "if only the school [i.e., university] were better, I would stay there despite everything, because it's beautiful." But academic prospects in the British zone looked better, and he landed in Braunschweig, where he and his friend Andrejs Bicevskis tried to enroll in the technical university. When they encountered problems there, they changed their sights to the Technical University in Hanover, also in the British zone, and were soon joined by other Riga University friends like Dailonis Stauvers. None of this should have been possible according to UNRRA's regulations, which banned interzonal travel to enter university and also forbade DP students to sign up directly with German universities. Nevertheless, Mischka and his two Riga friends were all registered at Hannover Technical University when the new semester began.

There was not a lot of social mixing with the German students, by most accounts, although they were all in classes together. In German universities attended by DP students, each national group had its own committee, and most socializing was done within that group. Even a non- (and, in later life, anti-) nationalist like Mischka Danos moved largely with his own group of Latvian friends from Riga as an undergraduate at the university in Hanover, although some of his German professors were important as scientific influences. He and his friends remembered relatively few contacts with German students, except for those who had German girlfriends met outside the university. It was not until his PhD studies at Heidelberg that German fellow students started to feature as individuals in Mischka's stories.[18]

Baltic DPs like Mischka and his friends—over a thousand of them in the winter semester of 1946 to 1947—were the largest group of DP students in German universities, with six hundred Poles in second place. In the previous semester (the first taking DP enrollments), Poles had outnumbered Baltic students in the British zone (though not the American or French). But in what Raphael Cilento described as "a sop to the Soviet Cerberus," the Americans had started restricting the number of Polish DPs who could study in German universities, and in the British zone UNRRA was facing objections to DP departure for university from Polish repatriation officers. From the standpoint of the Warsaw and Soviet governments, giving DPs the option of university was just another obstacle on the path to repatriation.

Russian and Ukrainian DP students are harder to tease out of the available statistics, but almost certainly they were fewer than Baltic students. Russian émigrés ("stateless") were a recognized nationality for purposes of university enrollment, and in the winter semester of 1946 to 1947, 218 out of almost 2,000 DP students enrolled in German higher educational institutions in the British zone were so classified. Neither "Soviet" nor "Ukrainian" was a category in the enrollment statistics. At a meeting at the UNRRA European office on June 30, 1946, a Soviet representative referred to "a large number of Soviet displaced persons going to German universities." While the discussion that followed dealt only with students from the Baltics, some of them are likely to have been Russian or Ukrainian. One who shows up in IRO's eligibility files was Viktor Werbitsky, born in Odessa in 1927, nationality not stated but probably Russian or Ukrainian rather than Jewish, as he seems to have been under suspicion of collaboration with the Nazis. Werbitsky had left the Soviet Union with his parents and sister in December 1944 (presumably with the retreating Germans), entered the Schleissheim DP camp in November 1946, and enrolled as a student at the Technical University in Munich in November 1947.

Jewish DPs were studying at German universities as well: in the American zone, there were said to be more than seven hundred Jewish students enrolled in higher education, most of them from Poland; and there was even a Jewish Students' Union based in Munich, with smaller branches at Darmstadt, Erlangen, Frankfurt, Heidelberg, Marburg, and Stuttgart. A memoir of one of these students recalled how important it was for these young DPs to get out of the DP camps and recover some sense of autonomy. "Entering a university, which meant being placed among the German population as boarders in Germany homes, was a way to restore a sense of agency and a vision of the future." The Jewish DPs also had an option not available to any other DP students, namely going to university outside Germany: as of April 1946, the Hillel Foundation, working with the JDC on site, had forwarded one hundred applications for study in universities in the United States.[19]

Before German universities had opened for DP students early in 1946, an "UNRRA university" had been set up in Munich as an initiative of the DPs themselves. This was the brain-child of some uprooted academics (the first rector, Professor Mitinsky, was a Russian who had taught engineering at the University of Prague before the war), and the Munich department of UNRRA helped them set up the new institution in the old Deutsches Museum. Instruction was in German, as the lingua franca of the DPs. Of the university's 2,378 students as of July 1946, 618 were Ukrainian and 334 "stateless" (émigré Russian). Despite the positive DP response, UNRRA was divided on the desirability and sustainability of the enterprise; the American occupation authorities were not supportive, and there were constant problems obtaining equipment and teaching materials. The US Army closed the university down abruptly just before the beginning of the new term in January 1947.

The UNRRA University was not the only diaspora-based institution offering higher education to DPs. Munich also became home to the Free Ukrainian University, described by a historian as "the center of Ukrainian intellectual life in the German diaspora," whose antecedents were in various higher educational institutions established in Western Europe by Ukrainian émigrés between the wars. Professor Vadym Shcherbakivsky led its reestablishment in Bavaria, and it commenced teaching in February 1946. In this case, the American military command was supportive, as was the Catholic Church. Premises were found in a German public school, and in 1950 the Bavarian state government recognized it as a "private university." It survives in Munich up to the present day.[20]

In the British zone, a "Baltic University" was set up in Hamburg in March 1946, with an enrolment of fourteen hundred by the end of the year. In contrast to the Ukrainian Free University in Munich, it was not allowed to grant degrees and diplomas. The first location was the bombed-out Museum for Hamburg History, but early in 1947 the university moved to better premises: a former Luftwaffe barracks at Pinneberg in Schleswig-Holstein. All the teachers were from the Baltic states, with Latvians predominating. The Baltic University was basically an UNRRA initiative, taken in response to suggestions made by Latvian DPs. Sir Raphael Cilento, UNRRA director in the British Zone at the time, described it in his memoirs as one of a series of measures taken to give the DPs something to do. But for many of the DP participants its significance for national spiritual survival was much greater. The students, according to one of their UNRRA supporters, were "some of the most liberty-loving individuals I have ever met." A more critical commentator found his fellow DP students "pathetically nationalistic" but conceded that it had helped preserve morale and a sense of dignity.

As of 1947, the university claimed seventy-six graduates (this in violation of the British ban on granting degrees!), with about 170 professors and 1,200 students. But dissatisfaction grew with the conditions of work, with DP scholars teaching without pay and receiving lower rations than school and even kindergarten teachers in the DP camps. Attempts were made to secure support from the American authorities, and there was even a desperate effort to move the entire enterprise, teachers and students and all, to the United States and take over an abandoned town in Maine—"at least until all the Baltic states are free and independent again." But all these efforts failed, and the university was closed down at the end of September 1949.[21]

Enthusiasm about higher education for DPs in general had already been on the decline for several years, as UNRRA started to realize that DPs who were able to study at some of the best universities in the world were not likely to be interested in repatriation, either immediately or upon graduation. UNRRA's European office stated early in 1947 that the primacy of UNRRA's commitment to repatriation implied that it should "prohibit any activities which . . . might impede repatriation." American Jews and Zionist organizations started criticizing UNRRA and the occupation authorities for allowing or encouraging Jewish DPs to study in German universities. In addition, it was noticed that some DPs were abusing the system by switching to another university faculty immediately on graduating from the original one (for example, finishing law and going on to enroll in medicine). As of December 1946, UNRRA ruled that, while DPs might choose to study at German universities, they would henceforth be offered no "special privileges" beyond those available to all DPs, such as accommodation and maintenance in a camp. The occupation authorities concurred, and the initial requirement that German universities should take in a DP quota of 10 percent of enrollments was dropped to 2 percent in the winter of 1946–47 and then phased out altogether in 1949.

Meanwhile, the game plan for DPs had changed with the replacement of UNRRA by IRO in mid-July: resettlement, not repatriation, was now the mission. But university education did nothing for a DP's resettlement prospects: indeed, a number of recipient countries specifically indicated a preference for manual workers, making no bones about their lack of interest in university graduates and students as migrants. "Most countries of resettlement are primarily interested in agricultural and skilled workers, and are reluctant to accept intellectuals, including those who have either recently completed their studies or are in the process of doing so," an IRO official wrote in 1949. "Accordingly, IRO has not considered it wise to encourage or sponsor higher education unless it leads to a better resettlement plan than could otherwise be achieved."

Reverting to Cilento's original skeptical assessment, and lacking UNRRA idealists' humanistic view of education as a good in itself, IRO came to see higher education simply an impediment to resettlement and a way for DPs to evade the reasonable expectation that they "get down to work at the earliest opportunity."[22] This stopped new DPs enrolling in German universities, but it didn't stop existing DP students graduating. The damage (or its opposite) had already been done. Mischka Danos and his friends from Latvia all managed to finish their degrees at Hanover Technical University and all then found re-settlement places without difficulty, most of them in the United States. Mischka himself was one of the last to leave (in 1951): he had to finish his PhD in physics, working with world experts in his field at the University of Heidelberg. But he still got his DP free passage to the United States from IRO.

5

Other DP Activities and Entertainments

UNSYMPATHETIC OBSERVERS called DPs who were neither working nor studying idlers. But that was far from the case for many of them, even though the activities in which they engaged were self-chosen and not always fully approved by the authorities. In the case of men, apparent idleness often covered an active life working in the black market. The case of women was different, partly for reasons of culture and tradition (DP women from the Soviet Union may have been used to the idea of paid employment, but those from most other countries were less so) and partly for biological reasons, namely their ability to bear children. The main occupation of a large proportion of young women DPs was having babies and bringing up small children. This was facilitated by the fact that the camp system functioned like a welfare state, providing guaranteed lodging, food, clothing, childcare, and medical services. In addition, social mores were much more relaxed in the camps than in the societies the DPs had come from, and there was no great stigma in having a child without a husband.

Young women might find themselves living the high life for a few years, dating US and British Army personnel and supping in officers' clubs. Some of the young men (and a few women) were seizing the unexpected opportunity of a Wanderjahr to see the world, setting off on a variety of adventures with the DP card in their back pocket. Others used time off their jobs or classes to do a bit of tourism by train or bicycle in the (still beautiful) German countryside. Young people of both sexes were competing in sports and even attempting to get DP-land recognized as the equivalent of a country for the purposes of international competitions. Almost all the DPs—or so it seems from the multiplicity of accounts—were engaging in various cultural pursuits with a strong nationalist bent, the better to preserve the national identity in exile.

It was these pursuits, above all, that led some resettled DPs in later life to remember the halcyon days of the DP camps with such nostalgia—an interval of freedom and hedonism that separated wartime misery from the strains and uncertainties of settling in a new country. This interval, for most, lasted only about three years. As the occupying armies—whose soldiers were the source of much of the bounty and good times—prepared to withdraw, the imminent necessity of organizing an advantageous relocation became the DPs' primary preoccupation. What had felt to some like a holiday was coming to an end.

Options for Young Women

Over 40 percent of adult DPs in UNRRA's camps as of April 1946 were women, a majority of them were of child-bearing age, and lots of them were bearing children. As of December 1946, 21 percent of the camp population were children under eighteen, about two-thirds of them under six, thus born during or after the war. The cohort of babies in the first year of their life was particularly impressive. Poles were the most fertile DP nationality at this point, one out of every eleven women over eighteen having had a baby within the past year. By 1948, the proportion of young children in the DP population had risen even further, due to an "extraordinarily high birth rate" of thirty-two per thousand—over ten times as high as England's in 1934.

Of the women giving birth during the war, most would have been working in Germany as forced laborers (Ostarbeiter), the fathers being either German or fellow Ostarbeiters from various countries. Germans were not supposed to have sex with foreign workers, but this rule was applied less strongly to German men than German women, and rape of foreign women generally went unpunished. Many Ostarbeiter women became pregnant by Germans, which faced them with the three options of having an abortion (not illegal for foreign laborers, although it was for German women), keeping their babies as single mothers, or giving them up for fostering by German families. It must be assumed that the rate of wartime child-bearing, and even child-keeping, among Ostarbeiter women was high, although no systematic statistics are available. One indicator would be the number of children repatriated to the Soviet Union (mainly with their Ostarbeiter mothers) immediately after the war. As of March 1946, over seven hundred thousand children and 1.5 million women had repatriated—in other words, one child for every two women. In a later data set, covering an additional six months repatriation up to August 1946, the ratio had risen to two children to every three women.[1]

Sexual mores were relatively relaxed among DPs, but this meant different things for men and women. For men, sexual promiscuity was something expected of soldiers—and, by extension, others away from their homes—in time of war and therefore not a major deviation from behavioral norms; for women, on the other hand, the loose sexual mores of the DP camps were in stark contrast to the norms of the societies they had lived in before the war. The outcomes were also different for the two sexes. For men, casual sex, even resulting in a pregnancy, was usually without serious consequences. For women, pregnancy was a major life event, requiring either that they bear the child, with or without a husband, or have an abortion (possible, but it cost money and was not without danger). On the plus side, the DP camps provided much more practical support for child bearing, and less social censure for unmarried mothers, than most social environments, including those the women had come from and those they would later settle in.

There was a degree of stigma after the war on women who had "slept with the enemy." But in the case of Soviet DPs this seems to have been manifest mainly in the repatriation process and after the return home. In the camps, it was as easy to accept—if indeed the matter was discussed at all—that the father of a wartime child was a Polish or Italian Ostarbeiter—as to suspect it was a German. Sleeping with the enemy was only one of many forms of collaboration of which DPs might be accused, and DPs themselves seemed disinclined to dwell on any of them.

Outsiders might be more judgmental. Sex and pregnancy were prominent in Raphael Cilento's report after a tour of the former Bergen-Belsen concentration camp, which was also functioning as a DP camp in the British zone, in July 1945. He noted that "according to hearsay, promiscuity is extraordinarily rife with a correspondingly high degree of venereal disease and a high rate of pregnancy. The statement was made that there were 500 pregnant girls in the Belsen camp area," though others said this was exaggerated. There were many reports from Western personnel that "sexual irregularity had reached appalling proportions," producing an "epidemic of births" to unmarried mothers. Observers on the ground in 1945–46 all commented on the enormous baby boom among DPs. Births in the Polish camp of Wildflecken were running at two a day by September 1945; by early 1946, a special maternity hospital had opened in the camp, staffed by three DP doctors, three midwives, and ten nurses.

In terms of nationality, the relatively small group of Jewish DPs led the field, with almost six children for every ten Jewish women. Their situation to be sure, was unique; and the Jewish baby boom, which has been seen in political terms as a form of national self-assertion, was undoubtedly connected to a conscious desire to rebuild the population after the Holocaust. Rather surprisingly, Russian "stateless," another small group, were almost as prolific as Jews. In the large Polish contingent, as well as the small Soviet one, the ratio was a bit under five children per ten women; for Latvians, it was lower, at four to five children for every ten women.[2]

Along with the epidemic of births there was also an epidemic of marriage among DPs. As one Jewish DP remembered, "people who had survived singly in all age groups were struck with a strong desire to be married." In a "steady rush of weddings," DPs married, seemingly almost randomly, "neighbors in the next barrack or distant kin or acquaintances from what had once been home." There were "so many marriages, sometimes really strange marriages that never would have happened before the war." People would meet, and five minutes later would ask, "Are you married?" Ramona Koval's mismatched Polish-Jewish parents emerged from hiding when Soviet troops arrived in their Polish town at the end of 1944, met accidentally on the street, and married in a hurry—"not for love but for pity and loneliness"—so that they could get passports to travel together. Although marriage was on a "wholesale" scale, many DPs made great efforts to get white cloth for brides' dresses and dark suits for men, courtesy of UNRRA, or sometimes borrowed from local Germans. Since Ostarbeiter had not been allowed to marry under the Third Reich, there were also comparatively long-established couples who now married with their children standing by.

Since marriage was easy, and most DPs were young and on their own, many DPs—perhaps even the majority—got married. This did not mean that the marriages lasted, or even that the new couples resettled or repatriated together. It also did not mean that the marriages were strictly speaking valid, since wives and husbands who had been left back home, on the other side of an "iron curtain" forming between East and West, were generally conveniently forgotten. In other words, DP marriage was a contingent concept, though women—who, when the partnership broke up, would be left with the children—were more likely to take it seriously than men.

Opinions vary as to the degree of social pressure on couples to marry in the camps. According to one social worker's report, most DPs regarded extramarital sexual relationships and births outside of marriage with "a kind of tolerant regret, and tried to keep them as much in the background as possible." But the stigma probably increased as camp administrators of conservative, nationalist views worried about upholding the national reputation with UNRRA and the occupation regimes increased their moral and political control in the camps. There were always some disapproving fellow DPs, often middle-aged women, ready to denounce immorality in the camps and point the finger at women who were promiscuous or had abortions. An American UNRRA official remembered the Balts as stricter than the Poles and other Slavs, as well as than Jews. If cohabiting Poles were under pressure to marry if they wanted to move together to another camp, "they usually made a civil ceremony, which they didn't regard as real."

Some DPs, like Mischka and his friend Andrejs Bicevskis, followed a different pattern, waiting to marry until they had graduated from university, had the ability to support themselves "on the German economy," and were within hailing distance of resettlement. Andrejs married another DP, also a Latvian, whom he had met in a DP camp—an "appropriate" marriage, as her father had been a district administrator in the same region as Andrejs's father and she had known his brother, Peteris, back in Latvia. Mischka married a young German woman from a solid middle-class family whom he had met through the sports club. Both Mischka and Andrejs resettled with their new wives within a few years, respectively in Australia and the United States, within a few years, and had their first child in the new country.[3]

Mischka's and Andrejs's situation—as young, healthy Latvian professional men, not threatened by forced repatriation, and with at least some family support structures and friendship networks intact—was very different from that of many other DPs, notably women of Soviet origin who did not want to repatriate. For the women, it was often a matter of finding someone to marry (or "marry") who would save them from forcible repatriation and maximize their chances of resettlement. While under Soviet law, women who were Soviet citizens retained that status even if marrying someone of another citizenship, the Allies took the view, based on British and American law, that women automatically acquired the nationality of their spouse and were registered accordingly in resettlement applications.

These circumstances meant that the citizenship/nationality of a prospective partner was highly relevant in DPs' calculations. Soviet nationality was clearly a good one for DP women to marry out of, and many did. The most advantageous marriages for Soviet women were not to other Soviet DPs, who were equally liable to repatriation, or to Germans, who were not eligible for

IRO resettlement, but to foreigners—DPs of other nationalities, usually East European, or soldiers and other personnel from the Allied occupation forces. On the other hand, some Germans regarded marriage to a DP as advantageous, since that conveyed potential eligibility for resettlement. But this applied almost entirely to German women, who would then be able to take their DP husbands' nationality. In one rare case where a German married a Jewish DP (after a quick divorce from his German wife, and evidently in order to travel with her as a migrant to Australia under Jewish sponsorship), he was deported back to Germany after a public outcry.[4]

For women DPs, members of the occupation forces were counted the best catch, both for affairs—which might involve living it up at the officers' clubs and having indirect access to the desirable goods available at PX stores—and, even better, for marriage. Glamorous nights out with Americans were part of many young DP women's experiences in Germany. Some children of DPs I interviewed decades after their resettlement had been surprised to find photos hidden away of their young fashionably dressed mothers drinking cocktails in American or British officer clubs, before marrying another DP and leaving for resettlement with him. As a repatriating DP woman told Soviet interviewers, "there was a lot of champagne and wine and . . . meals were free" for a good-looking girl in postwar Germany. She herself had made the mistake of marrying another Soviet DP and having a child by him around 1946, which did not prevent her from frequenting dancehalls and meeting Latvians, Poles, Ukrainians, Russians, and Germans who were eager to show her a good time but must have limited her options when it came to resettlement.

A fascinatingly unvarnished picture of the DP/GI dating scene in Bavaria is offered in the memoir of a teenage daughter of Soviet-German refugees, Ella Schneider:

> Amis were visiting different girls in our camp. It was a constant flow day and night. Some of the soldiers were black. All looked clean-shaven, wore clean uniforms and boots . . . The girls in our camp who ran with Amis talked openly about how to pick up a soldier and taught anyone who wanted to learn just what American catch words or phrases to use. Of course, my girlfriends and I were in our early teens and eager listeners. We wanted to learn American, just in case . . . Amis yelled at pretty girls. Their favorite saying, "Fräulein, Kommen sie hier (Miss, come over here.]" Sometimes, "Do you want a Yankee dime?"
>
> . . . The whores [her mother's word, the meaning of which Ella did not know] always seemed to have fun. They laughed, wore makeup, had money

for movies and beautiful clothing and good food for their families . . . I was determined to find out how one could become a whore. One evening I found the nerve and asked [the next-door neighbor's daughter] . . . what I had to do to go out with an Ami. She explained to me in great detail how she did it, from beginning to end. She stood at the corner of the street (in white high heels), after dark, waited until an Ami car came by and stopped. "Schokolade" [chocolate] was the key word, then hold up fingers for each bar. Usually they drove to a hotel for the night. In the summertime, they went to the Danube. There they ate, drank, and had sex in the grass. Sometimes, in the wintertime, her mother agreed for her to bring the soldier home and they would use her mother's army cot.

This was the lower end of the spectrum, where marriage was not the most likely outcome, although it sometimes occurred. Cohabitation for the duration of the tour of duty (or, optimistically, longer) was common: two Soviet DP women in this situation, living respectively with an IRO staffer and an American (with a child by him), firmly rebuffed Soviet repatriation officers, without claiming to be actually or even prospectively married. But there were many sad stories of DPs jilted by American and British soldiers, who might return home at the end of their tour of duty in Germany without even saying goodbye to a pregnant girlfriend. One such DP took the child that she subsequently bore to the forest and left it to die. Another, an Estonian nurse who got pregnant by an Englishman working with her at the Red Cross in Hamburg, found herself pressured by English colleagues to have an abortion or at least put the child in an orphanage without disclosing the name of the father, who had a wife back home in England.[5]

Mischka's Riga girlfriends "Baby" Klumberg and Waldtraut Herrnberger were higher on the DP social spectrum, although their situation was a lot more precarious than Mischka's because of their Baltic-German origin, which technically speaking should have made them ineligible for DP status. Waldtraut, in particular, had had moments of sheer panic and despair in the German years, struggling with a difficult relationship with an older German lover and worry about her mother, lost in the Soviet Gulag. Nevertheless, she managed to marry a Canadian, while Baby married an American GI from Chicago. Both went with their husbands to their husbands' native countries and started their families there.

Marriage to an American GI was as good as it got for a DP woman (at least until she started life with the GI's wary family in suburban Chicago). On the basis of Soviet figures, a Russian historian estimated that thirty thousand

Soviet women DPs in Europe were in foreign marriages as of 1949, mainly living in the husband's country of citizenship. France, Belgium, the Netherlands, and Italy were among the destinations. The great majority, however, married Eastern Europeans and usually went to live in those countries. At the beginning of 1952, the Soviets counted 7,973 Soviet women in Poland, Czechoslovakia, and Romania alone, with a total of 8,514 children. The largest number of Soviet wives were in Poland, with big concentrations living in Breslavl, Lodz, Złotoryja, and Wroclaw. Typically, these were women who had met a Pole who was a fellow Ostarbeiter, often working in the same factory, during the war and married him after it, generally with a child arriving along the way. There were also many Soviet DP women who had married Yugoslav DPs and gone to live in Yugoslavia. They would run into major problems when Tito broke with the Soviet Union in 1948 and many Soviet citizens were either expelled or sought to leave.

Not all the Soviet DPs who married East Europeans returned with them to their countries. At the predominantly Polish Vainberg DP camp near Stuttgart in 1949, there were twenty Polish men married to Soviet DP women, obviously not planning to repatriate to either country. When it came time for selection for resettlement, the East European marriages were generally an advantage for former Soviet citizens. The outward paths of Olga Ianovich from Kiev, Natalia Kashchenko from the North Caucasus, and Lydia Jankowski from Siberia were undoubtedly made easier by their assuming the nationality and last names of the husbands—respectively Polish, Serbian, and Czech—they met and married as DPs, since Russians were regarded with suspicion in Cold War Australia, their new home.[6]

Tourism and Adventure

At various points in his European odyssey, Mischka went off on trips to see the sights in places he hadn't been before. As a Latvian exchange student in Dresden in the winter of 1944–45, just a few months before the Dresden bombing of which he wrote a vivid account, he went south to Munich, Garmisch-Partenkirchen, and Innsbruck, fell in love with the mountain scenery, and decided that southern Germans were a lot friendlier than the northerners. There was a war on, and the Allies' devastating bombing of Dresden was just a month or so in the future, but Mischka's mood was buoyant, and in a letter to his mother he described his tourist experience as "positive to the highest degree." At the end of 1945, when train travel opened up again for civilians and DPs, he revisited Munich and once again marveled at its beauty. Bicycle rides with girlfriends to neighboring scenic sites were a staple of his later DP years. His friend Andrejs, on the road to resettlement in Australia via Naples a few years later, took time out while waiting for the boat in a DP holding camp for a trip to visit Capri as well as the ruins of Pompeii, a historical site he had always wanted to see. Ivan Popowski, a Russian DP from the Soviet Union, did the same, selling a blanket to pay for the bus ticket. As he explained to his sons, "they would have another opportunity to do this in their lifetimes but that this was his one chance to go."[7]

If Mischka and his friends could sometimes turn displacement into a tourism opportunity, other young DPs managed to make their DP stint into the equivalent of a gap year—a chance to see the world between childhood and the responsibilities of adult life. Young men were most likely to do this, though one remarkable woman's adventure story has come my way. Such stories rarely show up in memoirs of resettled DPs looking back on their wartime experience much later in life, partly because such memoirs usually emphasize victimhood. But a few of the DPs who chose to repatriate to the Soviet Union after their Wanderjähre outside the country told exactly such stories in their reentry interviews, presumably seeking to explain why, despite their fundamental Soviet loyalties, they tarried so long outside the country before returning—or sometimes, the tone of the interviews suggests, simply to boast about their adventures.

Not all were boastful or appeared to take pride in their adventures. A few told their stories poker-faced (or at least were so recorded by their Soviet interviewers), with no attempt to project the persona of an adventurer. This was the case with a Pole (a real one, for once) who had become a Soviet citizen after the region in which he was born (Bialystok, in the northeast of prewar Poland) was transferred from Polish to Soviet sovereignty under the Nazi-Soviet Pact of 1939. Andrei Rutkovsky, a soldier in the Polish National Army before the pact, was sent to the Gulag in 1940 with other dubious Poles from the newly incorporated regions but amnestied soon after, leaving the Soviet Union (legally) with the Anders Army during the war and ending up in Palestine, where he worked for four years as a watch repairer. This might have been the end of his short Soviet life, but in fact he fell ill in Palestine and was moved by IRO from the hospital to a German DP camp along with other former Anders Army soldiers. He did not care for life in the DP camp, but it was there that he met and married a West Ukrainian girl, and the two of them decided to repatriate to the Soviet Union to live with her mother in the Dorogobych region of Ukraine—he now a Soviet subject, by virtue of Bialystok's Soviet incorporation, but still (as the Soviet system allowed) identified as Polish by nationality (ethnicity).

A. I. Kuntaras from Western Belorussia had an even more adventurous story to tell, related in a spirit of righteous indignation against many of the obstructive people and institutions he encountered on his travels, and with an undertone of self-congratulation at his resourcefulness in dealing with them. A member of an unnamed, possibly Baptist, sect, he was a strong religious believer, and when he involuntarily became a Soviet citizen by virtue of the Nazi-Soviet Pact, he was arrested for refusing military conscription for religious reasons. After being amnestied, he spent some time working on a state farm in Samarkand (Central Asia) before falling ill and then being evacuated, apparently involuntarily, as a patient in a hospital attached to the Anders Army, to Iran. From Iran, he was sent to Tanganyika in East Africa.

Living in a Polish DP camp in Africa, Kuntaras made himself unpopular with other DPs by speaking out against the Catholic camp leaders and the pope. He tried to get away from the Poles and back to the Soviet Union by writing to the Soviet consulate in Teheran requesting repatriation, which duly forwarded his case to its counterpart in Cape Town. The Cape Town consulate sent him the necessary forms, but his enemies in the camp administration intercepted them. He then decided that his only way to get to the Soviet Union was through Poland; and so, accepting his involuntary status as a Pole, he signed up with IRO for repatriation to Poland. Once arrived in Poland, he managed to contact the Soviet mission in Rome and apply for repatriation to the Soviet Union, which was accepted and led to his repatriation two months later, in May 1950. But what should have been a success story ended in disaster when, on entry to the Soviet Union, he was arrested—one of the few voluntary repatriates of the early 1950s to suffer this fate—for illegally bringing in religious books and other items pertaining to his faith.

The younger the male DP telling his story, the more likely it was to be related as a series of adventures. Grigory Kudinov, a twenty-four-year-old Russian from Moldavia, crossed the Soviet border by accident in February 1945, having been drinking on the train with Soviet officers and then passed out, coming to only when the train was in Romania. The Soviet Union's international borders had been closed since the 1920s, so that the chance to see the world offered incidentally by displacement was a rare one, not to be missed by an adventurous spirit. "Finding himself in such a position," his interviewer noted laconically, "Kudinov decided to spend some time in other European countries"—which turned out to mean several years touring around Romania, Bulgaria, Yugoslavia, Hungary, Czechoslovakia, France, and Germany, finally landing in a DP camp in Austria more than three and a half years later. Perhaps he had in mind to return ultimately to the Soviet Union, perhaps not. His story was that he had expressed a wish to repatriate to an acquaintance, and as a result was picked up, interrogated, and beaten by American police who thought he was a Soviet spy, imprisoned, and released only on condition that he leave Austria and his DP camp. He did not immediately do that, but he did change camps and cities, finding a new berth in a Jewish DP camp in Salzburg where he became part of a black-market ring, dealing in cigarettes. Then he was imprisoned again for stealing a motorbike. Apparently this was his personal signal that the party was over. On his release, he went straight to the Soviet mission asking for repatriation, which was granted.

A young Ukrainian, Ivan Gladyshev, aka Granin, taken to Germany as a forced laborer during the war, managed as a displaced person in the years 1947–51 to visit Switzerland, Luxemburg, France, Belgium, Holland, Denmark, Sweden, Norway, and North Africa. The last destination was courtesy of the French Foreign Legion, which he had joined; and in that capacity he even had the chance to fight in Vietnam. But ultimately, having somehow retained his DP status throughout his wanderings, he decided that resettlement in Australia, with free passage provided by IRO, was a better bet. Australia, however, was a disappointment (jobs hard to find, and medical care poor)—or perhaps he had simply slaked his wanderlust and decided it was time to go home. He approached the Soviet embassy in Canberra for a free passage home in 1952. Untypically (since the Soviets were generally ready to organize free repatriation for anyone who was willing), the interviewing official's response was wary—"with such a man, it is hard to believe in the sincerity of his intentions"— but they did not turn him down outright. The archival story peters out here, but it seems likely that he did not in fact repatriate, at least not in the early 1950s.

Grigory Salnikov aroused even more skepticism in a Soviet interviewer, who clearly had his doubts about the veracity of the adventure stories Salnikov related with gusto. Salnikov, a Jew born in Vinnitsa in Ukraine who had always presented himself as a Russian, was an Ostarbeiter in East Prussia when Soviet forces occupied the area in February 1945. He then worked for a time for the dreaded counterintelligence agency SMERSH, or so he claimed (despite being unable to remember the name of his unit or anybody in it). SMERSH or something else took him back to the Soviet Union, where he moved around apparently aimlessly in the western border region before illegally crossing the border into Hungary in April 1946 and making his way to Austria, where he registered as a DP in a Jewish DP camp, before moving on to Germany. Vienna, Linz, Nuremberg, and Stuttgart were all stops on his itinerary, but then he decided in October 1947 to go to Paris. As with his other moves, no explanation for this move was offered, but as he claimed to have traveled shortly thereafter to Oran in Algeria and then Casablanca in Morocco, it looks as if he may have gone there to join the French Foreign Legion. His own version, which the interviewer unfortunately failed to push him on, was that he was transporting Jewish refugees from France to North Africa. Whatever he was doing, it landed him briefly in prison early in 1949 in Morocco.

By September 1948, however, he was traveling again, this time on the high seas, since his next stop was Australia. He presumably went there as a DP on the IRO resettlement scheme, but why is unstated—perhaps to add another continent to his list? While much in his account may be chimerical, his account of life in Australia is sufficiently circumstantial to suggest that he was actually there. Not for long, however, since he claimed to have been back in England by April 1949 (how he managed this given the shortage of shipping berths for regular passengers and the fact that he does not appear to have been deported by the Australians is unclear), and, shortly thereafter, to have spent twelve days in prison in Liverpool. Perhaps it was the prison experience that sent him off almost immediately to the Canary Islands and then to the Gold Coast in West Africa, which ended in another prison term, this time six weeks. After that he returned to England, only to find himself back in jail in Liverpool for a month. He gave no reason for any of these prison spells. But the last of them evidently led to a decision to repatriate. He made contact with the Soviet embassy in London, and they had him on the boat to the Soviet Union nine days later.[8]

Women telling their life as an adventure story showed up less often in the repatriation interviews. This was not necessarily for lack of adventure in their DP lives. Dvora Borman-Babaevo, a young Jewish woman born in a Polish shtetl, had certainly had her share, but the emotional thrust that comes through her narrative is not a celebration of adventure so much as a degree of self-satisfaction at the rightness of her choices in a series of difficult situations. Having become a Soviet citizen involuntarily as a result of the Nazi-Soviet Pact in 1939, she was evacuated from the western border region in 1941 and ended up in the distant Urals, where she and her family spent the war years. At the end of the war, the family left the Soviet Union (legally) for Poland, along with other Polish and Polish-Jewish evacuees in 1946. They did not stay in Poland, however, but like many others in this contingent moved on to Austria, where in 1947 Dvora married Magomet Babaev, a Soviet POW from the Muslim ethnic group of Lezgins in Dagestan. The couple then moved on to Italy, where they lived under the care of a Jewish organization. Although her parents and sister were recruited by the Jewish organization for settlement in Palestine, Dvora and Magomet decided to repatriate to the Soviet Union. She was pleased to report to her interviewer that her warnings about life in the Middle East had been proven right and the family in Palestine were now living in tents.

Anastasia Egorova definitely told her story as a series of adventures. This was perhaps how she was used to viewing the world, since by occupation in the Soviet Union she was a tramp (*brodiaga*), who probably used storytelling as her coinage in interactions with local populations. Born in 1912 a village in the Vyazma region of Smolensk province in the family of a railroad worker, she spent her youth in and out of orphanages and on the streets. After joining one of the gangs of homeless children that were a feature of Soviet life in the 1920s, she made her way south to Sebastopol and Yalta, living by begging and petty theft, by her own account, when disaster struck in July 1927: she injured her leg so badly in a car accident that it had to be amputated. The years that followed took her (according to her account) to Vladivostok on the Pacific (where she had a Chinese lover), back to the Caucasus, and then on to Central Asia and Siberia (perhaps the result of a sentence of internal exile rather than of her own choice, although she insisted on agency in her story).

World War II had more or less passed Egorova by, at least judging by her narrative, but towards its end she heard, rather belatedly, that Bessarabia (formerly part of Romania on the Soviet Union's western border), had become part of the Soviet Union by the terms of the 1939 Nazi-Soviet Pact. This presented itself to her as a new travel opportunity: "Hearing of the liberation of Bessarabia by Soviet forces, she decided to acquaint herself with that region and got herself by trains and road transport to Czernowitz, where she remained until May 1945, going from village to village, after which she went to Lvov," the biggest city in Western Ukraine. This was actually not far from her natal village in Vyazma, and she called in there too, but "found her mother's farm ruined, and her sister wouldn't take her in but kicked her out."

It was after this unhappy event that Egorova left the Soviet Union, a supposedly impossible feat for a Soviet citizen without special authorization, and all the more remarkable for someone with only one leg. She did it by hopping on a military train repatriating Polish and Polish-Jewish citizens (like Dvora, above) from the hinterland as it happened to be passing through Smolensk on its way to the West ("Deciding to travel with the Poles, [Egorova] got on the train and traveled toward Poland"). She had absolutely no right to do this, being ethnically Russian and without any Polish connections, and this fact was noted when the train got to the border and her anomalous presence was noted by border guards. But when she told them she was "going to her aunt's," they let her through without further questioning, though warning that she wouldn't be able to get back into the Soviet Union. Once in Poland, "ruined Warsaw did not appeal to her," so she did a bit of a tour of other Polish cities by rail—presumably using her extensive experience of getting on trains without a ticket, successfully fighting her way (one-legged) through the crowds that were thronging all major railway stations in these first postwar months—arriving on July 20, 1945, at the Austrian border. "She was not detained on the journey, since whenever she was questioned she answered that she was a Soviet citizen looking for her relatives." But now it was not an aunt she was allegedly looking for but an émigrée mother who was probably living in Italy, and she was now claiming Bukovina in prewar Romania as her birthplace.

Having successfully crossed the border into Austria (occupied by the Western Allies), she abandoned trains as a mode of travel and started hitchhiking, evidently on military trucks. The American occupation police picked her up and took her to a camp in Linz, where she possibly registered as a DP, but in any case she soon moved on, joining a group of Yugoslavs on their way home to Zagreb. Once there, the Yugoslav police picked her up, but she told them that she had been working since 1942 in Linz and was now going to her find her mother in Italy, at which point they helpfully gave her "a paper giving her the right to leave Yugoslavia." This she did, heading for Rome, where she sought help from the Soviet consul, to whom she identified herself as a Soviet citizen and gave her "exact address" (whatever this might mean for a professional tramp). The consular officials naturally thought she wanted immediate repatriation, but she corrected them: she wasn't finished with her travels yet ("the Italians are a good people and I still want to see Italy"). They apparently accepted this and sent her on her way without impediment.

After this high point of successful self-assertion, Egorova's story took a downward turn. On August 29, 1945, "ragged and barefoot," she got to Naples. Staggering along the streets of the city she was picked up by American police. At that point she had a hysterical fit and was taken to the "Leonardo Bianchi" psychiatric hospital in the city of Naples, where she remained for more than four years. Then representatives of the Soviet repatriation mission came by and told the hospital's four Soviet patients that they would shortly repatriate them. Exactly what Egorova thought of this is unknown, but in any case, she was sufficiently buoyant to tell the repatriating officials a good, if inaccurate, story of how she lost her leg. As her interviewer recorded, from her words:

> to make a better impression, she told the version that in her time she had escaped from German camp, fought the Germans in the ranks of Yugoslav partisans and that during flight from Germans she was shot, as a result of which she lost a leg. She also gave incorrect information about her departure from the Soviet Union, claiming that she had been forcibly taken to Germany in 1942.

She was repatriated via the Black Sea on February 14, 1950. Following standard procedure, the repatriation agency sent her back to her native village, now a kolkhoz chaired by her brother Ivan. The welfare of disabled kolkhoz members was a responsibility of the kolkhoz, not of state agencies. From the standpoint of the Repatriation Agency—if not that of Anastasia Egorova or her brother—it was an ideal repatriation outcome.[9]

Sports

Sports were a central part of the life of young people in the DP camps, encouraged by UNRRA as a way of keeping the DPs healthy and cheerful. UNRRA organized competitions within the camps and also between camps, soccer being the most popular. Arrangements were made for DP schoolchildren to do weekly gymnastics in the gymnasium of the local town and for DPs to have the use of sports fields and tennis courts several days a week. It was normal for the big camps to compete with other DP camps in soccer, basketball, volleyball, boxing, swimming, track, and gymnastics; sometimes there was the chance to play against teams from non-DP clubs and Allied military units. A Polish DP team was playing in an impromptu league with four others in the region, including one British Army team. Baltic DPs held annual "Baltic Olympics" featuring soccer, basketball, and track events; in 1949, 750 competed at the Funk Kaserne in Munich.

Jewish DPs were particularly active in sports, which were seen by Zionists as a way to "raise physical capabilities and . . . prepare our youth for the tasks that await them in the near future in the land of Israel." The Belsen camp had soccer, table tennis, tennis, and boxing teams that competed within the DP circuit. At the Jewish Leipheim camp near Munich, DPs built their own swimming pool. Boxing was a Jewish DP specialty. The finals of the Jewish boxing championships held in the big Zirkus Krone arena Munich—a favorite of the Nazis in earlier times—in January 1947 attracted a crowd of two thousand and began with the singing of a Zionist anthem.

The sources are silent on any manifestations of nationalism in the intra-camp games, which suggests that it was probably strongly discouraged by UNRRA. But there are reported issues of eligibility for competitions that mean that sports were not wholly cordoned off from the political issues of the wider world. The memoirs of a Russian émigré from the Parsch camp in Austria noted intriguingly in passing that "our football team was praised throughout Austria, although we weren't allowed in the official DP competitions," presumably because not all members were formally DPs.[10]

For Mischka Danos, the eligibility problem was whether, being a DP, he could compete in German teams or just DP ones. Sport was at the center of Mischka's DP life and that of his friend Andrejs Bicevskis, vying only with university study as a basic preoccupation. This had also been the case when they were students at the University of Riga during the war—both had been nationally competitive sportsmen, Mischka in track and pole vaulting and Andrejs in basketball—but it is surprising to find how seamlessly they continued the pattern as DPs. After Mischka's arrival in Germany to study at Dresden Technical University in mid-1944 (a move made to avoid call-up to the Waffen-SS in Riga), one of his first actions was to join the local (German) sports club; in the summer of 1945, he competed in a regional athletics competition in Dresden. When he went on to Flensburg in the spring of 1945 (having survived the Dresden bombing and anticipating the imminent end of the war), he again immediately joined the local sports club, competing in the four hundred meters and relay that summer. His involvement in sports as a displaced person thus preceded his formal induction as a DP.

Bichevskis had been on the Latvian national basketball team in Riga, and his escape from Latvia as the Soviet Army approached in the fall of 1944 was arranged through his old basketball coach, who smuggled him into a retreating German unit. Once in Germany, he signed up as a DP, but his subsequent sporting life as he told it was oddly disconnected from the big story of war and displacement. "After staying at other Camps, Andrejs went to Luebeck in North Germany and rejoined his old basketball team," he wrote in the third person of himself. He had the chance of going to France to play basketball professionally (this must have been in 1945–46) but decided instead to go back to university.

One of the first things Mischka did on arriving in Hanover in 1946, true to his usual form, was to join the Hanover sports club (Turnklub zu Hannover). That was the local German club, not a DP one. It was there that he met his German girlfriends, including Helga, a sprinter, whom he later married. Dailonis Stauvers, one of the Riga friends, also joined the Turnklub: his sport was table tennis. Mischka's main events were pole vaulting and the eight hundred meters in track, but he did some high-jumping and broad-jumping as well.

In his first summer in Hanover, Mischka was obsessed with finding a good pole for pole-vaulting. He wanted a bamboo one, but an aluminum pole—acquired with help from a Danish welfare officer in UNRRA—was the best he could do. At the Hanover championships in 1946, pole vaulting was not on the agenda, so he competed in the high jump and in the relay. One of his jumps was filmed for a newsreel, but unfortunately he "completely bungled" it. There was a huge audience for this competition, as it was run in the intermission of a football game. Mischka was obsessively trying to rethink and improve his technique at this point, in Bicevskis's opinion not necessarily to the advantage of his performance. Still, in August 1946, Mischka won the pole vaulting competition at the British zonal championships with a personal best of 3.7 meters.

Mischka competed in the zonal competitions in Cologne in March 1947, having been fortunate in finding a private house to stay in (by ringing doorbells until some friendly stranger agreed) rather than the bunker [sic] planned for his team's night residence. He really wanted to get to Paris for the student world championships—a big step up from DP zonal competitions—scheduled for August 1947, but it didn't come off. This may have been the more galling in that Bicevskis was away in Paris in the summer of 1947 competing with his basketball team. The next year was also disappointing for Mischka. He was really hoping that he would be eligible to compete in the German team (picked from the universities of the Western occupation zones), which was scheduled to play a British team from Oxford in "the first international light-athletics competition since the war that a German team entered" in August 1948; but then pole vaulting was eliminated because Oxford had no pole vaulter to compete. It is not clear whether, had pole vaulting been part of the competition, Mischka would have been "counted as a German and . . . therefore be able to take part," or on what grounds he hoped this would happen (because he had left DP status to "go on the German economy" when he moved to Heidelberg to do his PhD?). But at least toward the end of the summer he was able to take part in a competition in Bremen organized by a Swedish club touring Germany—it was the first athletic meet with foreigners, except the Oxford event in the summer, which had "a more than half-official character," and Mischka found it "extraordinarily interesting": the Swedes had a new type of pole, much better than the ones being used in Germany.[11]

Cultural Nationalism

Individual DP camps (or, in the case of some large camps, individual sectors within camps) soon acquired particular national colorations through the ingathering of DPs of the same nationality, and this was usually quickly followed by the election of camp administrations of strong nationalist bent, whether these DP leaders were Latvians, West Ukrainians, or Russian émigrés. Their mission, as they came to see it, was to preserve the spirit of the nation in exile and inculcate national patriotism among the DPs. This had both political and cultural ramifications. In the case of politics, UNRRA/IRO and the occupation regimes looked with some anxiety at some of the extreme nationalist and anti-communist developments in the DP community, but in the case of cultural nationalism—expressed in the form of high-cultural activities with national overtones, the cultivation of folk arts like weaving and folk singing and dancing, patriotic history classes, the conspicuous embrace of the national church, and the growth of patriotic youth groups (notably Boy Scouts)—they generally saw it in a more positive light, fostering moral uplift and education and at the same time keeping the DPs harmlessly occupied.

The camps with high morale all featured strong nationalist and national-religious training, organized on site; and most of them had something like a Scout troop to back it up. There was a physical-training aspect to Scout activity, but the aspect of inculcation of patriotism was very important, and sometimes accompanied by military training. Latvians had the largest number of Scout troops in the DP camps, followed by a smaller number of Polish, Yugoslav, Russian, and Ukrainian troops. The Latvians generally had separate Scouts and Girl Guides, whereas the Russians combined them. All the Slavic and Baltic national DP groups saw scouting as a means of patriotic indoctrination of youth. Among the Poles, for example, "older DPs used scouting to organize and instruct Polish youth in traditional knowledge. They held campfires twice a week, singing folksongs and reciting Polish literature and poetry."

Russian émigrés were familiar with the Scout movement from the interwar years, but those that came from the Soviet Union were not, as the Soviet Union had banned Scouts as "bourgeois" (substituting a communist equivalent, the Komsomol and Young Pioneers organizations, whose uniforms and rituals resembled those of the Scouts). Russian émigrés had launched a Scouts movement in Europe by Russian émigrés in the early 1920s, though its dominant figure—Chief Scout Colonel Oleg Pantuckoff, who moved in New York in 1922—was not well regarded in Europe. The Boy Scouts International Bureau withdrew recognition from the Russian Scouts in the late 1930s, perhaps partly in the hope of enticing the Soviets into the international movement. After the war, the British remained wary of encouraging Scouts in the DP context. While the Foreign Office was "anxious to prevent demoralisation among displaced persons and would support the spread of Scouting as a means of preventing such demoralisation," it recommended early in 1946 "not to recognise officially any Scout Group or Troops formed among displaced persons." This may explain the relative paucity of Russian Scouts in the occupation zones.

But in the few Russian camps where Scouts troops existed, they were treasured. The Scout movement at Mönchehof was the first step in the camp youngsters' civilization, a back-up to the school. "We [scoutmasters] didn't need to teach anything except our ideas, paths and laws, the hymn, our songs and, as the pivot around which the rest revolved, 'Be prepared for everything big and beautiful, Scout! / Be prepared!'" When they emigrated, the DPs took the Scouts movement with them as a key marker of national identity in their new homes.[12]

Religion was another key marker, central to the nationalist moral project in the camps, especially for nationalities like the Russians with a church that was basically national. The end of the war saw something like a religious revival among DPs:

> Churches sprouted rapidly—in old barns and barracks, in former SS meeting halls, in schoolhouses. Materials for church construction were picked from rubbish heaps and lovingly transformed by DP artisans. Latvians at a camp in Schleswig-Holstein built a chapel from discarded ammunition cases; when forced to shift to a different locale they reconstructed the chapel in a garage . . . Ukrainian Orthodox DPs at Hersfeld, Germany, changed an abandoned barn into a chapel by cleaning, painting, and decorating during one busy week.

Church attendance was high: a 1949 Vatican investigation found that three-fourths of the Ukrainian Catholic DPs regularly attended mass on Sundays. Priests emerged from among the former Ostarbeiter DPs to serve in them.

Theological centers, including a Jewish yeshiva at the Landsberg camp, were set up to train more. The national churches with which many of the churches in the DP camps were affiliated were often closely associated with nationalist movements, sharing leadership of community organizations with them. Catholic clergy and former members of the Christ Democratic party of Lithuania jointly dominated the Lithuanian Exile Community, established in March 1946. Sometimes different churches and denominations became involved in fierce factional activity within the national exile movement, as in a complex case involving the Belorussian Autonomous Orthodox Church, the Belorussian Central Administration in Regensburg, and an Autocephalic Belorussian church that, according to its opponents, had no historical existence.[13]

The religious marker of identity was nowhere stronger than among the Russian DPs. But this was an unusual situation in that many of these Russians were in fact disguised Soviet citizens, coming from a country where Orthodoxy and other religious observance had been marginalized and sometimes persecuted since 1917. Those who came from villages probably retained a basic knowledge of Orthodox rituals, but young people from the towns were likely to have been brought up as atheists, with very little understanding of or experience with Orthodoxy. Thus, one of the nationalist/cultural indoctrination tasks carried out by Russian émigrés in places like the Mönchehof camp must have been to teach, in a quite literal sense, the faith, just as they were having to teach the young DPs an unfamiliar version of the national history. Part of the educational process in Mönchehof was the visit of Archbishop Antony, bearing the miracle-working icon of Vladychitsa, supported by Great Princess Olga Aleksandrovna ("very modestly, even poorly dressed"), with the camp's Scouts troop in attendance. In Regensburg, Katharina von Dostojewski (daughter-in-law of the great writer) worked simultaneously for the establishment of a local Russian Orthodox parish and to defend DPs in the local camp against accusations of collaboration.

In the Soviet Union, the Moscow Patriarchate—now, after decades of conflict, allied to the state by a wartime concordat—was the supreme authority of the Orthodox Church. Outside the Soviet Union, there were several competitors for authority, but the dominant one as far as the DPs were concerned was the Russian Orthodox Church Abroad (ROCA). There were many Orthodox priests among the DPs, probably the largest number from the Western Ukrainian and Belorussian areas that had been under Poland between the wars, which lent a particular flavor to the anti-communist nationalism of

ROCA in the camps. Some of the most influential figures in ROCA in Germany were of this background: for example, Athanasy Martos from West Belorussia, educated at a Russian gymnasium there, ordained into the Belorussian Autonomous Church before the war, who continued to serve under the German occupation and left with the Germans at the end of the war. In January 1946, while a DP, he was received into ROCA as a priest and quickly became Bishop of Hamburg, in which position his activities included organizing false documents for Soviet DPs.

DP priests who came from Soviet Russia had imbibed a larger dose of Soviet culture than the West Ukrainians, although the experience of prison and exile that many of them shared had left them equally anti-communist in politics. Many had served as priests under German occupation, sometimes in recently reopened churches. Some had been chaplains for the Cossack forces whose refusal to repatriate in mid-1945 was dramatized at Lienz. Father Isidor Deresa, for example, was a parish priest in Donbass until the closing of his church in 1930s; spent a year in Soviet prison; returned to service under German occupation; and then in 1943 evacuated with the Cossacks as regimental chaplain. He survived the Lienz massacre to become a DP serving as a priest at the Parsch camp.

The clergy was a social estate in the traditional Russian social structure that had formally been dismantled with the abolition of serfdom in the 1860s but in fact persisted in many ways, including the likelihood that sons of the clergy (which, in its lower ranks, allowed married priests) would enter the family trade. Many of the DP priests were from the old clerical estate, but in the camps, and subsequently in the diaspora, they worked side by side with a smaller group of noble and/or intelligentsia origins, who had entered the priesthood during the war or in emigration, often after receiving a higher secular education. One such was Abbott Athanasios Mogileff, who had graduated in science from Moscow State University before being ordained under the German occupation in his hometown of Odessa, retreated with the Germans, became chaplain to the Russia Corps regiments (fighting with the Germans during the war), and then served as a priest under ROCA in a Bavarian DP camp.

The old Soviet contingent of clergy had, of course, worked under the Moscow Patriarchate in the past, while those from the Western provinces had been ordained by a variety of authorities, including the Belorussian Autonomous Orthodox Church. In postwar Germany and Austria, most of them were received into the Russian Church Abroad and worked as priests in the DP camps with majority or substantial Russian populations such as Fischbek, Schleissheim, and Parsch. From the Allied viewpoint, they were simply displaced persons themselves; and they were in due course resettled along with other DPs to the United States, Australia, Canada, and various other destinations.[14]

The Jewish DPs were in the unique situation of emerging from the Holocaust at a time when a Jewish national state was in the making. While synagogues were built in the camps, Zionism held center stage. Even the following of dietary laws and celebration of religious holidays, generally central to Jewish self-assertion in alien communities, was comparatively low key. The JDC duly brought in prayer books and special foods for festivals as well as organizing kosher butchering and kosher canteens in the DP camps, and "a donation of ten million pounds of kosher beef from the Irish Republic helped through a difficult period in 1947," but the focus was elsewhere—on Zionism as practical action. The Jewish state needed people, and the Jewish DPs needed a new home. The two ways in which people could be produced was through having babies (which Jewish women DPs did with a will) and migration.

In the first postwar years, legal passage to Palestine, still under the mandate, was impeded by the British, although some young DPs were smuggled out illegally to Palestine by the Jewish organization Bricha. Zionism flourished in the Jewish DP camps, helped on by the visit of Ben Gurion in 1945 and a steady stream of emissaries from Jewish organizations in Palestine. This was not so much the old idealistic Zionism of the diaspora as a new one that in a very literal sense involved "inventing nationality" for a new nation as well as, in practical terms, preparing Jewish citizens to live there. The physical conditioning that would prepare young DPs for their future pioneering life was central to the endeavor. It was a matter of wonder and encouragement for observers to witness an "aimless, amorphous body of youngsters transform itself into a highly organized society displaying a clear sense of purpose and direction for the future." It seemed to many in these first years that "the overwhelming majority" of young Jewish DPs had embraced the Zionist path and would naturally proceed to Palestine to live as soon as it became possible.

Military training to fight in Palestine was paramount under Bricha's influence, with the result that "the US military authorities were constantly issuing bans on paramilitary or military training in the Jewish DP camps." The JDC staffers in Europe also had doubts about "the indoctrination of damaged minds in political kibbutzim, where children bonded with leaders . . . not much older than themselves, filled with [Zionist] partisan zeal," and feared a "'totalitarian' imposition of 'disciplined unity.'" This opposition from the established authority structure led many young Jewish DPs—estimates range between a third and half of the fifteen to twenty-four age group—to leave the DP camps and prepare themselves for migration to the Jewish homeland in ad hoc collective settlements known as *kibbutzim* and *hakhsharot* (training farms).[15]

Latvian DPs were deeply involved in the invention of nationality too, but in their case on the basis of a lost nation, not one that was waiting to be built. That nation, founded in 1918 with the break-up of the old Russian Empire, had still been relatively new and in the phase of self-conscious identity creation: the intense cultivation of folk arts that went on in the camps was a continuation of prewar Latvian intelligentsia practices. Churches played a role in Latvia's cultural nationalism: "in foreign parts," according to Teodors Grīnbergs, archbishop of the Latvian Evangelical Lutheran Church, "Latvia is in Latvian churches." His church had at least 120 pastors in the various DP camps, as well as assuming a political role in making representations to the US authorities in support of Latvian DPs excluded from the camps by screenings. But the Latvian Lutherans were not an established national church as the Russian Orthodox Church had been under the Russian Empire. In the 1930s, only 55 percent of Latvians were Lutherans, with Catholics a substantial minority and Orthodox also well-represented.

This distribution reflected the diverse ethnic make-up of the country and the overlapping traces of Russian, German, and Polish historical presence. Mischka Danos, with his Hungarian Jewish father, Latvian mother who had nearly married a Russian, and education in a German gymnasium, may have been more cosmopolitan than most, but he was not a complete anomaly. Riga's Germans, Russians, Poles, and Jews, as well as Riga's Latvians, had developed their own social and cultural institutions in the early twentieth century. One of the tasks of cultural nationalism in the Latvian DP camps was forgetting about those historic differences and producing a homogenous national identity to present to the outside world: Latvian. As one historian puts it, "the minorities of interwar Latvia, politicians, intellectuals and communities faded in the émigré collective memory."[16]

Culture—particularly in the form of folk song, national costume, and folk arts such as weaving—was central to this project, which drew heavily on earlier Latvian nationalist cultural tradition. A Latvian song festival held at the Fischbach camp in Nuremburg in 1948, drawing thousands of attendees and featuring choir members parading streets of town in folk costumes and headdresses, marked the seventy-fifth anniversary of the first song festival in Latvia, which itself had been a milestone in the early nationalist movement. As one Latvian woman DP recalled, "We all sang. We also danced the folk dances. That's where I made myself the Latvian national costume, before the Song Festival."

Making and wearing national costumes and sewing national banners were characteristic activities of DP women in a number of national camps, not just Latvian. Women in the Ukrainian Lysenko camp, for example, had made a present for British princess Elizabeth on the occasion of her marriage in 1947 using "a traditional Ukrainian pattern" designed by one of their number. But in the Latvian case weaving in traditional style was particularly important. "Tradition" in this case was not something that had been handed down over the centuries in peasant families and maintained by peasant DPs in the camps but rather something that had been invented, as part of a nation-building project, by educated Latvians in the prewar period. Elga Kivicka and Anna Apinis painstakingly built looms and produced cloth in their camps (Fischbach and Memmingen respectively) on the basis of their activity as young women in the 1930s reviving lost handicraft traditions as part of a self-conscious creation of national identity. They used their looms to produce national costumes for the camps' theater groups and choirs, as well as to sell locally and send for exhibition by UNRRA, which regarded such demonstrations of DP artistic skills as good propaganda for DP resettlement, as well as a plus for the resettlement prospects of individual weavers.[17]

"Let's show everyone that we are cultured people, that we deserve our own nation," a Latvian DP newspaper exhorted in 1945. In this implicit competition between DP groups, it was the Latvians who won, with a truly spectacular volume of high-cultural achievements. In addition to establishing a Latvian ballet company in Lübeck, a Latvian opera in Oldenburg, and the Baltic University in Pinneberg in the British zone, they founded a Latvian People's University at the Bettenhausen camp near Kassel in the American zone, whose curriculum paid "special attention to religious-philosophical questions that enable us to understand eternal problems and carry us nearer to God." The Latvian diaspora in Germany, Sweden, and Denmark, numbering about 100,000 people, managed to publish 1,179 books between 1945 and 1950. It is said that more books were published in the camps—with the help of UNRRA subsidies and honoraria—than in the two decades of independent Latvia. Latvian DPs were energetically called on to contribute to this literary outpouring, with even Olga Danos, who had no previous background in writing, being encouraged to publish a few poems and fairytale translations. She appeared occasionally as a singer at DP concerts as well, standing in for a more frequent performer, her sister Mary, who was transforming her earlier profession as an opera singer into a more folksy presentation in national costume.

The cultural nationalism of the DP camps had a strong performative aspect that UNRRA, IRO, and the occupation governments all encouraged, regularly showing DP folk arts to visiting dignitaries such as Eleanor Roosevelt and General Eisenhower. This was meant to solidify Western perceptions of the DPs not as undisciplined savages from the East but rather as cultured, civilized people, Christians and anti-communists proud of their heritage, who would be welcome at Western tables. The DPs themselves embraced this idea, with each national group striving to present itself in the best and most cultured light. The Baltic groups, in particular, were indignant at what they saw as their "spoiled" national identities, as the result of war, loss of independence, displacement, and suspicion of Nazi collaboration and wanted to redress the balance. Latvian camp leaders felt it necessary to take on the role of "moral guardians" to prevent "unworthy Latvians" from tarnishing the group image by dissolute behavior, and a Latvian DP journal urged its readers "not to forget that our entire nation is being judged in terms of how we are seen to behave. We are responsible not only for ourselves, but for all our people." In Lithuanian camps, similarly, camp elites kept a watchful eye out for manifestations of "DP idleness, illegal profiteering, drunkenness, gambling, loose sexual behaviour, hooliganism, crimes against private property, evasion of work, violence, lack of solidarity and denunciation of other nationals" that might hurt their image with UNRRA. "Before showing up to strangers, we must ask ourselves . . . whether our performance will unveil the Lithuanian spirit." It was the same in the Jewish camps, where "camp committees continually admonished camp residents about their obligations as representatives of the Jewish people," whose reputation might be sullied by reports of black-marketeering and sexual promiscuity.[18]

PART III

Solving the Problem

6

IRO and Its Mandate

IRO HAD a long gestation in a context of increasing hostility between Soviets and Western allies. By the time of its operational arrival on the scene in mid-1947, the patterns of the Cold War were already becoming fixed, a distinct contrast to the hopes of a continuation of the wartime alliance in which UNRRA's postwar operations with displaced persons began. The bill to support it financially reached the US Senate at the beginning of March 1947, just as the US administration was gearing up to take over from the British in propping up Turkey and Greece to "contain" Soviet communism—a Cold War watershed. IRO, like UNRRA, was seen as a temporary body, but with a different basic mission as far as the DPs were concerned: where UNRRA's task had been to repatriate, IRO's was to resettle. The Soviet Union, objecting to the whole policy of resettlement, did not join the new organization, and its representatives and those of East European nations often denounced IRO's activities at the United Nations. The fate of DPs was now to be determined in a new, bipolar Cold War world.

UNRRA's relationship to the UN had been anomalous enough, given that it had been set up as a "United Nations" institution before the United Nations Organization came into existence. But IRO was, formally speaking, at a slightly further remove: although categorized as a "nonpermanent specialized agency of the UN," it was nevertheless to operate "outside UN supervision, with its own budget and membership." In Michael Marrus's words, "the United Nations kept the new organization at arm's length, reflecting the sharp divisions provoked by its establishment." The United States was in effect its sponsor as well as its major funder. As far as American preponderance of funding was concerned, IRO was in the same situation as UNRRA had been, although with a much smaller budget, reflecting its diminished scope (IRO's mandate was specifically to deal with the displaced persons, whereas most of UNRRA's budget went to field missions in war-devastated regions). According to the Truman administration's pitch to the US Congress, IRO was going to cost only one ninth of what UNRRA was costing.[1]

Another key point for Congress was that this time the Americans would be in charge. "We must avoid getting into another UNRRA," argued Undersecretary of State for Economic Affairs Will Clayton. "The US must run this show."[*] The new reality—soon to be graphically demonstrated by the Marshall Plan—was that the United States wasn't going to leave Europe to its own devices, as it had done after World War I. IRO's top leadership was American, as was its organizational style. At the same time, it would be an oversimplification to put the institution too straightforwardly into the "Cold War" box, even though some disgruntled former UNRRA staffers were inclined to do so; the "New Deal" element that had been notable in American's UNRRA staffing was present, if constrained by Cold War pressures, in IRO as well. Even the resettlement policy, so strongly resented by the Soviet Union as "theft" of its citizens, initially had underlying rationales that cannot be reduced to Cold War ones (though those were certainly present). US policymakers were concerned that the DPs—mainly congregated in Germany—would impose an impossible economic burden on the German regime that must, in time, succeed the occupation regimes. In addition, the administration's pitch to Congress noted that a major advantage of a resettlement policy involving a wide range of international destinations for the DPs was that it would reduce pressure on the United States to take them all.

There was a shift in the definition of the mandate as UNRRA gave way to IRO. UNRRA had had the charge of caring for persons displaced from their usual residence by the war or the wartime actions of the Germans, pending their repatriation. The possibility of individual resistance to repatriation had not been considered in UNRRA's foundation documents, whereas in IRO's constitution—as a result of the clashes in the human rights commission between Vyshinsky and Eleanor Roosevelt—it was explicitly acknowledged:

> A displaced person should normally return to his country when the reasons for his displacement were those mentioned above, since it may be presumed that such reasons have ceased to exist. If, however, a displaced persons refuses to be repatriated, he may remain within the mandate of the IRO (and thus be resettled or otherwise assisted, as appropriate) providing his reasons for refusing to be repatriated constitute "valid objections."

Such valid objections were "persecution on grounds of race, religion, national-ity or political opinions," or a reasonable fear of it, and "objections of a political nature judged by the Organization to be 'valid.'"

Equally important was an extension of the definition of eligibility. Only "dis-placed persons" had been eligible for UNRRA care, but IRO's mandate ex-tended also to "refugees"—"victims of a political regime" or "broadly speaking dissidents, expatriates and exiles" outside their country. This was foreshadowed in the earliest discussions of the new body, when it was accepted that its criteria would be "very much wider than" and "different . . . from the categories accept-able at present to UNRRA." The difference between the two categories was that "refugees are persons who left or remain outside their country for reasons of race, religion, nationality or political opinion, whereas, displaced persons are those who were forced to leave their country or were deported."[2]

One practical consequence was that Russian émigrés—who had left Rus-sia for political reasons after the Russian Revolution—now became eligible for IRO protection, including resettlement. UNRRA had regarded them as a problematic category, in part because many of them had served under Ger-man command during the war. UK foreign minister Ernest Bevin had even suggested "transferring them to one of the dominions and, if necessary, hold-ing them in a camp there" so as to facilitate negotiations with the Soviet Union, which attached "exaggerated importance" to the group. "When this Soviet grievance is out of the way," he said toward the end of 1946, "we shall be in a stronger position in pressing Russia for a treaty with Austria." He was still thinking in these terms a few months later when he proposed "that the White Russians be transferred to camps in North Africa, in an attempt to please the [Soviets]."

IRO continued to have problems with White Russians and others tainted by collaboration with the Nazis, but these tended to fade over time. Those in the new category of "refugees" were largely in flight from the Soviet Union and other countries now in the communist bloc—the same countries from which the majority of "displaced persons" had come. The new arrivals no doubt intensified the anti-communism and anti-Sovietism that were already firmly rooted among the great majority of DPs (except for the Jews), provid-ing the rationalization for the refusal to repatriate that was their common bond. IRO was substantially more sympathetic to such views than UNRRA had been, aligning itself much more unambiguously with the United States in the developing Cold War than its predecessor had done. Increasingly, the DPs were seen, as well as seeing themselves, less as victims of war and fascism (UNRRA's original definition) than as victims of communism.

When IRO began formal operations in July 1947, it took over all of UNRRA'S remaining staffers, although admittedly that number was only a quarter of what it had been, owing to rapid reduction at the end of UNRRA's life. The UNRRA contingent made up 80 percent of the new organization's two-thousand-odd staffers, with IGCR—the Intergovernmental Committee on Refugees set up before the war, and disbanded along with UNRRA to make way for IRO—providing another 15 percent. Myer Cohen, a veteran of the New Deal Farm Services Administration as well as UNRRA, was one of those who made the transition, having been acting chief of displaced persons operations under UNRRA from mid-1946 and promoted to assistant director-general under IRO. Social worker Kathryn Hulme was another, moving out of Wild-flecken, a large and boisterous Polish camp focused on repatriating its residents, to Aschaffenburg, whose mixed nationality inhabitants had apathetically settled in for the long haul (from her memoirs, it feels as if some of the fun had gone out of it for her). Of the IGCR people who transferred, the most senior was Swiss Gustav Kullman, IGCR's assistant director, who became a major player in the eligibility determinations that became a major preoccupation in IRO's last years.

Just as UNRRA had had two American directors (Lehmann and La Guardia), so did IRO: first William Hallam Tuck (August 1947–July 1949) and then Donald Kingsley (1949–52). This was said to be a disappointment to some non-Americans in senior positions in UNRRA who had hoped for the top job in the new body. Compared with Lehmann and La Guardia, Tuck and Kingsley were lesser figures in terms of stature back in the United States. Tuck was a Quaker philanthropist and friend of Herbert Hoover, with a background of international relief work in Hoover's American Relief Administration after the First World War. He came to IRO after working in Hoover's Food Mission in 1946–47 and would go on to work on a commission headed by Hoover (on the organization of the executive branch of government) in the 1950s. Kingsley, aged forty-one when he took the IRO job, had a New Deal background like Cohen's, having moved from an academic position at Antioch College in 1942 for work in Washington; after his stint with IRO, he would go on to lead the UN reconstruction agency in Korea. The highest-ranking non-American—deputy to Director-General Tuck—was British civil servant Sir Arthur Rucker (private secretary to Prime Minister Neville Chamberlain 1939–40). Another highly placed Briton, General Evelyn Fanshawe, headed IRO's mission in the

British zone of Germany, after having served in an equivalent position in UNRRA's last year.[3]

Prehistory of Resettlement

IRO's resettlement program was a bold initiative that historian Daniel Cohen has described as "an unprecedented instance of planned population redistribution." But it was not the first example of population engineering in the twentieth century: Stalin had relocated millions of kulaks and some minority nationalities in the Soviet Union in the 1930s and 1940s, and there had been a series of projects, accomplished or mooted, to move Jews to a particular territory—the Crimea and Birobidzhan in the Soviet Union, the Kimberleys in Australia—before the big Jewish relocation project that actually came off, the creation of the state of Israel in Palestine in 1948. In the United States during the war, a little-publicized "M Project" (Migration Project) had canvassed the possibilities of resettling unassimilated minorities at odds with the states in which they lived, with specific reference to mass resettlement in Latin America. After the war, millions of people were involved in ethnic resettlement projects designed to make national populations more homogeneous via population exchanges such as those between the Soviet Union and Poland involving Poles and Ukrainians.

These state-organized ethnic resettlement projects were the subject of major postwar studies on population movements by two demographers who had worked on M Project, Eugene Kulischer and Joseph Schechtman. But IRO's resettlement program for displaced persons was not mentioned in these studies; and, for all its ambitious scope, that program seems to have been devised with little or no theoretical underpinning or awareness of its place in a broader context of planned movements of population on an international scale. IRO's approach was wholly pragmatic: the mass of displaced persons in Germany and Austria presented a diplomatic-political problem that needed to be solved by moving them elsewhere. Where they would be moved depended on where they were willing to go, and which countries would take them.

Mass resettlement of the DPs was IRO's policy innovation. But smaller, focused resettlement efforts had been made even in the UNRRA period, when the main focus was on repatriation. For Jewish DPs, resettlement in Israel had been on the table, resisted by the British but favored by the Americans and Soviets and pushed by Zionist representatives of the Jewish Agency for Palestine working with the Jewish DPs in Europe. For other non-repatriable groups like stateless Russians, UNRRA's agreements with the occupation regimes identified the IGCR as an agency that might undertake small-scale resettlement in anomalous cases, while UNRRA got on with repatriation for the DP majority.[4]

IGCR had been formed on American initiative at Evian in 1938 as an international organization whose primary task was to deal with the Jewish refugee problem. But British opposition to Jewish resettlement in Palestine led IGCR to stonewall and, in effect, withdraw from resettlement activities on behalf of the Jews. An unkind assessment was that IGCR "demonstrated a consummate inability to accomplish much of anything." The appointment of Sir Herbert Emerson, formerly high commissioner for refugees under the League of Nations, as its director put it primarily in the British sphere of influence. Its budget, to which United Kingdom and United States were the main contributors, was small.

After UNRRA came into existence in 1943, the agreement was that it should provide temporary care for "stateless and non-repatriable" refugees at the time of liberation, that is, when they came out of camps, and "for a reasonable time" afterwards (defined in April 1945 as six months), until such time as IGCR could take over. In the event, of course, with regard to the Jewish refugees who were initially IGCR's main concern, UNRRA ended up taking open-ended responsibility, while IGCR confined itself mainly to marginal groups like Russian émigrés who, by virtue of having been displaced before the outbreak of the Second World War, were not eligible for UNRRA care.

When the British and Americans proposed in the summer of 1946 to increase IGCR's budget and expand its resettlement work with DPs, the Soviet Union resigned as an IGCR member, saying this was outside the organization's mandate. Negotiations with Brazil, Argentina, and other Latin American countries occupied IGCR for the rest of the year but produced no significant results. UNRRA came to regard IGCR as an annoying impediment to repatriation programs because of its connections with anti-communist nationalist groups and the fact that, however ineptly, it kept the resettlement possibility open. IGCR was proposed by some as a possible replacement for UNRRA in the lead-up to the establishment of IRO, but the British considered it too pro-Jewish and the Soviets, no doubt, too anti-communist and linked with the émigrés.

Small-scale as IGCR's resettlement efforts were, they nevertheless kept alive the sense that resettlement was a possibility. A more important contributor to that sense was the Truman Directive of December 1945 that allowed twenty thousand DPs to enter the United States outside normal immigration quotas. Raphael Cilento was probably right in saying that the United States' humanitarian gesture in 1946 spelled doom for UNRRA's repatriation program. From the time of its announcement early in 1946, any DP could hope that the golden gates of the United States would open for them—and in fact, after hastily closing again and remaining shut for more than two years without any promise to reopen, they finally did.[5]

Meanwhile, another form of resettlement was proceeding more or less covertly, but publicized on the DP grapevine, namely settlement of Jews in Palestine. Of all the DPs, the Jews were the most adamant against repatriation to their former homes, and nobody contemplated it as a possibility. Many Jews in Palestine fighting and planning for a Jewish state saw the DPs as a heaven-sent immigration source, but the British, still not reconciled to a Jewish state and holders of the mandate over Palestine, were not willing to admit substantial numbers. A smuggling network set up to smuggle Jews out of Europe gathered DPs from the camps in Germany, as well as newly arrived Jewish "infiltrees" from Eastern Europe for whom Salzburg was a major transit point, and transported them to Italy for departure by ship for Palestine. The British made energetic attempts to prevent this traffic, but on the ground the Americans, and apparently many UNRRA officials too, helped or at least turned a blind eye. When the smugglers dispatched five thousand Jewish DPs—the largest contingent yet—in the *President Warfield* (renamed *Exodus 1947* for the occasion), the British declined to accept the boat or its passengers and turned it back, leading to an odyssey of several months as many of the passengers repeatedly refused to disembark at any port but Haifa, its original destination. This was an international scandal, and by the time it ended the British were almost ready to bow to the inevitable. The foundation of the state of Israel in May 1948, opening the way to mass resettlement of Jewish DPs there, was close at hand.

The US-based JDC, the largest Jewish organization dealing with DPs, contributed a substantial amount behind the scenes to the movement of Jews from Europe to Palestine, despite its traditional attitude of neutrality on the question of Zionism. Its smaller competitor the Hebrew Immigrant Aid Society (HIAS) dealt with migration to Latin America and other resettlement countries, but not Palestine. While the JDC had generally good relations with the governments and international organizations involved in resettlement, HIAS sometimes incurred censure, notably from the Australians, who were annoyed by its success in evading what was meant to be a restrictive national policy on Jewish immigration.[6]

By mid-1947, when IRO took over from UNRRA, it was evident that no further significant repatriation was likely and that the capacity and desire of Western European countries to absorb the displaced persons (via schemes like Britain's *Westward Ho!* and the Belgian mines) was not enough to meet the need. The DPs could not be left in Germany, since the Germans had their own ten million German expellees from Eastern Europe to absorb, and the Allies, increasingly seeing West Germany as a future bulwark against the Soviets, wanted the country in good economic shape. (The miracles wrought by the currency reform of June 1948 and Wirkschaftswunder of the 1950s were still in the future; only a congenital optimist would have expected things to have worked out as well as they did.)

So where were the DPs to go? Overseas was the answer, and the United States the destination desired by most DPs. But the United States was chary of accepting this burden: the Truman Directive of December 1945 had been a one-time initiative, and it was not until months after IRO started functioning that the US Congress passed the DP Act and opened the way for large-scale immigration there. Meanwhile, IRO had been canvassing the possibilities of resettlement in countries with space and a demand for labor—Canada, Australia, and the big Latin American countries being the obvious targets. The pitch was not humanitarian but economic: you need workers, we can supply them. Australia, which first signed up with IRO in July 1957 and would end up taking more DPs than any country except the United States, made no bones about the fact that it wanted manual workers, to whom for the first two years it would assign unskilled jobs where they were most needed in the economy, making them in effect indentured laborers to the Australian state. Canada also wanted manual workers, though it proposed to assign them to the private sector rather than have the government find them jobs. In IRO's negotiations with various nations on resettlement, DPs were treated primarily as a workforce, that is, as economic commodities. IRO rarely if ever suggested that a country should accept them for resettlement on humanitarian grounds.

IRO's Overseas Resettlement Policy and the Cold War

While it was generally assumed that IRO was breaking the repatriation impasse by shifting to a policy of resettlement, this was not spelled out too crudely, in deference to Soviet sensibilities. To be sure, the Soviet Union did not join IRO. But it was involved in all the preliminary negotiations at the United Nations, of whose Security Council it was a member; and the UN remained a significant feature of the political landscape, even though IRO was not strictly a UN institution. Formally speaking, moreover, IRO had not disavowed repatriation: its founding charter stated that the "re-establishment of refugees" should be contemplated only in certain circumstances, and that repatriation remained the agency's priority—even though everyone knew this was not the case. Preserving the facade of cooperation, IRO's preparatory commission assured the Ukrainian branch of the Soviet repatriation agency in June 1947 that it remained "interested in repatriation of displaced persons" and was "therefore willing to assist Ukrainian [repatriation] officials in negotiations with military authorities for entry" to DP camps—an apparently favorable answer that at the same time passed the buck to the military governments.

But Cold War antagonisms and suspicions were hardening. In the United States, this was linked with a rising "Red scare" regarding the activities of domestic communists, a phenomenon that would lead Senator McCarthy to finger senior diplomats and State Department officials as tainted and force President Truman to agree to loyalty tests to combat the danger. From the Soviet standpoint, resentment over the abandonment of repatriation of its citizens and anger at the new plans to resettle DPs overseas were a part of the hardening of Cold War attitudes, though not a central one. For the United States and Britain, the consolidation of Eastern Europe as a Soviet sphere of interest, the development of Soviet atomic capacity, and fear of Soviet expansion were major factors, with the fate of DPs essentially incidental. Behind the scenes, US policymakers generally agreed that, in the short term, the Soviet Union was not in a position to start a major war even if it wanted to (which most thought it probably did not) because its army and economy had to be brought back up to strength after the devastation of the world war. This meant that the West had a window of opportunity to assert its primacy in the postwar world, since the Soviets were not yet strong enough to oppose it effectively, and, particularly in the United States, this approach was a winner in terms of domestic politics.[7]

After the end of the First World War, the United States had quickly withdrawn from Europe, and some expected that pattern to be repeated after the conflict that ended in 1945. The crucial US decision after the Second World War to stay involved in Europe was announced to the world in June 1947—the same month that IRO started operations, as it happened—when Secretary of State George C. Marshall spoke of the need for a European recovery plan in an address at Harvard University. The Soviet analysis was that the United States was headed for another big economic depression, which would both render such a plan unfeasible and push Europe deeper into crisis. But it soon became clear that these Soviet predictions were wrong: no great depression was imminent in the West; the Marshall Plan for European economic recovery would go ahead; and Britain, a major beneficiary of US largesse under the plan, would remain a close US ally rather than (as the Soviets had earlier hoped) become estranged from the United States as a result of capitalist competition.

It was also clear that both Europe and Germany were going to be divided into more or less antagonistic Western and Eastern zones for the foreseeable future. At Potsdam, the Allies had signed off on a vague agreement that Germany should be treated "as a whole," which allowed the West to see its future in the capitalist camp and the Soviets to see it as socialist. In practice, however, Germany had been divided since the war into four occupation zones, which meant in reality three plus one, with the Soviet zone as the odd one out. With military withdrawal not too far off, the Western Allies started to move to build a new German state on the basis of their three zones. "Bizonia" was the first step, achieved through the economic merging of American and British occupation zones starting on May 29, 1947; a currency reform for all the Western zones, including those in Berlin, was introduced in June 1948; and the recalcitrant French were finally drawn into an economic "Trizonia" not long before the formal establishment of the Federal Republic of Germany (West Germany) on May 23, 1949. For the Soviets, these developments constituted an almost existential threat—"a resurrected lethal enemy [Germany], backed by the world's strongest economy [the US]" to rebuild its prewar industrial might. "The Western powers are transforming Germany into their stronghold and including it in the newly formed military-political bloc, directed against the Soviet Union and the new democracies," a Soviet foreign policy analyst concluded.

The Soviet Union had long since decided that the United States was bent on deepening the growing divide between the two countries. In a long telegram to Moscow dated September 27, 1946, and written under Molotov's supervision, the Soviet ambassador to Washington characterized postwar US policy as "striving for world supremacy" (Molotov underlined this in his copy), taking advantage of Europe's and the world's "colossal need for consumer goods, industrial and transportation equipment," which America could supply. The US government's policy aimed "at limiting or dislodging" Soviet influence in Eastern Europe, seeking to overthrow pro-Soviet governments and open the region's countries to American investment. Not only was there talk about a "third war," there were direct calls for such a war and threats to use the atomic bomb. "Preaching war against the Soviet Union" was no longer a prerogative of the "far-right yellow press" but of respectable organs such as the *New York Times*.

The Marshall Plan, also known as the "European Recovery Program," exemplified both the US intention to remain active in Europe and the exclusion in practice of the Soviet Union and associated countries from the sphere of American largesse. Ultimately delivering $13 billion (well over $100 billion in current values) to eighteen European states, with the lion's share going to Britain, France, and West Germany, the plan was approved by the US Congress in March 1948. Dean Acheson, then US undersecretary of state under Marshall, described the plan as "an outgrowth of UNRRA," meaning a continuation of international (US) efforts to help European postwar reconstruction—but from the Soviet standpoint, it was a completely different animal, implicitly hostile to the Soviet Union. The Marshall Plan firmly pulled a future West Germany (whose outlines were already visible behind the framework of "Bizonia") into its orbit. There was at first no formal exclusion of the Soviet Union or Eastern Europe from the plan's beneficiaries. But the US assumption was that the Soviets would probably decline to participate, for fear of the power over them that US money would give, and this turned out to be correct. East European countries like Czechoslovakia and Poland were definitely eligible, and it would have suited US global interests to have them thus partially detached from the Soviet bloc, but the Soviet Union forbade them to sign up.[8]

In parallel with the US move toward a Cold War stance against the Soviet Union was the Soviet move to a similar stance against the United States. The Soviet Union had always had the ideological premise that the developed world was divided into two camps, the capitalist and socialist, whose interests were, in the long-term, necessarily opposed. But that did not prevent short-term cooperation, as the wartime alliance with the United States and Britain had demonstrated; nor did it necessarily imply that divergent interests would lead to war. In the years after the Second World War, Stalin, however angry he might be with his wartime allies, was not planning a military conflict, if only because he did not think that the Soviet Union currently had the strength to win. That meant that a Cold War, as opposed to a hot one, suited his bill: "He would push, demand, and bully, short of provoking warlike reactions on the part of his former allies."

A belligerent revival of "two camps" rhetoric, launched not by the Soviet Union itself but the Soviet-dominated Communist International (Comintern), was part of this approach. This is often interpreted as the Soviet dog barking without intending to bite. But, while the Soviet Union knew it had no current plans to launch a new hot war, it could not have the same assurance about the United States; and the Soviet leaders' suspicions about Western subversion were rising to a new height. Here the displaced persons issue, generally far from central in Cold War thinking, did play a role, since the specific causes of alarm cited by a Russian historian, on the basis of classified Soviet documents, were "covert operations by the newly established Central Intelligence Agency, the use of émigré groups to prepare anti-Soviet revolts in eastern Europe should war erupt, growing contacts between anti-Soviet immigrants and US government officials, and American usage of the former Nazi intelligence network specializing in Soviet affairs."

Among the visible manifestations of rising Soviet suspicion and xenophobia were the prohibition on Soviet citizens marrying foreigners in February 1947, and the "anti-cosmopolitan campaign," aimed first at Soviet contacts with foreigners and later primarily at Jews, that started around in the autumn of 1946 and developed into an unprecedented antisemitic campaign from 1949 until Stalin's death in 1953. This can be seen as a counterpart to McCarthyism in America, and in the Soviet case it reached even higher in terms of the political leaders who were directly threatened. If, in the United States, Secretary of State Dean Acheson was in trouble because of his friendship with Alger Hiss, in the Soviet Union it was Molotov and his foreign trade counterpart, Anastas Mikoian, both Politburo members (with Molotov the longtime no. 2 to Stalin) who were threatened. Not that Molotov was a closet dove, any more than Acheson was a secret Soviet-lover, but he had the dangerous characteristics of an outspoken Jewish wife who had had contact with Zionists and extensive (job-dictated) contacts with the West. Within a few years, Molotov and Mikoian would both lose their jobs, and probably come within hailing distance of losing their lives, with contacts with the Americans and the British among the counts against them.[9]

Continuing Conflict over Repatriation and Resettlement

Even as IRO's resettlement program got under way, the Soviet Union continued to push for cooperation in the repatriation of its citizens. The USSR never made any concessions or offers of compromise, for example by quietly dropping efforts to get back the "new" citizens of 1939–40 vintage and focusing on the "old" citizens, where their claims might have been more easily acceptable. They persevered doggedly and fiercely; as several historians have remarked, it

was a comparatively small issue in the broader canvas of international relations, but one that the Soviets were passionate about and not willing to drop.
As the American presence in Europe showed no signs of disappearing, the
European economy improved, and the Allied commitment to a functional,
Western-oriented West Germany strengthened, hopes that the Allies would
finally get sick of maintaining the DP camps and just walk away must have
dwindled, but the Soviets plugged on regardless—in fact, they would continue
trying to persuaded DPs to repatriate even after they had been resettled in
distant countries like Australia and Venezuela.

In the competition between repatriation and resettlement, however, resettlement was winning hands down. The first year of IRO's existence, mid-
1947 to mid-1948, was a time of treading water: the aim was resettlement, but
to what destinations was still unknown. But even in the first half year of IRO's
operations, when the resettlement policy had been introduced but there were
still few countries offering to participate, more than twice the number of DPs
were resettled as were repatriated. The news simply got worse, from the Soviet
standpoint, after the American and Palestinian logjams were broken in 1948,
with the new state of Israel now able to take Jewish DPs and the "DP Bill"
authorizing large-scale acceptance of DP immigration going through the US
Congress. Soviet figures for the period November 20 to December 31, 1948,
showed a ratio of ten "Soviet" DPs resettled for every one repatriated.[10]

IRO was worse than UNRRA, in the opinion of Soviet repatriation officer
Alexey Brukhanov; it was "an instrument of Anglo-American policy" pure
and simple. Having written off repatriation and (Brukhanov claimed) fired
all the staffers who supported it, the organization "was nothing less than a
supplier of a cheap labor force without rights for capitalist countries." "Slave
market" became the dominant theme in Soviet rhetoric against resettlement,
with IRO filling the function of "slave traders." The national selection committee scrutinized the DPs as if they were a slave market, "looking in their
mouths and fingering their muscles." Out in the colonies, they would be
"sweated like slaves."

Conflicts over the repatriation of Soviet children continued and were exacerbated when the overseas resettlement of children (along with other DPs)
got under way. Not surprisingly, Brukhanov seized on the (true) story that
Ukrainian DP children had died on an IRO boat taking DPs to Australia in
September 1949; he expressed grave fears for the new batch of two hundred
children, many of them sick, who had left Naples for Melbourne in December.
There was international publicity when, in September 1948, fourteen-year-old

Helena Kerlenko, a victim of "infantile paralysis" who had been in hospital in the American zone of Berlin since the end of the war, was removed by Soviet ambulance for repatriation, with the consent of American zonal authorities but against the wishes of IRO.[11]

The Soviets retained their repatriation missions in the Western zones, but the British and Americans were becoming increasingly impatient with them. More obstacles were put in the way of visits by Soviet repatriation officers to DP camps, which required the military authorities and/or IRO to provide escorts. Western authorities questioned the continuing need for repatriation mission at a time when there were scarcely any DPs in the camps registered as Soviet citizens (which, as the Soviets knew, meant little, given the prevalence of false self-identification). Moreover, it irked the Western authorities to have to put up with these Soviet beachheads—which they suspected as being cover for espionage—in their zones, when they had no equivalent offices in the Soviet zone.

The British froze the Soviet Repatriation Mission out first, with General Sholto Douglas ordering all Soviet repatriation officers out of the British zone within a month, that is, by October 1, 1947. Rhea Radin, of IRO's Repatriation Division, pointed out that if, as seemed likely, almost all Soviet repatriation officers were to be removed from the British and US zones, this would make it impossible to carry out IRO's mandate "of providing free access for representatives of countries of origin to all displaced persons of their nationality under our care." At the same time, General Clay requested a reduction in the number of Russian repatriation officers in his zone from thirty-four to four, to be accompanied by the routing of all repatriation arrangements through IRO, to which the Soviet response (from the deputy head of the Soviet military government in Berlin) was that "he has no cognizance of the IRO and will not deal with it."[12]

The Americans then went one step further, and, to Soviet outrage, actually closed the Soviet Repatriation Mission down. General Lucius Clay had warned his Soviet counterpart, Marshal Sokolovsky, that as of March 1, 1948, the mission would no longer be accredited, as "sufficient time has passed since the capitulation of Germany for the completion of voluntary repatriation," and he ignored Sokolovsky's angry response that ("as you know") there were still one hundred thousand Soviet citizens "awaiting repatriation" in the DP camps. When the due date came, eight Soviet repatriation officers (plus one Soviet soldier) hunkered down in the mission refusing to leave, at which point US military police cut off their electricity, water, gas, and telephone. Someone had evidently alerted the press, since there were newspaper reports that armed American police had climbed the fence into the garden and surrounded the building, giving staffers of the Soviet mission a dramatic ultimatum: "Immediately leave Frankfurt on Main or die of hunger." Even the Western Reuters news agency described this as "gangster-like" behavior, according to Sokolovsky's reports to Moscow. When the mission staffers still refused to budge, armed American police cordoned off the area with barbed wire. Along the way a "strong wind" removed the five-pointed Soviet star adorning the mission. Sometime during the day, the Soviets gave in, and at 6:20 a.m. on March 4, they left Frankfurt, headed for the Soviet zone. It is not clear whether, as earlier threatened, the Soviet car was escorted to the border by American troops.

This was a great blow for Soviet pride, a "shameful operation," in Marshal Sokolovsky's words, whose aim was to force resettlement on Soviet DPs, dooming them to "powerlessness, humiliation, and ruin." Evidently, despite the low rate of voluntary resettlement in past months, the Soviets were still hopeful that IRO's demise, already under discussion, would leave the DPs with no option but to repatriate—in other words, that "a mass return to the native land of the majority of the Soviet citizens who are still in DP camps in the American Zone" was on the cards in the near future, had the Repatriation Mission only been there to organize it. In fact, the closing down of the Repatriation Mission did not make it impossible for Soviet DPs to repatriate, but it certainly made it more difficult, as they had to make their own way to a Soviet embassy (London, Paris, or Rome, for example) or cross the border illegally into the Soviet zone of Germany.[13]

Tolstoy Foundation

Meanwhile, Soviet DPs who did not wish to repatriate had gained a new active champion with increasingly good ties with the US administration—the Tolstoy Foundation. The Tolstoy Foundation's activity was partly practical, facilitating selection for US immigration and lobbying for the Russians (both "Vlasovites" and Russian émigrés) in a US domestic context. But it also played a role in developing the Western "liberation" rhetoric about the DPs and reframing the Vlasovites from collaborators to democrats.

The Tolstoy Foundation, based in New York State, was the creation of writer Leo Tolstoy's youngest daughter, Alexandra Tolstoy, who had settled in the United States in 1931, established the Tolstoy Foundation in 1939 with her friend Tatiana Schaufuss, and made a number of influential friends for the

Russian émigré cause, including Eleanor Roosevelt and Allen Dulles. Even before the war's end, Alexandra Tolstoy was already in touch with IGCR and the American Council of Voluntary Agencies for Foreign Service about the plight of Russians in Europe, with IGCR's Deputy High Commissioner Gustav Kullmann addressing her respectfully as "Dear Countess." But her efforts to get a foothold in Europe were stymied for some time by worry about the political delicacy of work with Russian émigrés (who were, for the most part, not covered by UNRRA's mandate). IGCR tried to facilitate the foundation's plan for Tatiana Schaufuss to come over to Germany to work with the Russian refugees in 1946, but at first the problems encountered both with UNRRA and the military authorities seemed endless. Did the foundation have clearance from the US State Department? Was it planning to work just with the émigrés or with Soviet Russian displaced persons as well? If the latter, what would UNRRA's Soviet representative Menshikov think of that?[14]

Despite several rewritings of her proposal to clarify with whom she sought to work, Mrs. Schaufuss's plans to get to Germany in August 1945 seem to have fallen through. It was not until 1947 that she arrived, as a representative of the Tolstoy Foundation attached to the Church World Service (the overseas service program of the National Council of Churches of the USA); and it was probably not until after the passage of the US Displaced Persons Act in mid-1948 that the foundation became a real player in Europe, having been designated as one of the select group of voluntary organizations charged by the US Displaced Persons Commission (set up as to implement the DP Act that had just been passed by Congress) with securing sponsors and assurances for DP migrants. When it did finally arrive in Europe, the foundation established its base on the continent at Munich-Pasing.

As prospective US immigrants, many of the Tolstoy Foundation's Russian DP clients had a problem: they had fought under German command during the Second world War. Some of them were émigrés who had fought with the Russian Corps; others were former Soviet citizens who had joined the Vlasov Army, generally after falling prisoner of war to the Germans. Both groups claimed that their objective had been to fight Bolshevism, not to fight with the Nazis, but of course it complicated their postwar situation. The Tolstoy Foundation—which, under the IRO resettlement regime, could act on behalf of both émigrés and former Soviet citizens under their general mandate to look after "Russians"—took a clear and unapologetic line on this that would have made little headway in UNRRA days but was now well fitted for the new climate of Cold War. Russians who had had to fight under German command to fulfill their wish to fight against the Soviet Union should be seen not as pro-Nazi but rather as anti-communists—indeed, democrats. "These DPs have been suffering four and a half years" but "haven't lost their faith either in God or in the justice of human beings," Alexandra Tolstoy wrote in 1950. "They are suffering for the same principles that this country is based upon-freedom, human rights; of which they were deprived in Soviet Russia."

Tatiana Schaufuss was equally forthright in dealing with the related problem that many Russian DPs had made false statements of identity to Western authorities: as she explained to Ugo Carusi, head of the Displaced Persons Commission in Washington in 1950, they were desperate to escape forcible repatriation. "Can they be blamed and branded as forgers of documents, as fraudulent criminals for having tried to pass as Balts, by adding an 's' to their names (Davidow-Davidows etc), by assuming new names and having themselves declared dead by friends and relatives in Russia, by filling out UNRRA and IRO forms so made out, that their place of birth would protect them from repatriation squads?"[15]

"Liberalizing" Eligibility Criteria:
The Case of the Baltic Waffen-SS

The Tolstoy Foundation's understanding of Russian and Soviet DP collaborators as predominantly anticommunist rather than pro-fascist fitted the political culture of the late 1940s, which was rapidly evolving in a Cold War direction. It meant that former Vlasovites or Russian Corps members were no longer ineligible for resettlement. Russian immigrants were not a security risk, Alexandra Tolstoy told a US Senate subcommittee in 1951, but "a positive security asset," since they knew the evils of communism at first hand. This increasingly made sense to the British and Americans and, perhaps with a certain time-lag, to IRO.

Now that mass resettlement had been adopted as the general policy for dealing with DPs, it was obviously administratively rational to resettle them all, rather than mandating exclusions that would only make more work in the short term and, in the longer term, create a group that could neither be resettled nor repatriated, for which no one would be responsible after IRO went out of business in a few years. So far, such people, if identified, had been held in special non-DP camps in the British and American zones of Germany and Austria, or else were living among the Germans without IRO support and keeping their heads down. If they were to be resettled by IRO, they would first need to be moved to DP status. But IRO was hampered by a constitution that appeared to ban the granting of such status to collaborators, including anyone who had fought under German command. Something would have to change.

IRO's shift in attitude was delicately noted by its official historian. The original guidelines, as laid down in IRO instructions on eligibility in 1947, were that Estonians, Latvians, and Lithuanians who "joined the Wehrmacht before 1944 should be regarded as volunteers and ineligible," as were Russians, Ukrainians, Cossacks, Georgians, Azerbaijanis, and others who had fought under Germany command in auxiliary units like the Russian Corps and Vlasov Army. But with increasing difficulties with the Soviet government in the new context of Cold War, IRO's general council started to find this too restrictive: as IRO's official historian wrote, there was growing appreciation "that many persons might technically have collaborated with the Germans and yet were in refugee status." This implied a situation where recognition was often occurring de facto, despite the formal prohibition. It was no longer the political moment to insist on enforcement of IRO's original principles; the change had to be in the opposite direction, namely a "liberalization of eligibility" for DP status in line with the changing attitudes of IRO's member states. An additional consideration for IRO was the fact that "in the last stages of the Organisation's existence," the "benefit of the doubt" should be given wherever possible in order, essentially, to enable the displaced persons to be removed from Germany—in other words, the camps needed to be emptied before IRO closed down.

The term "liberalization" was initially used by Donald Kingsley, IRO's director-general, summing up the situation as of the cessation of IRO activities early in 1952. At first, he wrote (in a notably awkward and circumlocutory text that perhaps reflects the uneasiness of an old New Dealer protecting Nazi collaborators), there were "limitations . . . in line with the general idea at that time as to who should be considered as a deserving refugee or displaced person," but "during the course of time, a marked evolution has taken place in the attitude of the international community," as witnessed by the broader and "more liberal spirit in the conception of a refugee deserving of international protection" manifest in the founding statute of the successor body, the office of the United Nations High Commissioner for Refugees. Although restricted by its own constitution from support of "war criminals," IRO, "in the last period of its operation, had endeavoured to liberalize the interpretation of its own definitions, in order to fall into line with the wider conception of a refugee."

There were, of course, countervailing voices, which in the long term would have substantial impact, though they were little attended to at this point. The Soviet Union complained loudly and repeatedly, but to little effect. Jewish community pressure in the countries of resettlement, which would later be a significant major factor in raising consciousness about war criminals, was still in the process of formation. In Europe, Simon Wiesenthal, a young Buchenwald survivor working for the US Office of Strategic Services, became aware through participation in the screening of refugees in Austria in 1945 that thousands of Nazi collaborators were applying, and often being approved, for DP status. He founded the Jewish Documentation Center to gather material against such people, creating his own network of young Jewish volunteer investigators from the DP camps. But he soon became disillusioned with the Allies' good faith. What has happened to all those former collaborators? Wiesenthal rhetorically asked Alexander Bedo of IRO's eligibility board. "You, dear Mr Bedo have to know, as well as we do, that with a very few exceptions all these people are now 'United Nations DPs'. Many of them are living now in IRO DP camps, others have stolen enough to live outside of the camps." With IRO's help, many had already emigrated and would "spread their poison" elsewhere. Wiesenthal appealed to Bedo to intervene on behalf of "our killed parents, wives, children *who were murdered by some of the present 'United Nations DPs.'*" But the mood of the time was against him, his DP volunteer helpers departed for resettlement, and for some years his remained almost a lone voice.[16]

The first to benefit from IRO's increased tolerance of collaborators were the Latvian legionnaires. The British were subjected to energetic lobbying by Charles Zarine, independent Latvia's last minister in the Latvian Legation in London who had remained in the United Kingdom after Soviet occupation of his country in 1940, enjoying "a curious diplomatic half-life in which he continued to act as if an independent Latvian state still existed." His attitude from the beginning was that Latvians who had fought in the Latvian Legion/Waffen-SS under German command were "victims of circumstances"; and the British government, initially cautious, soon effectively acquiesced. Alfred Valdmanis, who as minister of justice in the collaborationist General Directorate functioning under the German occupation of Latvia had encouraged young men to register for military service with the Germans, was another active lobbyist. From 1947, large numbers of Latvian Waffen-SS veterans, including those with SS tattoos on their arms, were admitted to Britain with no real screening under the EVW scheme.

There was always room for dispute about members of the Latvian Legion, since it had initially recruited on a voluntary basis before switching to conscription, conducted by the German occupiers, around 1943. (Mischka Danos's notice of call-up had been the reason for his departure to study at the University of Dresden in 1944.) Their units had been labeled "'Waffen-SS" by the Germans, but what if any relationship with the real SS existed was disputed. Earlier, UNRRA had been inclined to treat all legionnaires as volunteers unless proven otherwise, and at first IRO continued on the same lines, although not without complaints that conscripted Latvian Legion members were being unfairly treated.

Throughout 1946, the British were steadily transferring 16,500 Baltic Waffen-SS veterans held in POW camps in their zone to DP status, essentially without screening. The same was happening with ninety thousand Baltic POWs in the US zone, although the perception was that they were less favorably regarded by the Americans than by the British. The Americans did make some effort to screen their Baltic POWs, as UNRRA policy required, before transferring them to DP status, but to little effect. Valdmanis himself passed a second security screening by the US military government in March 1946, receiving a certificate that described him as "a person believing in democratic ideals" with a record of anti-Nazi activity (this was his version of bureaucratic conflicts he had had with the Germans while working with them).

UNRRA's British chief of operations in Germany, Sir Frederick Morgan, was aware that UNRRA's policy was being flouted but lacked the will to enforce it—or perhaps simply recognized that if the British and American military authorities decided to offloaded over a hundred thousand Baltic Waffen-SS members into the DP camps, there was not much that UNRRA could do about it. At the end of September 1946, the international Nuremberg War Crimes Tribunal ruled that the Waffen-SS was a "criminal organization" involved in wartime atrocities, but this did not substantively change the situation on the ground with regard to treatment of its members. After IRO came on the scene in mid-1947, it began to shift its policy on these groups to correspond with practice. Reconsideration of the Baltic Waffen-SS issue in October 1947 led to a new ruling from IRO—for which Alfred Valdmanis, who had testified before the council on the matter, claimed credit—that "Baltic nationals, who from 1943 on had 'volunteered' for service in the German armed forces, be considered mobilized by force." Over the next six months, the eligibility board changed tack accordingly, and appeals of legionnaires against earlier rejections of applications for DP status began to be accepted.[17]

The United States, similarly, shifted ground in its immigration policies. Under section 13 of the 1948 Displaced Persons Act, "no visas shall be issued under the provisions of this Act to any person who is or has been a member of, or participated in, any movement which is or has been hostile to the United States or the form of government of the United States." This was at first construed to include the Latvian Legion and Waffen-SS units, for which some young men in the Baltics had volunteered and others been conscripted. But in a process similar to the one IRO went through in Europe, this prohibition became less and less politically tenable. Latvian émigré organizations campaigned to protest the exclusion of Baltic SS men from US visas and citizenship, arguing that they were not "real" Nazis, only patriotic Latvians and Lithuanians. The US State Department finally ruled that, although the Latvian Legion had fought alongside the Germans, "its purpose, ideology and activities" were separate, meaning that ex-Latvian Legion DPs were now suitable candidates for immigration to the United States. In September 1950, after internal arguments, and against the opposition of its Jewish member, the Displaced Persons Commission recommended dropping the Latvian Legion and the Waffen-SS in the Baltics from the list of organizations whose membership implied hostility to the United States.[18]

Ukrainian and Russian Collaborators

Modification of policy with regard to Baltic DPs naturally raised the hopes of those pushing for relaxation toward collaborator groups from other nationalities, among them the Ukrainian Fourteenth SS Galician Division. This was a volunteer unit raised in the Ukraine during the occupation, trained by the Germans, and assigned to the Waffen-SS. Nine thousand of its members wound up in May 1945 under Allied control in the Riccione-Rimini camp, having surrendered as a unit, priests and family members in tow. Their fate was a matter of international Ukrainian lobbying, including from Canada and Brazil, as well as pressure from the Vatican, responding to pleas from Bishop Ivan Buchko of the Ukrainian Greek Catholic Church. In March 1946, British foreign minister Bevin and Sir Frederick Morgan of UNRRA agreed that they should be protected, "since they could have come from the area of the Ukraine under Polish rule before 1939." With the announcement of *Westward Ho!*, the Foreign Office seized on the chance of a way out of the predicament about what to do with them. With minimum security screening, they were shipped en masse to the UK in April–May to be used as labor. In July 1948, eighty-three hundred Ukrainians in Britain were converted from POW to EVW status.

Some members of the division remained in Europe, however, and their cases continued to come before IRO's eligibility board. When in 1951, following the removal of the Baltic Waffen-SS units from the US Immigration's proscribed list, an instruction came down through IRO to accept the Galician division men as eligible for DP status, the Belgian head of the board, Marcel de Baer, was outraged and recorded his protest in an internal memo of September 13, 1951. To give DP status to members of the Galician Division, as well as to Russians who had served in Vlasov units in France, was a violation of IRO's constitution, he wrote, and "as a judge and as chairman of the United Nations War Crimes Commission," which had listed them as war criminals, he felt obliged to put his dissent on record.[19]

One Russian group that had fought under German command during the war was of particular concern to the British and the Tolstoy Foundation. Referred to in British documents as the Rogozhin (Rogoshin) group, these were the remnant of the Russian Corps, raised by émigrés in Yugoslavia at the beginning of the war, that had surrendered to the British in southern Austria in 1945 under the leadership of Colonel Anatoly Rogozhin and been warehoused in Camp Kellerberg in Austria since. The Rogozhin group had its admirers among British officers working with IRO in Europe. Peter Gibson, a British officer with a background in IGCR who later headed the IRO mission in Austria, raised their case sympathetically. Another British officer regretted that IRO had not yielded to pressure on the Rogozhin group: they were "by far the highest type of DPs in our Zone" and "our oldest customers," that is, second-generation refugees. "My personal interest must be excused and attributed to the fact that in the period 1920–1922 I worked in Constantinople with the Allied Occupation and I took a personal part in getting 600,000 White Russians out of Russia under the aegis of Dr Nansen," he wrote to London in April 1949. "For all I know [I] may have helped some of these very same people whom I now meet 26 years later."[20]

The Tolstoy Foundation was deeply interested in the Rogozhin negotiations, providing both an ideological rationale and practical help in getting such newly legitimized DPs sponsors to immigrate to the United States. They were a noble group, Schaufuss argued, even if on the face of it they were "prima facie ineligible" according to IRO rules: "In their heroic stand for Freedom and Liberation they look towards the West as the sole hope of the World in this crucial struggle against all forms of dictatorship and political terror." No doubt the appeals for revaluation of eligibility forwarded by the foundation reflected their coaching, as those who wrote the appeals explained that they had joined the Schutzkorps for motives of anti-communism and the wish to fight the Soviets: "There was no question of joining the lines against the Allied forces."

The foundation's director, Alexandra Tolstoy, was a tireless lobbyist for the Rogozhin group with political leaders, notably Ernest Bevin. She urged the British government to take up its cause at the IRO General Council, arguing that "one cannot blame the Russians for the fact, now recognized the world over, that non-cooperation with the Reds meant collaboration with the Germans. To those Russians who had consciously aligned [sic] themselves against Communism 35 years ago, and had reared their families in the same belief, mobilization into the Russian Protective Corps of Yugoslavia was the only logical step to take." At a lower level, the Tolstoy Foundation was involved in constant correspondence and backroom politicking with various Western authorities on the disposition of Russian DPs and refugees, including the all-important provision of US sponsors for the Rogozhin members and assurances that places would be available for them to immigrate to the United States under the Church World Service program in case of an affirmative outcome on their eligibility.[21]

The Tolstoy Foundation was not the only lobbyist for the Rogozhin group. Humanity Calls, a US nonprofit organization to aid victims of communism whose members included the journalist Eugene Lyons, published a brochure in 1950 entitled "Stop Crimes against Humanity" protesting IRO's failure to certify the Rogozhin group in Kellerburg Camps as DPs and thus allow them to emigrate to the United States. The brochure noted that IRO was the successor to UNRRA, an organization dissolved after its cooperation in DP repatriation, which was "a crime against humanity," and moreover had inherited much of UNRRA's personnel, plus a constitution framed "in collaboration with Soviet representatives." IRO had deliberately twisted the definition of "displaced persons" to fit the communist party line, claiming that these people were refugees from the Nazis when they were actually "refugees from the Soviet Union." "Four years after the war ended, IRO still speaks of Nazi persecution but never a word about Soviet tyranny."

IRO was indeed more hesitant about the Rogozhin group than about the Latvian Legion. Although the question of their eligibility came up at the executive committee of IRO's general council in September 1949, and apparently elicited some sympathy, nobody was prepared to initiate a motion. As of April 1950, the outlook was still grim: Schaufuss had reported to IRO that "prospects for the resettlement in the US had been dashed by the retention of IRO eligibility as a prerequisite for a visa under the new DP Act"; and she was beginning to doubt that, under these circumstances, the Tolstoy Foundation could even find sponsors for the Rogozhin group. IRO considered looking into the United Kingdom as a possible destination (presumably informally, as the Rogozhin group was not under IRO's mandate). Count Bennigsen, a senior figure in the Russian emigration in Britain, dropped by the Foreign Office Refugee Department to suggest sounding out Australia as a destination for all the "out of camp White Russians" in Germany and Austria, though the Foreign Office preferred to focus on the three to four hundred Rogozhin group members still in the Kellerberg camp.[22]

The Rogozhin issue was never quite resolved—at least not officially. As a British official reported to the Foreign Office in March 1950, the eligibility review board had concluded that there was no way to get round the fact that the "the [Russian] corps had been formed at German instigation from the start, that is members knew of this when they volunteered, that there was no particular pressure for them to join and that the sole purpose of the corps was to help wage war against the Soviets, there being no mention of self-defence in any of its war-time pronouncements"; in other words, there were no grounds to contest their status as collaborators. For this reason, the IRO secretariat had decided to drop the idea of a motion conferring eligibility on them. Instead, it decided to circumvent its own rules by secretly supporting the efforts of the Tolstoy Foundation to resettle the Rogozhin group. As a member of the British delegation to an IRO meeting in Geneva wrote back to the Foreign Office, "IRO would make available to the Tolstoy Foundation and any other bodies who can procure visas for the ineligibles sufficient funds to meet the cost of shipping them to any country (such as Argentina) which may be prepared to accept them. They intend to cover this up by making payment in the guise of a refund to us in respect of unspecified services to refugees in general."

Six months later, internal UK Foreign Office correspondence reports that at recent IRO meetings in Geneva "a resolution was adopted which *in effect* [my italics] grants eligibility status" to the Rogozhin group. The Tolstoy Foundation "have a very large number of assurances for immigrants to America, some of which they now hope to use in connection with the Rogozhin group. There is also a possibility that some of them may be moved to England under the scheme announced by the Home Secretary under which 2,000 hard-core cases will be admitted from Germany and Austria." May 24, 1950, saw the first move of a family of the Rogozhin group out of Austria, travel arrangements being made not by IRO but through a private travel agency, Thomas Cook.

The status of Vlasov Army fighters was still more delicate, in that they were former Soviet citizens, which meant that if they were acknowledged to be war criminals, Western authorities were bound to return them to the Soviet Union for punishment. According to IRO's historian, Vlasov Army members were among those benefiting from "the more liberal assessment of eligibility" adopted by IRO in its last years, a statement that accords with some individual testimonies. For example, "Vladimir," a Soviet officer taken prisoner by the Germans who subsequently joined the Vlasov Army, survived years "full of dangers" immediately after the war ("he barely escaped being lynched by a mob, was hunted by the Soviet Repatriation Commission, and spent some time in hiding"), but then had his status "legalized" and was accepted as a DP.[23]

In sum, IRO's mission was resettlement. When this came in conflict with earlier restrictions on admitting former Nazi collaborators to DP status, the resettlement mission trumped doubts about the desirability of collaborators as migrants. The rebranding of the DPs from "victims of Nazism" to "victims of communism," initially pushed on behalf of the Russians by the Tolstoy Foundation, became common currency of the Cold War, thus allowing the United States—IRO's major funder—to open its own doors for resettlement, as well as enabling other countries to become mass resettlement destinations.

7

Resettlement as Policy

RESETTLEMENT HAD never been part of UNRRA's mandate. "It is not UNRRA's function to arrange the resettlement of displaced persons in countries other than those of their previous residence," the European office directed in October 1945. "Thus, UNRRA should not undertake any general plan of resettlement." To be sure, if other organizations offered resettlement opportunities to individual DPs, "it would be wrong to hamper their efforts"; but repatriation, not resettlement, was UNRRA's mandate, and staff should not "suggest resettlement as an alternative to repatriation in dealing with DPs." Only in "exceptional cases" might UNRRA provide "limited assistance (such as transport)" for resettlement. This was a reference to Jewish DPs with immigration certificates for Palestine, where, as even the British conceded, it was probably UNRRA's business to help them.

By the end of 1945, however, the waters had been seriously muddied by President Truman's announcement, in the wake of the Harrison report, that the United States would accept a limited contingent of DPs more or less immediately. This was, in fact, a resettlement program, albeit one that came without guarantees of future continuance. UNRRA, which was assumed to be the body organizing the program in Europe, was taken aback. As Hansi Pollack of UNRRA's relief section wrote to the organization's headquarters in Germany, if the director-general of UNRRA agrees to Truman's request, that would imply that UNRRA was up for "a great deal of the work that was formerly interpreted as being resettlement," that is, not just transport support but "investigation of individual cases regarded eligibility for immigration visa, visa affidavit, documentation etc." Given UNRRA's dependence on the United States, it was scarcely possible for the director-general to refuse, and he did not. This was the first substantial resettlement prospect to be offered to DPs, and for several years the only one.[1]

UNRRA's successor, IRO, came in with resettlement as its mandate. It was open for offers on resettlement from mid-1947, but it took a while for countries to get their act together. Australia was one of the earliest solid prospects, ahead of the more tentative Brazil and Canada. But business was slow until mid-1948, when two major logjams were broken: the United States and Palestine/Israel.

The first breakthrough was the resettlement of Jews from DP camps to Palestine. The British, who had held the League of Nations mandate over Palestine, fought a stubborn battle against large-scale entry of Jewish DPs, despite American pressure to admit them; and even after they surrendered the mandate to the United Nations early in 1947, lack of agreement on the proposed partition of Palestine into Jewish and Arab states kept the immigration issue in suspension. The State of Israel was formally established on 15 May 1948, opening the way in principle to unrestricted entry of Jewish DPs. Even then, however, there were obstacles, since the outbreak of fighting between Jews and Arabs in Palestine led IRO (backed by the British, but opposed by the Americans) to refuse to resettle DPs there on the grounds that it was a war zone. But this was ironed out by the beginning of 1949, with a full resumption of IRO assistance and financial aid for Jewish resettlement in Israel from April of that year. This paved the way for Israel to become the top recipient of Jewish DPs and the third largest recipient of DPs in general by the end of IRO's resettlement program in the early 1950s.

The second breakthrough was the passing of the Displaced Persons Act by the United States Congress on June 25, 1948, after much internal haggling. The United States was the preferred destination of a majority of non-Jewish DPs, and of many Jewish DPs as well. The DP Act in its initial form allowed for the entry of 205,000 DPs from Europe over a two-year period, and the numbers were raised in a 1950 amendment.[2]

As these possibilities of resettlement outside Europe opened up, options inside Europe were diminishing. Britain, having taken in some seventy-thousand under *Westward Ho!*, felt it had shot its bolt. The Belgian mines had not proved attractive to the DPs, and the French came so late into the act that the US and Israeli options were already available. Overall, there was a swing away from the postwar sense of a labor shortage in Europe to an opposite mindset, according to which Europe was overpopulated, even without counting the DPs, and that out-migration should be encouraged. Thus the resettlement of the mainly East European DPs in the years 1947–52 turned out to be a prelude to the assisted emigration of well over half a million West Europeans from the same territories (Italy, Germany, and Austria) to the same destinations (the United States, Australia, Canada, Argentina) in the five years that followed. In several of these countries, Volksdeutsche—Germans expelled during and after the war from their previous places of residence in Eastern Europe, not eligible for DP status under IRO rules—were presented by opponents of DP (and particularly Jewish DP) resettlement as a hard-working, clean, and easily assimilable alternative.[3]

While IRO supervised and organized the resettlement of DPs, each of the countries that signed up as recipients had their own immigration procedures and selection preferences. Most had political criteria, expressed as security concerns, aimed to exclude Nazi collaborators and communists. But increasingly only lip service was given to the exclusion of collaborators, with the negative emphasis in practice on communist sympathizers. Recipient countries each had their own preferences with regard to the age, marital status, and work qualifications of their immigrants. IRO accepted this but tried to maintain the fiction that selection was made without regard to race, religion, or nationality, when in fact that was far from the case. In a disconcerting echo of Nazi racial preferences, almost all the recipient countries preferred Balts (the closest to Aryan on offer) and were disinclined to take Jews. "Without openly declaring their unwillingness to accept Jewish immigrants," a United Nations report of June 1948 noted, "the various missions invariably reject all the Jewish candidates." (Sometimes, as in the case of British *Westward Ho!* recruitment, Russians were lumped in with Jews as an unwanted group.) IRO was forced to accept this, although not without undertaking some evasive maneuvers to circumvent the Jewish quotas.[4]

Occupational preferences were important, as most of the recipient countries wanted labor of particular types. It was not only the Soviets who caught "a whiff of the slave market" in the selection process. This phrase comes from the *London Times*, while the *New Yorker*'s correspondent quoted cynical comments from DPs that "what is wanted is the pounds of flesh—young, strong, male and single." Relief workers made similar remarks, and a popular US magazine wrote that "governments may thumb through IRO's DP 'catalogue' like farmers through a Sears, Roebuck annual; their representatives prowl in the camps as if in department-store bargain basements, where the marked-down price tags feature race, size, family status, age, skills, muscles." IRO tried to convey to recipient countries that, in addition to providing themselves with manpower for their economics, they were also fulfilling an international civic duty that involved accepting some of the halt and maimed who were on nobody's wish list, but this had little success until the very end of the process, when a few European countries stepped up to take limited numbers of left-overs. It was not only the ill, disabled, and elderly who were hard to place. According to the official in charge of DP selection for the United States, "the problem of intelligentsia is almost as difficult as the problem of the blind and crippled."

DPs were, on the face of it, almost wholly at the mercy of the resettlement market. But this impression is in part misleading, since the DPs, being apprised of the selection committees' preferences, could be very creative in tailoring their self-presentation to meet them. They evaded age limits by misstating their age, claimed to be single when single men were preferred, rewrote their biographies to produce the desired nationality, and ditched university degrees to become experienced laborers and farmhands. In the destination countries, especially the United States, ethnic lobby groups strove to increase their nationality's share in DP immigration. In the case of Jewish DPs, the least favored group for all countries but Israel, they ended up with significantly larger proportions of the total DP immigration in countries like the United States and Australia than the countries' stated preferences would have suggested. At the other end of the preference scale, Baltic DPs were in such a favorable position that they could often make a choice. Since the United States was most DPs' preferred destination, a disproportionate number of Baltic DPs—over 100,000 out of a total of about 160,000—went there, with lower-ranking Latin American countries that also preferred Balts getting comparatively few.[5]

United States

Generally speaking, the selection preferences of different countries were worked out on the ground by selection committees sent by their governments' immigration departments. The US case was unique in that the entrance of DPs was governed by a specific legislative act, and the lengthy passage of that legislation was in effect a drawn-out process of negotiation and lobbying about national, religious, and occupational preferences. It was American Jewish representatives, concerned about the fate of the surviving Jews in Europe, who spearheaded the pressure for a DP act. But because of the strength of anti-Jewish feeling in Congress and the public, they had to camouflage this lobbying and temporarily accept partial defeat at the hands of other lobby groups in 1948 (although they were able to reverse this with a 1950 amendment). The bill faced powerful and vocal opposition, despite President Truman's support. In the opinion of Representative Ed Gossett from Texas, the DPs were "a new Fifth Column" and the camps in Europe were "filled with bums, criminals, black-marketeers, subversives, revolutionaries, and crackpots of all colors and hues." The main veterans' association in the United States, the American Legion, was against the bill on the ground that "migration should stop until all foreign immigrants were thoroughly Americanized," and so were patriotic societies like Sons of the American Revolution. The ostensible fear was that the act would enable communists and Soviet spies to enter the United States, but "communists" and "Jews" were often conflated: according to *Newsweek*, many Americans asked, "Weren't the DPs Jews? Didn't they come from Eastern Europe? And didn't that mean that most of them were probably communist?"

Marvin Klemmé, a backwoods Oregonian who had worked with UNRRA, expressed his reservations about admitting Jews to the United States more freely than many. They tended to be the kind of people who would vote for Henry Wallace, he surmised; had Soviet and communist sympathies as well as intellectual pretensions; and tended to criticize everything about the American way of life. The Jewish intellectuals ("Trotskyites at heart") were the worst and "should be selected [for immigration] with even greater care than ordinary working people, because of the fact that they have greater possibilities of engaging in mischief."[6]

President Truman publicly urged adoption of the bill in his State of the Union messages of 1947 and 1948, and it was also supported by influential members of the East Coast liberal establishment, the Federal Council of Churches of Christ in America, and a number of Catholic groups (mindful of the fact that a substantial proportion of DPs, including virtually all Poles, many Lithuanians, and some Latvians, were Catholic). Various ethnic groups lobbied energetically for the bill, of course with the interests of their co-national DPs foremost in mind. Propaganda from the Latvian organizations included the claim that 60 percent of the country's population had fair hair and blue eyes. Lithuanians emphasized the "desperate situation of the Baltic peoples under Soviet rule," subject to a persecution the president of the Lithuanian-American Council described as "genocide." The Russian lobby, represented primarily by the Tolstoy Foundation, had not really found its feet in the lead-up to the bill's passage and felt itself hampered by the popular equation of "Russian" and "Soviet"/"communist" and outmaneuvered by lobbying groups from the areas annexed by the Soviet Union just before the Second World War, primarily the Baltic groups and West Ukrainians.

In the event, Latvians and other Baltic groups did very well according to the provisions of the act, and Jews comparatively poorly. Preference was to be given to people from regions annexed by the Soviet Union as well as to farmers (both favorable categories for Baltic DPs), with a definition of DP adopted that excluded persons who had entered the camps in 1946 and early 1947 (that is, the Jewish "infiltrees"). Liberals were left unsatisfied, with some condemning the act for smacking of "hate and racism"; both Catholics and Jews felt they had been discriminated against; and President Truman found the bill as passed to be "flagrantly discriminatory." He signed it, albeit "with very great reluctance," because it was better than nothing.

Having made the immigration of displaced persons a matter of congressional legislation, the Congress set up the Displaced Persons Commission (DPC) in Washington to coordinate the selection process. Its three members—a Protestant, Catholic, and Jew—were appointed by the president and shared his favorable attitude to DP immigration. The commissioners' work "reflected their liberal biases and undercut the letter and spirit of the law passed by Congress," as was the president's intention; their internationalist instincts were also visible in the hiring of staff "who had formerly worked for UNRRA, the IRO, and the voluntary agencies." The commission's head, Ugo Carusi (the Protestant member of the DPC) was a former US commissioner of immigration. Edward M. O'Connor had been active in Catholic relief work. Harry N. Rosenfield, the Jewish member, was a lawyer, born in New York to Russian-immigrant parents, who had got his start working for Republican (and future IRO head) Fiorello La Guardia in New York. His formative Washington experience was working for the Federal Security Agency (a New Deal administration dealing with health, education, and welfare) during the war.[7]

The US approach to selection was to do it by sponsorship—individual if that was available, but more often institutional, with various voluntary agencies, charities, religious, and national organizations providing "corporate affidavits" guaranteeing that the DP immigrants would be placed in jobs, helped with housing, and not allowed to become a public charge. The American Friends Service Committee, HIAS, and the Tolstoy Foundation were among the many institutions approved as givers of affidavits. Jewish organizations were particularly active, and Catholics were also mobilized: after the passage of the DP Act in 1948 "every Catholic bishop in America received instructions to appoint a diocesan resettlement director." Protestants, except Lutherans (the dominant church in Latvia) were generally less keen, with the Church World Service allocating only about $1 million for refugees 1948, as against $10 million from Jewish organizations. But Lutherans assisted the entry of over thirty thousand DPs, mainly from the Baltic states.

The sponsoring agencies in turn would have to drum up hosts who were looking for cheap labor or moved by charitable instincts and would provide work and initial accommodation. Working with IRO, their representatives would organize selection and transport. A US visa, issued by the State Department, was necessary in addition to the affidavit, and sometimes this caused problems, as the US consular officials tended to be less favorably inclined to DPs than was the DPC. In addition, the DPs selected had to go through a security check by the US Army in Germany, as well a physical examination organized by IRO.

After his reelection in November 1948, and with a democratic majority in Congress, President Truman immediately urged a liberal revision of the act, with removal of restrictions; and the DPC took this on board as one of its major tasks. The amended bill to admit four hundred thousand displaced persons almost without restrictions was introduced by Emmanuel Celler, a Jewish representative from New York, but, as Commissioner Rosenfield later attested, it was the DPC that had rewritten it—"we carried the ball completely." Progress was blocked, however, by Senator Pat McCarran, newly returned from a visit to the DP camps in Europe in the fall of 1949, who warned against allowing "the entrance of millions of aliens, from the turbulent populations of the entire world, who are seeking admission into the United States under the guise of displaced persons" and proposed the Volksdeutsche as an attractive alternative. It was not until June 2, 1950, that the amended DP act was finally passed, allowing 301,500 displaced persons to be resettled in the United States, more or less without restrictions, over the next two years.[8]

The amended Displaced Persons Act banned persons who had been members of either the Nazi or the Communist Party, as well as their subsidiary organizations like the Nazi youth organizations for boys and girls, Hitlerjugend and Bund Deutscher Mädel, and their Soviet counterpart, the Komsomol. This affected DP collaborators comparatively little, since neither the Latvians who fought in the Latvian Legion or Waffen-SS nor the Russians from the Vlasov Army and Russian Corps were likely to have joined the Nazi Party, even if they were sympathizers and/or willing to fight under German command. But for former Soviet citizens who had been communist party members (which included most men who had been officers or held civilian responsible jobs) or members of the Komsomol (which included a high percentage of the relevant age group) it was a major impediment.

By the time the revised act passed, the United States was deep in the anti-communist hysteria associated with the Cold War, which affected the terms of the discussion. While rules against admission of collaborators and former members of Nazi organizations were relaxed with time, vigilance against communist sympathizers intensified. In fact, according to Rosenfield, individual Waffen-SS members had *never* been on the Immigration Department's "inimical list": "that was mostly the Communists." A parade of US senators touring the DP camps had expressed concerns that they might become breeding grounds for communists, as well as for black marketeers. In an atmosphere of rising anti-communism, the Internal Security Act of 1950 expanded the authority to screen DPs and other aliens for potential subversion. This almost halted the flow of DP immigration to the United States for six months (from the fall of 1950 to the spring of 1951), although it picked up again from the middle of 1951.

Assessing the DPs' political reliability by nationality, the US Army's European Command found a range between 100 percent reliability for Baltic DPs to 50 percent for Jewish ones. Russians were not included as a category in this assessment, but it was generally thought that Russians had had a harder time than anyone else from the European DP camps getting into the United States, and that migrants of Russian origin were probably particularly liable to fall under suspicion of "un-American activities." Still, there were some grounds for optimism about the future. Alexandra Tolstoy's argument that "White" Russians were cultured and religious people, "suffering for the same principles this country is based on—freedom, human rights; of which they were deprived in Soviet Russia" was beginning to gain some traction. It was argued strongly by witnesses called before the Subcommittee on Amendments to the Displaced Persons Act in September 1949 that the "White Russian" contingent from China, whose admission was under consideration at the same time as the DPs, were lifelong fighters against the Soviets, "bitter and strong enemies of communism, excellent fighters for freedom and prospective defenders of the Constitution of the United States."[9]

Australia

Australia, despite its small population, (not much over seven million in 1945, as compared with the US 140 million) proved to be the second-largest destination for DPs. Its preferences and political biases resembled those of the United States, though there were some significant differences in political culture: Australia had a Labor government during and after the war, as well as a significant communist party, which, after being banned in the years of the Nazi-Soviet Pact, achieved considerable popularity during the war before losing much of it in the postwar years. The Cold War came later to Australia than to the United States, and in somewhat moderated form.

There were also important differences in the approach to immigration. Having historically depended largely on British immigration, Australia had no prewar experience of large-scale non-British migration and no conception of itself as a "melting pot" to draw on. As of the end of the war, Australian citizenship was still not formally distinct from British, and the majority of the population still called Britain "Home." The postwar immigration was unprecedented both in its scope and in the "foreignness" of the migrants. It was an initiative of the Commonwealth (= federal) Government in Canberra from beginning to end, part of a broader postwar economic and social reconstruction project. Ethnic and religious lobby groups played little role, business and private enterprise virtually none.

Arthur Calwell, the immigration minister, went to Europe in July 1947 specifically to look for immigrants suitable for blue-collar work. Disappointed in his hopes of Northern Europeans, and aware that British supply could no longer meet Australian demands, he made do with East European DPs and signed a "mass resettlement" agreement with IRO. Immigration officers working under the supervision of the Australian military mission in Germany would make the selection from among DP applicants gathered by IRO. The successful applicants would then undergo a security check and a medical examination and sign a two-year contract for work to be assigned by the Australian government. Then, assuming they passed, they would be shipped out of Europe in vessels provided by IRO for the long voyage to Australia. The laboring jobs assigned to the DPs were mainly infrastructural, located far from the big population centers: railways, roads, and the state-run Snowy River Hydroelectric Scheme, the pride of the national postwar reconstruction plan.

Australia was a predominantly Protestant country with a Catholic minority that was largely of Irish origin. Immigration was not yet on the Australian Catholic agenda at the end of the Second World War; there was no visible awareness among the (mainly Irish) hierarchy that a whole new constituency might be available in the form of Polish displaced persons, and no recorded lobbying to bring them in. The Orthodox Church, either in its Greek or Russian iterations, was not yet a presence on the Australian scene. There was a small Jewish community, mainly long-established and of British origins, which had viewed the prewar arrival of a few thousand (mainly Central

European) Jewish refugees under the prewar Évian Accords with uneasiness, worried that they would arouse antisemitism among Anglo Australians. Only a left-wing minority in the small community actively lobbied for the postwar admission of East European Jews.

In their selection methods, the Australians were notable for the thoroughness of their medical inspections and their intense focus on getting healthy, strong, young immigrants capable of manual work. Even minor physical abnormalities like varicose veins or conjunctivitis might get an applicant rejected by the Australian teams. Overall, Australia rejected over half of the applicants it interviewed on medical grounds, a higher percentage than any other national selection committee. The other Australian peculiarity noted by IRO was a very strong objection to accepting intellectuals, even if their professional specialties were "useful" ones like engineering or medicine. As Calwell put it, Australia wanted "horny-handed toilers," not educated people or "traders and retail merchants" (surely partially code for Jews).[10]

Australia's agreement with IRO included the stipulation that "DPs and refugees" would be selected "without discrimination as to race or religion." This could potentially have been in conflict with the country's "White Australia" policy, which excluded Chinese and others on racial grounds, since within the multinational Soviet population—hence, presumably, among "Soviet" DPs—there were not only Russians (classified as "European") but also people whom Australia would have identified as "Asiatics" (Buryats, Kalmyks, Tatars, and others), had they known about them. This never emerged as a real problem with regard to DP immigration, however, largely because of Australian ignorance. In practice, as far as DP immigration was concerned, the "race" issue was about Jews.

While IRO did not allow discrimination on grounds of "race," it did accept preferences relating to "nationality," and the nationality preferences that guided Australia's selection had clear racial overtones. These preferences were known to IRO and used in the selection process, although not publicly made explicit in detail. According to internal Australian immigration memos, Balts (Estonians, Latvians, and Lithuanians) were at the top of the list, followed by three categories of Slavs (Slovenes and Ukrainians first, Yugoslavs, Czechs, and Poles added later). Jews were at the bottom. Russians were not on the list at all, since—as a result of misstatement of nationality and the classification of Russian émigrés as "stateless—Australia did not realize how many it was getting. Belatedly, "White Russians" were added, although there was some uncertainty as to whether this meant people from Belarus (literally, White Russia) or prewar émigrés.

Australia's preference for non-Slavic Northern Europeans was underlined by the confidential instruction that the first shipload of "mass resettlement" migrants should consist entirely of Baltic DPs (single men) from the British zone. On his July 1947 visit to Europe, Immigration Minister Calwell had been favorably impressed by the "beautiful Balts" he had encountered: good-looking, tall, blonde, blue-eyed, clean, and polite. His thinking was that, once they were supplied with decent clothes to make a good impression on first arrival, they would reassure the Australian public of the assimilability of the whole contingent of "New Australians."

His prudence was partly dictated by fears that the visible arrival of East Europeans, including Jews, would arouse an adverse public reaction. There had already been something of an outcry in 1946 about shiploads of refugees, mainly Russian Jews, from China; and, to avoid further pushback, Calwell (who was not personally antisemitic) introduced a 25 percent Jewish quota on migrants arriving on any one vessel. Since this was often reduced in practice, access to mass resettlement to Australia became difficult for Jews. With the help of American Jewish agencies HIAS and JDC, and the covert cooperation of IRO, many Jewish DPs chose the alternative path of migrating to Australia on "landing permits," which meant paying for the ticket instead of the free passage provided by the country's Mass Resettlement program, finding individual sponsors, and not being subject to the two-year labor contract.

In Australia it was often hard to draw a strict line between antisemitism and a broader xenophobia directed at all non-English-speaking and foreign-looking migrants. In trade union circles, there was also a suspicion of the "Mass Resettlement" migrants as cheap labor who might be used to undercut the wages of Australian workers. In general, in the major blue-collar unions, some of which were communist-led, the DP migrants were treated with suspicion as right-wing, anti-union, and anti-communist. There was significant anxiety in the Left about bringing in Nazi collaborators among the Baltic and East European DPs, and Calwell frequently had to defend his department from such accusations, as well as from the counteraccusations of the Right that he was bringing in communists.[11]

Canada

Unlike Australia, Canada was not experiencing an acute labor shortage immediately after the war and there was no strong consensus that the country needed to build up its population. It was Hugh Keenleyside, the newly appointed deputy immigration minister, who "moved to open the door to displaced persons" in the spring of 1947. To be sure, W. L. Mackenzie King's liberal government declared its belief that "a large increase in the Canadian population is desirable and that an expanded movement of immigrants will contribute to that increase," but this seems to some degree to have been pushing against the grain. In addition, there was the suspicion that subsidized migrants who came from Europe were likely to regard Canada as a stepping stone for the United States. As in Australia, many people thought it would be best to stick with immigrants from Britain (or, in the case of Quebec, from France), and there were fears that "public opinion in Canada did not favour the absorption of large numbers of refugees, especially East Europeans and Jews." Still, Canada, unlike Australia, already had a substantial Ukrainian population (over 300,000 in a total of 11.5 million in 1941); and there was an active Ukrainian as well as a Jewish lobby on immigration questions.[12]

In contrast to both Australia and the United States, Canada adopted a "Sponsored Labour Scheme" in June 1947 whose salient characteristic was that Canadian industries, not the state, would place "bulk" orders for a particular number of DPs with particular skills, not for named individuals. The quotas would be filled by selection officers in Europe working in cooperation with IRO. The work obligation (evidently to work in the particular industry the DP was selected for, rather than a specific enterprise) was for twelve months and would be enforced by the industries, not the state—though, in a development noted by the Australian government, the Canadian Department of Labour felt obliged in November 1947 to contradict the false rumor that, once arrived and placed in a particular industry, they could buy themselves out before their term was up. Logging, lumbering, and mining were among the industries involved, with the Canadian Metal Mining Association and Canadian Forestry Association among the sponsors, but domestic service and farm work were soon added, and over the life of the scheme accounted for half the arrivals. The very first request received was for one hundred DP girls for a spinning mill.

Canada took a strong line on the chosen worker coming alone, without dependents. This was similar to the British approach in its *Westward Ho!* scheme but unlike that of Australia which, while initially preferring single migrants, was less systematic in rejecting family groups. When a DP was interviewed by the Canadian selection commission, he (or she) was explicitly asked "whether, if he and his family were selected, he was prepared to leave his family behind until he could nominate them for call forward."

Canada's agreement with IRO, like Australia's, stipulated that there would be no discrimination on the basis of country of origin or religion, only occupation, but, as in the Australian case, ethnic preferences were nevertheless well in evidence, and the preferences were basically the same. Canada's informal wish list as far as DPs were concerned also put Balts at the top ("clean, hardworking, conscientious, and resourceful") and then went down the lists of Slavs, from Ukrainians to Poles, with Jews at the bottom.

As in Australia's Mass Resettlement scheme, Jewish DPs (or at least those identifying as such) were underselected for Canada's Sponsored Labour Programme, though some came in under the guise of Catholics or Protestants. A distinctively Canadian twist was the "subtle intertwining of profession-related and 'ethnic' criteria," which enabled supporters of Jewish immigration to get Jewish DPs in by way of labor requests from industries like tailoring where they were likely to well represented. (This could also have its farcical side when the furriers' trade group, finding and no doubt primarily looking for Jewish tradesmen, was urged to beat the bushes for non-Jews with the required specialties to make the ethnic breakdown look better.)[13]

The Ukrainian part of Canada's postwar immigration story had some interesting complications. The Ukrainian DPs who went to Canada were, as elsewhere, a mixture of West Ukrainians (former Polish citizens, strongly anticommunist) and East Ukrainians (former Soviet citizens). The prewar Ukrainian community, part of it hailing from the Austro-Hungarian empire in the late nineteenth and early twentieth centuries rather than from the Russian Empire, included socialists and even communists in its ranks, and they strongly objected to the admission of DPs whom they regarded as "war criminals" and "fascists." There was some reflection of these attitudes even in the mainstream Canadian press, where references could be found to "Nazi zealots" who "could no more be expected to be loyal citizens of this country than they were of their own native land." Friction within community increased after the arrival of Banderite (anti-Soviet wartime collaborationist) DPs in 1949.

On the security side, Canada, like the United States and Australia, was concerned about admitting communists, but its level of concern seems to have been lower than that of the United States, despite a certain uneasiness about the loyalty of (Russian-speaking) Jewish immigrants provoked by the defection of Igor Gouzenko, a cipher clerk and undercover intelligence man at the Soviet embassy in Ottawa, and information on his contacts in Canada. The Canadian government explicitly forbade the entry of "communists" into the country but not that of fascists or war criminals.[14]

Other Destinations (Latin America, Israel, Morocco)

Latin America did not live up to early hopes that it would prove one of the top destinations for DPs. Negotiations were started with refugee organizations from 1946, with Venezuela, Brazil, Guatemala, and Argentina all looking like good prospects. But few countries ended up signing formal agreements with IRO, and all the Latin American countries together took under 100,000 (9 percent of total numbers resettled). The largest contingents went to Argentina (32,712), Brazil (28,848), and Venezuela (17,277). The poor uptake was all the more disappointing for Russian DPs, who, untypically, were favored candidates, particularly in Argentina.

In the 1920s, Argentina already had over 160,000 settlers from the Russian Empire, and Brazil over 100,000. The local Russian Orthodox community worked to organize invitations to compatriots. But it was President Juan Perón's enthusiasm for Russian émigrés that was really unusual. He liked their antidemocratic values and valued their professional skills. The collaborationist shadow of many of them was no bar from Perón's point of view: he had become a (qualified) admirer of Mussolini's fascism when sent on a military mission to Italy before the war, and after the war his country became notorious for offering haven to Nazis fleeing Europe.

In an early trial run, the Argentinian government instructed its consuls to give visas to DPs of Slavic origin, especially Russians, up to the age of forty-five. According to Soviet officials disapprovingly observing the process, their selection favored "members of the Vlasov and Anders armies, former police and war criminals." In September 1947, the Soviet Foreign Ministry noted that the Argentinian government was thinking of taking in more than fifty thousand DPs from the Anders Army. The British Foreign Office was picking up similar information, although in this case it was the Rogozhin (Russian Corps) group that the Argentinians were allegedly interested in, and the negotiations were being conducted by a mysterious Colonel Evgenii Nagaetz (Nogaets), whose sister, Princess Zulita, was allegedly married to Perón's Minister for War. The Tolstoy Foundation helped in procuring and paying for visas for Russian DPs to go from Italy to Argentina, while the Orthodox Church activists in Argentina, working with the American Red Cross, estimated that they had got approval for over forty thousand invitations.

But all this fell apart when Argentina suddenly closed the doors on immigration, invalidating the visas that had already been issued to the Russians. According to a Soviet Foreign Ministry source, in February 1949 the Perón government "greatly restricted" the intake of Soviet DP (presumably Vlasov Army people) and then stopped it altogether. Argentina ended up taking only about forty thousand Russians, half identified as stateless and half as Soviet.[15]

Argentina's preference for Russians was unusual in a Latin American context, as in an international one, but two small countries, Venezuela and Paraguay, showed a similar bias in their selection. Venezuela had an extraordinarily large postwar migrant intake, given its small population. The country basically wanted manpower for its petroleum industry, but it also accepted professionals and offered free schooling and university tuition to immigrants along with the local population. Whether by accident or design, the postwar intake was notable for including a comparatively large percentage of Russian migrants—11 percent of its entire DP intake. Paraguay's intake was small (under six thousand in all), but almost half identified as Soviet citizens.

Apart from these idiosyncrasies, the prejudices and preferences of the Latin American countries were generally in line with those of other major resettlement destinations. Brazil, Argentina, and Chile favored Baltic DPs as well as Germans over East Europeans and had "an unusually strong animus against professional people" (this went even further than Australia's similar bias, since in Brazil foreign doctors, engineers, and a number of other professionals were forbidden by law to practice). Brazil wanted farmworkers as immigrants and felt cheated when it emerged that some DPs who had come in under that guise were actually "opera singers, painters etc."

Most Latin American countries were unwilling to take Jews and even threatened in their dealings with IRO to halt all DP immigration rather than take them. Paraguay was again an exception, since almost a third of its DP intake was Jewish. The majority of the Jewish arrivals came in 1947–48, and an IRO report of 1951 noted disapprovingly that some of them were remaining only a few days in the small country before moving on clandestinely to its larger and more prosperous neighbors, Argentina and Brazil.[16]

Palestine/Israel was the anomalous resettlement destination in that it was an option only for Jewish DPs. Of the 231,548 Jewish DPs resettled by IRO in the period 1947–51, 56 percent (130,408) went to Israel, almost twice the number (according to official figures that are probably underestimates) that went to the next most popular Jewish DP destination, the United States. But until the creation of the state of Israel in May 1948, and even for some months after it, the process of Jewish resettlement there was not simple.

Britain, formally in charge of Palestine's intake of migrants under the Mandate, determined the number of DPs admitted and did its best to keep them low. Fifteen hundred migration certificates for DPs were issued per month in 1947, but the actual number of completed migrations IRO paid for suggests that not all the slots were filled. An American Jewish observer saw IRO—in which British citizens held the majority of administrative positions—as acting here as "the instrument of British policies" in holding migration back. For a while after Israel's foundation, IRO stopped funding DP resettlement there because resettling in a war zone was against its rules. But the Palestine/Israel-based Jewish Agency for Palestine and the US-based JDC continued their resettlement work, and early in 1949 IRO reconsidered its position, paying the Jewish organizations' costs in retrospect as well as budgeting for a future Jewish resettlement in Israel of fifty thousand DPs.

Another anomaly with regard to Jewish resettlement was that Jews who before the war had been German or Austrian citizens qualified as DPs eligible for resettlement. (No other former German or Austrian citizens were admitted to the status of DP.) The numbers of German- and Austrian-Jewish DPs resettled in Palestine/Israel were nevertheless comparatively small (under 6,000 in total). The largest group (almost 55,000) identified themselves as coming from Poland, with 1,768 listing the Soviet Union, Ukraine, or Belarus as the country of origin, 1,238 from the Baltics, and 783 listed as stateless.[17]

Morocco, then a French protectorate, was only a minor destination for DPs, mainly Russians, but its story is worth noting because it was so untypical. Konstantin Boldyrev, the NTS activist who headed the Russian Mönchehof camp, conceived the idea of moving NTS's center of operations from Germany to Morocco, and managed to sell this idea to the French government and IGCR in 1946. The first group of Russian DPs—134 people plus dependents—left Germany for Morocco in mid-1947, and by the end of the year there were 600, including Boldyrev (now no longer formally a DP but IGCR's official representative in Morocco), other NTS personnel, a priests, two doctors, and a choir director.

Morocco proved to be a way station for the Russian DPs, not a permanent home. Boldyrev soon left for the United States; others remained for a few years until the end of French rule in Morocco in 1956, when most of them moved to the United States, Australia, or France. It had been a strange and perhaps a desperate choice from the beginning. Ivan Nikolajuk, an engineer from Mönchehof who arrived in Morocco in September 1949 and left for Australia in 1956, wrote in his diary in March 1948 that "taking account of a possible new war . . . it is best to get as far away as possible from Europe," and Morocco was the only place taking Russians. Later Nikolajuk wondered why he had left

Germany in the first place, when he had a well-paid professional job there, a place to live, and access to social security, health care, and a good education system for his young son, and concluded that it was a kind of psychosis associated with the "new 'cold war'" and a sense of Germany as haunted by ghosts of war and hostile toward foreign refugees.[18]

Race Issues: Turks and Kalmyks

When Raphael Cilento saw the Soviet Army advancing westward in 1945, he was strongly reminded of "their Mongol ancestors." That was not a politically correct thought in UNRRA terms, but he surely was not the only person to have it. Bubbling along below the formal diplomatic consensus that Soviet citizens were "Europeans" were several underground streams of racial concern about Soviet "Moslems" ("Turks and Mongols" of Islamic faith) and Kalmyks.

The Soviet Union's many Turkic peoples (sometimes called Turko-Tatar) were mainly to be found in the republics of Central Asia and the Caucasus (Azerbaijan), and their recent political past was checkered. They were disproportionately represented in military collaboration with the Germans during the war, providing units of Soviet Osttruppen fighting with the Germans numbering over eighty thousand men, a seventh of the total. Crimean Tatars (who provided ten thousand Osttruppen) were punished for their "treachery" by deportation as a people into the interior of the Soviet Union after the Soviet reconquest of Crimea from the Germans in 1944.

UNRRA first encountered the problem in the summer of 1946 when a group of over two thousand people, most of them evidently from the Soviet Caucasus, Crimea, and Azerbaijan, gathered in the Mittenwald DP camp in Bavaria claiming Turkish nationality and demanding to be sent to Turkey. The Turkish government was taken aback, and UNRRA even more—particularly given the fact that, if they were really Turkish citizens, they probably had no right to DP status and UNRRA protection (until February 1945, Turkey been on the wrong side in the war). The Soviets offered help in identifying their citizens, with a view to their speedy forcible repatriation, which UNRRA politely declined. Turkey sent a mission with similar intent but found it hard to communicate with the "Turks," since "some speak only Russian, some neither language"). It wasn't just Soviet Turko-Tatars (speaking a variety of local Turkic languages, more or less comprehensible to a Turkish speaker) who claimed to be Turkish citizens: Georgians and Armenians—non-Turkic peoples, though also from the Soviet Caucasus—were making the same claim. Under cross-examination by IRO's eligibility board, "it was revealed that they were all Soviet citizens who appeared to have valid objections against return," had destroyed their documents, and "lied from fear of forcible repatriation."[19]

Turkey, after initial hesitation, "decided, in principle, to allow the entry into their country of displaced persons or refugees who claim to have links with Turkey." This offer, which came with offers of "free transport, immediate acquisition of Turkish nationality, freedom from taxes, freedom from military training, Government assistance, an immediate monetary grant, free grant of land and lodging and equipment," looked too good to be true to IRO's chief of mission in the Middle East, and indeed his skepticism seems to have been justified. The agreement the Turkish government actually signed with IRO a year later (on June 24, 1948) did offer immediate citizenship but put all expenses of moving the group on IRO. According to Turkish sources, 3,384 Moslem DPs were resettled there, treated as members of other Turkic minorities in the country, with some unconfirmed reports of "great material distress."[20]

A small group of Moslems from the Soviet Crimea and the Caucasus were taken under the wing of Prince Amr Ibrahim and brought to Egypt from DP camps in Italy at the prince's expense in October 1947. Two years later, the prince had evidently lost interest in them, and they were living in an abandoned army camp, supported by an Egyptian benevolent society. IRO was under pressure to do something about them and thought of Australia as an appropriate destination—but there was the race problem. Australia's "White Australia" policy was essentially anti-Chinese, but there was uneasiness about anybody not clearly European. "Asiatic" (Sephardic) Jews, for example, were considered less desirable even than "European" Jews (Ashkenazi). Other Middle Eastern groups causing alarm were "persons of Asiatic origin who are Lebanese, Syrians, Turks and Armenians" (a category that probably included Turkic people from the Soviet Caucasus and Crimea). IRO hoped Australia would take a few of the from the Middle East contingent on landing permits, although anticipating objections that they were "not of pure European race (they are mainly rather dark-skinned and of simple peasant stock) and/or that they are Moslems."[21]

The United States did not have an official "White America" policy, but it still wanted its DP immigrants to be of "European race." Russians were considered Europeans, all the more demonstrably if they were "White Russians" (though the Congressional Record had to clarify that a Russian witness's testimony that potential Russian immigrants were "really White people, absolutely unquestionably White people" referred to "the political, anti-Communist persuasion of these refugees, rather than their color"). But Tatars and other Soviet Turkic groups were not so unquestionably white, let alone the Buryats of Siberia, originally from Mongolia ("as Mongol in appearance as the retreating Japanese," UNRRA's Raphael Cilento had noted at the end of the war). US Immigration initially turned down a young Soviet POW of "Tartar race" [*sic*] "on ground that he had not shown that he was of preponderantly white blood" and that Tatars, as "Asiatics," were ineligible to enter under the "Soviet quota." Armenians were another dubious group, although the United States had concluded by the early 1950s that their "racial characteristics" were generally understood to "identif[y] them with Europeans."[22]

But it was the Kalmyks (also rendered as Kalmuks, Kalmooks, Kalmycks, Calmooks) whose racial status and acceptability for resettlement became a long-running issue with the US Immigration Department. A nomadic Mongol people whose religion was Buddhist, they had migrated from northwest China to the lower Volga region of the Russian Empire in the seventeenth century. Some later enrolled as Cossacks policing the border for Moscow. Come the Bolshevik Revolution of 1917, these Don Cossack Kalmyks often chose the White side in the Civil War, earning Soviet enmity, and some Kalmyks left Russia after the Civil War and lived in Yugoslavia and Bulgaria between the wars. In the Soviet Union, they were a recognized nationality, allocated a Kalmyk autonomous region on the Volga, which during the Second World War was part of the large area of the Soviet Union that fell under German occupation. During this time some Kalmyks were taken to Germany as Ostarbeiter and others—about five thousand, as of December 1942—joined cavalry units, which, when the Germans retreated, crossed the frontier with them. This "treachery" was the basis for the Soviet deportation of the remaining Kalmyks to Central Asia and Siberia in 1943. Those that had left, serving under German military command, surrendered to the Allies and were put in POW camps for a few years, after which most found their way into DP camps. As of 1951, IRO estimated that there were still around eight thousand Kalmyks in Germany.

With such a complex backstory, there was plenty of material for competing claims that the Kalmyk DPs were, on the one hand, "Asiatics," or, on the other, "Whites" whose love of freedom made them essentially "European." According to an IRO source, the majority were former Soviet citizens who had served the Germans in military or police capacities, but the standard story told by individual DPs themselves—one historian called it "consistent, if fabricated"—was that they had been émigrés in Yugoslavia or Bulgaria before the war. IRO found them a handful. The community in Germany was organized, politicized, and internally divided and prone to mutual denunciation as communist spies.

Kalmyk resettlement cost IRO "five years of endeavors," all the more weary-ing in that the factious Kalmyks insisted on being resettled as a group (or several groups) rather than as individuals or families. The basic problem was that they were considered "Asiatic" by most potential resettlement countries, including the United Kingdom, Australia, and other British Commonwealth countries, and the United States. Destinations tried unsuccessfully by IRO were "Siam [Thailand] (1948), France (1948–49), French Morocco (1949), Alaska (1950), Paraguay (1950), Madagascar (1951) and Ceylon (1951)," and some Kalmyks had also made fruitless overtures to China for resettlement in Sinkiang (bordering Russia). They were "the people nobody wants," according to a sympathetic US reporter:

> ideal immigrants . . . except—well, they are yellow people. The Kalmucks, on one occasion, presented a humiliating brief to show that they weren't as yellow as other yellow peoples. They were, they claimed sort of roof-of-the world Nordics, with folk sagas like the Norse epics, forthright, non-wily natures, and, most pitiable assertion of all—the skin under their clothing was quite white, really. Even this self-debasement moved no nation.[23]

A common approach in individual applications was to argue that one's an-cestry was in fact as much Russian (hence European) as Kalmyk. This was sometimes complicated by the fact that the same person might, a few years earlier, have presented themselves as essentially Turkic in an effort to gain admittance to Turkey. In such cases, DPs wanting to get to the United States in the late 1940s/early '50s often made statutory declarations on their racial origins. Sandza Ahremov, for example, put on record that although his father was "Kalmock," his mother and all her family were Russian ("direct line white race," making him "more than 50 [percent] of white race blood.") For those who reached the interview stage, appearance played an important role. When DP Wladimir Andrejew applied for a visa to the United States in 1949, the vice consul noted in his favor not only that he had two Russian grandparents (the others were Kalmyk and Tatar) and a Ukrainian wife but also that he had fair hair, albeit with "Mongol eyes" and high cheekbones, and that his children "look even less Mongoloid than Andrejew himself." Another applicant with three out of four Kalmyks grandparents did not qualify—"looks Mongol."

The 1940 US Nationality Act, Section 303, limited the right to naturaliza-tion "only to white persons, persons of African nativity or descent, and descendants of races indigenous to the Western Hemisphere," thus apparently excluding Kalmyks. But the Kalmyks were not without well-wishers and useful contacts, particularly among church and human-rights groups, who ended up mounting a remarkable campaign in their support in the United States. The Tolstoy Foundation was active on their behalf, as was the New-York-based Russian American Union for Protection and Aid to Russians and the United Committee to Aid Russians in Europe. The Kalmyks gained friends and advocates in the World Council of Churches; the US Church World Service; the Brethren Service Commission (which had helped conscientious objectors during the war); the International Rescue Committee, founded in 1933 to help refugees from Nazi Germany; and the Unitarian Service Committee. They also had crucial support from within IRO in the person of Oliver Stone, a lawyer in its Washington office.

The American support group came together in the fall of 1950, after hearing from Kalmyk spokesman in Paris, Badma N. Oulanoff, that IRO—closing its own camps in Europe, and having failed to find resettlement for the Kalmyks— had told Kalmyk DPs that they were about to be "transferred to the German economy," that is, left to fend for themselves in Germany. The original focus of the American group's efforts was Paraguay, where it was hoped that the Kalmyks could move as a community to work in agriculture. But that came to nothing after unfavorable publicity in the local press (evidently on racial grounds).[24]

The second prong of attack was the US courts, where IRO (represented by Oliver Stone) brought an action against the Immigration Service's refusal to admit Kalmyks Dorzha and Samsona Remilev on grounds of race. The Remilevs were "first-wave" Russian-speaking Kalmyk émigrés, he a former officer in the Russian Imperial Army, who argued that the Kalmyks had been assimilated to a European culture (Russian) over three hundred years of living alongside and marrying Russians. Dorzha Remilev submitted a passionate statement describing himself as a "fighter against the communism" in Europe for thirty years who now longed to go to "free democratic America" and could not comprehend that "the country of true humanism and the creator of the Charter of Rights could refuse the shelter to a person only, because he is but half yellow, and not quite white."

Oliver Stone argued before the court on March 30, 1951, that the Immigration Service had wrongly classified the Remilevs as Mongol by race, and therefore ineligible, because they and the whole group of Kalmyks seeking resettlement in the United States were actually "of white race" ("more or less europeanized in terms of blood and custom") as a result of their long-term residence in Europe, regardless of the distant Mongol (Asiatic) origins they shared with Tatars, Hungarians, and others. The issue was ultimately decided for the Remilevs—and the Kalmyks as a whole, and by extension a range of other Soviet Turko-Tatar groups—after the intervention of Deputy US Attorney General Peyton Ford, who accepted Stone's remarkable arguments in toto. The decision that Kalmyks were "racially eligible for naturalization and, therefore . . . racially admissible into the US as quota migrants" was confirmed by the acting attorney general on July 28, 1951. The first contingent of Kalmyk DP immigrants arrived triumphantly in the United States in October, and by April 1952 a total of 560 Kalmyks had been resettled in the United States by the Church World Service, the Brethren Service Commission, and the Tolstoy Foundation.[25]

Security Concerns

Collaboration with the Nazis never entered the US discussion about the Kalmyks, although on a purely factual level it should have: they were as much involved as the indisputably "white" Latvian legionnaires, Ukrainian Waffen-SS, and Russian Vlasovites. The omission was partly a question of timing. By the 1950s, Western governments and IRO had largely lost interest in excluding collaborators, focusing instead on communist sympathizers. But even earlier, as we saw in the previous chapter, screening for collaborators had usually been perfunctory and ineffectual. When UNRRA tried its own screening operations in 1947, DP leaders bombarded the US military with complaints and "vitriolic attacks" about alleged left-wing bias, and UNRRA backed off. In the same year, Brigadier Fitzroy Maclean, sent by the British Foreign Office to screen Ukrainian Waffen-SS troops in Italy with a view to their resettlement in Britain, concluded that his mission was impossible. There was no evidence but the men's own statements, and, while all admitted to having fought with the Germans, they justified this in terms of their anti-Soviet convictions and denied any war crimes.

Rumblings of unhappiness about admitting DP collaborators as immigrants could be heard in the resettlement countries, mainly from Jewish communities, but their impact was relatively small. In the United States, an article published in the New York Post in 1948 alleged that most nonrepatriating DPs, apart from the Jews, were collaborators. But this provoked such a storm of criticism and repudiation from Catholic and Protestant organizations that Jewish organizations decided not to pursue the issue. In Australia, Immigration

Minister Calwell angrily rejected "gross libel on a fine type of people" and said it was unthinkable that Australia's selection teams in Europe would have admitted anyone "even remotely suspected of collaboration with our enemies." Australia's lack of official concern about collaborators (as well as a hint of uneasiness on the part of some staff on the ground) can be judged from the memoir of a Soviet Russian engineer who had worked voluntarily with the Germans during the occupation and left the Soviet Union with them when they retreated. As he remembered, the interviewer at the Australian consulate in Germany in 1949

> looked at my papers, then looked me straight in the eye, "You're a collaborator . . . You, an engineer, helped the Germans to fight against us." Certain that I would not get a visa, I replied curtly, "It depends how you look at it and who's talking." The interview was short and tense, but in the end the man simply said "Go to Australia."

A final medical check of DP immigrants bound for Canada in September 1947 from the British zone, found that twenty-five of them had either SS tattoos or marks of their removal under their left arms. It was two hours before scheduled departure, and, given that they had already passed both a security examination and a basic medical check, IRO's international movement officer did not feel "it was in my power to stop these men from sailing." It was decided, in the equivalent of a shrug, to send a list of their names to Canadian immigration officials and let them decide what, if anything, to do about the situation.[26]

Rejection was in fact relatively rare, and clear explanations of the reasons in individual cases much rarer. Australian selection teams in Europe reported rejecting only about only about five hundred of twelve thousand applicants on security grounds, but this would not have included the probably more frequent cases where another box was checked. According to data for the US zone of Germany, about 6 percent of almost seventy thousand DPs applying for resettlement as of late 1948 were rejected, but the proportion of these rejections that were security related is not clear. Certainly some applications aroused suspicion in the US Displaced Persons Commission and were carefully investigated. A DPC investigator, Norbert George Barr, interviewed such people in Germany, finding out a lot about the complexities of individual cases but often coming down on the positive side. A Latvian who admitted having belonged to the Latvian Waffen-SS but said that his service was not voluntary and did not involve combat duties convinced Barr of his good faith when he was able to produce his Latvian wartime ration book, showing that he had drawn civilian rations until February 1944, about the time when the Waffen-SS stopped relying on volunteers in Latvia and started drafting people. Barr concluded that "subject made the impression of a reliable individual and . . . does not appear to constitute a security risk." He was less favorably impressed by a Russian, claiming to be a stateless prewar émigré, who was suspected, along with his Soviet Tatar wife, of collaboration. Barr thought the pair of them had most likely been Nazi collaborators but did not consider the husband a security risk. The wife, in his view, was a sufficiently dubious character to warrant further investigation, but even with her his report does not come down unambiguously on the side of rejection.

Increasingly, the predominant security concern of the resettlement countries was keeping out DPs who were communists and communist sympathizers. That created major problems for former Soviet citizens who, back home, had been members of the Soviet communist youth organization, the Komsomol (a large proportion of the age group) or of the Communist Party itself (most of the professionals and managers). The US Internal Security Act of 1950 made it necessary for immigrants, including DPs, to sign "loyalty oaths"—affidavits affirming their lack of connection or sympathy with communism—on arrival. As Alexandra Tolstoy later testified, the act "effectively stopped" Russian DP immigration, albeit temporarily, with professionals coming under particular suspicion. In Britain, an internal review of Home Office screening of two hundred thousand refugees, DPs and immigrant workers who had entered the country between 1945 and 1950, found that it had been mainly directed against "Communists and pro-Soviet fifth columnists," with interviewers ignoring even direct admissions of wartime military collaboration.[27]

In October 1950, fifty DP passengers were held at Ellis Island under the Internal Security Act because they had served a "communist or totalitarian government." IRO was surely not happy with this, but its Washington representative merely suggested that "until [the] correctness [of] this provisional INS interpretation [of the] internal security act has been determined you may wish consider screening out such potential detainees" from future sailings. Given that UNRRA had been widely felt to have been discredited by suspicion of softness on communism, IRO's caution was understandable. IRO itself did not exclude communists or communist sympathizers, ipso facto, from eligibility for IRO care and resettlement. Individual countries might make this judgment,

IRO's top lawyer (Gustav Kullman) advised in March 1948, but as far as IRO was concerned

> neither actual affiliation to a communist party, nor adherence to the tenets of what is deemed to be communism by word or deed are relevant in the determination of eligibility. The overwhelming majority of DPs and refugees who prefer resettlement to repatriation may be held to be out of sympathy with the political tendencies now prevalent in their countries of origin in Eastern Europe, but it is by no means excluded that persons who were once affiliated with the communist party or who hold communist beliefs have demonstrated valid objections to return. Even high officials of several East-ern Governments, members of the Communist party have gone into political dissidence while on mission abroad. . . . It must therefore be held that IRO may well in the proper discharge of its constitutional obligations, declare Communists eligible and give them assistance in resettlement.

Such people, Kullman considered, should be "sharply distinguished from . . . the genuine political agent who attempts to penetrate into a country under the disguise of a genuine refugee," though he did not seem unduly alarmed even by that ("It is normal to expect that in mass movements [of refugees] as now organized by [IRO] a small number of such men may slip through."

This was still IRO policy early in 1949, at least for the purposes of in-house discussion. In November 1948, the issue was raised whether, when one na-tional resettlement mission turned down a DP applicant for security reasons, other potential resettlement authorities (notably, United States, Canada, and Australia) should be informed of this by IRO. A letter on the topic was drafted, probably by L. Michael Hacking (of IRO's Division of Mandate and Repara-tions, later its chief historian), with the accompanying comment "that Com-munists, as such, are not excluded from our concern; indeed, a number of the Spanish refugees specifically within our mandate may perhaps be Communists and, in principle, the possibility of a Trotsky-ite or a convert like Kravchenko being our concern should not be neglected. This matter of Communists should not be exaggerated; it does not often arise."

Hacking's conclusion was optimistic: there may not have been many com-munists in the DP camps, but there were plenty of problems involving *suspi-cion* of communism in the migrant screening process of individual countries. This presented IRO with a dilemma.

Was it IRO's responsibility to inform other countries of potential resettle-ment that a DP had been rejected on security grounds by the country of his first choice? It is clear from the (strictly internal) discussion of the issue that IRO staffers thought it more likely that such exclusions would occur as the result of anti-communist moral panic than anything more substantive. "It is a most regrettable fact," Hacking wrote, "that our experience with some security officers and organisations is such that we cannot unreservedly accept as accurate mere assertions from them," since these were often based on hearsay, not facts, and "grave injustice has been done to individuals as a result of unsubstantiated allegations." None of the other participants in the discussion was enthusiastic about IRO taking a proactive role in passing on security suspicions. "Might it not result in some kind of black list?" Marie D. Lane asked, while F. C. Blanchard from Planning and Field Services proposed that, to minimize damage to individuals, it would be prudent to "avoid such expressions as 'Communist' or 'Sympathizer', and replace them by 'undesirables.'"

The draft letter was never circulated, probably because IRO decided that sharing security rejections was a can of worms best left unopened. Its approach in practice seems to have been hands-off: if resettlement countries are worried about communists, let them do their own dirty work. Some staffers may have informally shared information about security rejections in their dealings with individual resettlement countries, but such information was likely to circulate among Western intelligence agencies in Europe, regardless of IRO's actions. The exact number of DPs rejected for resettlement for unstated security reasons will probably never be known. Along with the elderly, disabled, physically and mentally ill, "Asiatics," intellectuals, and the aged and infirm, they would form part of the "hard core" that, at the end of its tenure, IRO could find nobody to take.[28]

8

DPs Weigh the Options

GOVERNMENTS AND INTERNATIONAL ORGANIZATIONS might make plans, but for the DPs these were not hard-and-fast outcomes but rather parameters within which to operate. Resettlement might be on offer, but to where, and under what conditions? Repatriation remained a possibility for all Soviet DPs (broadly construed to include citizens of the Baltic states), but it was important to learn as much as possible about the fate of those who had gone before. Staying in Germany was the default option for DPs who were "hard cases" for resettlement, as well as those for whom staying suited a personal agenda.

By the late 1940s, it was time to decide on the next move, or at least to try to influence the decisions taken on one's behalf, for example, by national selection committees for resettlement. The occupation regimes were closing up shop, leaving a new and untested entity, the Federal Republic of Germany, to cope with in their stead. After many false alarms, IRO really was approaching the end of its mandate; funding was definitively running out. On top of that came the war scare over Berlin in 1948, which many DPs took to be the prelude to a Third World War and thus a sign that leaving Europe for a destination as distant as possible was prudent. All of this made choices about departure more urgent.

Some had already tried to take matters into their own hands. These included Jewish DPs departing more or less surreptitiously for Palestine and others taking up work opportunities in Belgium and the United Kingdom in the hope that these would lead to permanent residence. A group of Latvians acted even more dramatically, setting off for the Americas on their own initiative in small boats.

The first "Viking boats" manned by Baltic refugees sailed illegally from Sweden in the autumn of 1945, before the DP camp system in Europe was fully established. *Emma*, with sixteen passengers, made it to the United States in December of that year. Channeling the image of the Pilgrim Fathers, whose arrival in Massachusetts in the early seventeenth century was celebrated in the United States as a foundational event, *Newsweek*'s story on their arrival was headed "The Pilgrims." The boat had been one hundred and twenty-eight days at sea on a voyage that went from Scandinavia via Scotland and the Madeira Islands. It was followed by over thirty boats sailed across the Atlantic by DPs in the period 1945–51, most landing in US or Canadian ports but a few going to Argentina. Total arrivals, mainly Latvian and Estonian, numbered close to fifty thousand.

Half a century later, "boat people" arriving from across the seas to make unauthorized landings were generally treated as illegal immigrants who constituted a threat to the communities they sought to join. But these refugees were white and Christian, and the majority response was welcoming. "The sheer audacity of the Estonians in risking the Atlantic in tiny boats for a chance at freedom helped win the hearts, if not the minds, of many Americans," President Truman said of *Emma*'s arrival. "This is the pioneering spirit that built this nation." The refugees, mindful of the importance of a good public image, dressed their children in national costume, made sure to shave before public appearances, and described themselves as fleeing communism. Boston's Latvian Lutheran community took up their cause, and in 1948 future president Kennedy, then a Massachusetts member of the House of Representatives, weighed in on behalf of a Latvian group newly arrived in Provincetown whom some spoilsports had identified as Waffen-SS members.[1]

Looking for the Right Exit

IRO's resettlement program started in 1947. Given that the Soviet and Baltic DPs were in DP camps because they had decided not to repatriate, it is clear that most of them were hoping for resettlement. Their reasons, as they would give them to selection committees and immigration officials, involved a principled repudiation of communism. But the long interviews conducted by the Harvard Project revealed a more nuanced picture. Some DPs who described themselves as ideological anti-communists had quite positive things to say about the Soviet system in terms of welfare, education, and opportunity, while pragmatically recognizing that their own wartime actions and circumstances constituted a black mark that would be hard to live down in the Soviet Union. "Alexei," a skilled worker in his early thirties, told interviewers that he "would not have hesitated to return to the Soviet Union if he could have been certain of his safety," but, as a realist, he did not believe rumors about clemency for repatriates, all the more for someone like him, who had been a Red Army officer when he was taken prisoner of war by the Germans in 1942. Usually unspoken when DPs talked of their decision to not to repatriate, but nevertheless a factor in many decisions, was the fact that living standards were generally higher in the West than in the Soviet Union.

If repatriation was ruled out, that basically left resettlement or remaining in place and hoping for the best. Life in the DP camps was comfortable enough, but the camps were not going to last forever. As more and more DPs left, the psychological pressure on the rest to go became stronger. Doors for emigration out of Europe were open now, but they might close. Procrastination might mean that you missed the last boat (and the last free passage) and were stuck forever. Even German-speaking DPs, living outside the camps with jobs and prospects in Germany, felt the pressure to leave, as their DP friends steadily departed. Some were torn, recognizing that the new life (and new language) to be found abroad might in fact prove harder than the one they had. In the Russian Schlüsser family, living in Germany since the 1930s, Paul wanted to go, but his wife, with a good job as a doctor and an established set of friends, would rather have stayed, and so probably would their teenage children. In the Danos family, Olga would have preferred to stay, once she set up her church-sculpture business in Fulda, if Mischka had not been set on leaving. And Mischka himself, essentially a native speaker of German, finishing a PhD in physics with a supportive supervisor and a nascent reputation in his field in Germany, not to mention a German wife and generous in-laws, had plenty of reasons to remain—indeed, he would surely have had an easier time professionally if he had done so—but, as he later remembered, he felt he "had to" leave; living in Germany had somehow become intolerable for him.

IRO was surprised to find itself with new applicants in its final months, as refugees who had never applied for DP status before, fearing forced repatriation and perhaps also wary of accusations of collaboration, hurried to sign up so that they could be resettled. The number of DPs on the books in Germany and Austria actually rose by over 20,000 in the first half of 1948, despite 150,000 DPs being resettled or repatriated in that period. Most of the newly registered were Russians from the Soviet Union, according to an IRO report, probably former Vlasovites. With IRO due to go out of business, and the threat of US doors closing at the end of 1951, "a final rush . . . saw long lines winding through the camps. Some DPs were carried on stretchers. All clung to precious documents as they desperately tried to get papers approved before the end of 1951 and the US DP Act."[2]

"Everyone wanted to go to America," an IRO officer commented wryly. Apart from the generally held impression that it was the land of opportunity where the streets were paved with gold, individual DPs had their own particular reasons. Agathe Nesaule's Latvian mother was determined to go to the United States, despite the fact that her Lutheran pastor husband had been offered a church position in Latin America, because she saw it as the land of women's equality where her two daughters would get a good education. Mischka Danos wanted to go there to study physics.

The DP rumor mill, including the journals published by DPs in Russian and other languages, attempted to keep readers apprised of the current state of the options, as well as providing (often highly unreliable) information on life in the countries in question. The DPs "want to go to the America of their dream," an American journalist reported. "They fear that the Argentine is too far, Morocco too hot, Canada too cold, England too harsh, Australia too full of horned toads—which it is, according to a startled convoy of D.P. Lithuanians who lately arrived there." And Sweden, a gathering place for many Russian refugees though not formally in the IRO orbit, was simply "too close to Moscow."

Still, some had other preferences; and there was the additional consideration that other doors (Canada, Chile, Australia) opened before the United States, meaning that DPs had to make judgements about birds in the hand versus the bird in the bush. In Mischka Danos's circle, friends and acquaintances had already started to leave by 1948, and news was filtering back about their impressions of Argentina, Palestine, and Brazil. One of his closest friends was off to Australia with his extended family, including a brother-in-law who was a ship doctor and had actually seen the place; another had gone to Chile. His mother, Olga, favored Argentina—the language would be easier (given that she knew Italian), and she was "simply frightened of the US," which she saw as "a big factory populated with heartless robots."[3]

IRO tried to discourage DPs from playing the field. A Jew who had fled to China in the late 1930s accepted IRO's offer of resettlement from Shanghai to Israel, but when the ship reached Naples he disembarked and headed for a DP camp, hoping that IRO would resettle him in the United States, which had always been "his real objective." His ploy failed, as IRO refused to change his classification as "eligible for resettlement in Palestine only." A Soviet Russian returned from serving out a contract in Belgium was also knocked back: "Petitioner has been given the chance for resettlement and he has refused to accept the offers that were made to him because he unreasonably considered that they were not good enough." That was at the beginning of 1950. Eighteen months later, he might have had better luck, if he were prepared to take something other than his first choice: an internal IRO memo of mid-1951 noted that, while the US DP Commission usually refuses the returnees from Belgium, on the grounds that they were not in the US zone of Germany on the January 1, 1949, cutoff date, they still had a chance to get into Canada or Australia.

Even in the Jewish DP camps, many favored the United States, despite the Zionist pressure to go to Israel, since many had relatives there while Israel was an unknown and dangerous quantity. Where one had relatives in the world was a key consideration for all DPs. In the Jewish case, ambivalence about Israel as a destination is nicely captured in the probably apocryphal story of a Jewish DP in Belsen asked by the local Zionist committee why, given his sympathy for Zionism, he had registered for resettlement in Uruguay. The answer was simple: "the Jewish people should go to Palestine," no doubt about it, but, with his last surviving relative in Uruguay, "I am going to Montevideo."

One of the concerns about Israel as a destination was that there was a civil war going on there with the dispossessed Arabs. Joseph Berger's mother actually wanted to go to Israel but was persuaded that New York was safer. "Daddy's friend Moshe Granas advised him not to go there [to Israel]. 'In Israel the new immigrants sleep in tents,' he said. 'There is not enough milk for the children. There are no jobs for tailors like myself. I was afraid there would be another war with the Arabs.'" That changed her attitude. "I was tired of struggle," she told her son later. "Israel would be more struggle." Besides, there was an uncle in New York City.

For some, the important thing was to get out of Europe, to whatever destination would take them. Paul Schlüsser and his wife were professionals who had the triple problem of not strictly being DPs, having a German name, and, on Paul's part at least, having probably been a Nazi sympathizer. The family managed to get classified as "stateless" but failed in their applications for DP status. In his capacity as elected chairman of the Frankfurt Russian Immigrant Committee, Paul was in fact a virtuoso at the creation and presentation of (often false) documentation and helped many people jump through the required hoops in that capacity, but ironically he couldn't make it work for his own family. He did find "cousins" (first-wave Russian émigrés, actually unrelated) in New York who were willing to act as sponsors for the family's immigration to the United States, but the application was mysteriously rejected, despite the fact that he seems to have had connections with US counterintelligence. When in 1947 the Soviets arrested Paul's brother's wife in Berlin as a spy and sentenced her to twenty-five years hard labor, his fears of being targeted and kidnapped by the Soviet Union intensified, and he started desperately looking into other possibilities: Canada, Venezuela and even Morocco and Madagascar. But for several years nothing came through.

Against the odds, Ella Schneider's family was luckier. Her mother had been a Soviet citizen of German nationality when she crossed the border but decided it would be safer to register as Volksdeutsche (which, strictly speaking, she was not, being from the Soviet Union rather than from Eastern Europe, and not having been expelled from her country of origin). This protected her against repatriation but also made her ineligible for the DP camps. The family lived in inferior refugee camps in Bavaria and suffered discrimination from "real Germans." After a few years, she simply wanted to leave—"I don't care [where]. America, Canada, Australia, any of those places would be better than this place. Besides we are too close to Russia and the Communists. If they don't know where we are, then they cannot get us back. You know these Real Germans will sell us out to the Communists just to be rid of us." To their astonishment, and that of others in their camp, the Schneiders drew the lucky ticket: the United States gave their family of six a visa.[4]

Telling a Good Story

Whatever their preference, in order to get to the destination of choice, DPs needed to present themselves to a national selection committee or its equivalent and be accepted as a suitable immigrant. The most desirable characteristics in this process were youth, lack of dependents (or willingness to leave them behind), good health, laboring skills and experience, and anti-communism. It was preferable to have arrived in Germany not of one's own volition, that is, as a prisoner of war or Ostarbeiter; not to have a traceable record of collaboration; and to explain one's unwillingness to return to the Soviet Union in terms of a principled objection to the Soviet form of rule.

Since not everyone possessed these attributes in real life, DPs had to work hard in tailoring their resumés to suit the requirements of the resettlement countries. Naturally this often involved taking liberties with the truth, thus creating a huge workload for IRO's eligibility review board, which was the initial screener of applications passed on to the national selection committees. The board's chairman, Marcel de Baer, sighed at the "numberless adventurers, economic emigrants, deserters, collaborators, war criminals, and fugitives from justice, most of whom had forged papers, and all of whom claimed the status of political refugees," with whom he had to deal.

Two male DPs of Polish or Ukrainian origin, tailors by profession, presented themselves to the Brazilian selection committee as a farmer and carpenter respectively. They were admitted, and soon after entry, both were working at their real trade of tailoring, "extremely busy finishing the many orders they had received." Another Ukrainian DP was selected as a "gardener and machinery technician," although he was actually an intellectual with experience in editing and journalism. When sent along with six-hundred-odd other Ukrainian and Polish DPs to work in agriculture deep in the Brazilian provinces, he acquired a small plot of land in a Ukrainian colony, but soon found a job as editor of a Ukrainian paper and moved to the city.

Many false statements of identity and occupation were left to stand indefinitely, confounding all attempts to gather accurate statistics. Some were later corrected, however, usually by DPs applying for US entry who had been advised that such correction would further their chances. The corrections were made in statutory declarations before the legal counsellor of IRO that all DPs were invited to make; Tatiana Schaufuss of the Tolstoy Foundation reassured the US DP commissioner in 1950 that, since the establishment of the new immigration regime in the United States, thousands of Russians had "straightened out" their records.

One such record-straightener was a Russian from the Crimea, a former Ostarbeiter, who had registered himself and his Polish wife as Volksdeutsche, thinking that this would give them better options in Germany. But then came the possibility of emigration via IRO, for which Volksdeutsche were ineligible, so in 1949 they admitted the previous deception and registered as respectively Russian and Polish DPs. A former Soviet citizen from Taganrog, who had left the Soviet Union with the Germans in 1943 and identified himself to UNRRA as a Pole, wanted to be resettled in the United States and found a sponsor there via the Russian émigré paper *Novoe russkoe slovo*. This forced him to decide which identity to use for his US application:

> We had long been thinking about how to register. Whether or not to tell the truth, as it is, that we come from the Soviet Union, or still the old story that we are from Poland . . . A staff member of the IRO to whom we described our situation advised us that it would be better for us, if we would write the truth as this would be of the utmost importance for emigration to America. So we did and the future showed that this was the right decision.

Joseph Berger's parents, Polish Jews, had spent the war in the Soviet Union, where they married and where Joseph was born. Repatriated to Poland before moving on to Germany as DPs, they registered as Polish and destroyed his Soviet birth certificate and their own marriage records before applying for resettlement in the United States in 1950. His mother later told him that this was because of America's suspicion of communists and of any kind of Soviet connection: "If the Americans knew we had been in Russia during the war, they would not have let us come here."[5]

For a woman, marriage to the right person (or the right documents) was a good way to get out of Germany. We have already explored numerous cases of Russian/Soviet women marrying Frenchmen, Italians, and Americans and thus gaining legal residence in their countries. North American husbands were top of the line in terms of resettlement. But even marriage to DPs of other nationalities could be helpful. Anna Lipowoy, a Soviet citizen from Ukraine, had two children with another Soviet DP, registered as a Pole, who was blind and therefore had very limited resettlement prospects. They had not disclosed the marriage to UNRRA/IRO. Then in 1947 Anna saw a chance to link up with a Polish DP approved for resettlement in Australia; and after a quick, perhaps bigamous, marriage, she and her children were able to leave with him as a family. Her former husband complained to IRO, but it was too late—the ship had sailed.

In a similar fraud, a Romanian refugee (ineligible for DP status because his country had been on the Axis, not the Allied, side in the war) almost lost his wife and two children when the wife found a Yugoslav DP willing to take her and the children with him as his family when he resettled in Australia. But in this case, the real husband's complaint to IRO came in time for their departure to be halted at the Resettlement Processing Center at Fallingbostel just before sailing. A third case involving Ukrainians had its own twist, since the husband and wife had colluded in his departure to Australia with another woman, who was traveling as his wife. Before departing, he registered his original wife and their son as his sister and nephew, and the agreement was that, after settling in Australia, he would sponsor their emigration as family members. The original wife contacted the authorities some years after her husband's emigration, complaining about his failure to live up to their agreement.

The possibilities of creative self-fashioning practised by DPs are illustrated by the first boatload of 869 Baltic DPs shipped off to Australia on the SS *Gen. Heinzelmann* in October 1947. The selection committee wanted young single manual workers, particularly farm workers and builders' laborers (who "must have had some experience in these trades") along with "general labourers." Domestic servants and nurses were later added. Accordingly, the group that sailed from Bremerhaven officially comprised 142 farm workers, 76 builders' laborers, and 510 general laborers on board, along with a small female contingent of domestics, waitresses, and nurses. But by the time the boat arrived in Fremantle, a miraculous transformation had occurred: its DP passengers had become overwhelmingly middle class and educated.

"The girls almost without exception, are very good types indeed," reported the immigration official who interviewed them on board when their arrived. Among the "waitresses" were Lisa Melkus, a museum archeologist with very good English and a history degree from the University of Riga, and Irina Vasins, a philosophy graduate who had taught theology back home. The "domestics" were almost equally impressive: Stase Jakaviciute was a former art student at Kaunas University, while Helma Liiver had studied mechanical engineering as well as working for a year in Germany with the US Counter Intelligence Corps. The men "also appear to be, generally, very fine types," the immigration official noted, "who, although recruited as farm labourers, building labourers, etc., may have qualifications for much better types of work." Indeed, the male group included two sons of a Latvian diplomat who were both qualified as lawyers; two professional singers; an architect with English as one of the languages spoken at home; and a former director of the Estonian President's School for children with weak lungs, famed throughout Estonia.[6]

Finding Supporters and Sponsors

Helma Liiver's securing of a coveted place on the *Heinzelmann* was very likely helped by a recommendation from her US counterintelligence colleagues, and the same was surely true of many of the other women who reported having worked in Germany as typists for UNRRA and IRO. In going through the hoops of resettlement, it helped at every stage to have backing from a Westerner in Germany working with UNRRA, IRO, the occupation military, or foreign voluntary organizations like the JDC. This was an informal process, and only traces remain scattered through the archives. The Estonian Roman Koolmar, an architect by profession, thus hard to place, was recommended for resettlement as a "hardship case" in light of his large family (wife and four children) by Miss Berta Hohermuth, of IRO's migration office in the US zone, who noted that "he has been working with UNRRA and IRO since 1945." Miss Hohermuth also did her best for an Estonian bookkeeper (with a wife and three sons) who "is employed with IRO Augsburg since April 1947."

Resettlement in the United States required sponsors to give "assurances" of support for the future migration. These were of two types: those that named an individual DP, and the "blanket" assurances where the sponsor's details and requirements were filled in and it was up to selectors in Europe to find the appropriate people. American relief worker Kathryn Hulme gave a typically lively account of the latter process as it played out in her Wildflecken camp.

The voluntary agency people swarmed into the field with thousands of un-named assurances and began the greatest matching operation ever seen in human affairs—a veritable man-hunt to find in the flesh the exact type of worker described on each affidavit, with a family of specified size that would fit into the house or rooms held in readiness. At last we could see the usefulness of the exhaustive studies we had done on our DPs. If any volun-tary agency wanted, say fifty blue-eyed Balts in a hurry, each with a family of no more than six and dependents over sixty-five years of age, we could produce the people from our statistical Himalayas in nothing flat. You want a Lithuanian skilled in violin repair—we have him. You want a hundred tractor drivers—We have them . . . A neat clean old lady agile enough to be an invalid's companion—Here she is. We had everything the employer-citizens of the States were asking for and thousands more besides.

In the case of "blanket" sponsorship, the motives were various. A lot of sponsors were recruited by churches at parish level, with appeals to sympathy with suffering coreligionists, or else by émigré associations such as the Tol-stoy Foundation, looking to help fellow nationals. There were undoubtedly idealistic sponsorship offers from Quakers and the like. There were also offers with perhaps a tinge of idealism but also a real need for labor, for example, from farmers. And then, particularly from America's Deep South, there were sponsors who appear to have largely been after cheap indentured labor to replace that of blacks on cotton and sugar plantations, which subsequently became something of a scandal. In addition, there were some sponsors look-ing not just for labor but for brides. In the US context, it was not possible to state this overtly, but in Southern Rhodesia—where IRO had a presence ser-vicing over sixteen thousand DPs, mainly Poles, refugees brought to East Africa pro tem until they could be settled elsewhere—IRO implicitly con-doned it. When local (white) prospectors wrote to IRO camp commanders in the territory "proposing marriage to any suitable girl who was prepared to share their life," these proposals were duly posted, without IRO comment, on the camp's notice boards. It was believed that more than three hundred marriages resulted.[7]

With regard to individual sponsorship, staffers of the voluntary organizations often "helped to write to relatives in America, even to remote shirttail relatives, as potential sponsors." But other DPs (like Schlüsser) had the savvy to take the initiative themselves, looking either for actual relatives or for people (usually of the same nationality) who were willing to claim to be such. The NTS journal *Posev* released a special guidebook on emigration, specifying opportunities in different countries of destination and listing addresses of important organizations concerned with Soviet DPs in Europe and elsewhere. One would-be US immigrant, perhaps wishing to burnish his anticommunist credentials, cited *Posev* as his source of information when he wrote to Kapatsinskii's New York-based United Committee to Aid Russians in Europe seeking help with sponsorship. This was one of many enquiries the Committee received from Russian DPs in Europe. And not just Russians: an elderly Latvian of Orthodox faith wrote begging for help with emigration early in 1949, saying he was at the end of his tether from unemployment and "the threat from the east." A Russian who identified himself as a DP camp administrator from the US zone wrote to Kapatsinskii to plead his own cause as a potential US immigrant, along with that of his "sister-in-law" (a DP from Kiev with a child born after the war), not-ing as a self-recommendation that he had worked for two and a half years with UNRRA and IRO and was a friend of Archbishop Serafim, metropolitan of the Orthodox Church in Germany. The Tolstoy Foundation's office received similar petitions, also clearly tailored for what the writer hoped was the appropriate model. One Soviet DP, whose IRO identification was as a Ukrainian wartime Ostarbeiter, presented himself to the Tolstoy Foundation as a Russian POW and Vlasovite fighter against communism.

The Danoses, as usual, were lucky—but whereas in general their luck was often partly due to Olga's resourcefulness, in this case, it was also a virtuous act on her part that was responsible. In Riga, back in 1941, she had saved the life of a young Jew, Simon Mirkin, by employing him and sheltering him in her house and thus saving him from the slaughter of Jews from the Riga ghetto. After the war, having survived Stutthof concentration camp, he worked as a DP in the American zone for HIAS and the US Army, and this enabled him to get to America early, in 1947, on the initial Truman quota. A few years later, now living in New York, he offered to sponsor Olga, and subsequently Mischka and his new German wife, as immigrants under the DP Act. It was this offer that tipped the scales for Olga, finally persuading her to overcome her distaste for the United States and give in to Mischka's pressure to go there rather than to Latin America.[8]

Collaborators known to have borne arms under German command in theory posed a particular problem for IRO and the resettlement countries. In practice, they also enjoyed considerable protection in high places and from international intelligence agencies. Members of the Rogozhin Corps, for example, were ineligible for DP status on grounds of collaboration, but we have already seen how IRO covertly arranged their departure from the Kellerburg camp in the British zone of Austria to the United States, courtesy of the Thomas Cook travel agency (the arrangements were so secret that even the group's leader, Colonel Anatoly Rogozhin, believed that some private group in England, not IRO, was paying).

Vlasovites were in a similar predicament, stuck for some years in special camps from which, according to one report, "you could get out only by going to work in the Belgian mines." But relief was coming for them too, as IRO liberalized its approach to eligibility of collaborators. Ivan Bogut, a former Soviet POW who was probably a Vlasovite, and Yuri Domansky, formerly of the Russian Corps, were both unexpectedly summoned in the early 1950s and told to get ready for immediate resettlement in Australia.

These two were the kind of collaborators whose wartime choices could be seen as anti-Soviet rather than pro-Nazi, but others like the Russian orientalist Nikolai Poppe were liable for more serious war crimes accusations. Poppe had left his position at Leningrad University in 1941 to go to the Caucasus, where he offered his services to the occupying Germans as an expert on the local topography and peoples. When the Germans withdrew in 1943, he went with them to a position at the Wannsee Institute in Berlin, a center of intelligence research on the Soviet Union. After the war, he found himself in the British zone, hunted by the Soviets, but the British refused to hand him over and instead enlisted the cooperation of US State Department officials, including George Kennan, to have him shipped off secretly to the United States under a new identity.

Ukrainian Mykola Lebed is said to have been responsible for organizing the killing of thousands of Jews and Poles as commander of the Bandera OUN group during the war. In Rome at the end of the war, he contacted the American military offering his files on communist agents in Ukraine, his contacts with anti-communist fighters behind the iron curtain, and information about Ukrainians in the DP camps in exchange for US protection. The offer was accepted. When Soviet agents discovered his presence in Italy, the American army moved him and his family to Munich, where American intelligence recruited him to work on the organization of underground resistance groups in Ukraine. In the fall of 1949, with a false name, false papers, a concocted past, and Army CIC clearance that was obtained with the assistance of the CIA, Lebed secured a visa as a displaced person and migrated to the United States.

Several leaders of the émigré anti-Soviet group NTS, actively involved with the CIA in the early postwar years, found themselves offered US immigration visas that, in their telling, came as a surprise. Boldyrev was one; another was the NTS president, Viktor Baidalakov. As one of his close associates related, "something . . . quite strange, happened . . . In February 1947 [Baidalakov] un-expectedly received a telegram from a woman representing the World Council of Churches under the American consulate in Frankfurt" telling him that "an affidavit for his migration to the United States . . . had arrived." Given that (as a collaborator) he had been deprived of DP status in Germany, he could not pass up the opportunity and went to the consulate to fill out his questionnaire. The consul, evidently unaware of what was presumably a CIA operation, refused him a visa, but a few days later had to back down and issue it, with the result that Baidalakov set sail for New York in April 1947.

It was, in fact, CIA policy to reward its Russian collaborators (many of whom had formerly collaborated with the Nazis) with resettlement in North America or Australia, often under new names. This was initially done covertly, but it acquired legal status when Congress, on the CIA's request, established a new category of immigrant, the "Displaced Persons National Interest case," for émigrés "whose presence in the US was deemed in the national interest as a result of the prominent or active part they played in the struggle against Communism." The CIA had asked for authorization of the entry of fifteen thousand CIA-sponsored refugees, over and above those coming by regular channels under the DP Act, but Congress whittled this down to five hundred. Private organizations like the Tolstoy Foundation, however, were able to pick up some of the slack.

For those collaborators who had missed out, there was further help available when the US Refugee Relief Act of 1953 offered 205,000 "special non-quota immigrant visas" to refugees and escapees, the latter defined as "any refugees who, because of persecution of fear of persecution on account of race, religion or political opinion, fled from the Union of Soviet Socialist Republics" or other communist states. This was particularly aimed at recent defectors but also covered any remaining DPs with problematic pasts, whose departure from the Soviet Union, whether or not under German patronage, was now reinterpreted positively as flight from Communism. About seven thousand Russians appear to have entered the United States under the act.

The CIA used it to bring a number of leaders from its stable of anti-communist Russians in Germany to the United States. Among Russian anti-communists arriving in 1955 was the prominent Vlasovite Nikolai Troitskii, the first director of the CIA-supported Munich Institute for Study of the History and Culture of the USSR, who, ironically, went to the United States after resigning his job in Munich in protest against "open interference by the Americans" in the institute's affairs.[9]

Belatedly Choosing Repatriation

After the resettlement programme was established, the Soviets continued their efforts to persuade Soviet DPs in Germany and Austria to return, though now with an extra edge of anger in the propaganda and warnings of the dire fate that awaited those who accepted resettlement to distant places. In one propaganda leaflet distributed among DPs in Germany, "Nikolai P," recruited to the French Foreign Legion in Indochina, is quoted as writing to a friend in West Germany of the terrible conditions he found himself in: unbearable workload, pressure to sign new contracts, etc. the resettled DPs were allegedly mercilessly exploited as labor, not treated as human beings. "In USA, Brazil, Canada, Morocco—everywhere the DP remained just as rightless and humiliated as in the camps of West Germany."

Another leaflet cited the regret of a resettled Russian DP who wrote to his father in Kursk of his misery in "this cursed Venezuela. Don't believe their promises." "They want to take you over the ocean and promise all kinds of good things. But you know that there even without you there are millions of unemployed. They need you as cheap labor force in the mines, for breaking stones, and in plantations." The commissions just pick the physically strong. You will have all the rights "of a healthy horse, which is valued as long as it can work. What awaits you is homeless wandering without family and tribe." Return to the native land, the leaflet urged, where "among those close and dear to you, you will find your real human happiness."

Voluntary repatriation was very much a minority choice in the later 1940s and early '50s, but it was a choice nevertheless made by about nine thousand Soviet citizens—Russians and Ukrainians, as well as citizens of the former Baltic states and other republics, on whom, by happy archival accident, we have quite detailed individual data from their reentry interviews. The largest contingents came from the British and American occupation zones of Germany and from the United Kingdom, whose contribution of over one thousand voluntary returners included repatriating Anders Army personnel and disappointed *Westward Ho!* recruits.[10]

It wasn't always easy to repatriate, given Allied tacit noncooperation and the active hostility of many camp administrations. No doubt exaggerating a bit along the way, many returning DPs, interviewed on arrival, told harrowing stories of the difficulties they had faced in trying to contact Soviet representatives or even getting their addresses. A number had had to make long journeys to Soviet consulates, in the absence of a functioning repatriation mission nearby. A young man who had been in a DP camp in Italy said that DPs there "want to repatriate, but the Italian government doesn't let them out . . . I got out of the camp by deceit—by registering with IRO for emigration. They took me to Rome, and there I went to the Soviet Mission." A returnee from the French zone of Germany had a comparatively easy exit, managing—though not without difficulty—to make contact with a Soviet repatriation officer visiting his camp. Even so, the camp administration tried to talk him out of it and impede his departure. An adventurous teenage girl, failing to make contact with repatriation officials, illegally crossed the border into the Soviet zone on her own.

One might expect that returning DPs would tell their Soviet interviewers a story of Soviet patriotism and ideological commitment—in other words, the opposite story told by their DP counterparts presenting themselves to resettlement selection committees. This happened only rarely, however, and was greeted with skepticism when it did. A habitual criminal, whose repatriation had been a choice of the Soviet Union as a free man or imprisonment for theft in the British zone, stated that "everything foreign had already become disgusting to me, I couldn't bear their 'democracy,' I wanted to live like a human being," but his interviewer was unimpressed. The same was true when a repatriating daughter of the Latvian artistic intelligentsia, full of anger against her parents and their elite friends in the camp, claimed that she had come "to start a new life in a new country, the Soviet Union" out of a newfound sympathy with communism. One DP repatriating from London, Grigory Salnikov, took the trouble to write up an account of the joy he felt on the boat at escaping the horrors of capitalism and returning to the best country in the world (clearly hoping to become a poster boy for the Soviet repatriation campaign), but his interviewer brusquely dismissed it as of no interest.

The DPs who repatriated to the Soviet Union in the late 1940s and early 1950s had obviously taken time to make up their minds. In explaining their decisions, many spoke of worry about what would happen to DPs once IRO pulled out, the camps were closed, and residents were left to fend for themselves, while others expressed fears of resettlement in strange, faraway countries. A Lithuanian man said he decided to repatriate in order to avoid "forced emigration to Australia, to which he was obliged to agree in February 1949 as otherwise he would not have been accepted in the camp." A Latvian who returned to an IRO camp in Hamburg after a stint working in the French mines said that he had almost no friends left in the camps because they had all emigrated. But he was deterred from doing the same when he received a letter from a DP who had gone to Australia and regretted it: "They live in tents [there] and have completely forgotten what a human house looks like," his friend wrote. (Tents—including tents in Palestine—often featured in such reports of unhappy resettlement.)

The weighing of the options evident in this case could often be glimpsed in the repatriates' reentry interviews. Among the "pull" factors cited as drawing them back to the Soviet Union, the strongest was the desire to reunite with family back home. Parents were most often mentioned by the young, spouses sometimes. Several women said that they returned because of the torment of having left a child behind when they were forcibly taken to Germany. A few repatriates mentioned that their decision to return had been clinched by hearing a personal appeal from a family member broadcast on Moscow Radio or receiving a letter from parent, spouse, or child back in the Soviet Union. But such appeals—often regarded in the DP camps as falsifications, written on command—were not necessarily taken as gospel. One man said he had discounted a number of letters he had received, allegedly from family, asking him to return, because he thought they were just propaganda documents, but then received a long and circumstantial letter from his daughter that he thought was genuine, which had determined his choice.

Among "push" factors, the most frequently cited with lack of employment prospects or unsatisfactory employment in Europe. This was usually described in nonemotive language, unlike the horror stories of the propaganda leaflets. Judging by the sample in these files, one of the experiences most likely to produce subsequent return was accepting contract work in the Belgian mines in 1947. Conditions of work were bad, but, in addition, the original contracts were expiring in 1949, and it was hard to get other work in Belgium because of the current economic crisis.

Another "push" factor quite often mentioned by those who had lived outside the camps was suspicion of being Soviet spies. DP women who had married foreigners and gone to live in their country were particularly vulnerable, especially if their marriages broke down. A repatriating Estonian claimed to have actually been arrested and imprisoned as a spy in Sweden in 1949 after he visited the Soviet embassy to enquire about repatriating. A Jewish nurse from Voroshilovgrad who had gone to England to work said that her decision to repatriate was made after she was denounced in the local Ukrainian community as a "Bolshevik, a Russian spy" as well as being a victim of antisemitism in this community.

Complaints about material conditions in the DP camps were rare in the re-entry interviews of 1948–50. But there were other kinds of problems in the West, particularly for those living outside the camps. DPs were not popular with the local German population, especially blue-collar workers, and one Latvian repatriate reported being taunted with comments like "Why do you sit in camps?" "Why don't you go back home?" and "Are we going to have to feed you for long?" Swedes were suspicious of foreigners, one Estonian returnee said, and paid them lower wages.[11]

As we have seen in an earlier chapter, some repatriates recounted their international travels as adventure stories, explaining their return simply of terms of their having had their fun and now being ready to return. Occasionally, the decision to return was described more or less as happenstance, as in the case of the young man who, after various adventures, went to Italy to try to enlist in the French Foreign Legion, settling for a DP camp and subsequent repatriation only when this proved impossible. But many repatriates made clear that the decision to repatriate had been a tough one, and they were still scared about its consequences. They reported being subjected to, and scared by, talk in the DP camps that if they returned to the USSR they would be arrested and sent to Siberia; and some said that IRO personnel had given similar advice. A fair number said frankly that this had led them to delay their return, and that even now they still had traces of apprehension. A twenty-three-year-old, who had been working at a textile plant in Poland with many other Soviet girls (most married to Poles), said the girls were discouraged from returning by rumors that life was hard in the Soviet Union, "that the culture is very backward, that the women's hair would be cut off at the border, so that they don't bring back foreign hairdos, and that children will be taken from their mothers."

Frankness, however, had its limits. None of the 1949–50 repatriates mentioned the Soviet famine of 1946–47, particularly devastating in the Ukrainian lands from which many of them had come, as a reason for earlier nonreturn, although it surely was a significant factor in discouraging repatriation in previous years. Famine was clearly not a permissible topic, along with anything related to politics (Stalin, the Communist Party, the secret police). The DPs' mood during the process of repatriation was often described as nervous and jumpy. The Repatriation Agency in Moscow frequently had to complain to the security services about the impact on apprehensive repatriates of individual arrests by the MGB at the collection points, leading not only to low morale but also to flight. Many repatriates remained apprehensive that they were actually being tricked and would be sent to Siberia right up to the time of arriving back in their home region. Even then, they were worried about whether they would find their families, get work, and generally reintegrate, concerns their interviewers often noted sympathetically. A buoyant mood and joyful arrival was evidently sufficiently rare for interviewers to report it with satisfaction, as when twenty-seven-year-old Vera Moskaltsova was "joyfully greeted" by family, friends, and neighbors on her arrival home in Makeevka. She may well have been joyful at being reunited with her seven-year-old son; the only downside was that she had had to come back without her Polish husband, who was still waiting for a visa.[12]

As with those seeking resettlement in the West, the DPs returning to the Soviet Union faced an audience that might be skeptical about their account of the process that got them to Germany in the first place, preferably avoiding any suggestion of collaboration, and they basically told the same story as the resettlers: "the Germans took me against my will." The repatriates had another potential hurdle to get over, namely, why they had taken so long to decide to return, but this was dealt with perfunctorily in most cases, and sometimes not at all. The interviewers, it seemed, had little difficulty understanding why the DPs might have stayed away. Those who provided a detailed explanation were generally women, attributing their actions to a failed marriage or relationship to a man, usually a foreigner, and these stories seemed to be insistently offered rather than solicited by the interviewers. It was taken as a given (for all the long-established Soviet rhetoric about women's emancipation) that in any marriage or relationship, the man's interests were decisive, and this applied even when it meant that the woman went to live in a foreign country with her husband. A common story was that of a Soviet woman taken to Germany as an Ostarbeiter during the war and who while there met, married, and had a child by a DP of another nationality (Polish, Yugoslav, Czech, or sometimes Italian), moved with him to his country after the war, and was then left stranded when the marriage broke up (or he died, or she found he had married her bigamously and had another family at home).

Among the men, many were repatriating because of criminal charges—
either to get out of prison in the Allied occupation zones or because a criminal
record made resettlement unlikely. A former Russian POW who admitted
"systematic" engagement in criminal activity, including armed robbery and
two murders during his time in the British zone, was reported by his Soviet
interviewer to be "afraid to emigrate" and therefore deciding to "hide from his
crimes by way of returning to the native land." Two men in their twenties, released from prison in the French zone, were characterized by the interviewer
as "habitual thieves." Another, the son of a Soviet journalist killed by the Germans in Ukraine in 1941 according to his story, spent the war imprisoned, first
in Bucharest and then in Prague, but escaped in January 1945 and fled to Italy,
where he was imprisoned again for assault. He decided to repatriate on his
release from Italian prison in 1950.[13]

Contrary to the general picture that citizens of the Baltic states, independent
before the war, were unlikely to want to repatriate to the Soviet Union, the
admittedly small sample provided by 1949–50 reentry interviews shows Latvians, Lithuanians, and Estonians to be *over*represented, at almost a quarter of
the total. There were manual workers among them, but the Baltic group was
overall better schooled than other Soviet repatriates (no doubt reflecting
higher educational standards, at least in Latvia and Estonia) as well as including a higher proportion of intellectuals and professionals. They included a few
quite puzzling cases, such as the young Latvian who threw up his studies of
medicine at the University of Tübingen to repatriate, citing difficulties with
his studies and a fear of "moral humiliation" if he emigrated and had to work
in some degrading job, as he had heard happened to some DP students who
went to Canada. His behavior in the transit camp was described as "withdrawn," and he refused to be interviewed about his experiences on radio.

Most of the Baltic DPs claimed to have been taken to Germany as Ostarbeiter (a claim less likely to be true than in the case of Ukrainians and southern
Russians). But they also often gave August–September 1944 as the time of departure, which strongly suggested a voluntary departure with the Germans as
the Soviet Army approached. Of those who made this claim, one Latvian man
said he had been drafted into the German army in Latvia and left with his unit
in August 1944, while others said they had served in the German Army, but in
noncombat roles. An Estonian nurse said she had been taken to Germany along
with the hospital where she was working, as did a laundress with regard to her
Army laundry. But not everybody thought it necessary to claim coercion in
their departures. One Latvian woman in her twenties said that she and her

parents, from whom she was now estranged, had left Riga voluntarily. A Latvian man, born in 1912, actually admitted to volunteering for the German Army in 1942 and fighting with it on the Eastern Front before being wounded and de-mobilized. (His interviewer clearly thought him a tricky character but seems to have waved him through regardless.)[14]

The Process of Departure

Getting accepted for resettlement in a particular country might seem like a happy end, but for some DPs it was the beginning of months of anxiety. There's many a slip twixt the cup and the lip, as the old proverb says. That was some-thing to which many DPs, even with all the documents in order and their luggage packed, could attest from hard experience. The actual process of de-parture was quite extended—from three to more than twelve months—which meant that all kinds of unexpected things could happen.

Criminal convictions were one thing that could throw a spanner in the works. A young Latvian woman with a child born during the war, and a postwar relationship with an American Army officer that went nowhere, had received a sponsorship assurance from her more fortunate sister, who had married a US Army lieutenant and moved with him to New Mexico. But the whole process was thrown into jeopardy by her conviction in Germany for using a forged ra-tion card. IRO's legal advisor recommended that this not be held against her in her resettlement, but that was up to US immigration, so who knows what hap-pened. A Russian was held up for three months in a transit camp near Hamburg while German police investigated an accusation of black-marketeering against his former German employer. In the files of the special investigator for the DPC, the most common holdup was a record of theft as a DP, although the files included one case of a Latvian doctor arrested on suspicion of performing an abortion (though later acquitted) in the French zone of Germany, to whom the investigator gave a positive endorsement.

There were also the shoals of "moral turpitude" to steer through. A thirty-three-year-old Lithuanian professional woman, divorced with an eight-year old son, was sponsored for immigration by a former DP whom she planned to live with and marry, but she ran into trouble with INS (the Immigration and Naturalization Service) in 1950 when it suspected that she was entering the US for immoral purposes. Other "moral turpitude" refusals—an eighteen-year-old caught picking grapes, a woman who had taken a dress from a bombed-out dwelling which she was using as a temporary refuge, a DP who had thrown a stick that accidentally killed a chicken—were overthrown after voluntary societies appealed them on the DPs' behalf.

Health was a frequent cause of setbacks and delays. One family member's negative result from a TB X-ray, or even the discovery of old TB scars, could stop a whole family, all set for departure, in its tracks. NTS leader Prianishnikov's departure for the United States was suddenly thrown into jeopardy by a TB diagnosis, but, perhaps thanks to American intelligence connections, the outcome was unexpectedly positive: he was sent off to Switzerland for treatment for a few weeks, and the family duly departed for the United States on his return. Worst of all was when one family member received a last-minute rejection on health grounds that put the departure in question. A Latvian family, accepted for resettlement in "all good faith" in May 1949, were in Naples awaiting embarkation for Australia when it was discovered that one of the children was "showing signs of spastic palsy," which disqualified the whole family. In other cases, where one child in the family was blind or otherwise physically or mentally disabled, the family was encouraged to put them in an institution in Germany and proceed for resettlement.

Olga Danos had a last-minute health crisis. Already cleared for emigration to the United States, she developed a stomach problem, which she tried to ignore, treat herself with homoeopathic medicine. After hemorrhaging for weeks, she finally went to a doctor in Fulda and was immediately put in hospital and told she had to have an operation. Her letters to Mischka are characteristically lacking in self-pity (luckily none of her family was around, since "I don't know how to put up with being sick with elegance—I mean spiritual elegance"), but it was a terrible blow, taking up all her savings and more, as well as putting her ability to depart in question. Her summons to the transit camp in Butzbach—one hundred kilometers away by train, with a long walk at the end—came shortly after her release from hospital, but she somehow made it, "miserable as a dog," as she wrote to Mischka. "I don't know why I have to go to America. And yet I am going to do it."[15]

After an anxious two months waiting for a response to their visa application for the United States, the Schneider family finally, in January 1951, "received a big brown envelope stamped Dringend [urgent]. The postman on his bicycle delivered it personally. Pages of precise instructions, what we should do and not do, pack or leave behind, in order to report to Munich to start processing for our trip to the land of our hopes and dreams. They gave us six weeks' notice." Her stepfather quickly made a wooden box for their possessions: "Mama loaded it with pictures, papa's Hohner accordion and the few thin summer dresses we owned. We had no shoes to pack. We wore the only shoes we owned. We took our aluminium pots from Russia, lace tablecloth, my real papa's embroidered Russian shirt (just in case he returned from Siberia some-day!) . . ." With the last money we had, Papa bought two suitcases to carry a change of clothing for each of us."

> At the immigration collection point in Munich while waiting, Mama and Papa became very uneasy. All around us were people from Russia, as well as from Romania, Czechoslovakia, Poland, and Yugoslavia, which were now occupied by the Russians. Surely they were not going to load us on trucks and carry us back to Russia like the Americans did to those people in that guarded camp near Passau? Even though it was 1952, none of us really knew what Americans were liable to do . . . But the die was cast. It was too late. Whatever the outcome, we had no choice but to deliver our collective lives into American hands.

In Funk Kaserne, they were given a room of their own, and incredible and abundant American food like pancakes, ice cream, and oranges. ("Papa was still suspicious. They are fattening us up before the slaughter, he insisted.") Then came the last-minute crisis: Ella's mother was discovered to be pregnant, and the Americans would not admit pregnant women. Her mother and step-father decided on an abortion, and somehow it was procured in time for the family to sail on schedule.

For Mischka Danos and his German wife, Helga, it took eight months to go through all the hoops for US Immigration, even with sponsorship from Olga's protégé Simon Mirkin and the change in US policy that made Helga's teenage membership in the BDM (the Nazi youth society for girls) no longer an obstacle. It was March 1951 when they received their letter announcing that they were cleared for resettlement in the United States and instructing that within fourteen days they must register with the resettlement office in Mannheim, submit all documents, go through medical inspection, and then "wait to be assigned transport." Mischka's job in Heidelberg ran out in June. But in mid-July, although they had been assigned a departure number, they still had not been called for medical inspection. The reason for the holdup turned out to be a bureaucratic technicality: they were departing from the American zone, but Mischka's DP registration had been in the British zone. This was somehow cleared up, and a final security screening took place in late August. In mid-October their clearance went through, and they were told to report to Ludwigsburg with luggage for departure on the next transport to

United States. They sailed out of Bremerhaven on the *General Ballou* on November 3, 1951.

Of all the last-minute setbacks, death had to be the worst. Paul Schlüsser's long wait had finally ended when Australia gave a provisional acceptance to the family: two parents, a young adult daughter, and three adolescent children. After an interview in Butzbach with an Australian immigration officer, for which the whole family dressed in their Sunday best, they were cleared for departure and set off to Bremerhaven with all the possessions they were allowed to bring, waiting for the next available boat. But then tragedy struck: at the Bremerhaven camp, fifty-year-old Paul had a heart attack and died. This plunged everything into turmoil, not only because Paul had been the family member who was really set on leaving but also because his death had technically disqualified the family from entrance to Australia: immigration rules required at least an equal ratio of working adults to dependents, but Paul's death had changed the family ratio from 3:3 to 2:3. While Paul's widow struggled to decide whether she wanted to go or not (job and apartment in Germany given up, possessions sold), the family was shunted off to another holding camp pending an official decision on eligibility. In the end, unhappily and uncertainly, they sailed off to Australia, a distant and unknown country that none of them had any active desire to live in.[16]

The Schlüsser family's voyage must have been a particularly miserable one. But in any case, the Australian trip, which took about a month in overcrowded and unsanitary former troop ships that were often ready for the scrapheap, tended to be harrowing for everybody but young single people who made their own fun. The Latin American run was not much better. Valentin Lekhno, a White Russian lawyer from Kharkov, made the voyage from Bremen to Rio de Janeiro in January 1949 in a rundown British ship with more passengers than berths. IRO put him in charge of a fractious bunch of DPs on board, most of them Soviet peasants in an earlier life, to handle all the quarrels and complaints about poor food and sanitary conditions. His account contains the unexpected information that, although DPs were supposedly allowed only essential luggage, a number of people brought sewing machines, and two entrepreneurial types managed to get on board the equipment for an entire knitting factory and radio workshop.

In the confined circumstances aboard ship, intergroup tensions could mount and denunciations multiply. On the long Australian run, the usual conflicts were between Jewish and Baltic DPs, who accused each other of being respectively communists and Nazis. The same scenario played out on the *Marine Fal-*

con, sailing from Hamburg to New York in 1949 with 550 passengers, when a Polish Jewish passenger accused another passenger, a Lithuanian DP, of having been a Nazi storm trooper, personally responsible for his own incarceration in a concentration camp. US Immigration investigated and concluded that the Lithuanian had indeed served as a concentration camp guard in Poland and moreover had lied about the date of his enrolment in the Waffen-SS (1941, not, as he had stated, 1944). He was then held imprisoned, but after a change of US policy on admission of Baltic Waffen-SS members he was "paroled to the home his wife and children lived at in Bridgeport, Connecticut." It was by this time too late for him to be admitted to the United States as a displaced person, but intervention by his local congressman secured his admission "under the Lithuanian quota."

The trip across the Atlantic was comparatively short, and children sometimes enjoyed it. "To me, the ship was like a house," Ella Schneider remembered. "It had everything: bedroom, bathroom, playrooms, kitchen, shower rooms, reading rooms, and so many more rooms. American cowboy films were shown nightly in a huge auditorium on the upper deck," and there was even a library where she could chat to her friends. She did not mind their beds being three floors down and stacked in threes but rather recalled the "good mattresses" and the "great big bathroom": "we could shower with hot running water and good-smelling non-eye-burning soap anytime we wanted."

The Danos family's experiences were less positive. Olga's trip across the Atlantic late in 1950 was on a former troop ship filled with DPs living in sordid conditions, with fetid air, pushing and shoving at meals, and vomit in the hallways. After twenty-four hours of acute sea-sickness in her top bunk, and still recovering from her operation, Olga spent most of her time on deck, "look[ing] for hours at the water and the sky," wearing two jackets and her fur coat. Misha and his wife Helga made the same trip a year later on another former troop ship carrying over a thousand DPs to New York. The *General Ballou* had come direct from Korea, where war had recently broken out, adding to sense of a world on the brink of another catastrophe. The gently bred German Helga found the voyage nightmarish: all the vomiting was disgusting, especially at meals; the American food was strange (no sauerkraut, pickled cucumber or herring); and their fellow passengers—mainly Polish, Ukrainian and Russian DPs—were "impertinent and undisciplined," "almost without exception very primitive and dirty people," and "Germany can be happy" to have been able to offload them to America. Despite the ready availability of showers with running hot water, "70 [percent] of the people on this ship have still not bathed a single time during our trip. You can probably imagine how badly these people stink," she wrote indignantly to her parents.

For those going back to the Soviet Union, the Baltic trip was less of a physical ordeal. As the SS *Sestroretsk* steamed from London to Leningrad across the Baltic, repatriate Grigory Salnikov spent his time on literary composition, describing his happiness at leaving the "rotten and decaying" world of the West after almost six years; the pleasure of hearing "joyful Russian songs" over the ship's loudspeaker system; and the envy with which English passengers looked at the homeward-bound Soviets. This was a bravura performance for official ears, covering who knows what mixed emotions.

The DPs headed for resettlement had mixed emotions, too. Olga Danos's sponsor Simon Mirkin, meeting her at the dock in New York, launched into a whole spiel to waiting reporters about how a poor Jewish refugee had "paid his debt of gratitude to a Christian woman" who had saved his life in Riga in 1941 by sponsoring her immigration to the United States. The *Spokane Daily Chronicle* ran the story, but Olga seems to have been unimpressed: "a complete novel," she called Mirkin's performance in her letter to Mischka back in Germany.

The standard story of immigrant arrival to the United States culminates in the sight of the Statue of Liberty ("give me your huddled masses") as the boat approaches New York. Olga's view was obscured by "night and cloud." On Ella Schneider's boat, lots of DPs in their best clothes were "shouting, dancing, and hugging each other." Ella herself was fascinated by the sight of New York's skyscrapers but felt "afraid of the unknown." On her parents' faces, there was "quiet resignation."[17]

9

Unfinished Business

BY 1951, IRO HAD RESETTLED MORE THAN A MILLION DPS, about a third of them (around 350,000) identified as coming from the Soviet Union, Ukraine, Belorussia, and the Baltic States or as being stateless Russian émigrés. This was certainly an underestimation. Four hundred fifty thousand—the Soviet estimate of "lost" citizens (including those from the Baltic states, West Ukraine, and West Belorussia)—is probably closer to the mark.

The United States—the preferred destination for the majority of DPs—turned out to be the largest recipient, taking a total of well over 300,000 DPs of all nationalities, including close to 150,00 of the "Soviet" group. Australia was the next, taking over 180,000 DPs of all nationalities and almost 70,000 "Soviets." Israel was next in absolute numbers, with over 130,000 Jewish DPs settled there, although only a few thousand of these identified themselves as coming from the Soviet Union or having been stateless émigrés before the war. Canada was in fourth place, taking over 120,000 DPs, including over 45,000 Soviets. The UK took more than 85,000, including over 30,000 Soviets. Thus, with the exception of the Jewish DPs going to Israel, the great majority of DPs were resettled in First World countries, over half in North America, and most of the rest in Australia and the United Kingdom.

Latin American countries took somewhat more DPs in total than the UK (ninety-four thousand), but their intake of Soviet DPs was smaller. Argentina and Brazil were the biggest recipients among Latin American countries, but they took in only about seven thousand and ten thousand Soviet DPs respectively. Their share of Baltic DPs was strikingly low, given that these were preferred nationalities in most of the countries' selection processes. Reflecting their desirability as immigrants, compared to Slavic DPs, almost half of the Baltic DPs went to the United States, a quarter to Australia, and most of the rest were divided between Canada and the UK.[1]

So here was a big problem that, by the time IRO went out of business in 1951, had been remarkably successfully solved. But of course there were loose ends to be tied up. The immediate one was what to do with the "hard core" of DPs—around 190,000 in Germany, Austria, and Italy by IRO's count—who did not wish to repatriate, could not be resettled, or simply had their own plans.

Hard Core

In the waning months of IRO, dedicated employees tried desperately to find homes for the "hard core," consisting primarily of the aged, the sick, disabled, and mentally ill, as well as the professionals who were unwanted by most of the host countries. The "classes" of people particularly liable to find themselves in the hard core were those suffering from physical or mental ill-health; men over forty-five and women over forty; unmarried mothers and widows with children; persons with a criminal or security record; members of particular groups such as "Asiatics, non-Turkish-speaking Moslems, Armenians"; professionals over thirty-five, particularly priests, pastors, and professional soldiers; clerical workers over forty; persons with "poor physique or personal appearance"; persons of "bad repute" (this presumably covered security risks as well as convicted criminals); and persons whose locations made it difficult for the resettlement missions to get to them.

DPs with criminal records could find themselves in double jeopardy, unless they were of Soviet origin and willing to repatriate. A thirty-year-old Ukrainian from Poland who had multiple sentences for black-marketeering in his time as a DP might still have been acceptable to IRO for resettlement, given the minor nature of the offences; "however, no country wants to accept any person with such records of punishments and Mr MB became a 'hard core' case." DPs rejected as security risks by resettlement countries also formed part of the hard core.[2]

In the health field, TB was a major problem. An IRO report of July 1950 stated that the organization had four thousand TB cases on hand, accompanied by two thousand dependents. There was the possibility of getting them cared for and even cured in sanatoria in Germany and Switzerland, but someone would have to pay for it, since IRO could not. IRO was hoping that Canada would step up for some of the burden (one thousand cases) and guarantee both to pay for treatment and to take them as immigrants once cured; the Canadian government was considering it. A 1951 report from Salzburg noted as one of the most difficult groups "the TB cases, calcified, inactive or active, which have few chances for emigration on the one hand and recovery in Austria on the other." On Tubabao, DPs' resentment against a doctor who discovered higher than expected rates of TB, and thus imperiled their resettlement, developed into open warfare. Venereal disease, similarly, was on most countries' immigration black list, although by mid-1951, the United States and Brazil were accepting cases that had received the new Wasserman treatment. Australia was still refusing them, but IRO hoped to persuade the New Zealand government that it could safely accept afflicted individuals.[3]

Psychiatric illness or breakdowns were common among DPs, with depression and paranoia being the most common forms. For mental cases, "the only possibility seemed to be continued care in their present location," according to Director Kingsley in mid-1950. This, however, had not yet been agreed with the new German government, though a guarantee of permanent care to mentally ill patients was being sought. Earlier, however, strenuous efforts had been made to repatriate mental patients. According to IRO's assistant director-general for repatriation and resettlement in 1949, repatriation "is believed to be the normal and, in most cases, the best solution for mentally ill displaced persons and refugees;" he further noted that "the future of a mental case who does not speak or understand German, in a German mental hospital, with German doctors, is indeed sombre." But the mentally ill were not always welcome as repatriates, let alone for settlement in other countries. The Soviet Union was unusual in its unqualified acceptance of them—but, as so often, politics intruded, and some Western officials were unwilling on principle to allow DPs to be repatriated to the USSR from German hospitals, while Baltic and Ukrainian nationalist groups strongly objected on behalf of their nationals.

Mental illness seems to have been even more or a problem out in the jungle of the Philippines, increasing as time passed and the Russian DPs remained stranded. In 1949, IRO even thought of sending the Tubabao "hard core" round the world to the DP camps of Germany in 1949, although this plan seems to have been abandoned after suicide attempts and hunger strikes. Several DPs who had not previously been regarded as insane were now observed to have "lost their mind," and an internal IRO memo on the mental condition of refugees in the Philippines reported twenty "mentally deficient and epileptic" DPs in the camp hospital; ten chronic alcoholics, most suffering from delirium tremens; and four attempted suicides. Even some of the TB cases were now showing "signs of insanity."[4]

The disabled were also part of the hard core, very difficult to resettle and sometimes even to repatriate. Australia was upfront in not wanting migrants with disabilities. The United States was willing to accept them in principle, as long as their disability did not prevent them earning a living, but IRO officials neverthe-less feared that a restrictive approach to the admission of the disabled might "creep into the immigration laws." There were particular problems with children, whose disabilities sometimes prevented the whole family from leaving, or forced the parents to leave one child behind in an institution. A Ukrainian child named Nina, described as an "intelligent epileptic" child, was serially abandoned, first by her single mother, then by her first foster family when they emigrated, and finally by a second foster mother who simply left her on a tram. A Good Samari-tan took her to the nearby Soviet consulate, where staffers "regaled [her] with food and toys" and arranged her repatriation to the Soviet Union.

The aged posed an equal problem. Resettlement countries mainly had age cutoffs for independent migration, although if elderly DPs had younger rela-tives, they could hope in some cases for sponsorship under family reunion schemes. For many, the departure of their children for resettlement in foreign parts was the beginning of an anxious wait to see if the children, and their host governments, would actually honor their promises. In addition there was the "Over-age group"—"too young for an Old Age Home, yet too fatigued and worn out to support themselves on their own—often intelligent and skilled people whose special skills cannot used." A poignant example came from IRO's resettlement officer in the Philippines. Latvians Eustachius Juras and his wife Elisa Juras had applied unsuccessfully for resettlement in America, Co-lombia, Paraguay, Brazil, Australia, and Argentina. "Due to the worry about his future, Juras is becoming a little unbalanced and cannot remember names and places and finds it difficult to give a coherent account of anything and in my opinion it would be quite impossible for him to earn a living for himself or his wife in any country." The IRO official handling the case was looking for a local Lutheran old-age home that might take the couple.

In March 1950, the former Lithuanian minister in London, Bronius Kazys Balutis, appealed to the British for help and humanitarian treatment of an estimated five thousand Lithuanians, both DPs under IRO care and others deemed ineligible for it, for whom resettlement places had not been found. Most of them were aged, crippled, or had contagious diseases; some had been stranded after returning from Belgium when their work contracts expired.

In the very last months of its tenure, IRO redoubled its efforts to dispose of the hard core, with some sympathetic responses, especially from northern

Europe and Scandinavia. This was painstaking work with individual cases—9 blind DPs accepted by Norway, 16 mentally defective children by Belgium, 42 TB patients by Sweden, some aged DPs by the Little Sisters of the Poor in the United Kingdom—but that left 4,655 unprovided for in the US zone of Germany alone. Other countries, such as Australia, were less responsive to IRO's pleas, insisting on the necessity of its "stringent requirements" on age and physical and mental health," while boldly claiming a humanitarian record second to none as far as DPs were concerned.[5]

Remaining in Germany and Austria

Failure to repatriate or be resettled usually meant, ipso facto, staying in Germany or Austria, and this was the fate of the nondistributed hard core of DPs after IRO's closure. The number of DPs (all nationalities) who remained in Germany after IRO's withdrawal and the closing of the DP camps is generally accepted to have been around 100,000 to 150,000. Of this residuum more than 13 percent needed long-term institutional care. The comparable figure for "non-German speaking refugees" remaining in Austria as of September 1952 was 43,000. Given that the Russian/Soviet/Ukrainian/Baltic group had comprised about a third of the DPs under IRO care, this would suggest that perhaps 50,000 were left in Germany and Austria, though Soviet estimates were higher. Some of the remainers were people who, for whatever reason, preferred to stay in Central Europe rather than repatriating or resettling, but probably the majority remained simply because they had found no other place to go when the time came for IRO camps to close.

There had been a time when the Allies, still in a wartime mindset, were worried that if DPs remained in Germany indefinitely, they would form "an undesirable addition to German manpower." By early 1950s, however, IRO wanted nothing more than for West Germany to absorb the hard core it was leaving; and the willingness of the new West German state (the Federal Republic of Germany, established in 1949) to take the residue was a matter for relief and gratitude. The handover took place in 1950–51. The FRG government issued a statement on June 30, 1950, that they would take on the responsibility for hard core DPs, who would be called, rather chillingly, "homeless foreigners" (*heimatlose Ausländer*). This was followed on April 25, 1951, by a document entitled "On the Legal Position of Homeless Foreigners" that, after extensive discussion and negotiation with IRO, formalized the situation. It guaranteed the erstwhile DPs' right to acquire property and education, to work, including in their specialties, and to receive welfare and unemployment benefits, as well as promising preference in citizenship applications.

Austria was on a different timetable from Germany, having no comparable handover from departing occupation powers to be negotiated. Its Ministry of Interior took over financial and administrative responsibility for the DP camps with the departure of IRO in 1951. Austria offered fewer guarantees to the remaining DPs than Germany, and the presence of a large number of Volksdeutsche—to whom Austrians were somewhat more welcoming than to the Slavic and Jewish DPs—was a complicating factor.[6]

Those DPs still living in camps in Germany were being energetically encouraged to move out of them and offered help in finding normal apartments, but it was not until 1961 that the last camps were closed. A Hamburg source picks 1957 as the key year when former DPs started entering the German workforce and getting to know Germans. This was the time many DP families moved out of the camps into their own apartments, changed their employer from the British Army to a German civilian one, and, in the case of DP children, found their first German girlfriend or boyfriend. Getting a job was very hard for most of the former DPs, with fluency in German being a major problem, and it often took a long time. Many in the professional group, particularly ex-military and academics, never managed to re-establish themselves. Although contemporary commentators and even later German historians tend to play down popular hostility to the "homeless foreigners," it is clear that the strong anti-DP sentiment of the immediate postwar years (dirty, criminal, unfairly privileged in ration terms) persisted. Not everybody, including some parts of the German legal profession, thought it appropriate to give the range of rights and benefits offered by the 1951 law to this group. Their assimilation into German society has been characterized as a "half-hearted integration." Some resentments increased rather than dissipating over time. Latvians, who often felt a cultural kinship with the Germans (and a shared superiority over Slavic and Jewish DPs) were unhappy that they had to pay a substantial fee to receive German citizenship and felt stigmatized as a group when the West German government launched a serious pursuit of Nazi war criminals in the late 1950s.

In Austria, where the large refugee population of the 1950s former DPs included Volksdeutsche and Jews as well as Slavic DPs, popular preference was strongly in favor of the Volksdeutsche, with Slavic DPs seen as only marginally better than the much-disliked Jews. A differentiated welcome was manifest in the fact that in the period 1945–52, 150,000 Volksdeutsche received Austrian citizenship (admittedly out of a larger group of refugees) as against 35,000 non-Jewish DPs and a mere 12 Jewish DPs. The DPs continued to be seen as "black marketeers, freeloaders, criminals, delinquent, and alcoholics who offended the cultural sensibilities of native Austrians and threatened public order"; in addition, the left-wing press kept up a flow of attacks on DP former collaborators.

A Bavarian official overseeing the change from DP to homeless foreigner remarked optimistically that camps were bad for people, and that former DPs who had been transferred to German jurisdiction were "generally happier under the new circumstances than under IRO administration." Who knows if this was the case for Lithuanian Marija Bendicaite, taken to Germany as labor in 1944, when she was sixty-eight years old, who found herself in her seventies quite alone in Germany in 1951 after the departure to the United States of her only known relative, a widowed fifty-two-year-old brother-in-law, in 1951. But at least Germany provided her with a place in a home for the aged.

For the handicapped, West German residence, even without citizenship, sometimes looked preferable to resettlement outside Europe, in that in Germany they were eligible for a disability pension that might not be available elsewhere. (IRO Hamburg reported in May 1951 that "a number of handicapped persons have decided to give up their resettlement rights voluntarily," even having been registered as eligible, on these grounds.) On the other hand, there were the unfortunate cases that fell between the cracks, as in that of the disabled Romanian, a former POW, who was rejected not only by all resettlement commissions (as having been an Axis prisoner of war, not an Allied one) but also for repatriation by his country of origin, and, on top of that, deemed ineligible for welfare support in Germany because his disability was acquired as a POW.[7]

Twelve to fifteen thousand Jewish DPs opted to remain in West Germany, and as of the beginning of 1951, Austria was housing another five thousand or so, of whom thirty-five hundred wanted to stay in Austria. Several thousand of the Jews in Germany were still living in DP camps, with no plans to leave. The Jews at the Föhrenwald camp in southern Bavaria were notable for their stubborn refusal to fall into line. They opposed the transfer of their camp from IRO to German authorities in October 1951, then clashed violently with German police after the camp was raided for black market activities. Five years later, the problem was still unsolved as, for a variety of reasons, many residents had failed to emigrate, despite the availability of Israel as a destination and the fact that the JDC would pay their resettlement costs. Worried observers

diagnosed dependency problems, especially those of "the group of an estimated 250 children of 'hard-core' [who] had no idea what life was like outside
of Föhrenwald. Their parents had never worked, they thought that supplies
such as food and clothing came in boxes with JDC marked on the side, and
they only really knew the small community that had lived within the gates of
the center." It was not until 1957 that Föhrenwald finally closed its doors.

Worse still, from the standpoint of the authorities, was that Jewish DPs who
had been resettled in Israel, North and South America, and Australia were
starting to return to Germany. Some of the returns may have been legal, since
the 1951 law on stateless foreigners specified that stateless individuals who had
formerly lived in Germany could return to the country within two year of their
departure, but others were not: as of August 1953, Föhrenwald had eight hundred illegal returnees living in the camp, and by the end of 1953, three thousand
returnees had passed through it. These returns took everybody by surprise and
were disapproved of by both the JDC and the Western German government,
as well as IRO and its successors. But they were part of the re-formation of a
permanent Jewish community in Germany, one of whose best-known leaders
of the 1990s was Polish-born former displaced person Ignatz Bubis.[8]

Returns and Deportations after Resettlement

Jews returning to Germany from Israel were not the only resettled DPs who
either changed their minds or were rejected by their new countries and deported back to Germany. There were DPs who, after resettlement in one country, moved on to another as soon as they had saved up enough money to pay
for the passage. The United States was the most popular second resettlement
destination. Another possibility, discussed later in this chapter, was belated
repatriation from the resettlement country to the Soviet Union, which was
free. Both of those options were choices made by DPs. But it could also happen
that a DP was rejected by his new country as an unsuitable immigrant and
returned to Germany. This was normally done at the port of entry, on the
judgement of immigration officials.

Mental illness seems to have been the most common reason for enforced
return. In 1949, Canada sent back two Polish schizophrenics to Germany,
where they were put in mental hospitals. The year before, the same country
had deported back to Germany a sufferer from epilepsy (then considered a
mental illness) who had concealed his condition from the medical examiners
but, with the excitement of the trip, had a bad attack on board; as a "possible

charge on public funds in Canada," he could not be accepted as a migrant. IRO's Director-General Kingsley tried to persuade the Canadian government not to insist on returning such cases to Europe, but found it adamant. Australia, similarly, refused to allow the disembarkation of four DPs from one transport ship in December 1947. Two of them had "developed during the voyage symptoms of mental instability" and a third had a complication of conjunctivitis that had caused loss of sight in one eye. The fourth was a Latvian woman, barred from landing on "security grounds" after unspecified information was received from Germany. A fifth man on the same ship discovered to have venereal disease was in danger of being barred but was finally admitted on the grounds that he would "respond to treatment in one week." IRO's medical director found these returns "reasonable."

In other cases, the DPs were let in initially but subsequently issued deportation orders on the basis of unsatisfactory conduct in their new country or newly discovered information against them. The question of whether the resettlement countries had the right to return people to Europe was moot: it was an issue that it had not been in IRO's interest to clarify in advance, and a tug of war ensued in the late 1940s, which ended only with the dissolution of IRO and the departure of the occupation regimes, leaving no entity that could conceivably be held responsible for handling the human rejects. The Australian government, which in 1949 had asserted its right to deport unsatisfactory migrants, regardless of their length of residence in the country, felt fully within its rights deporting those who showed "poor conduct or character" and, with regard to DP immigrants, cited an informal agreement between IRO and the British Control Commission that Australia could return to the British zone of Germany any "nasty" individual who might mistakenly have been admitted. It did in fact deport forty or fifty of the DPs resettled by IRO, mainly for work offences related to the two-year contract, but including some for murder, assault, theft, rape, homosexuality, epilepsy, and mental illness.[9]

IRO was at first tolerant of this, as long as returns remained relatively rare and the rejecting country paid part of the cost of return, since its primary concern was not to "jeopardise the success of the mass migration scheme," currently in full swing. Later, particularly in light of the mass resettlement to the United States following the passage of the 1948 Displaced Persons Act, IRO toughened its stance, worried that the numbers of returns might become unmanageable. When in March 1949 the Australian government sent back sixteen Ukrainian and Polish deportees to Germany for refusing employment offers and generally showing themselves to be unsuitable as "future Australian citizens," they omitted to clear this in advance with zonal authorities in Germany, and IRO called their bluff: the men languished at a camp in Naples, their European port of entry, for months before finally being allowed to proceed to Germany. In May 1949, IRO's Department of Mass Resettlement sent out a memo to recipient countries noting that reentry would not be permitted without advance clearance and that captains of ships and aircraft would be instructed not to accept such passengers without such clearance being presented. Toward the end of the same year, IRO issued the warning that "deportation should not be resorted to for reasons of fluctuations of the labour market, occupational diseases, or mere undesirability which is not warranted by considerations of national security," and that it should not be initiated without the individual in question being "given a hearing before a competent authority."

One deportation that caused something of an international scandal, particularly in the United States, was that of the Russian Mikhail Kolosov, aka Gregor Lach, who in his DP days in Germany had managed to publish a memoir of his life in the Soviet Army in a New York Russian-language journal. This was one of the rare security deportations on which details are available. Arriving in Australia for resettlement in 1949, Kolosov/Lach made the mistake of telling immigration officials that he had come under a false name and was a former Soviet officer and Communist Party member. As a result, a few months later the Australians deported him back to Germany. An outcry in the anti-communist Russian emigration ensued, with testimonials to his unimpeachable anti-Sovietism coming from recent Soviet defector Viktor Kravchenko and the leader of Russia's short-lived Provisional Government in 1917, Alexander Kerensky, but to no avail. Deported back to IRO's care in 1950, he lived for some years in Germany, closely watched by US military intelligence and no doubt by the Soviets as well, before perhaps emigrating to Canada in the mid-1950s.[10]

From 1951, signatories to the Convention and Protocol Relating to the Status of Refugees (1951) (including all the major IRO resettlement destinations) were barred from deporting refugees "unless they threatened national security or public order." By this time, entry visas to Germany were being refused to returned migrants, or rather to the governments that sent them, and Italian authorities were taking a similar position. With its mission basically accomplished and the need to conciliate host countries diminishing, IRO "was categorically refusing to facilitate the repatriation of deported displaced persons; some deportations had to be attempted twice." After IRO's departure from Europe in 1952, Australian immigration officials tried to insist that the Federal Republic of Germany was bound by an agreement to accept their undesirable DPs, but when asked to produce the agreement, "they could not, as none existed." But if it was not possible to deport undesirable East European immigrants back to Germany, how could they be got rid of? The Australian Immigration Department considered trying to return them to their countries of origin, but this was promptly vetoed by the Ministry of External Affairs, which pointed out that "sending DPs back to countries behind the Iron Curtain would invite international censure and political embarrassment."

The political impossibility of sending undesirable migrants back to the Soviet Union from the United States was made clear in a notorious failed-deportation case in the United States, that of Russian poet and literary scholar Rodion Akulshin, a former POW and then DP in Germany who on entry to the United States in 1950 had misstated his name and nationality (he called himself Rodion Berezov, of Polish nationality) but subsequently confessed the fraud. This public admission won him a deportation order from the INS, but Alexandra Tolstoy and others in the Russian community took up his case, as did Senator John Kennedy, and the order was not enforced. In fact, testifying to the US Congress about Russian concealment of identity, Alexandra Tolstoy made the surprising statement that she regularly counseled Russians in Berezov's situation to make a clean breast of it "because even though they would be subject to deportation proceedings, nothing, no effective follow-up, could be carried out upon the part of the immigration authorities, because they have no place to be deported to."

Deportation is, on the face of it, one of the quintessential powers governments have over their country's residents. But here, as so often, it turns out to be a two-edged sword—in other words, a procedure that DPs could also use to obtain their own ends. The known cases of DPs doing so involve Australia, a particularly distant destination, that was not most DPs' first choice and had an unpopular two-year requirement of manual labor on arrival. For those who arrived and found it had all been a terrible mistake, return as a matter of individual choice was very difficult: not only was the passage expensive and berths scarce, due to the shortage of postwar shipping, but an Australian passport and exit visa were required. If it was the Australian state shipping them out, however, those problems immediately disappeared. To some, not surprisingly, provoking the authorities to deport them looked like a good option.

Mstislav Chlopoff, a Russian émigré from Belgrade passing as a Pole, was successful in getting himself deported back to Germany a year after his 1948 resettlement in Australia on grounds of unsatisfactory work performance, although his subsequent efforts to get himself resettled by IRO in the United States—or, as he became increasingly desperate, Canada, or Brazil or anywhere—appear to have failed. In several other cases, a DP's earlier statement of a desire (or "demand") to be returned to Germany, coupled with conspicuous bad behavior, preceded their deportation, although officials naturally formulated the deportation order in terms of punishment rather than fulfilment of wishes. The Estonian DP Robert Talts boasted of this stratagem on repatriating to the Soviet Union after he had got himself deported from Australia. Or course, not all such efforts were successful. The request of an epileptic Polish DP consigned to a Melbourne mental hospital to be sent back to Germany was met with some skepticism by the Australian authorities (although Australia had deported DPs on grounds of epilepsy, they thought this one was "using his epilepsy for the purpose".) In any case IRO and the Germans had refused to take him back.[11]

Continued Soviet Attempts to Repatriate Its Citizens

From the Soviet point of view, resettlement of its DPs was a mistake that still needed to be corrected. To that end, it did its best in the late 1940s and early '50s to let resettled DPs know that it was not too late to return, however far away they had landed. If the results were meager, this was not for want of trying.

Most DPs were uninterested in Soviet offers of repatriation, often reacting with fear or hostility. But, as always, there were a few who saw possibilities in the Soviet willingness to repatriate its citizens, particularly if their experience in the first years of resettlement had not been happy. Russian Vasily Chistokhodov, aka Aleksandr Muravsky, had resettled in Argentina, courtesy of IRO. Unemployed and dissatisfied, he visited the Soviet consulate in Buenos Aires three times in August 1951 to talk about the possibility of repatriating, although he was worried about the possibility of punishment (not unreasonably, as he had past contacts with the CIA). At the same period, Chistokhodov was visiting the US embassy to explore the option of emigrating to that country. But it turned out he would be liable to be drafted for US military service in Korea, which attracted him no more than Gulag did. As far as the archival records shows, he stayed in Argentina.

There were also resettled DPs who genuinely wanted to go home. The Estonian DP Maria Nelson had met and married a British serviceman, Sam Nelson, in Germany, and they had gone to live in his home town in England. This worked out badly because Sam had become a communist, and his family disapproved. Similar problems developed when they emigrated to Australia (disapproval from Sam's aunt; suspicion on the part of a landlady seeing Soviet stamps on letters to Maria), so in 1949 they returned to England, now with two young children, but relations with the family remained difficult. They decided that they should go and live in the Soviet Union, since Maria could get a free passage with her children as a repatriate. The hope was that Sam—a communist, after all—would be allowed to follow.

Maria's wish to return to the Soviet Union, and her English communist husband's eagerness to accompany, would have puzzled Western readers, had they known about it. This was the height of the Cold War "Red scare," and the Western press made clear that the Soviet Union was a country so repressive that nobody would willingly live in it. A story that hit the headlines throughout the Western world was that of the Soviet woman in New York who jumped out a third-floor window of the consulate rather than succumb to pressure to repatriate. Oksana Kasenkina was a teacher at the Soviet school in New York recalled to Moscow along with other teachers when, at the height of US-Soviet tensions over Berlin in 1948, the school was closed. The school's head defected, but Kasenkina dithered, first apparently accepting refuge at the Tolstoy Foundation's Reed Farm and then writing a distraught letter to the Soviet consul asking to be rescued from the anti-Soviet company into which she had fallen.

It is hard to interpret Kasenkina's contradictory actions in terms other than psychological distress and confusion, but the effect was to plunge Alexandra Tolstoy and Soviet consul Jacob Lomakin, as well as herself, into a media frenzy. Accusations, counteraccusations, and complex court proceedings followed, in what United Press rated as the fourth biggest international news story of the year, topped only by President Truman's election, the Berlin airlift, and the high cost of living. The sensational story was linked from the beginning to the plight of nonrepatriating Soviet DPs, who, as renowned commentators Joseph and Stewart Alsop wrote, had, in their hundreds of thousands "obeyed precisely the same impulse as moved Mme Kasenkina to her desperate expedient"—that is, to stay out of the Soviet Union at all costs. For the Soviet DPs' supporters in the United States such as Alexandra Tolstoy, Kasenkina's "leap to freedom" had been essentially made by them all.[12]

Soviet embassy personnel throughout the world must have thanked their lucky stars that they had not been in Lomakin's shoes. Even as it was, they found the repatriation tasks that had been added to the previous workload onerous. In the absence of legally recognized repatriation missions in the resettlement countries, the Soviet embassies and consulates had to handle repatriation, including propaganda among the resettled. This was fraught with problems. As the Soviet embassy in the United States complained in 1952, it was hard to locate the DPs since many of them had entered the country under false identities. Once they were found, attempts to visit their apartments often produced unwelcome publicity in the press. Only a few were willing to approach the embassy and talk about repatriation, and on the rare occasions when this happened, the authorities did their best to squash it. The Soviets claimed that after a seventeen-year-old Russian girl had contacted the embassy seeking to repatriate, she had been arrested by the Americans as a communist.

The Soviet legation in Canberra had similar problems. When in 1948 it published a small notice in the local paper informing DP migrants from the Baltic that they had the same rights to free repatriation as other Soviet citizens and inviting them to register with the embassy, a torrent of protests followed from émigré organizations against what was claimed to be coercive registration. This in turn prompted the Australian government to issue a statement advising DPs to ignore the invitation. After that, or so the embassy claimed in its reports to Moscow, it was not allowed to put any announcements about repatriation in the Australian press. That meant that the only way to get the message was through DPs who might, on their own initiative, visit the embassy and then possibly spread the word in the migrant camps. For the whole of 1949, however, there had been only six such visits.

Both the Soviet embassy in the United States and the legation in Australia felt overwhelmed by the extra workload associated with repatriation, and urgently requested some extra staff for the purpose. The Washington embassy's problems seem to have been ignored, but in February 1951, the Soviet Foreign Ministry approved the extra slots for the legation in Canberra, accepting Ambassador Lifanov's recommendation that the staffers in question should go under diplomatic cover. Australia thus became one of a number of resettlement countries to which the Soviet Union sent undercover repatriation agents.[13]

The repatriation agents encountered considerable resistance from within the émigré communities. In Argentina, on one occasion conflict between repatriates and their sponsors and anti-communists came to the point of fisticuffs at the Buenos Aires port. One anti-communist activist, a survivor of Lienz, actually organized observation on the visitors to the Soviet embassy in Buenos-Aires: "From morning to late at night a 'duty officer' sat in an apartment from which the entrance was visible, writing down all those who crossed the threshold and even photographing them if conditions allowed." The reports of Soviet repatriation agents abroad reflected this attitude of hostility and suspicion, and sometimes reciprocated it. In Venezuela, Colonel Morozov characterized the fifty-nine DPs with whom he had been able to make contact in Venezuela in unfavorable terms such as "speculator," "bourgeois, served in Gestapo," and "worked for Germans; beat up Jews."

Nevertheless, some individual resettled DPs were sympathetic to the Soviet approaches. In Canada, the Soviet embassy's Third Secretary N. Poliakov made a special trip from Ottawa to Toronto to meet representatives of an unnamed "progressive" organization that he hoped would be helpful in contacting potential repatriates. In Australia, the left-wing Russian Social Club in Sydney was one of the few places where the Soviet undercover agents were welcome and could make contacts.

Anatoly Gordeev, seconded to the Soviet Repatriation Agency from military intelligence, arrived in Australia as an undercover agent at the end of 1951 and worked there for about a year on repatriation (despite his intelligence background, he appears not to have combined this with systematic espionage work). He found it a hard slog. Internecine conflicts within the embassy impeded his work. The Australian authorities were uncooperative and suspicious. Making contact with the DPs was difficult, partly because many of them were still in migrant camps in regional New South Wales and Victoria, and he was not sure if he was allowed to go there. Most of the DPs avoided him. Of those who contacted him, several were psychiatrically disturbed. Relatively young himself, Gordeev had most success in establishing friendly relations with young men at odds with their anti-Soviet fathers.

For all his efforts, Gordeev managed to organize only eight individual and family repatriations—a mixture of Ukrainians, Russians, and DPs from the Baltics—in a year of hard work. The DPs he interviewed told various stories of disappointment about their lives in Australia. A teenage Ukrainian peasant was sent to work on sugar plantations in the north, living in a tent and eaten by mosquitos; he fell ill, "experienced mockery from the children of the local bourgeoisie," and was so lonely he was ready to kill himself. Another Ukrainian, a PhD from Kiev University, found it intolerable to be forced to work as a laborer living in a "large unused poultry feed-shed" with his wife, in another life an industrial chemist. One of the few women in the group was the wife of Mstislav Chlopoff, the DP who had provoked his own deportation back to Germany earlier. Rather than join him, as they had apparently planned together, she had married an Australian, presumably bigamously, and then for unknown reasons abandoned him as well in favor of repatriation to her parents' home in Ukraine. Another repatriate with his own agenda was a young Lithuanian who had told Gordeev that his reason for repatriation was fear that the Australians would put him in a psychiatric hospital. During the stopover in London en route to the Soviet Union, he absconded and was never seen again.

None of Gordeev's repatriates expressed ideological reasons for repatriating. But there were a few earlier and later repatriates from among DPs resettled in Australia whose return was a political choice. Juris, a Latvian who had become politically radicalized after arriving in Australia, was ostracized by others in his migrant camp before deciding to return to the Soviet Union. Jascha Zelensky, a young Ukrainian member of the Russian Social Club, whose repatriation arrangements were already underway when Gordeev arrived, went back with the aim of joining the Red Army and fighting for the Soviet Union.

Gordeev's lack of success with repatriation was not untypical. His counterpart in Argentina did not much better, reporting that for all his efforts, only fifteen individuals repatriated in 1950 and ten in 1951—"moreover six of those repatriating ran away on the trip back to the Homeland." The Soviet Repatriation Agency's data as of mid-1952 showed only a few hundred repatriates from the resettlement countries, with Venezuela in first place (twenty-eight), followed by Argentina and Canada.[14]

It is scarcely surprising that Gordeev and the other repatriation agents did so poorly, given the lack of any formal amnesty for collaborators and the fear of punishment and social ostracism. This changed somewhat when, after Stalin's death, there was a renewed push to get repatriates back, the brain child of KGB head Ivan Serov, who was worried about intensifying CIA efforts to use émigrés as a Cold War weapon. An amnesty was announced in September 1955 for returning DPs who had worked with the Germans, even those who had served in the military under German command (with the exception of officers, whose punishment on return would be limited to five years exile within the Soviet Union). Families, regardless of citizenship, could now accompany repatriates. A Soviet Repatriation Committee (Komitet za Vozvrashchenie na Rodinu) was established in East Berlin and given its own journal, *Za vozvrashchenie na Rodinu* and radio station. The committee established branches in Latin America in the 1950s, which existed in a state of perennial warfare with the local Russian anti-communists.

There was at least one Cold War repatriation coup: the return from Argentina in the mid-1950s of Iury Slepukhin, previously one of brightest figures of solidarist (NTS) youth in postwar Argentina. Back in Europe, he had managed to dodge forced repatriation by escaping from a Soviet transit camp with the help of émigré relatives. Later, he became disillusioned with NTS, realizing, in his sister's recollection, "that it's all a mirage and self-deception, just games." "I could not live in the West with its two-headed freedom and with its material well-being turning man into animal," Slepukhin said after his repatriation. He managed to make a Soviet life for himself in Leningrad, publishing in Soviet journals from the late 1950s, being admitted to the Soviet Writers' Union in 1963, and becoming a cult hero to some of the city's young littérateurs.

For the Latvian DP Juris, radicalized in Australia after being ostracized by other DP, repatriation worked out less well. Back in Soviet Riga, he had changed his mind about the move within a year, but his efforts to persuade Australia to take him back with his wife and five children were unavailing. Lecturing the Soviets on the superiority of Australian trade unions, he was committed to a Soviet psychiatric hospital as a dissident. While he was released from the hospital after a year or so, he never left the Soviet Union again.[15]

Extradition and Punishment of "War Criminals"

"War criminals" were another piece of unfinished business for the Soviets, who continued their efforts to locate, extradite, and punish them. For decades the West rebuffed these efforts, assuming that the accusations were without merit—until, in the 1970s, attitudes in the West started to change. The initial automatic dismissal of Soviet claims reflected both a general reaction to the Cold War enemy and a more specific uneasiness with Soviet "show trials" of war criminals, reminiscent of the Great Purge trials of the late 1930s, which had clearly served political ends rather than the interests of justice.

For a new round of trials in the early 1960s, the Soviets sought the extradition of DPs who had been resettled in the United States, Canada, England, Australia, and elsewhere. The message to the West was twofold: on the one hand, a rebuke to Western governments for harboring Nazi collaborators; on the other hand, a warning to diaspora communities and their anti-Soviet activists that "the long arm of Soviet justice was about to corral those who had collaborated with the Nazis."

The United States, Canada, the United Kingdom, Australia, and all the other host countries regularly refused such extradition requests. In response to a request to extradite Estonian Ervin Viks, allegedly a former commandant of a wartime concentration camp in Tartu, Australian attorney general Garfield Barwick stated that Australia stood by "the right of this nation . . . to enable men to turn their backs on past bitternesses and to make a new life for themselves." Although Australia was also firm in refusing extradition requests for Ukrainian war criminals, there was a particular edge in its responses to Soviet requests for extradition of people from the Baltic states, since Australia, like the United States and the United Kingdom, did not recognize the incorporation of this region into the Soviet Union as legitimate. In the early 1960s, the British adamantly refused to extradite Ain-Ervin Mere, a former chief of the Estonian Security Police who had found refuge there under the *Westward Ho!* program in 1947. A decade later, on receiving a Soviet request for extradition of the Ukrainian Kyrylo Zvarich, said to have killed Jews in his native village as part of a German police unit, the Foreign Office did not even bother to reply, let alone investigate.

Public reaction in the resettlement countries to this lack of concern about war criminals was minimal, coming mainly from Jewish organizations and the civil-libertarian Left. As early as 1948, David Nussbaum raised the issue in the *New York Times*, but his article was strongly rebutted on behalf of the Baltic migrants by the National Catholic Resettlement Council, which claimed that Nussbaum was "trying to discredit the whole [DP resettlement] program." In the absence of hard data to support the allegations, Jewish organizations in the United States backed off. In Australia, similarly, the mainstream Jewish community "failed to maximize its efforts" to bring Nazi collaborators to justice for many years.[16]

The West's refusals to extradite alleged war criminals for prosecution became part of the propaganda war on the issue of war criminals that the Soviet Union continued to wage in the 1960s. A much-circulated text was *Daugavas Vanagi—Who Are They?* (1962), with lists of alleged Latvian war criminals produced by the Latvian Committee for Return to the Homeland. The Soviet journal *Return to the Homeland* not only regularly published the names of alleged war criminals living under false names in the United States but also, in an ingenious act of intimidation, sent copies to their home addresses in that country, addressed to them by their original names.

Soviet propaganda made little headway with mainstream opinion in the resettlement countries of the West, which had no appetite for investigating or prosecuting past DP crimes. Israel was a notable exception, but its most famous war crimes trial, the Eichmann trial of 1961, was of a senior German Nazi official who had escaped under a false name to Latin America, not a displaced person from the Baltics, Ukraine, or Belarus, and did not involve cooperation with the Soviet Union or use of Soviet testimony. Another exception was the

Federal Republic of Germany, which, dealing with its own specific political issue of German guilt, set up a special unit to handle war crimes in 1958. Latvians from the Waffen-SS were particularly on the German unit's radar, something that caused resentment among Latvians who had remained in the country, who felt they were being ethnically profiled as likely war criminals.

In the German Latvian community, there were a few oddballs who made the hunt for wartime collaborators an avocation. One such man, inspired by reading *Daugavas Vanagi*, spurred on the Hamburg police to reopen the case of Viktors Arājs, a leader of the Arājs Commandos who were accused of participating in the murder of three hundred thousand Jews from the Riga ghetto in Rumbula Forest. Arājs, protected by the British and rumored to have escaped to Latin America, had in fact been living quietly in West Germany under a false name with documents supplied by the Latvian legation in London. The German police found and arrested him in 1975, and a few years later a German court sentenced him to life imprisonment for the Rumbula Forest murders.[17]

Western attitudes to war crimes started to change dramatically from the 1970s, first in the United States, and then in other resettlement countries in the West. This was basically a product of heightened awareness of the Holocaust coupled with détente between the United States and the Soviet Union; and the initiative came from the US Congress and the legal profession, backed by the Jewish community. The primary US concern was crimes against Jews, while that of the Soviet Union was crimes against the Soviet population—but the people they were going after, Nazi collaborators hidden among the DPs resettled in the West, were essentially the same.

In the 1970s, a special war crimes unit of the US Immigration Department launched an investigation of Latvian Vilis Hāzners, accused of lying at his 1956 entry into the United States about his involvement in the murder of Jews in Riga. This was a highly charged case, since Hāzners—a Latvian Legion fighter who, as a POW, was one of the founders of the militantly anti-Soviet veterans' organization Daugavas Vanagi—was a pillar of the Latvian emigration in the United States and worldwide, president in the 1950s of the international Committee for a Free Latvia and one of the driving forces behind the Captive Nations movement. The Soviet Union had long sought to prosecute Hāzners, who was one of those accused in *Daugavas Vanagi—Who Are They?*, as well as four alleged war criminals who were the subject of a Soviet documentary. The immigration authorities denied using information supplied by the Soviet Union, but the Latvian community was convinced that it did, and that the whole thing was a KGB operation. As in most of the cases brought by the INS unit, the result was an acquittal, but with great reputational damage to the defendant.

A peculiarity of the US approach, run through the Immigration Department, was that those accused were not charged with war crimes but rather with making false statements about themselves and their political pasts on entering the United States. As we have seen at many points in this book, such false statements from DPs were by no means confined to war criminals, so this was a minefield as far as the DPs were concerned. Hāzners's warning that such accusations could "affect any one of us" struck home. From the standpoint of the immigration authorities, the disadvantage of the approach was that, even in the case of a guilty verdict, deportation was often unenforceable because it would have been to an iron curtain country.

By the late 1970s, the Immigration Department's war crimes unit was on its way out, perceived as ineffective because of its poor record of success in prosecutions. In 1979, the activist liberal congresswoman for Brooklyn, Elizabeth Holtzmann, introduced into the US House of Representatives a bill on the deportation of Nazi war criminals, under which responsibility was transferred to a new Office of Special Investigations (OSI) under the Justice Department. Within a few years, OSI, headed by Allan Ryan, had a crusading staff of fifty, including twenty lawyers, seven historians, and four investigators, and a raft of ongoing cases receiving huge publicity. The new body would have a better record of convictions: out of 134 individuals against whom charges were advanced, 83 persons lost their US citizenship and 62 departed permanently from the United States, either of their own volition or as the result of a deportation order.[18]

A concurrent shift was occurring with regard to use of Soviet evidence in Western war crimes trials. Prosecutors in West Germany were already using witness testimony, identity documents, and forensic evidence supplied by the Soviet Union in the 1960s, but the United States took some time before tentatively following their lead. The first request to the Soviets for war crimes information was made by the US embassy in Moscow, on behalf of INS investigators, in 1976. From then on, the Soviets regularly gathered witness statements and sent them to INS via the embassy, although INS still hesitated to use this information in its prosecutions. As for OSI, Ryan was in Moscow within months to negotiate a more formal process of information gathering, and from 1980 and Soviet witness testimony subsequently became a key component of the agency's prosecutions.

The Soviet Union was not the only source of witness testimony: the American investigators worked closely with Jewish investigators from the Simon Wiesenthal Center and Yad Vashem as well. Nevertheless, in the period 1980–83, OSI used Soviet testimony in over half its cases, the great majority of defendants being former DPs from the Soviet Union (predominantly Ukrainians and Belorussians) and the Baltic states (predominantly Latvians), resettled by IRO in the United States. In response to criticism of the use of Soviet documentation, OSI argued back, saying the documents they had were originals and signatures had been authenticated. Even the unofficial ban on deporting war criminals back to the Soviet Union was starting to erode. Ukrainian Feodor Fedorenko, a former guard at Treblinka, was first convicted by the INS and denaturalized, and then deported to the USSR in 1984, where he was prosecuted, convicted, and executed in 1987. The Estonian Karl Linnas was also deported—by the Reagan administration!—for war crimes prosecution in Tallin, capital of Soviet Estonia, in 1987, but he died in Leningrad before the trial could take place.[19]

The Latvian Konrāds Kalējs, an Arājs Kommando member, was arrested living in retirement in Florida in 1985 and had a successful deportation action brought against him by OSI using filmed testimony from his trial in absentia in a Soviet Riga courtroom. His original resettlement country had been Australia, where he had been naturalized a few years after arrival, so that was the country to which the United States deported him. But he quickly removed himself to Canada, only to have the Canadians deport him back to Australia. Once again, he wriggled free, this time going to the United Kingdom, where he took refuge under a false name in a Latvian nursing home. Discovered again, he returned voluntarily to Australia.

Belatedly following the US lead, Canada, Australia, and the United Kingdom all established their own commissions of inquiry into war crimes between 1985 and 1988. In all three countries, most targets of investigation were former Soviet (Ukrainian and Belorussian) or East European DPs, and the crimes with which they were charged related to killing Jews in the Second World War. Use of Soviet documentary testimony and other evidence had by now become standard, along with official cooperation with Soviet prosecutors and other officials. In a striking turnaround, a new quasi-consensus was emerging in the West (at least in the liberal-center part of its political establishment) that, regardless of the "political spectacle" aspect of the postwar Soviet war crimes trials, they were nevertheless based on "real investigative data" that were "basically accurate" and constituted "the main basis for contemporary knowledge" of war crimes in the West as well as the East.[20]

Not everyone was happy with the acceptance of Soviet evidence in war crimes trials, however. Americans for Due Process, an organization primarily representing the diaspora groups most affected by Nazi war crimes allegations (Latvian, Lithuanian, Estonian, Ukrainian, Romanian, and Croatian), did its best to discredit OSI and defend individuals accused of war crimes by "inform[ing] the American public about Soviet methods of fact gathering and witness testimonies." It became a standard defense ploy—often successful—to argue that the Soviet evidence was ipso facto unreliable and unacceptable. When the Ukrainian Ivan Polyukhovych was put on trial under the Australian War Crimes Act in 1991, an Adelaide judge disallowed almost all the evidence from Soviet Union.

Doubts about the validity of Soviet evidence were one reason for the failure of almost all these belated prosecutions, along with the infirmity and mortality of the aged former DPs on trial and, after a few years, declining public enthusiasm for expensive long-drawn-out investigations and prosecutions that generally failed to produce a result. The collapse of the Soviet Union in 1991 introduced a new twist to an already complex story, since the successor states in the Baltic were less eager than their Soviet predecessor to pursue Second World War war criminals, although they were under some international pressure to do so. In the case of Konrāds Kalējs, who had ended up back in Australia after a series of deportations and escapes that had confounded authorities in the United States, Canada, Australia, and the United Kingdom in the 1980s and '90s, Latvia finally seemed ready to prosecute, albeit on only one finite issue, in 2001; and Australia, which had always ignored Soviet extradition requests, was ready to comply. But it ended up as another piece of unfinished business: Kalējs died, aged eighty-eight, before the deportation could be executed.[21]

Conclusion

HANDLING THE DP PROBLEM after the Second World War must count as one of the great achievements of diplomacy and international organization in the modern era. Who could have predicted that out of the chaos of millions of displaced in Europe in 1945, and the unexpected crisis sparked by refusal of repatriation, a solution would emerge, within five years, by which the great majority were resettled free of charge in First World countries?

The outcome of the DP question was spectacularly different from the other big refugee problem of the period, that of Palestinians displaced in the Middle East by the foundation of the state of Israel, which has not yet been solved almost eight decades later. The contrast with the millions of present-day refugees trying their luck in leaky boats on the Mediterranean in the hope of getting into Europe and elsewhere from North Africa and the Middle East is also stark.

After the first turbulent months, the DPs in Germany and Austria were housed, clothed, and fed adequately and often well. Life may have been sometimes boring in the DP camps, but it was also safe—residents were not at risk of being shot by roving groups of soldiers, or executed on trumped-up political charges, and, despite DP fear, there was not even a statistically significant chance of them being kidnapped for repatriation by the Soviets. The Allies gave the DPs in Germany better rations than the local population; and among the crowds of other people displaced in Germany at the time, including ten million Volksdeutsche expelled from Eastern Europe, they were by far the best off: "DP" status was, literally, a privilege. The DPs sometimes complained of being disrespected by Allied personnel—but at the same time, they were allowed to run their own camps, with elected officers whose salaries were paid by the Allies. These "camps" were not camps in the literal sense but solid accommodations (formerly schools, barracks, and other institutional buildings;

sometimes requisitioned private houses) with amenities such as water, electricity, and heating. When some DPs, resettled in Palestine or sent to work off their contracts in the Australian outback, were housed in tents, they were outraged.

Why, in comparative perspective, did the DPs do so well? One possible hypothesis is that they were white Europeans, and that their good reception had the same basis as that of Ukrainians crossing the western border after Russia's invasion in 2022: namely that they belonged to that rare species of refugee that can be perceived in the First World as kith and kin. But that hypothesis fully fits only the DPs from the Baltics, universally regarded as clean, cultured, disciplined, and assimilable. East European DPs of Slavic origin (Poles, Yugoslavs, and so on) were not so positively perceived; and Soviet DPs (including, in the 1940s, Ukrainians) were seen as barely white and only marginally European: they were often regarded as "Mongols" and "Asiatics," who, on top of their racial inferiority, had been brought up under communism.

The DPs were certainly fortunate in that their displacement occurred at a rare time of hope and commitment to international organizations (notably the UN) and their problem-solving potential. They were doubly fortunate in that the United States could afford to pick up the tab and was, at this point, willing to do so. But that willingness itself needs explanation. The Soviet Union complained that the West was stealing its citizens, via resettlement, in order to exploit their labor. This had a grain of truth in some cases (Australia, some Latin American countries) but it did not fit the case of the United States, which ended up taking the largest number of DPs, and whose financial support was essential to IRO's functioning. The US Congress's decision to admit DPs en masse was to some extent the result of lobbying by ethnic and religious communities on behalf of their own, each seeking preferential admission for DPs of their own persuasion (Latvian, Ukrainian, Russian, Jewish, Catholic, Lutheran, and so on).

But it was the Cold War, and the possibility of framing DPs not as victims of war and fascism but of communism, that was crucial in convincing the US Congress to fund the Displaced Persons Act of 1948. In the propaganda battles of the Cold War, the DPs' refusal to repatriate, signifying an urgent need and desire to be rescued from the horrors of communism and embrace the free world, together with the US ability and willingness to effect this rescue, constituted irrefutable proof of the superiority of Western democracy. The successful solution to the problem of displaced persons after the Second World War was possible only because of the US embrace of a Cold War paradigm that conceptualized the postwar order in terms of bipolar ideological antagonism and competition rather than international cooperation.

This, is, of course, a gloomy conclusion for anyone looking to history to teach lessons on how to solve international problems. Up to a point, to be sure, the DP story shows us that well-funded international bodies such as UNRRA and IRO can do a good job looking after refugees in the short term. UNRRA was an idealistic institution. IRO, more politically constrained, still retained a larger share of its predecessor's decency and moral commitment than might have been expected. Neither institution was short of dedicated and empathetic staffers with the welfare of their DPs at heart. But it is not within the capacity of such bodies to find long-term solutions without major financial support, which in the context of the late 1940s could only come from the United States. UNRRA lost the support of the US Congress both because it had reached an impasse in its repatriation mandate when significant numbers of DPs refused to repatriate and because Congress felt no particular interest in maintaining for an indefinite period a million or so uprooted East Europeans defined as victims of war and Nazism. IRO came in with a new mandate, resettlement, which came with an end date, which was one major advantage. The other advantage was the rebranding of the DPs from victims of war and Nazism to victims of communism—in retrospect, the sine qua non for the continuance of congressional funding that made the resettlement program realistically achievable.

It would be possible to hypothesize a wily Machiavelli within IRO or the US State Department who in 1947 saw that just such a rebranding would solve the problem and worked behind the scenes to accomplish it. No such Machiavelli emerges from the archives, however, to claim credit. There is no foundational document to mark the shift. The "victims of communism" template seems to have emerged spontaneously within these institutions as they reactively adjusted their thinking from the wartime paradigm of alliance with the Soviet Union to the new paradigm of suspicion, zero-sum competition, and Cold War.

This brings us back to the DPs themselves. It has been a major argument of this book that the DPs were not simply "pawns of fate" but exercised more agency, collective and individual, than is normally assumed. A key example of this is the refusal of many DPs to repatriate, overturning the assumptions of the great powers in the immediate aftermath of the war that speedy mass repatriation would be the mechanism for removing the DPs from Europe and solving the DP problem.

But there is another example of DP agency that is equally crucial. Who originally thought of the DPs as victims of communism? Not IRO, not the military occupation regimes, and certainly not UNRRA. But from the very beginning of self-government in the DP camps, this was the self-conception of the anti-communist Slavic and East European nationalists who assumed leadership in all but the Jewish camps and served as the DPs' spokesmen. "Victims of communism," the rebranding which ultimately enabled the solution of the DP problem, came from the DPs themselves, not the governmental and international actors that were their carers; and its initial function was to justify their refusal to repatriate to countries that were now under communist control. If that refusal was their first great act of agency, their collective self-reinvention from victims of Nazism to victims of communism was their second.

In scholarship on the DPs, Slavic and Baltic DPs have traditionally played a secondary role, with Jewish DPs occupying center stage. In some ways, the Jewish DPs' experience matched that of the non-Jewish DPs, but in a number of important respects it did not. The Jewish DPs were quite clear about their identity as victims of Nazism. The "victims of communism" trope was irrelevant to them, and was also, to many Jewish DPs who had spent the war years in the Soviet Union, uncongenial. They disliked and feared the aggressive nationalist sentiments that reigned in the Polish, Ukrainian, Russian, and Baltic DP camps—sentiments that the Jews associated with antisemitism. The emerging Cold War offered no particular opportunities to them and, if anything, complicated the situation, since their Zionist objectives had US and Soviet support, but not British. As a group, the Jewish DPs had their own clear idea of what the Great Powers needed to do for them, which was to allow them to settle in Palestine. This, after some diplomatic back-and-forth, was what happened—another outcome in which DP agency was important, although in this case backed by strong support from the Jewish diaspora, especially in the United States, and Jewish international organizations.

The Slavic DPs, generally reciprocating the Jewish DPs' dislike, were a very different group in terms of political attitudes and aspirations. If the rank-and-file Russian and Ukrainian DPs who had been brought to Germany involuntarily as Ostarbeiter might see themselves as, to a degree, victims of Nazism, this was not the case with most of the anti-communist nationalist DP camp leaders, many of whom had been active or passive collaborators during the war. To such people, the original definition of DPs as victims of Nazism had been an actual or potential obstacle to their admission to DP status. "Victims of communism" was an identity that brought no such risks but, on the contrary, corresponded exactly to their own self-conception.

The Slavic and Baltic DPs, unlike the Jews, had no strong supporters in the world outside. They were staunch in their refusal to return to the Soviet Union, Poland, Yugoslavia, and so on, but there was no specific place that they wanted to go instead. Indeed, some of the most politically committed of them wanted to stay in Germany, the better to fight communism at first hand. For the Soviet/ Russian nonrepatriating DPs in particular, anti-communism (= anti-Sovietism) was an even more fundamental identity than nationalism. Their assertion of an identity as victims of communism was an act of agency that was not specifically directed toward achieving mass resettlement outside Europe, but, as an unanticipated consequence, made that resettlement possible.

It is never a fortunate situation to be a displaced person. In this book, I have tried to convey not only the global personal catastrophe of being displaced but also the endless stream of smaller-scale privations, disappointments, and anxieties that DPs had to cope with. These included physical and mental illness, loneliness, insecurity, worry about the fate of family members, remorse about leaving them, anxiety about missing opportunities, anguish at misfortunes like a child's disablement that might doom the whole family's hopes of rescue, frustrations at dealing with alien bureaucracies in a foreign language, the constant need for subterfuge coupled with a fear of being found out, and, for "Soviet" DPs, the additional fear, justified or not, of being snatched by Soviet agents and forcibly returned to the Soviet Union.

Nevertheless, in a comparative perspective, the "Soviet" DPs of postwar Germany were surely the luckiest of victims, however jarring this conclusion may be when one contemplates their individual experiences of loss and suffering. For the majority of DPs, their displacement ended, within six years of the war's end, in resettlement with free passage to a First World country, often the longed-for United States. This was an outcome that only the most optimistic could have dreamed of at the end of the war.

As for the great powers, the Cold War rebranding of the DPs produced a huge propaganda victory for the West that, as a bonus, brought associated economic benefit to Western countries short of labor. The political morality of this might be questioned, notably with reference to the admission of war criminals to the United States, Canada, Australia, and the United Kingdom under the guise of DP mass resettlement programs, which would become a contentious issue in all those countries from the 1970s. Redefining "victims of Nazism" as "victims of communism" (which, inter alia, made possible the inclusion of war criminals in IRO's resettlement scheme) involved a slightly dubious sleight of hand that simultaneously appealed to US public opinion and baffled the new Cold War enemy, the Soviet Union. But it was this conjuring trick, more than anything else, that made a speedy resolution of the postwar "DP problem" possible. Without it, the US Congress would never have financed the DPs' mass resettlement to the United States, let alone to the other countries involved. It was the Cold War that made possible the speediest and most successful solution to a major refugee crisis in twentieth-century history.

ACKNOWLEDGMENTS

I THANK the following scholars for generously helping me with advice and information on different aspects of this research: Warwick Anderson, Aleksei Antoshin, Nina Bogdan, Catherine Evtuhov, Peter Gatrell, Owen Hatherley, Andrew Janco, Edward Kasinec, Nadieszda Kizenko, Marina Moseikina, Benjamin Tromly, and Stephen Wheatcroft. I am particularly grateful to Aleksei Antoshin, in Russia, and Andrew Janco, in the United States, for generously locating and scanning materials for me.

A special debt of gratitude is due to several groups of scholars with whom I have worked closely on questions of displacement and migration in the past ten years. In Australia, Ruth Balint, Joy Damousi, Phillip Deery, Mark Edele, Elena Govor, Justine Greenwood, Christopher Hilliard, Mara Moustafine, Ebony Nilsson, Jayne Persian, and Nicholas Pitt have been wonderful collaborators, and I have also benefited from interactions with colleagues interested in migration at ACU's Institute for the Humanities and Social Science. Particular thanks go to Ruth and Joy for their quick and helpful answers to frequent email questions. It has been a source of great pleasure, as well as intellectual stimulus, to be part of this community of scholars and friends.

Internationally, I owe a great deal to Caroline Humphreys, Mollie Arbuthnot and participants in the Cambridge "Displacement" project, as well as to Jay Winter and others involved in the "Statelessness" project, and to my old friends and colleagues at the University of Chicago, Tara Zahra and Eleonor Gilburd. My Princeton editor, Priya Nelson, made a crucial suggestion about the presentation of my argument right at the end of my revisions, and Joy Damousi was the sounding border for the text (in place of a preface) that resulted.

My brother David Fitzpatrick, a historian of Ireland and migration, was my regular email interlocutor on this project before his untimely death in 2019. My husband Michael Danos, who died in 1999, is the former "displaced person" whose experience set me off on the study of DPs and remains central in my thinking about the topic.

The University of Sydney was my academic home during the pandemic lockdown when much of the work on the book was done. In 2020, I took up an appointment as a professor at the Institute of Humanities and Social Science at ACU in Melbourne. I am grateful to both institutions for their support, as well as to the Australian Research Council for the two "Discovery" grants that facilitated my research on migration in 2016 and 2022.

TABLE 1. IRO Resettlement of Russian / Soviet / Baltic and Jewish DPs, 1947–51, by Country of Destination

	Total all DPs	Total "Soviet" DPs	Number of total "Soviet" DPs					
			Ukrainian	Belorussian	"USSR"	Baltics	Stateless Rus / Nansen	Jews*
All	1,038,759	347,316	113,677	2,517	41,325	163,474	26,323	231,548
USA	328,851	148,471	45,044	1,135	14,506	77,454	10,332	64,930
Australia	182,159	68,996	19,607	854	4,944	39,695	3,896	8,172
Canada	123,479	45,749	14,877	152	8,158	21,296	1,266	16,021
UK	86,346	31,023	15,001	29	459	15,272	262	586
France	38,455	6,787	3,342	56	735	1,538	1,116	2,220
Belgium	22,477	10,401	5,650	1,826	1,872	825	228	
Latin America	94,027	28,820	9,935	383	6,965	4,463	7,074	5,027
• Argentina	32,712	7,188	2,283	0	2,071	1,043	1,791	736
• Brazil	28,848	10,234	4,609	336	1,427	1,350	2,512	803
• Venezuela	17,277	5,534	1,887	47	786	1,749	1,065	417
• Paraguay	5,887	2,595	146	0	2,265	71	113	1,685
• Chile	5,108	1,321	319	0	320	216	466	388
• Peru	2,340	179	86	0	33	14	46	98
• Uruguay	1,461	1,147	5	0	58	19	1,065	699
• Ecuador	394	21	0	0	0	5	16	201
Israel	132,109	3,789	35	44	1,689	1,238	783	130,408

Source: Calculated from Louise Holborn, The International Refugee Organization (London: Oxford University Press, 1956), 437–40 (annex 41); figures for July 1, 1947, to December 31, 1951.

Notes: 350,000 should be regarded as a minimum figure for DPs from the former Soviet Union and interwar Russian emigration for several reasons. In the first place, some Russians (both Soviet and émigré) would have identified themselves as Poles, Yugoslavs, or other East European nationalities. In the second place, IRO's statistics apply only to persons who were given the de jure status of DPs, eligible for IRO care and maintenance in Germany, Austria, and Italy. But there were also tens of thousands of de facto displaced persons who at the end of the war had found their own way from the Baltics or elsewhere to Scandinavia and Finland (over thirty thousand Baltic refugees in Sweden alone), in addition to those who had gone to Palestine illegally from Germany and Austria and others whose resettlement had been organized under other auspices of other institutions (IGCR, voluntary societies). For Sweden, see Cecelia Notini Burch, A Cold War Pursuit: Soviet Refugees in Sweden, 1945–54 (Stockholm: Santérus, 2014), 92, 140, 144–45. Diaspora sources for various nationalities similarly come up with substantially higher figures for resettled DPs than those of IRO.

For example, the Ukrainian diaspora estimate of 213,3880 Ukrainians resettled internationally as of 1952 was more than double IRO's numbers. See Wsevolod W. Isajiw, "The Ukrainian Diaspora," in *The Call of the Homeland: Diaspora Nationalism, Past and Present*, ed. Allon Gai et al. (Leiden: Brill, 2010, 293–94). Similarly, the Latvian Red Cross estimate of 125,000 resettled displaced Latvians resettled in the years 1947–51 is twice as high as the IRO figure. Daina Bleiere et al., *History of Latvia in the 20th Century* (Riga: Jumava, 2006), 424.

*It should be noted that IRO's figures for Jewish DPs are based on self-identification as such, and a DP who both identified as Jewish and gave a country of origin would be listed under both categories. According to these figures, 56 percent of all DPs identifying as Jewish went to Israel and 44 percent to other resettlement countries. Almost certainly, this proportion is too high. In addition to the factor of nonidentification as Jewish of entrants to resettlement countries other than Israel, the recorded numbers of Jewish migrants for all countries with policies restricting Jewish entry are likely to be substantially lower than the real numbers, because of effective measures taken by Jewish DPs, with the help of JDC, HIAS, and (covertly) IRO, to evade those restrictions. Thus IRO's figure for postwar Jewish resettlement in Australia is probably about half the real number because, to avoid the quotas on IRO entrants, many came on landing permits. See discussion in Sheila Fitzpatrick, "Migration of Jewish 'Displaced Persons' from Europe to Australia after the Second World War," *Australian Journal of Politics and History* 67, no. 2 (2021). IRO's figure for Canada appears to be similarly low. According to Louis Rosenberg's figures in "Canada," *American Jewish Year Book* 53 (1952), 258–59, and "Canada," *American Jewish Year Book* 57 (1956), 299, Canada gained 22,469 Jews ("most of them refugees and displaced persons") through immigration in 1946–50 and an additional 25,164 Jews in 1951–55. IRO's number for the period 1947–51 is around 16,000.

NOTES

Introduction

1. **Displaced persons (DPs)**. The term "displaced person," in general use in British relief circles by late 1942 for the victims of forced migration, was widely disseminated when demographer Eugene Kulischer used it in his book *The Displacement of Population in Europe* (Montreal: International Labour Office, 1943). The ten million estimate is based on figures in Lucius Clay, *Decision in Germany* (London: William Heinemann, 1950), 15.

2. **Agency**. For a comparable discovery of agency with regard to Jewish immigration to the United States in the face of restrictions on their entry, see Libby Garland, *After They Closed the Gates: Jewish Illegal Immigration to the United States, 1921–1965*. Chicago: University of Chicago Press, 2014.

3. **Jewish and other DPs**. A number of excellent and influential studies of DPs foreground Jewish DPs, sometimes almost to the exclusion of other groups: for example Michael R. Marrus, *The Unwanted: European Refugees in the Twentieth Century* (New York: Oxford University Press, 1985), part 5; Gerard Daniel Cohen, *In War's Wake: Jewish Displaced Persons in the Postwar Order* (New York: Oxford University Press, 2012); and David Nasaw, *The Last Million: Europe's Displaced Persons from World War to Cold War* (New York: Penguin Press, 2020). A more expansive concept of DPs, including the Slavic and Baltic groups, is used in Mark Wyman, *DPs: Europe's Displaced Persons, 1945–1951* (Ithaca, NY: Cornell University Press, 1998); Ben Shephard, *The Long Road Home: The Aftermath of the Second World War* (New York: Anchor Books, 2012); Ruth Balint, *Destination Elsewhere: Displaced Persons and Their Quest to Leave Postwar Europe* (Ithaca, NY: Cornell University Press, 2021); and the *Beyond Camps and Forced Labour* series, edited by Johannes-Dieter Steinert and Inge Weber-Newth (Osnabrück, 2003, 2005, etc.).

4. **Polish Jews in the wartime Soviet Union**: On the complicated circumstances that produced this situation, involving both voluntary (flight and evacuation in the face of German attack) and involuntary movement (deportation from the newly incorporated formerly Polish territories), see Yosef Litvak, "Jewish Refugees from Poland in the USSR, 1939–1946," in *Bitter Legacy: Confronting the Holocaust in the USSR*, ed. Zvi Gitelman (Bloomington: Indiana University Press, 1997), 123–50, and Mark Edele, Sheila Fitzpatrick, and Attina Grossmann, eds., *Shelter from the Holocaust: Rethinking Jewish Survival in the Soviet Union* (Detroit: Wayne State University Press, 2017).

5. **UNRRA and IRO**. The official histories of these organizations are George Woodbridge, *UNRRA: The History of the United Nations Relief and Rehabilitation Administration*, 3 vols. (New

York: Columbia University Press, 1950) and Louise Holborn, *The International Refugee Organization: Its History and Work* (London: Oxford University Press, 1956).

6. **Basic archival sources**. The core institutional archives used in this book are the UNRRA Archives (UA), held in the United Nations Archives, New York; the IRO archives in Archives Nationales (AN), Paris; British Foreign office archives in National Archives of the UK (NA UK); and National Archives of Australia (NAA), together with the State Archive of the Russian Federation (GARF), Moscow. For materials of the Soviet military government in Germany see GARF (*fond* 7317) and the Repatriation Agency under the Council of Ministers of the Soviet Union (GARF *fond* 9526).

7. **Michael Danos**. See Sheila Fitzpatrick, *Mischka's War: A European Odyssey of the 1940s* (Melbourne: Melbourne University Press, 2017); idem, "'Determined to Get On': Some Displaced Persons on the Way to a Future," *History Australia* 12:2 (2015), 102–23.

Chapter 1. UNRRA and Its Mandate

1. **Bevin's lament**: quotation from Alan Bullock, *Ernest Bevin, Foreign Secretary, 1945–1951* (Oxford: Oxford University Press, 1983), 196; **chaos in Germany**: quotation from Lucius Clay, *Decision in Germany* (London: William Heinemann, 1950), 15–16; **Soviet sensitivity on DPs:** Norman Naimark, *Stalin and the Fate of Europe: The Postwar Struggle for Sovereignty* (Cambridge, MA: Harvard University Press, 2019), 109 (quotation) and 252; **DP issue and human rights**: Gerard Daniel Cohen, *In War's Wake* (New York: Oxford University Press, 2012), 79–99.

2. **Molotov on Churchill's defeat**: quotation from 1970s interviews with Molotov in Feliks Chuev, *Sto sorok besed s Molotovym: Iz dnevnika F. Chueva* (Moscow: "Terra," 1991), 85; **British-US financial tensions**: Bullock, *Bevin*, 18, 121, 124; **quadripartite regimes**: Austria, as well as Germany, had one, but there the Western powers operated in concert rather than separately, and in cooperation with an elected national government that had no counterpart in Germany until 1949; **Soviet postwar predictions on capitalism**: these ideas were developed by Hungarian-born Soviet economist Eugen Varga, a major consultant to Stalin and other Soviet leaders in the immediate postwar years before a notorious falling-out. See Kyung Deok Roh, *Stalin's Economic Advisors: The Varga Institute and the Making of Soviet Foreign Policy* (London: I. B. Tauris, 2018), 134–40; **Soviet expectations**: Vladimir O. Pechatnov, "The Soviet Union and the World," in *The Cambridge History of the Cold War* (Cambridge, UK: Cambridge University Press, 2010), vol. 1, quotations 93, 95; **Molotov not to be duped:** Chuev, *Sto sorok besed*, 77–78.

3. **Clark Kerr and Soviets**: telegram of December 3, 1945, quoted in Bullock, *Bevin*, 199–200; (Clark Kerr's good relations with Stalin) see farewell conversation, January 25, 1946, in I. V. Stalin, *Sochineniia*, vol. 16, part 1 (Sent. 1945–dek. 1948) (Moscow: Izd. ITRK, 2011), 186–93l; (Clark Kerr's low opinion of Molotov) Bullock, *Bevin*, 134; **Molotov no diplomat**: Chuev, *Sto sorok besed*, 107; "**Old Stone Face**": this is Dean Acheson's version in Dean Acheson, *Present at the Creation: My Years in the State Department* (London: Hamish Hamilton, 1970), 78; within political circles in the Soviet Union, "stone-arse" was a popular variant. **Molotov's political problems at home**: see Sheila Fitzpatrick, *On Stalin's Team: The Years of Living Dangerously in Soviet Politics* (Princeton, NJ: Princeton University Press, 2015), 176–77.

4. **Bevin "not a gentleman"**: Stalin, *Sochineniia*, vol. 16, 332, 860; Bullock, *Bevin*, 134; Chuev, *Sto sorok besed*, 75; **abrasive Soviet style**: Acheson, *Present at the Creation*, 34, 78; Eleanor Roo-

sevelt, "Liberals in This Year of Decision," *Christian Register*, June 1948, in *The Eleanor Roosevelt Papers*, vol. 1, *The Human Rights Years, 1945–1948* (Detroit: Thomas Gale, 2007), 720, 830 (quotation), 914; **Generals' embrace**: Clay, *Decision*, 107, 138; **Jackson on working with Soviets**: Columbia University Library, Special Collections, Papers of Robert A. Jackson (C256) (henceforth, Jackson Papers), Box 1, File 58 (quotations from interview with Jonathan Power, 1983); ibid., Box 2, File 3, Oral History 1978.

5. **Origins of UNRRA**: George Woodbridge, *UNRRA: The History of the United Nations Relief and Rehabilitation Administration*, 3 vols. (New York: Columbia University Press, 1950), vol. 3, 23 (quotation from preamble to "The Agreement for the United Nations Relief and Rehabilitation Administration 9 November 1943") and vol. 1, 9–11, 21; Acheson, *Present at the Creation*, 65–66, 69; Ben Shephard, "'Becoming Planning Minded': The Theory and Practice of Relief 1940–1945," *Journal of Contemporary History* 43:3 (2008), 408 n. 15; **Lehman as director**: Woodbridge, *UNRRA*, vol. 1, 21; Shephard, "'Becoming Planning Minded'," 54, 414; Acheson, *Present at the Creation*, 43; **Hoover's rebuff**: Shephard, "'Becoming Planning Minded'," 153; Frederick Morgan, *Peace and War: A Soldier's Life* (London: Hodder and Stoughton, 1961). Robert Jackson later reflected that "in terms of getting results, the Allies might have done better to recall Herbert Hoover" than give the task to UNRRA: Jackson Papers, Box 2, oral history of Sir Robert G. A. Jackson (1978).

6. **UNRRA's financial backing**: Woodbridge, *UNRRA*, vol. 1, xxv–xxxv (listing of contributions in chronology), 105, 108–9; Arieh J. Kochavi, "British Policy on Non-Repatriable Displaced Persons in Germany and Austria, 1946–1947," *European History Quarterly* 21 (1991), 366; Bullock, *Bevin*, 143; **Stalin's offer**: Jackson Papers, Box 1, File 45: Thomas J. Mayock, preliminary monograph, confidential, not for circulation, "UNRRA and the Struggle for the Continuance of International Relief," 59–60; **problems with US Congress**: Acheson, *Present at the Creation*, 132; Kochavi, "British Policy," 366; Bullock, *Bevin*, 143; Andrew Harder, "The Politics of Impartiality: The United Nations Relief and Rehabilitation Administration in the Soviet Union, 1946–7," *Journal of Contemporary History* 47:2 (2012), 358; letter from Cmdr. Jackson to the Minister of State, London, August 25, 1947, Jackson Papers, Box 1, File 50; **cessation of funding**: Woodbridge, *UNRRA*, vol. 1, 46 (quotation); Jackson, letter to Minister of State, August 25, 1947, in Jackson Papers, Box 1, File 50; **criticisms of corruption**: University of Queensland, Fryer Library Manuscript Collection 44, Cilento Papers, Box 18, Folder 107: ms. "Escape from UN-Reality," 81; Marvin Klemmé, *The Inside Story of UNRRA* (New York: Lifetime Editions, 1949), 8; **Jackson's emergency mission**: Shephard, "'Becoming Planning Minded'," 413 (quotation); Jackson Papers, Box 1, File 50, letter to Minister of State, London, August 25, 1947.

7. **UNRRA staffing and procurement**: Michael R. Marrus, *The Unwanted: European Refugees in the Twentieth Century* (New York: Oxford University Press, 1985), 319; Jackson Papers, Box 1, File 50, letter to Minister of State, London; Woodbridge, *UNRRA*, vol. 1, 149, 164, and 166–67; **bonding in Middle East**: Jackson Papers, Box 2, oral history of Sir Robert G. A. Jackson (1978); **British influence**: Morgan, *Peace and War*, 228; Cilento Papers, "Escape from UN-Reality," 82–83; Klemmé, *Inside Story*, 216.

8. **Americans in UNRRA**: Morgan, *Peace and War*, 228; G. Daniel Cohen, "Between Relief and Politics: Refugee Humanitarianism in Occupied Germany 1945–1946," *Journal of Contemporary History* 43:3 (2008), quotations 442 (from Francesca Wilson) and 438; **"New Deal"**: staffers included (in addition to Myer Cohen) Conrad van Hyning, head of ERO's Displaced

Persons division, who had previously worked in another New Deal agency, the Federal Security Agency in Puerto Rico, Milton P. Siegel, chief of UNRRA's office of Far Eastern Affairs, who, like Cohen, had worked for FSA, and Karl Borders in UNRRA's Bureau of Supply, formerly of the Works Progress Administration, a New Deal institution dealing with unemployment: Woodbridge, *UNRRA*, vol. 3, 3–18: "Who's Who"; Cohen, "Between Relief and Politics," 441; **idealists**: Cohen, "Between Relief and Politics," 441; Susan T. Pettiss and Lynne Taylor, *After the Shooting Stopped: The Memoir of an UNRRA Welfare Worker, Germany 1945–1947* (Victoria, BC: Trafford Publishing, 2004); Kathryn Hulme, *The Wild Place* (Boston: Little, Brown, 1953); **UNRRA and UN**: Woodbridge, *UNRRA*, vol. 1, 45–46; **attitudes to socialism and the Soviet Union**: for warm appraisals of Soviet partners in field missions, see Cmdr. Jackson (a non-socialist recent convert to Catholicism!), Jackson Papers, Box 1, File 50, box 1 (end of job letter to Minister of State, London, August 25, 1947, 8) and Box 2, File 3, oral history (1978), and Marshal MacDuffie, in his *The Red Carpet: 10,000 Miles through Russia on a Visa from Khrushchev* (London: Cassel, 1955), as well as Harder, "Politics of Impartiality," 348, and Jessica Reinisch, "'Auntie UNRRA' at the Crossroads," *Past & Present* 218 (2013), 81.

9. **"Overstaffed with Communists and Jews"**: Klemmé, *Inside Story*, 4–7, 227 (Myer Cohen); Morgan, *Peace and War*, 222; Leonard Dinnerstein, *America and the Survivors of the Holocaust* (New York: Columbia University Press, 1982), 12 (Rifkind quotation); **loyalty to UNRRA**: Jackson Papers, Box 1, File 567 (1983 interview with Jonathan Power).

10. **DPs not UNRRA's central task**: Woodbridge, *UNRRA*, vol. 2, 470 (quotation); his UNRRA bio in vol. 3, 8. Out of a total of over fifteen hundred pages in Woodbridge's three-volume official history, the "Displaced Persons" department occupies a modest sixty-six pages in volume 2. It should be noted that no other sector of UNRRA's work employed so many people as displaced persons: Cohen, "Between Relief and Politics," 440; **DP care not foreseen**: Woodridge, *UNRRA*, vol. 2, 475; **UNRRA's relations with military governments**: Woodbridge, *UNRRA*, vol. 3, 197 (British), 202 (US), 189 (French).

11. **Gen. Patton on DPs**: Marrus, *Unwanted*, 321–22; **military preference for voluntary societies**: Shephard, "'Becoming Planning Minded,'" 413; Cohen, "Between Relief and Politics," 439; and see memo "Relief supplies for Germany," from Gen. Clay to Adcock of the US War Department" and other similar documents in *The Papers of General Lucius D. Clay, Germany 1945–1949*, vol. 1, edited by Jean Edward Smith (Bloomington: Indiana University Press, 1974) (the index to this volume, which covers the entire period up Clay's service in Europe, does not even have an entry for UNRRA); **Army would have done better job**: Klemmé, *Inside Story*, 47–48; **UNRRA and military governments**: Shephard, "'Becoming Planning Minded,'" 413; **agreements**: Woodbridge, *UNRRA*, vol. 3, 185–92, 194–201, 201–6, also Marrus, *Unwanted*, 321, and Dinnerstein, *America and the Survivors*, 10.

12. **Soviet attitudes**: Nasaw, *Last Million: Europe's Displaced Persons from World War to Cold War* (New York: Penguin Press, 2020), 318, citing SHAEF directive of April 1945; Marrus, *Unwanted*, 317–18 ("segregated" quotation); John G. Stoessinger, with the assistance of Robert G. McKelvey, *The United Nations and the Superpowers: United States-Soviet Interaction at the United Nations* (New York: Random House, 1967), 119–20 ("bi-lateral" quotation, from Arutiunian, August 1945; **souring relations**: Woodbridge (*UNRRA*, vol. 2, 486–87) calls this a disagreement between "the Slav nations and the other United Nations," since the Soviet position was shared by other Eastern European nations, notably Poland and Yugoslavia—an interesting variant on the framing that became established during the Cold War.

13. **First reactions to Jewish DPs**: Klemmé, *Inside Story*, 57 (quotation); Nasaw, *Last Million*, 116 (quoting Patton's diary entry, September 15, 1945; **Harrison mission**: Ben Shephard, *The Long Road Home: The Aftermath of the Second World War* (New York: Anchor Books, 2012), 110–12; Yehuda Bauer, *Out of the Ashes: The Impact of American Jews on Post-Holocaust European Jewry* (Oxford: Pergamon Press, 1989), 47 (quotation) (Bauer concludes that the Harrison Report was "not quite fair to the Army," since Eisenhower had already fixed many of the problems, including transferring Patton); **Truman's executive order**: Truman's directive #225 was published in the *New York Times*, December 3, 1945. As Nasaw notes (*Last Million*, 126), it did not give overt preference to Jewish DPs but stated that visas for US entry "should be distributed fairly among persons of all faiths, creeds and nationalities." While in practice Jewish DPs received a disproportionate share of these visas, Nasaw explains this by the fact that "the Jewish voluntary agencies in Germany were better positioned than the Catholic or Protestant ones to provide the displaced Jews with the documentation required to get their visas."

14. **Arrival of Polish Jews in Soviet Union during war**: UA: S-0411-0002 / S0411-0002-10 (report on infiltrees by Jay B. Krane, UNRRA CHQ for Germany, confidential to Chief of Operations, UNRRA, Germany, January 18, 1946); Mark Edele, Sheila Fitzpatrick, and Atina Grossmann, eds., *Shelter from the Holocaust: Rethinking Jewish Survival in the Soviet Union* (Detroit: Wayne State University Press, 2017); **US welcome**: Nasaw, *Last Million*, 242; **Soviet tacit support**: UA: S-0411-0002 / S0411-0002-10, April 2, 1946; **British anger**: Nasaw, *Last Million*, 249; Klemmé, *Inside Story*, 59 (quotation); **conflicts with British over Bergen-Belsen**: on Jewish protests against the employment of German nurses in the Belsen hospital, see Cilento Papers, "Escape from UN-Reality," 68, 82a; Susan Armstrong-Reid and David Murray, *Armies of Peace: Canada and the UNRRA Years* (Toronto: University of Toronto Press, 2008), 255, citing the unpublished memoir of Canadian Matron Lyle Creelman; **UNRRA and Bergen-Belsen**: on Jewish protests against inclusion of non-Jews in UNRRA team, see UA: S-1450-0000-0271-00001: "Jewish Problem in the British Zone," report from Lt.-Col. K. W. Charley to Rhea Radin, October 23, 1946, reacting to a World Jewish Congress report of August 28, 1946; **UNRRA accepts Jewish arrivals**: UA: S0523-0006-0017-00001: urgent cable to Dudley Ward from [Alfred E., General Counsel at UNRRA HQ] Davidson, Washington, DC, February 14, 1946.

15. **JDC in Europe**: Cohen, "Between Relief and Politics," 47; Bauer, *Out of the Ashes*, xvi; **JDC and American zone**: Dinnerstein, *American and the Survivors*, 47; **JDC and US military**: Bauer, *Out of the Ashes*, 201–2 (McNarney quotation); Nasaw, *Last Million*, 174 (citing Lucy Davidowicz, sometime JDC staffer in postwar Europe, later a distinguished historian of the Holocaust); **JDC in British zone**: Bauer, *Out of the Ashes*, xvi; UA: S-1450-0000-0271-00001: meeting of American and British Jewish voluntary organizations with UNRRA officials in the British zone, March 19, 1946, to discuss complaints from Josef Rosenhaft, writing on behalf of "the Central Jewish Committee in the British zone of Germany"; **Morgan's comments**: Morgan, *Peace and War*, 245; Shephard, *Long Road Home*, 159 (quoting London *Evening Standard*). Raphael Cilento, Morgan's subordinate in charge of UNRRA operations in the British zone of Germany, expressed similar sentiments in his unpublished memoir: Cilento Papers, "UN-Reality," 125–26; **Morgan's departure**: UNRRA director Lehman tried to keep him on with a warning, but when he continued to go off message to journalists, including the statement that "UNRRA missions in Germany are an umbrella for Soviet espionage and crime" reported by Doris Fleeson in Washington's *Evening Star*, August 27, 1946, he had to be "released" (not formally a dismissal) from the UNRRA position: UA: S-0411-0002-10.

16. **1943 Agreement**: "The Agreement for the United Nations Relief and Rehabilitation Administration 9 November 1953," in Woodbridge, *UNRRA*, vol. 3, 23; **UNRRA's responsibility**: Woodbridge, *UNRRA*, vol. 2, 471; **collaborators**: UA: S-0523-0006-0017, quotation from letter of Miss Radin of Welfare and Repatriation London to Arolsen HQ, February 11, 1946; **Agreements with zonal commands**: Woodbridge, *UNRRA*, vol. 3, 195 (British agreement), 201 (US agreement); **on Army responsibilities**: UA: S-0523-0006-0017-00001: cable from Whiting, Munich, to Van Hyning, February 22, 1946.

17. **Volksdeutsche**: UA: S-1021-0081-0002; DP-US 18: Eligibility and Screening, UNRRA Central HQ Germany, Administrative order of August 31, 1946; ibid., order of General McNarney, HQ of USD forces, European theater, May 16, 1946, on ineligibility of Baltic citizens who had voluntarily immigrated to Germany and taken German citizenship, or returned to Germany in 1949–41; UA: S-1450-0000-0075-0001, cable from Vienna to London dated February 22, 1946, assuring headquarters that they were "presently removing all Volksdeutsche German Balts Collaborators from DP Camps assisted by UNRRA." This, of course, leaves open the possibility that they were *not* removing Volksdeutsche German Balts who were *not* deemed to be collaborators. In any case, none of Mischka Danos's "Riga German" friends lost their UNRRA eligibility on these grounds. **Definition of "displaced person"**: AN: AJ / 43 / 148 (*Preliminary draft of Instructions on IRO Eligibility*. Volume I. Handbook [Rome: Eligibility Office of PCIRO—Italy, October 1947]); NAA: A445 / 1 / 2 ("Revised Policy—1947": "a displaced or persecuted person is one who has suffered at the hands of a Nazi or Fascist regimes by being placed in a concentration or forced labour camp, being deported from his usual place of abode [or being] forced to lead a clandestine existence during the war period"); **Jewish "persecutees"**: UA: S-1252-0000-0155-00001: submission to Second Session of the Council of UNRRA, Montreal, from Agudas Israel World Organization, signed Jacob Rosenheim President, n.d., proposing a general resolution that "Germans or stateless Jews or other victims of Nazi racial and religious persecution should not be considered enemy-aliens for UNRRA purposes, and, even if they are living in enemy territory, must be cared for by UNRRA in the same way as citizens of the United Nations"; Woodbridge, *UNRRA*, vol. 2, 481–82; **UNRRA in British zone reportedly not assisting**: UA: S-1450-0000-0271-00001: Selene Gifford, director, UNRRA repatriation division, ERO, to chief of UNRRA's German operation, BAOR, October 23, 1946; **"German Jews eligible"**: UA: S-0411-0002-10: memo from H. R. Pollak (Asst. Director Field Operations, UNRRA, British Zone, UNRRA HQ), November 1946.

18. **Classification by country of origin**: Cohen, "Between Relief and Politics," 448; **"Jewish" accepted as nationality**: Lynne Taylor, "Please Report Only *True* Nationalities': The Classification of Displaced Persons in Post-Second World War Germany and Its Implications," in David Cesarani et al., eds., *Survivors of Nazi Persecution in Europe after the Second World War* (London: Vallentine Mitchell, 2010), 41 (UNRRA directive); UA: S-0425-0010-02: Categories of DPs 1945–6, Annexe "B," HQ US Forces, European Theater, Office of Military Government (US Zone), November 16, 1945, "Determination and Reporting of Nationalities": "Those Jews who are without nationality, or those Jews (not Soviet citizens) who do not desire to return to their country of origin, will be reported as 'Jews.'" **Different understandings of term "nationality"**: For confusion within UNRRA on the "troubling" fact that under Polish (and other East European) law, nationality seemed to have "ethnological and racial" implications, see UA: S-0400-0003-01: memo from Paul Carter, Legal Adviser, to Acting Chief of Operations, De-

cember 10, 1946; **Baltic nationalities**: on US acceptance of Latvian, Lithuanian, and Estonian as nationalities, on grounds of nonrecognition of Soviet incorporation of their states, see UA: S-0425-0010-02: Categories of DPs 1945–6. Annexe "B," HQ US Forces, European Theater, Office of Military Government (US Zone), November 16, 1945; **British and American position on Balts**: Nasaw, *Last Million*, 135, and UA: S-0523-0006-0017-00001: memo "On eligibility of DPs for UNRRA care" from Conrad Van Hyning of the Displaced Persons division to Dudley Ward, ERO's general counsel, dated December 1, 1945 ("Balts should be considered as eligible on the theory that they are either of undetermined nationality or stateless. The date of their displacement was during the war which qualifies them on this basis and the manner of their displacement should be considered merely as a result of the war, thus making them eligible"); **French dissent**: Wolfgang Jacobmeyer, *Vom Zwangsarbeiter zum heimatlosen Ausländer: Die Displaced Persons in Westdeutschland 1945–1951* (Göttingen: Vandenhoeck & Ruprecht, 1985), 80–82.

19. **Morgan on Balts**: Morgan, *Peace and War*, 232; Klemmé, *Inside Story*, 248; **Valdmanis**: Ralph Price (UNRRA chief of reparations in the US zone), wrote indignantly on Mickelson's connection with Valdmanis in an internal report, "Displaced Persons US Zone. Repatriation Report," in UA: S1021-81-3, citing the latter's recent identification as a "quisling" in Gregory Maiksins, *The Baltic Riddle* (New York: L. B. Fischer, 1943, 205). For an overview of Valdmanis's extraordinary career, which continued in Canada after resettlement, see Gerhard P. Bassler, *Alfred Valdmanis and the Politics of Survival* (Toronto: University of Toronto Press, 2000). **Balts as collaborators**: Klemmé, *Inside Story*, 248; Dinnerstein, *America and the Survivors of the Holocaust*, 223 (quoting Middleton).

20. **Ukrainian nationality claims**: In a note of December 1, 1945, Van Hyning of UNRRA Displaced Persons suggested to the European office's General Counsel Dudley Ward that "if we could adopt the general policy that persons whose former residence is now under a different government from that which it was while he resided there may be given a free choice as to where they wish to go, we could consider them eligible pending much determination" (UA: S-0523-0006-0017-00001); **British position**: NA UK: FO 945 / 598: minute from Lieut-Col (no sig.), to Mr. Wilberforce, May 1946; UA: S-0400-0003-01: cable from Brig. W. Stawell, War Office, London, March 21, 1946; **Polish position**: UA: S-0400-0003-01—DPs—Ukrainians. W. Wolski, Gen. Plenipotentiary of Polish government for repatriation, Austrian Mission, and R.H.R. Parminter, chief, UNRRA Mission to Austria, November 1, 1946: clarification of position of Polish government on repatriability of individuals of Ukrainian nationality and Volksdeutsche; **Ukrainian-Polish conflict in camps**: Nasaw, *Last Million*, 166; **gradual recognition of Ukrainian nationality**: NA UK: FO 945 / 598: minute from Lieut-Col (no sig.), May 1946 to Mr. Wilberforce (including reference to lobbying for recognition of Ukrainian nationality from Canadian Ukrainian Committee); Anna Holian, *Between National Socialism and Soviet Communism: Displaced Persons in Postwar Germany* (Ann Arbor: University of Michigan Press, 2011), 103; Jacques Vernant, *The Refugee in the Post-War World: Preliminary Report of a Survey of the Refugee Problem* (Geneva: United Nations, 1951), 60; Taylor, "'Please Report Only True Nationalities,'" 44–45. Vernant dates the official acceptance of Ukrainian as a nationality category as March 1947, but UNRRA reports indicate that it was being used in the field, though not universally, some months earlier: UA: S-0437-0022-17 (memo from R. J. Youdin to S. K. Jacobs, November 18, 1946); **hair-splitting**: Morgan, *Peace and War*, 233.

21. **Belorussian claims**: UA: S-0437-0022-30 (Memos from "White Ruthenians" to UNRRA HQ, May 12 and October 15, 1946): signatory Dr. Jan Stankiewitsch described "White Ruthenians as "a nation with their own original language, history, culture" whose people were currently dispersed in Polish, Ukrainian and Russian DP camps" and ought to have the same recognition as the Ukrainians, since both had republics in the Soviet Union. According to another letter in the file, "White Ruthenians" were also known as "Kriviches," and UNRRA concluded that they must be Belorussians under another name. **Allied confusion on meaning of "White Russian"**: see Sheila Fitzpatrick, *White Russians, Red Peril: A Cold War History of Migration to Australia* (Melbourne: Latrobe University Press, 2021), 62–3; **Russian as a nationality**: Andrew Paul Janco, "Soviet 'Displaced Persons' in 1941–1945," PhD diss., University of Chicago, 2012, 210, 224–25; **Monchehoff**: see below, notes to chap. 3.

22. **Threats of UNRRA closure**: Nasaw, *Last Million*, 199; **staff look for new jobs**: Cilento Papers, "Escape from UN-Reality," 133. Cilento himself was one of those seeking UN jobs, leaving UNRRA for in New York in June 1946 (University of Queensland, Fryer Library Manuscript Collection 233: Fedora Fisher Collection, Box 4: Personal File for Raphael Cilento), although his hopes for the directorship of the new World Health Organization were disappointed. **Lehman's resignation**: Woodbridge, *UNRRA*, vol. 1, 44 (he ran unsuccessfully for senator for New York in 1946 but in 1948 was appointed to fill a vacancy in 1948 and was elected in 1950); **La Guardia appointment**: Woodbridge, *UNRRA*, vol. 3, xxxi (chronology); **assessments of La Guardia**: Jackson Papers, Box 1, File 36: letter of Robert Jackson to Edward Jackson, April 9, 1946; Klemmé, *Inside Story*, 219; **La Guardia's task**: Nasaw, *Last Million*, 261; Jackson Papers, Box 2, oral history of Sir Robert G. A. Jackson (1978) (Jackson agreed in this interview that La Guardia was brought in to wind up the organization but said he then "did a flip" when he saw it was doing a good job); **bias toward Jewish DPs**: Morgan, *Peace and War*, 255–56; **purge of antisemites in UNRRA**: Shephard, *Long Road Home*, 238.

23. **Operation Carrot**: Woodbridge, *UNRRA*, vol. 2, 515; **opposition to Operation Carrot**: Marrus, *Unwanted*, 322; Morgan, *Peace and War*, 255–56; AN: AJ / 43 / 140: Myer Cohen, in interview by Michael Hacking, December 20, 1951; **response at Wildflecken**: Hulme, *Wild Place*, 150–51 (quotation), 152; **Polish repatriation numbers**: Woodbridge, *UNRRA*, vol. 3, 426, table 13: "Repatriation of Polish displaced persons by month"; **US criticism**: Nasaw, *Last Million*, 265–68 (quotation 267): Democratic political bosses in Chicago and Illinois, with their large Polish population, were sympathetic to this claim.

24. **Field missions tour**: Woodbridge, *UNRRA*, vol. 1, xxxii; **Jackson's Soviet contacts**: Jackson Papers, Box 1, File 45: Thomas J. Mayock (Office of Chief Archivist and Historian), preliminary monograph, "UNRRA and the Struggle for the Continuance of international relief," n.d. [late 1946?]; **meeting with Stalin**: Stalin, *Sochineniia*, vol. 16, part 1, 393–97: "Beseda s General'nym Direktorom IuNRRA F. La Gardiia, August 29, 1946," marked "completely secret."

25. **Plan to save UNRRA**: the plan is outlined in a manuscript in the Jackson Papers, Box 1, File 45: Mayock, "UNRRA and the struggle for continuance of international relief," which includes a handwritten note states that the strategy was in fact thought up by Cmdr. Jackson. **Soviet willingness to pay**: Mayock notes that Soviet representative Feonov had indicated Soviet support for UNRRA's continuation and willingness to pay in a press interview at Geneva on August 6, 1946 (Jackson Papers, Box 1, File 45: Mayock, "UNRRA"), and Jackson later said that the Soviets were willing to make their contribution in gold, a substantial concession (Jack-

son Papers, Box 1, File 58; Transcript of interview with Jonathan Power, July 11, 1983); **Stalin's praise of UNRRA**: Stalin, *Sochineniia*, vol. 16, part 1, 393–97 ("Beseda"); **La Guardia's boasting**: UA: S-0411-0002-10 (UNRRA Daily Press Clippings USA no. 174) contains a cutting from the *Chicago Sun* of August 30, 1946, quoting La Guardia as saying that Stalin was open to helping solve the European DP problem by "accept[ing persons of non-Soviet nationality [presumably Jews] from among 830,000 displaced persons in UNRRA's European camps"—something at complete variance with Soviet policy, which had always been to accept any and all Soviet citizens as repatriates but to refuse to take anyone else; **La Guardia's resignation**: Woodbridge, *UNRRA*, vol 3, xxxi, chronology. Jackson later claimed that La Guardia "could have pulled off the US funding extension if he had tried, but he had made a deal with Secretary of State James Byrnes and others to sink UNRRA in return for nomination for the Senate seat in New York State (Jackson Papers, Box 1, File 50: letter of August 25, 1947, to Minister of State, London). Whether or not this was true, La Guardia may already have been a sick man: he died of pancreatic cancer in New York on September 20, 1947, at the age of sixty-four (*New World Encyclopedia*, "Fiorello H. LaGuardia," https://www.newworldencyclopedia.org/entry/Fiorello_H._LaGuardia, accessed October 11, 2023).

26. **Churchill's Fulton speech**: Text at https://www.nationalarchives.gov.uk/education/resources/cold-war-on-file/iron-curtain-speech/, accessed April 5, 2023.

27. **UNRRA funding Eastern Europe**: Acheson, *Present at the Creation*, 200–201; **cooling of relations**: Clay, *Decision in Germany*, 159, 161; American foreknowledge of text: Bullock, *Bevin*, 224–25; Daniel Yergin, *Shattered Peace: The Origins of the Cold War and the National Security State* (New York: Penguin Books, 1977), 175–76; **Stalin's reaction**: Stalin, *Sochineniia*, vol. 16, part 1, 317 (conversation with Boleslaw Bierut and Edward Osobka-Morawski, May 24, 1946).

28. **Congressional criticism of UNRRA**: Harder, "Politics of Impartiality," 359, 362; **"Communists and spies in organization"**: Reinisch, "'Auntie UNRRA,'" 88 (quoting Ambassador Arthur Bliss Lane); Morgan, *Peace and War*, 150, 160 (the phrase "Honeycombed with spies" is attributed to him in the *New York Times*, August 24, 1946, quoted Reinisch, "'Auntie UNRRA,'" 97); Rheinisch, "'Auntie UNRRA,'" 97, n. 101 (list of UNRRA personnel accused of being Soviet spies); Jackson Papers, Box 2, File 3: 1978 oral history (Jackson, working for the British government in the 1950s, reported that "literally dozens" of American former UNRRA staffers seeking jobs "approached me having been accused by McCarthy of being communists and traitors to the United States").

29. **Death knell**: Woodbridge, *UNRRA*, vol. 1, 46–47; **achievements**: Harder, "Politics of Impartiality," 368; **successor institutions**: in addition to IRO, which was not formally a UN institution, these included the World Health Organization (WHO), the United Nations International Children's Emergency Fund (UNICEF), and the United Nations Economic and Social Organization (UNESCO): Reinisch, "'Auntie UNRRA', 71; **closures of missions and offices**: Woodbridge, *UNRRA*, vol. 1, chronology on xxxiii–xxxiv.

Chapter 2. Repatriation to the Soviet Union and Allied Conflict

1. **Yalta Agreement**: AN: AJ / 43 / 148, p. 26 (Yalta Agreement "Application of Soviet citizens"; Combined Chiefs of Staff, "Reciprocal Agreement on Prisoners of War, 8 February 1945," in Argonaut Conference January–February 1945: Papers and Minutes of Meetings Argonaut

Conference (Office, US Secretary of the Combined Chiefs of Staff, 1945), at cgsc.contentdm .oclc/org/cdm/singleitem/collection/p4013coll8/id/3687, accessed February 19, 2019; **proportion of Soviet DPs from incorporated territories**: V. N. Zemskov, "'Vtoraia emigratsiia' i otnoshenie k nei rukovodstva SSSR, 1947–1955," in *Istoriia rossiiskogo zarubezh'ia: Emigratsiia iz SSSR-Rossii 1941–2001*, ed. Iu. Poliakov et al. (Moscow: Institute Rossiiskoi istorii RAN, 2007), 73–74 (note that this is only an estimate: because of false statements by DPs and inconsistent Allied and UNRRA record-keeping, the exact breakdown between those who before the war had held Polish citizenship, on the one hand, and Soviet, on the other, can never be exactly known); **no obligation to readmit repatriates**: UA: S-1451-0000-0074-00002 IGCR: T. T. Scott to Sir Frederick Leith Ross, December 17, 1944; Andrew Paul Janco, "'Unwilling': The One-Word Revolution in Refugee Status, 1940–51," *Contemporary European History*, 23:3 (2014), 435–36.

2. **"Unmixing of nationalities"**: Rogers Brubaker, "Aftermaths of Empire and the Unmixing of People," *Ethnic and Racial Studies* 18:2 (1995), 189–218; **repatriation of war criminals**: AN: AJ / 43 / 148, 29 ("Collaborationist group Russian Liberation Army," 29: "Members of this organisation . . . are repatriable under the Yalta Agreement"); **Soviet attitude to repatriation after World War I**: Reinhard Nachtigall, "The Repatriation and Reception of Returning Prisoners of War, 1918–22," *Immigrants & Minorities* 26: 1–2 (2008), 157–84, and Richard B. Speed III, *Prisoners, Diplomats and the Great War* (New York: Greenwood Press, 1990), 172–73; Mark R. Elliott, *Pawns of Yalta: Soviet Refugees and America's Role in Their Repatriation* (Urbana: University of Illinois Press, 1982); Peter Gatrell, *A Whole Empire Walking: Refugees in Russia during World War I* (Bloomington: Indiana University Press, 1999), 193–94 (denaturalization); **unwillingness of East European countries to accepted nontitular repatriates**: AN: AJ / 43 / 140 (interviews de fonctionnaires de l'OIR par Michael Hacking, historien à l'OIR 1950–52: Meeting in Palais Wilson between Mr. Jarrell and History Unit Potulicki, January 8, 1952).

3. **Number of Soviet displaced persons in 1945**: V. N. Zemskov, *Vozvrashchenie sovetskikh peremeshchennykh lits v SSSR 1944–1952 gg.* (Moscow: Tsentr gumanitarnykh initiativ, 2016), 16; **Yalta conversations**: Zemskov, *Vozvrashchenie*, 47; **resistance to repatriation**: Elliott, *Pawns of Yalta*, 88–89 (Fort Dix); Nikolai Tolstoy, *Victims of Yalta* (London: Hodder & Stoughton, 1977), 213–14; Nicholas Bethell, *The Last Secret: Forcible Repatriation to Russia 1944–7* (London: Deutsch, 1974), 135, 151; Jayne Persian, "Cossack Identities: From Russian Émigrés and Anti-Soviet Collaborators to Displaced Persons," *Immigrants and Minorities* 3:26 (2018), 131 (Lienz); **Soviet branding of POWs as traitors**: Richard Overy, *Russia's War* (London: Penguin, 1998), 80–81; V. N. Khaustov et al., eds., *Lubianka: Stalin i NKVD-NKGB-GUKR "Smersh'"*, *1939–mart 1946* (Moscow: Rossiia XX vek, 2006), 324–25 (Order no. 270 of August 16, 1941; resolutions of State Defence Committee [GKO] of December 24 and 27, 1941); **no Soviet amnesty**: GARF: 7317 / 20 / 145, l. 462 (Chernov-Reshetnikov interview, June 23, 1949). Something like amnesty promises were apparently issued at republican level, notably by the Lithuanian and Ukrainian republican governments: Aleksei Ivanovich Briukhanov, *Vot kak eto bylo* (Moscow: Gospolitizdat, 1958), 120–21.

4. **Suspension of Allied cooperation:** (**American**) Elliott, *Pawns of Yalta*, 108–10; GARF: 7317 / 20 / 1: "Kratkaia istoriia otdela repatriatsii i rozyska sovetskikh grazhdan SVA v Germanii za period 1 iiun' 1945–1948 g. Kn. 1, 35; (**British**) NA UK: FO 371 / 122678: BERCOMB [Gen. Sir Brian Robertson, deputy cmdr. of British forces, British zone of Germany] to TROOPERS,

October 12, 1945; (Montgomery): NA UK: FO 371 / 122678: PW & DP division, December 18 [1945], to Control Commission for Germany (British Element); **Gen. Patton**: Elliott, *Pawns of Yalta*, 106; UA: S-0437-0022-15 ("Restricted" order, November 17, 1945—Patton was removed by Eisenhower from command of the Third Army and military governorship of Bavaria in October 1945); **DP citizenship**: "Displaced Persons' Registration Instructions," cited Janco, "'Unwilling,'" 432 (quotation from Janco's paraphrase); **"no Soviet nationals left in camps"**: NA UK: FO 945 / 598 (Lt.-Col. D. C. S. Sinclair, War Office, undated, to Brimelow, Dir. Civil Affairs Commonwealth Office, citing directive of November 1945 from Prisoner of War Directorate); **McNarney-Clark Directive**: Janco, "'Unwilling,'" 434 (General Joseph T. McNarney had recently taken over command of US forces in Germany from Eisenhower and was military governor of the US zone of Germany; General Mark Clark commanded US forces in Austria); **total Soviet repatriations and numbers remaining**: calculated from Zemskov, "'Vtoraia emigratsiia,'" 72, and idem, *Vozvrashchenie*, table 7, 141.

5. **Soviet atrocity stories**: George Fischer, "The New Soviet Emigration," *Russian Review* 8:1 (1949), 10; **filtration process**: A. V. Riabova, "Organizatsionno-normativnaia baza 'fil'tratsii' sovetskikh grazhdan v 1940-e-nachale 1950-kh gg.," in *Marginaly v sovetskom obshchestve: Mekhanizmy i praktika statusnogo regulirovaniia v 1930-1950-e gody. Sbornik nauchnykh statei* (Novosibirsk: Novosibirskii gosudarstvennyi universitet, 2006), 136–39, and see Igor Vasilevich Govorov, "Fil'tratsiia sovetskikh repatriantov v 40-e gg," *Cahiers du monde russe* 49:2 / 3 (2008), 374–78; **women repatriates (statistics)**: Sheila Fitzpatrick, "The Women's Side of the Story: Soviet 'Displaced Persons' and Postwar Repatriation," *Russian Review* 81:2 (2022), 286; **labor shortages**: see Wendy Goldman and Donald Filtzer, *Fortress Dark and Stern: The Soviet Home Front during World War II* (Oxford: Oxford University Press, 2021); **arrests after repatriation**: Seth Bernstein, *Return to the Motherland: Displaced Soviet in World War II and the Cold War* (Ithaca, NY: Cornell University Press, 2023), 146–47; **repatriated POWs**: Zemskov, *Vozvrashchenie*, 111–12; Mark Edele, *Soviet Veterans of the Second World War* (Oxford: Oxford University Press, 2008), table 5.2, 118 (Edele gives the slightly higher figure of 16.7 percent handed over to the NKVD).

6. **Soviet Military Administration**: the classic source is Norman Naimark, *The Russians in Germany: A History of the Soviet Zone of Occupation, 1945–1949* (Cambridge, MA: Belknap Press, 1995) (but note that repatriation scarcely figures in his account of the agency in the immediate postwar period, an indication of its low priority in the institution); **Soviet Repatriation Agency** (official name: Upravlenie Upolnomochennogo po Repatriatsii pri Sovete Narodnykh Komissarov SSSR [Administration of the Soviet Council of People's Commissar's Plenipotentiary for Repatriation], set up in 1944): its mission was to locate and register Soviet citizens in Europe, arrange their return to the Soviet Union (providing housing, food, and medical treatment along the way), cooperate with the NKVD on filtration, and transport repatriates back to the Soviet Union: Iu. N. Arzamaskin, *Tainy sovetskoi repatriatsii* (Moscow: Veche, 2015), 29; **low clout of agency**: "Posetiteli kremlevskogo kabineta Stalina," in *Istoricheskii arkhiv*, 1994 no. 6 to 1997 no. 1, ed. A. V. Korotkov et al. (the 1945–51 log of Stalin's office, where the most important meetings took place, shows that Golikov or any other agency representative was rarely invited); **SMERSH**: set up on April 21, 1943, by the State Defense Commission, answerable only to Stalin, although working closely with the security agencies (Riabova, "Organizatsionno-normativnaia baza 'filtratsii,'" 137); **conflicts with SMERSH over kidnappings**: GARF: 7317 / 20 / 1 ("Kratkaia

istoriia otdela repatriatsii i rozyska sovetskikh grazhdan SVA v Germanii za period 1 iiun'
1945–1948 g. Kn. 1, 115); **rare cases of repatriation agency involvement in kidnappings**: Bernstein, *Return to the Motherland*, 196–67; **Golikov's promise**: Arzamaskin, *Tainy*, 30 (quotation
from TASS interview, November 11, 1944); **Soviet liaison officers**: UA: S-0523-0006-0017-
00001 (cable from Mr. Radin, Welfare and Repatriation, London) to Washington, February 23,
1946); (**Soviet view**) Briukhanov, *Vot kak eto bylo*, 184–85; (**UNRRA view**) UA: S-00399-0002-
06 (A. Genchington, chief PW & DP Division, "Facilities to Be Afforded to Soviet Liaison
Officers," September 5, 1946; George Woodbridge, *UNRRA* (New York: Columbia University
Press, 1950), vol. 2, 517.

7. **Soviet sympathizers in UNRRA: Ralph Price memo**: UA: S-1021-0081-0003; Repatriation Report May 1, 1947, by Ralph Price, Chief of Repatriation, UNRRA, US Zone, Germany.
In February 1947, Price had visited Warsaw (where a communist government had recently been
installed) in his capacity as repatriation head and expressed sympathy with Polish government
complaints about the obstruction of repatriation from Wildflecken by assertive anti-communist
groups: Ben Shephard, *The Long Road Home: The Aftermath of the Second World War* (London:
Vintage, 2010), 242; **Paul Edwards case**: UA: S-0523-0042-1 (letter of Myer Cohen, Acting
Chief of DP Operations at UNRRA HQ, to Dudley Ward, Deputy General Counsel of
UNRRA's European office, May 19, 1947, and Cohen, note to Ward, May 29, 1947); **Edwards's
survival**: Louise Holborn, *The International Refugee Organization* (London: Oxford University
Press, 1956), appendix 4, 762 (Edwards's appointment as head of mission in the American zone
of Germany, an office he held from July 1947 until August 1948); **other sympathizers**: (Cohen)
UA: S-00399-0002-06: meeting with Soviet mission representatives at UNRRA HQ on September 16, 1946 (in advising zone directors that, with respect to Latvian, Lithuanian, and Estonian
DPs, "the appropriate official . . . to consult with is the accredited Soviet representative," Cohen
appears to have made an unusual concession, adding, "I do not know whether the occupying
authorities will agree, but those are the UNRRA instructions to UNRRA personnel"); (Margaret Bond) UA: S-0402-0003-0001 (Margaret Bond, Chief Repatriation Officer, January 10,
1946, to Director-in-Chief, Austrian Operation).

8. **Anti-Soviet attitudes in UNRRA**: UA: S-00399-0002-06 (Resolution no. 99, Relating
to Displaced persons Operations, 5th Council Session, Geneva, [August] 1946); UA: S-0402-
0003-0001 (Cilento, Dir, British Zone, to Charley, Chief of German and Austrian Branch, Welfare &
Repat. Div., April 24, 1946, "On reports concerning alleged employment by UNRRA personnel
of unauthorized methods to induce repatriation"); UA: S-00399-0002-06 (Fanshawe to Chief
of Operations, British Zone, December 19, 1946, and letter on behalf of Zone Director [Fan-
shawe] to [Soviet liaison mission head] Brukhanov, December 1946); **complaints of Soviet
representatives**: UA: S-00399-0002-06 (Notes of interview at USFET between Maj.-Gen.
Davidov, Chief, Repatriation Mission, USSR, and Brig.-Gen. V. Meyer, deputy Chief of Operations, UNRRA, July 25, 1946); **Soviet general snubbed**: UA: S-00399-0002-06 (memo on
telephone message from Hansi Pollack to COG re Gen. Davidov; Fanshawe, Zone Director, to
UNRRA's PW / DP Division, September 9, 1946); **Cohen's apology**: UA: S-00399-0002-06
(meeting at Central HQ, September 16, 1946, attended by Myer Cohen, Gen. Davidov, Brig.
Cyrus Greenslade [Dep Chief of Operations] et al.).

9. **Fanshawe and Soviets**: (on wartime cordiality) UA: S-00399-0002-06 (meeting at Central HQ, September 16, 1946); **Fanshawe and Brukhanov**: UA: S-0409-0014-02 (Minutes of a

meeting between reps. of PW / DP Division, UNRRA, and the Soviet C-in-C's Mission held at the Fürstenhof, February 24, 1947); UA: S-00399-0002-06 (Fanshawe to Myer Cohen, June 26, 1947); Briukhanov, *Vot kak eto bylo*, 97 (note that the correct transliteration would be Briukhanov or Bryukhanov, but Brukhanov is the version used by the Allies); **Brukhanov on UNRRA**: Briukhanov, *Vot kak eto bylo*, 94, 97; **Soviet grievances**: UA: S-0411-0002-09 (notes taken at a meeting of General Davidov [Soviet liaison officer, USFET] and his staff [with USFET and UNRRA reps] Heidelberg, November 1–2, 1946); UA: S-0409-0014-02 (minutes of Fürstenhof meeting, February 24, 1947).

10. **Allied connivance in false registration of Soviet DPs**: Nikolajuk Papers, ms of S. V. Tribukh, "Menkhegof—lager' russkikh DiPi" (1989), 73 (the advice allegedly came from Col. Marquis Paravicini, head of the department of civilian administration in the US zone); **Soviet accusations**: UA: S-0411-0002-09 (Soviet liaison officer General Davidov at meeting with USFET and UNRRA representatives, Heidelberg, November 1–2, 1946); AN: AJ / 43 / 573 (telegram from Secretary of State for Dominion Affairs to Australian Department of External Affairs and Defence Department, January 8, 1947, reporting Soviet protest of September 19, 1946, on alleged UK obstruction in repatriation of Soviet citizens); **disappearance of DPs and mockery of Soviet liaison officer:** UA: S-0437-0022-17 (R. Blair, Maj. Inf., to HQ Third Army Liaison Section, February 11, 1946); **British position**: UA: S-00399-0002-06 (Vincent Meyer, Brig.-Gen. USA [Rtd], Dep. Chief of Operations, Liaison, Berlin, to Greenslade, acting COG, Arolsen, October 25, 1946, re Conference with USSR Reps. on October 8, 1946); **UNRRA's position**: UA: S-0399-0002-06 (Cyrus Greenslade, Acting Chief of Operations, Germany, to European Regional Office: attn. General Counsel, November 25, 1946); UA: S-0402-0003-0004 (Carl Martini, Director of UNRRA Field Operations, to Zone Director, Heidelberg, December 7, 1946); **US position**: UA: S-0399-0002-06 (Greenslade to ERO, November 25, 1946 [instruction of March 8, 1946]); UA: S-0411-0001-09 (notes taken at a meeting of General Davidov [Soviet liaison officer, USFET] and his staff [and USFET and UNRRA representatives, Heidelberg, November 1–2, 1946); UA: S-0402-0003-0004 (Paul Edwards, UNRRA's US Zone Director, to Myer Cohen, Director of Repatriation Division, January 30, 1947); **acid Soviet comment**: UA: S-00399-0002-06 (meeting held at CHQ, October 8, 1946: the comment was made by one of the four Soviet participants—Gen. Davidov and three deputies—to US zone director J. Whiting); **estimated number of Soviet citizens in Western zones**: UA: S-00399-0002-06 (meeting held at CHQ, October 8, 1946—statements by Fanshawe, Lenclud, and Brukhanov).

11. **Soviet DPs outside camps: (Fanshawe statement)** UA: S-00399-0002-06 (meeting held at CHQ, October 8, 1946); UA: S-00399-0002-06 (Genchington, "Facilities to be afforded to Soviet Liaison Officers," September 5, 1946); **(prohibition on Soviets making list of "free-living" DPs)** GARF: 7317 / 20 / 1 ("Kratkaia istoriia otdela repatriatsii i rozyska sovetskikh grazhdan SVA v Germanii za period 1 iiun' 1945–1948 g.," Kn. 1, 37—Soviet estimate of numbers); GARF: 7317 / 20 / 128, ll. 8, 5, 188—Soviet efforts to contact free-livers). On the broader issue of "free-living" DPs, see chap. 3.

12. **Soviet visits to DP camps**: UA: S-00399-0002-06 (Genchington, "Facilities to be afforded to Soviet Liaison Officers," September 5, 1946) (This memo specifically mentions "camps containing Balt DPs, and so called 'Ukrainians'" as being covered by this instruction. However, an attached sheet containing "questions to be elucidated" included the contradictory statement that Soviet Liaison Officers' right of access related only to "soviet citizens recognized as such

and as announced by the policy of HMG, i.e. persons of whom there is prima facie evidence of Soviet citizenship and who were citizens of and residing within the USSR on 1st September 1939."); GARF: 7317 / 20 / 1 ("Kratkaia istoriia otdela repatriatsii i rozyska sovetskikh grazhdan SVA v Germanii za period 1 iiun' 1945–1948 g.," Kn. 1; **resistance in camps to Soviet visits**: AN: AJ / 43 / 610 (memo from Brunswick officer, BAOR, to Lemgo HQ, December 13, 1949); (**Mönchehof**) Nikolajuk Papers: Tribukh, "Menchekhof," 78; AN: AJ / 43 / 610 (memo from Brunswick officer, BAOR, to Lemgo HQ, December 13, 1949); (Davidov comment) UA: S-00399-0002-06 (transcript of notes of interview at USFET between Maj.-Gen. Davidov and Brig.-Gen. V. Meyer, UNRRA, July 25, 1946); **UN report on harassment**: University of Queensland, Fedora Fisher Collections, Box 5 (cutting from New York Times, June 16, 1948: "Refugee Problems of Europe" by George Barrett, citing report to General Assembly of United Nations at Lake Success prepared by Carl J. Hambro of Norway and Pierce Williams of the United States).

13. **Distribution of Soviet newspapers**: UA: S-0409-0014-02 (minutes of a meeting between reps of PW / DP Division, UNRRA, and the Soviet C-in-C's Mission, Fürstenhof, February 24, 1947; information from Col. Wood); **bans in camps**: UA: S-00399-0002-06 (Genchington, "Facilities to be afforded to Soviet Liaison Officers," September 5, 1946); **dissenting French**: AN: AJ / 43 / 570 (Decisions prises à la conference de Moscou en ce qui concerne les personnes déplacées, May 1, 1947); **radio broadcasts**: UA: S-0409-0014-02 (Russian Affairs 1947).

14. **Letters to Soviet DPs from family**: UA: S-0437-0022-16 (memo from Soviet Liaison Officer for Repatriation of Soviet Citizens Tusa to UNRRA Director for the American Zone, Mr. Whiting, October 1946) (advertisements: note that the announcement is directed to Soviet citizens born in "the Ukrainian, Belorussian, Estonian, Moldavian, Lithuanian, Latvian and other Soviet republics" with no specific mention of Russians); **Allied noncooperation**: UA: S1021-0081-0003 (Ralph Price, "Repatriation Report," May 1, 1947) ("refusal to facilitate" exchange of mail in Western zones meant that Soviet liaison officers were often unable to deliver letters from the Soviet Union to DPs); **statistics on letters**: GARF: 7317 / 20 / 5 ("Istoriia otdela repatriatsii i rozyska sovetskikh grazhdan SVAG za period s 1-go iiulia 1948 g. po 1-e ianv. 1950 g.," 63–64); **censorship by Repatriation Agency**: GARF: 7317 / 20 / 1 ("Kratkaia istoriia otdela repatriatsii i rozyska sovetskikh grazhdan SVA v Germanii za period 1 iiun' 1945–1948 g.," Kn. 1, 116); GARF: 7317 / 20 / 5 ("Istoriia otdela . . . s 1-go iiulia 1948 g. po 1-e ianv. 1950 g.," 63–64; **letters as sources of DP addresses**: GARF: 9526 / 6 / 836, l. 124 (report from Consul Sadovnikov in Australia, March 15, 1950); **DP wariness**: GARF: 9526 / 6s / 889, l. 316 (report for 2nd quarter of 1952, Gordeev to Filatov); GARF: 7327 / 20 / 128, l. 18 (Finkman case, January 20, 1948); GARF: 7317 / 20 / 145 (interview with Leonid Chernov-Reshetnikov, June 1949).

15. **Official encouragement to write**: GARF: 8327 / 20 / 128, l. 5 (Ramanauskene case, January 10, 1948); GARF: 9526 / 6 / 917 (Filatov to Soviet Embassy, Argentina ["Secret"]); GARF: 7327 / 20 / 128 (repatriation department in Germany to Moscow, February 26, 1948); **skepticism in Danos family**: Sheila Fitzpatrick, Mischka's War: A European Odyssey of the 1940s (Melbourne: Melbourne University Press, 2017), 148–49; **Repatriation Agency admits clichés**: GARF: 7317 / 20 / 5 ("Istoriia otdela . . . repatriatsii i rozyska sovetskikh grazhdan SVAG za period s 1-go iiulia 1948 g. po 1-e ianv. 1950 g.," 63–64; **silence and mocking response**: GARF: 9526 / 6 / 888, l.83 (Gordeev memo, March 2, 1952); **allegations that Soviets offered money for repatriation**:

AN: AJ / 43 / 899, citing *Neue Zeitung*, October 9, 1948 (no confirmation found for this elsewhere in Western or Soviet archives).

16. **Labor needs, experience of World War I**: Geoffrey Best, *War and Law since 1945* (Oxford: Oxford University Press, 1997), 140–42; Richard B. Speed III, *Prisoners, Diplomats and the Great War* (New York: Greenwood Press, 1990),, 180–89; Heather Jones, "A Missing Paradigm: Military Captivity and the Prisoner of War, 1914–18," *Immigrants & Minorities* 26:1 / 2 (2008), 28, 42; **Vyshinsky on Soviet entitlement**: Gerard Daniel Cohen, *In War's Wake: Europe's Displaced Persons in the Postwar Order* (Oxford: Oxford University Press, 2012), quoted 26 (speech by Vyshinsky to UN General Assembly, February 12, 1946): **nations' need for labor**: Briukhanov, *Vot kak eto bylo*, 129; *Times* **on "slave labor"**: Quoted (without date) by Janet Flanner, "Letter from Aschaffenburg," *New Yorker*, October 30, 1948, 101; **retention of DPs for labor**: Reinhard Nachtigal, "The Repatriation and Reception of Returning Prisoners of War, 1918–22," *Immigrants & Minorities* 26:1 / 2 (2008), 172; Speed, *Prisoners, Diplomats and the Great War*, 171, and see discussion in chap. 4.

17. **DPs as war criminals**: Cohen, *In War's Wake*, 24; **Soviets on Western pressure against return**: Briukhanov, *Vot kak eto bylo*, 94; Zemskov, "'Vtoraia emigratsiia'," 75 (paraphrase of Vyshinsky's statement of March 1947); **Soviet spies' reports**: V. N. Khaustov et al., eds., *Lubianka: Stalin i NKVD-NKGB-GUKR "Smersh'"*, 1939–mart 1946 (Moscow: Rossiia XX vek, 2006), 550–52 (summary of reports in memo of S. N. Kruglov, Minister of Internal Affairs, to Stalin, Molotov, Beria et al., February 13, 1946); **Vyshinsky at UN**: quoted in Cohen, *In War's Wake*, 26–27; **Eleanor Roosevelt's response**: Eleanor Roosevelt, *The Eleanor Roosevelt Papers*, vol. 1, *The Human Rights Years, 1945–1948* (Detroit: Thomas Gale, 2007), 248 (speech at UN General Assembly Plenary Session, February 12, 1946).

18. **Lost children radio program**: A. L. Barto, *Naiti cheloveka* (Moscow: Geroi otechestva, 2005) (her show, "Naiti cheloveka" (to find someone) ran on Radio "Maiak" from 1964 to 1973; **"I Want to Go Home"**: Mark R. Elliott, *Pawns of Yalta* (Urbana: University of Illinois Press, 2012), 217–18; **rescue versus abduction**: The competing frames of rescue versus abduction has played out historically in a number of different settings, such as Australia's "stolen generation" issue, on the removal of indigenous children from their families, once seen by the authorities as benevolent and now excoriated, or most recently in the case of Russian/Ukrainian children taken to Russia during the Ukraine war, for which in 2023 the International Criminal Court declared President Putin a war criminal. **Soviet parents search for children**: AN: AJ / 43 / 610 (meeting between Soviet Repatriation Mission and HQ PWDP at Lemgo, November 30, 1948); GARF 9526 / 6s / 898, ll. 195–98 (missing gypsy boy); **definition of "child"**: Tara Zahra, *The Lost Children: Reconstructing Europe's Families after World War II* (Cambridge, MA: Harvard University Press, 2011), 8–9; **"germanized" children**: UA: S-0402-0003-0005 (Eileen Blakey, Child Welfare Consultant, "On unaccompanied children in Germany," June 24, 1946); Ruth Balint, *Destination Elsewhere* (Ithaca, NY: Cornell University Press, 2021), 84–85; UA: S-0437-0022 / S-0437-0022-16 (memo on Soviet visit from M. Jean Henshaw, Director, International Children's Center on Chiemsee, December 4, 1946).

19. **Children as national property**: Zahra, *Lost Children*, 242; **kidnapping**: UA: S-0402-0003-0005 (Eileen Blakey, Child Welfare Consultant, "On Unaccompanied Children in Germany," June 24, 1946) and Zahra, *Lost Children*, 146–72; **Soviet and Polish competition for "Ukrainian" children**: UA: S-437-0022-17 (memo of May 13, 1946, on Ukrainian children at

the Children's Center at Kloster-Indersdorf); Briukhanov, *Vot kak eto bylo*, 148–50; **Daria Kav-chak case:** GARF: 7317 / 20 / 5, *Sbornik po istorii Otdela ... za period s 1-go iiulia 1948 goda po 1-e ianvaria 1950 goda*, vol. 3, 37); **statistics on unaccompanied children:** UA: S-0402-0003-0005 (statistics for unaccompanied children in the US zone as of August–September 1946, and March 1, 1947) (a grand total of 11,861 cases had been handled thus far, of whom 2,316 were identified as Russian and 82 Ukrainian, not including "Ukrainian-Polish").

20. **Allies against child repatriation to Soviet Union:** Zahra, *Lost Children*, 216–21; **international market for children:** Balint, *Destination Elsewhere*, 81–82; **statistics on unaccompanied children:** UA: S-0402-0003-0005 (statistics for unaccompanied children in all three Western zones as of March 1, 1947, August–September 1946, and March 1, 1947); **statistics on child repatriation:** UA: S-0402-0003-0006 (Reports to Repatriation Missions, 21 / 11 / 1946-1 / 4 / 1947); **individual cases:** GARF: 7317 / 20 / 128, l. 50 (Kaliningrad, formerly German Königsberg, in the extreme west of the Soviet Union was evidently a drop-off place for retrieved Soviet children); GARF: 7317 / 20 / 128, ll.110–18; **"United Nations children" in German care:** UA: S-0402-0003-0006 (Cyrus Greenslade, acting Chief of Operations in Germany, to Gen. Vershinin, Russian Military Mission Berlin, November 22, 1946); **Soviet repatriation "rarely in the best interests of the child":** Zahra, *Lost Children*, 217–18; **Bobrowitsch case:** Zahra, *Lost Children*, 219–20.

21. **British and Soviet views on war crimes:** Arieh J. Kochavi, *Prelude to Nuremberg: Allied War Crimes Policy and the Question of Punishment* (Chapel Hill: University of North Carolina Press, 1998), 36 (1942 Molotov quotation), 95–100, 218, 239; Tanja Penter, "Local Collaborators on Trial: Soviet War Crimes Trials under Stalin (1945–1953), *Cahiers du monde russe* 49:2 / 3 (2008), 341–64; **Nuremberg Trials:** see Francine Hirsch, *Soviet Judgement at Nuremberg* (New York: Oxford University Press, 2020); **Soviet violence against alleged war criminals:** Norman Naimark, *Stalin and the Fate of Europe: The Postwar Struggle for Sovereignty* (Cambridge, MA: Harvard University Press, 2019), 261 (three to four Soviet kidnappings a month in Austria); UA: S-00041-0002-09 (memo of November 25, 1946, from HQ French Zone to CHQ Arolsen, reporting firsthand account by a Frenchman of attempting kidnapping by Soviet officers who may have been trying to meet a quota); Protoierei D. Konstantinov, "'Vtoraia volna'—vospominaniia i razdumi'ia o rossiiskoi emigratsii," in *V poiskakh istiny: Puti i sud'by vtoroi emigratsii*, ed. A. V. Popov (Moscow: RGGU, Istoriko-arkhivnyi institute, 1997), 65–66 (remembering the stepping-up of such activity—"murders of individual emigrants, kidnapping, discrediting, crippling people as the result of 'accidents,' poisonings, drownings and more of the same kind"—in 1946–47); **UNRRA resistance to military pressure to give collaborators DP status:** UA: S-0411-0002-01: "Eligibility, February–August 1946," telegram marked "Priority" from Dep. Chief of Operations Brig. W. A. Stawell, Central HQ UNRRA Arolsen, April 30, 1946, to UNRRA B. R. Cilento, UNRRA US Whiting, UNRRA French Leclud, on "Ex-Wehrmacht Released from POW Status"; **collaborators in camps:** UA: S-0402-0003-0001 (Margaret Bond, Chief Repatriation Officer, to Dir. in Chief, Austrian Operation, January 10, 1946); **Brukhanov quotation:** Biukhanov, *Vot tak eto bylo*, 111–12.

22. **Soviet lists refused:** NA UK: FO 1020 / 2846 (from War Crimes Section, HQ British Troops in Austria, May 29, 1946); **Soviets on Western concealment of war criminals:** UA: S-00399-0002-06 (meeting held at CHQ, October 8, 1946); Briukhanov, *Vot kak eto bylo*, 111–12; **British evasions:** (Todt employee) NA UK: FO 945 / 598 (Soviet Nationals: Repatriation of dissident displaced persons [1945–46]. Lt-Col D.C.S Sinclair, WO, to Brimelow, n.d.); (Azer-

baijanis) NA UK: FO 371 / 71663 [August 1948]; ("no trace") NA UK: FO 1020 / 2846 (General Staff Intelligence to PW & DP Division, June 4, 1946); (Vienna cases) NA UK: FO 371 / 71663 (Memo from Sir B. Jerram, British High Commissioners in Vienna, July 8, 1948); **Operations Keelhaul and Eastwind**: Elliott, *Pawns of Yalta*, 115–19; NA UK: FO 1020 / 2846 (memo from Director, PW & DP Division to DP Section, Land Steiermark, July 3, 1946, citing information from UNRRA, June 7, 1946); **Mayhew on British policy**: NA UK: FO 371 / 71663 (memo from Sir B. Jerram, British High Commissioner in Vienna, July 8, 1948); **arrested chaplain**: Konstantinov, "'Vtoraia volna'," 65.

23. **Soviet explanation of non-return**: GARF: 7317 / 20 / 1: "Kratkaia istoriia otdela repatriatsii i rozyska sovetskikh grazhdan SVA v Germanii za period 1 iiun' 1945–1948 g.," Kn. 1, 113; **1946–47 famine in Ukraine**: F. Slaveski, *Remaking Ukraine after World War II: The Clash of Central and Local Soviet Power, 1944–1953* (Cambridge, UK: Cambridge University Press, 2021); **DP grapevine**: Bernstein, *Return*, 140–41.

Chapter 3. Organization of DP Life

1. **"Pawns of fate"**: UA: S-0425-0010-17 (Statement of the Executive Staff of UNRRA US Zone Headquarters, [April 1946]); Janet Flanner, "Letter from Aschaffenburg," *New Yorker*, October 30, 1948, 98; **Mischka Danos's and Bichevskis's plans**: Sheila Fitzpatrick, *Mischka's War* (London: I. B. Tauris, 2017), 93, 107, 112–17; Andrejs Bicevskis, Family Memoir, in email to Sheila Fitzpatrick, May 6, 2008; **destination decisions**: Stanislavs Zmuidins, "From Izvalta to Insula," in *Insula Displaced Persons Assembly Center: A Latvian Memoir*, ed. Ventis Plume and John Plume (Minneapolis: Kirk House Publishers, 2004), 42; **Olga Danos's age**: ITS Tracking Records: Olga Danos (accessed online via Holocaust Museum, Washington, DC); University of Chicago Special Collections: Michael Danos Papers (IRO Certification, October 26, 1948); **DP grapevine**: Flanner, "Letter from Aschaffenburg," 98; **"wallowing" in camps**: Bella Brodzki and Jeremy Varon, "The Munich Years. The Students of Post-War Germany," in Steinert and Weber-Newth, *Beyond Camps and Forced Labour*, ed. Johannes-Dieter Steinert and Inge Weber-Newth (Osnabrück: Secolo-Verlag, 2005), 156.

2. **Allies policy on repatriation of Baltic DPs**: Laura Hilton, "Cultural Nationalism in Exile: The Case of Polish and Latvian Displaced Persons," *Historian*, 71:2 (2009), 287–92; **Jewish DPs**: Gerard Daniel Cohen, *In War's Wake: Europe's Displaced Persons in the Postwar Order* (Oxford: Oxford University Press, 2012), 134–36; UA: S-1021-0081-0003 (report by A. V. Taraska, Field Operations Officer, on the Jewish community in Regensburg, March 1947); **indifference to anti-communism**: Anna Marta Holian, "Between National Socialism and Soviet Communism: The Politics of Self-Representation among Displaced Persons in Munich, 1945–1951" (PhD diss., University of Chicago, 2005), 211; **Ukrainian DPs**: Hilton, "Cultural Nationalism," 289; **collecting information on the options**: Fitzpatrick, *Mischka's War*, 207–8; **reading employment ads**: Gary Nash, *The Tarasov Saga: From Russia through China to Australia* (Sydney: Rosenberg, 2002), 224.

3. **Types of housing**: Woodbridge, *UNRRA*, vol. 2, 500–501; **British arrogance**: Fitzpatrick, *Mischka's War*, 122 (quotation); **"total institutions**: Erving Goffman, *Asylums* (New York: Anchor Books, 1961); Tomas Balkelis, "Living in the Displaced Persons Camp: Lithuanian War Refugees in the West, 1944–54," in *Warlands: Population Resettlement and State Reconstruction*

in the Soviet-East European Borderlands 1945–50, ed. Peter Gatrell and Nick Baron (New York: Palgrave Macmillan, 2009), 27; **denunciation**: (in camps) AN: AJ / 43 / 806 (unsigned handwritten note, Munich, n.d. [1951); (in Soviet life) Sheila Fitzpatrick, *Tear off the Masks! Identity and Imposture in Twentieth-Century Russia* (Princeton, NJ: Princeton University Press, 2005), 205–61.

4. **Camp self-administration**: George Woodbridge, *UNRRA* (New York: Columbia University Press, 1950), vol. 2, 522; **UNRRA and "rehabilitation"**: Woodbridge, *UNRRA*, vol. 2, 522; **self-government statistics**: UA: S-1021-0081-0001 (L. Doughty, "Camp self-government," August 1947); **self-government in practice**: Balkelis, "Living in the Displaced Persons Camp," 35–39; Flanner, "Letter from Aschaffenburg," 98; **camp leadership**: (aggressive individuals) UA: S-1021-0081-0001 (Doughty, "Camp self-government," 1947); (nationalists); Kathryn C. Hulme, *Undiscovered Country: A Spiritual Adventure* (London: Muller, 1967), 266, 269.

5. **Bettenhausen**: UA: S-1021-0081-0005 ("A Short History of Junkers Camp, Bettenhausen, Kassel"); **Wildflecken**: Hulme, *Undiscovered Country*, 266, 269; UA: S-1021-0081-0003 (Edwards, Heidelberg, to UNRRA HQ, Arolsen, February 1, 1947); Kathryn Hulme, Dep. Dir. Wildflecken, Report, June 23, 1947); **Hanau**: Woodbridge, *UNRRA*, vol. 2, 532.

6. **Mönchehof**: Ivan Nikolajuk Papers: Ivan Nikolajuk, "Memoirs," 154–55; Andrew Paul Janco, "Soviet 'Displaced Persons' in Europe, 1941–1951" (PhD diss., University of Chicago, 2012), 198–99, 200; B. Priannishnikov, *Novopokolentsy* (Silver Spring, MD: self-published, 1986), 227–28, 241 ("typhus" trucks); **numbers of residents**: Prianishnikov, *Novopokolentsy*, 227, gives a figure of 1,500, possibly only counting the major Mönchehof camp; Janco, "Soviet 'Displaced Persons,'" 203, gives the total number of residents camps under Boldyrev's leadership, including Fürstenwald and Rothwesten and a smaller camp near the R-12 airfield, as 2,746; **émigré/Soviet breakdown**; Janco, "Soviet 'Displaced Persons,'" 197, 210, 215; **production of false documents**: Janco, "Soviet 'Displaced Persons,'" 198–99; **mecca for anticommunist Russian émigrés**: Sheila Fitzpatrick, *White Russians, Red Peril* (Melbourne: Latrobe University Press, 2021), 45 (these included future pillars of the Russian NTS community in Melbourne Yuri Amosov and Konstantin and Irina Halaffof, as well as members of their Melbourne social circle, Ivan Nikolajuk and family and their relatives the Klucharevs); **politically uncongenial turned away**: Janco, "Soviet 'Displaced Persons,'" 209; **housing**: Prianishnikov, *Novopokolentsy*, 254; **workshops and enterprises**: Janco, "Soviet 'Displaced Persons,'" 204; **Scouts**: Eugene Schlusser, *Escape from the Sun* (Melbourne: Australian Scholarly Publishing, 2017), 239; **cultural and educational life**: Irina Halaffof, *Svidetel' istorii* (Melbourne: University of Melbourne, 1988), 31–34.

7. **Mönchehof's spiritual richness**: Prianishnikov, *Novopokolentsy*, 228; Benjamin Tromly, *Cold War Exiles and the CIA* (Oxford: Oxford University Press, 2019), 47 (quoting US counterintelligence investigators); **Boldyrev's "dictatorship"**: Tromly, *Cold War Exiles*, 246; **battles with UNRRA**: Prianishnikov, *Novopokolentsy*, 241; **problems with Americans**: Janco, "Soviet 'Displaced Persons,'" 222–24; Tromly, *Cold War Exiles*, 44–45; **Moroccan adventure**: see chap. 4; **end of Mönchehof**: Janco, "Soviet 'Displaced Persons,'" 233, 241–42; Nikolajuk Papers: S. V. Tribukh, "Menkhegof—lager' russkikh DiPi" (ms.), 92 (quotation); **Morocco**: Nikolajuk Papers, "Boldirev's reminiscences," 307 (quotation), and see this volume, chap. 7.

8. **Praise for Baltic DPs**: UA: S-0402-0003-0001 (Harold Ingham, ex-Deputy Team Director, UNRRA, letter to the editor, *Manchester Guardian*, May 29, 1946); quotation, on UNRRA and displaced persons from Steinert and Weber-Newth, *Beyond Camps*, 834; **Esslingen: fond**

memories: Zmuidins, "From Izvalta to Insula," 42; **facilities:** Ieva Zake, *American Latvians* (New Brunswick: Transaction Publishers, 2010), 32; **origins of camp:** Feliks Krusa, "An Unrra Assembly Centre Esslingen o / Neckar [*sic*], September 1946," citing early camp history from 1946 camp director René Pinczon du Sel, available at https://latvians.com/index.php?en/CFBH /EsslingenUNRRA/ess-300-esslingen-view-all.ssi, accessed October 2, 2021; **professionals:** Krusa, "An Unrra Asssembly Centre"; **cultural life and education:** Inta Gāle Carpenter, "Memory-Theater as Cultural Generativity: *Eslingena*: A Musical in Toronto and Riga," *Journal of Baltic Studies* 38:3 (2007), 321; Zake, *American Latvians*, 32; **religious life:** Krusa, "An Unrra Assembly Centre"; **occupations:** Krusa, "An Unrra Assembly Centre"; Carpenter, "Memory-Theater," 320 (quotation).

9. *Eslingena* **musical:** Quotations from Carpenter, "Memory-Theater," 329–30, 326, 323; "Why Did We Cry at 'Eslingena'?" Latvians Online, https://latviansonline.com/why-did-we -cry-at-eslingena/); Krusa, "An Unrra Assembly Centre"; **darker views of Esslingen:** some in the Latvian diaspora strongly objected to the upbeat picture offered in *Eslingena*: for a very different picture of life in the Latvian DP camps, stressing demoralization, criminal activity, and casual sex, see the play by Janis Balodis (son of former Latvian DPs resettled in Australia), *Too Young for Ghosts* (Sydney: Currency Press, 1991), produced in Melbourne and Sydney in 1985. Rasma Prande's account: GARF: 7317 / 20 / 145, ll. 50–86, 99–101 (interviews February 2 and March 4, 1949 (comments on Sakss l. 69).

10. **Nationality changes:** O. I. Itsikson, "Vospominaniia o dvukh vydaiushchikhsia pevtsakh v Sidnee," *Avstraliada* no. 68 (2011), 8–10 (Kornilov); Nataliia Zhukovskaia, "Maria Pavlovna Karpovich (née Samoilenko), *Avstraliada* no. 77 (2013), 3; Evgenii Nikolaevich Zubrin, "Avto-biografiia," *Avstraliada* no. 73 (2012), 26–28; interview with Kristian Ireland, Berlin, November 3, 2015 (his maternal grandparents); Ivan Nikolajuk, "Memoirs," in Nikolajuk Papers; Fitzpatrick, *White Russians, Red Peril*, 9–11.

11. **Abundance in US zone:** Inta Gāle Carpenter, "Folklore as a Source for Creating Exile Identity among Latvian Displaced Persons in Post-World War II Germany," *Journal of Baltic Studies* 48:2 (2017), 209; ***Westward Ho!:*** see chap. 4; **French zone:** I. Bogut, "Pamiati Leonida Aleksandrovich Vertsinskogo," *Avstraliada* no. 12 (1997), 42; **housing moves:** Modris Eksteins, *Walking since Daybreak* (Boston: Houghton Mifflin, 1999), 184; **camp moves:** E. Iushchenko, "Dr Viktor Evgen'evich Istomin," *Avstraliada* no. 32 (2002), 13–14; Georgii Nekrasov, "Georgii Mikhailovich Nekrasov," *Avstraliada* no. 43 (2005), 32; **Mischka's travels:** Fitzpatrick, *Mischka's War*, 127–32, 158–59, 177–78 (I can only deduce the reasons for the Zeilsheim registration, since I found out about it only after his death, when I happened to see his name on a list of foreigners of Latvian citizenship compiled by the Jewish Community of Frankfurt); **movements of Olga Danos and her sister Mary:** Fitzpatrick, *Mischka's War*, 136–37, 233–34; **interzonal moves: (statistics)** AN: AJ / 43 / 806 (Comportement et délits des refugiés 1948–51) (in October 1948 and August–October 1949, detected illegal entry to the US zone from the Soviet one was running at about twenty thousand a month; in April 1950, it was less than half that. Traffic de-tected *out* of the US zones to all other zones was 1,549 in April 1950, about half heading for the Soviet zone); **(cases)** GARF: 9526 / 6 / 669, ll. 82–3; UA: S-0411-0002-01 (Memo from Jay B. Crane, Chief, Reports & Analysis division, to Morgan, August 20, 1946).

12. **"Free-livers": no good statistics:** George Fischer, "The New Soviet Emigration," *Russian Review* 8:1 (1949), 7 (Fischer was a member of the team working on the Harvard Project

on the Soviet Social System); Louise Holborn, *The International Refugee Organization* (New York: Oxford University Press, 1956), annex 13: "Displaced Persons in Germany, Austria and Italy, 31 December 1946," 197 (IRO figures for the end of 1946, presumably supplied by UNRRA, gave a figure of 168,261 DPs known to be living outside camps out of the total 859,774 DPs); UA: S-0409-0014-03 ("Clarification of 4 July 1946," with similar figures to IRO's above); AN: AJ / 43 / 397-8 ("D.G.9: Vital statistics—1949"): figures for February 1950 (not 1949, despite file title) are 228,000 living in camps and 145,000 outside them; **reasons for living out of camp: (fear)** Fischer, "New Soviet Emigration," 7; **(dislike of herd)** Eugenia Hanfmann and Helen Beier, *Six Russian Men—Lives in Turmoil* (North Quincy, MA: Christopher Publishing House, 1976), 97; **language skills:** Michael Danos papers (letters from Michael to Olga Danos, October 26 and November 2, 1945; Michael's diary and letter fragment, dated November 2 and December 14, 1945); **women living with foreigners:** see chap. 5; **moving between camp and private lodgings:** GARF: 9526 / 6 / 669, ll. 82–83 (Klanners); Michael Danos Papers (Olga's movements reconstructed from her letters to Mischka); Andrejs Bicevskis, interview, Brisbane, July 30, 2007, Dailonis Stauvers, telephone interview, April 10, 2007; Andrejs Bicevskis, email to author, May 6, 2008.

13. **UNRRA's efforts to control free living:** University of Queensland, Fryer Library Collections 233: Fedora Gould Fisher collection, Box 4, Folder 5 (4a) (Memo "On status and treatment of Displaced persons living outside Assembly Centers," May 14, 1946); UA: S-0409-0014-03 ("Clarification of 4 July 1946 on treatment and status of DPs outside Assembly centres"); AN: AJ / 43 / 841 (IRO Munich to Area Commander, Military Government Munich, October 7, 1948: "Request for eviction from private billets of IRO care Displaced Persons").

14. **Political indoctrination from DP elite:** Balkelis, "Living in the Displaced Persons Camp," 27–28; **socialism still on Jewish DP spectrum: (Bundists)** Holian, "Between National Socialism and Soviet Communism," 405; Atina Grossman, *Jews, Germans, and Allies: Close Encounters in Occupied Germany* (Princeton, NJ: Princeton University Press, 2007), 137; **(Leipheim):** UA: S-1021-0081-0003 (Miss E. Roberton, Director, "Jewish Camp Leipheim Airport," June 1947); **Ukrainian National Committee punished:** Jan-Hinnerk Antons, "Britischer Umgang mit militanten Antikommunisten, Kollaborateuren and mutmasslichen Kriegsverbrechern unter osteuropäischen DPs," in *Personnes déplacées et guerre froide en Allemagne occupée*, ed. Corine Defrance, Juliette Denis, and Julia Maspero (Brussels: Peter Lang, 2015), 64–65; **Soviet complaints:** A. I. Briukhanov, *Vot kak eto bylo* (Moscow: Gospolitizdat, 1958), 106, 112, 161 (quotations); UA: S-0409-0014-02 (minutes of meeting of PW / DP Division, UNRRA, and the Soviet C-in-C's Mission, Fürstenhof, February 24, 1947); AN: AJ / 43 / 610 (Summary of Meeting held with Soviet Mission, April 30, 1947); **some UNRRA officers sympathetic:** Briukhanov, *Vot kak eto bylo*, 111–12 (citing Major Safonov's report of conversation with British officer Greenwood); **UNRRA uneasiness: (national committees, DP leaders)** UA: S-0411-0002-01 (Carl Martini, Dir., Field Operations, February 19, 1947; **(dubious advisors)** UA: S-1021-0081-0003 (Repatriation Report, May 1, 1947, by Ralph Price, Chief of Repatriation, UNRRA, US Zone, Germany).

15. **National organizations morphing from welfare to politics:** AN: AJ / 43 / 807 (Folder on Political Dissidents General; list of organizations as of August 31, 1951); Aldis Purs, "'How Those Brothers in Foreign Lands Are Dividing the Fatherland': Latvian National Politics in Displaced Persons Camps after the Second World War," in *Warlands: Population Resettlement*

and State Reconstruction in the Soviet-East European Borderlands 1945–50, ed. Peter Gatrell and Nick Baron (New York: Palgrave Macmillan, 2009), 56; **Soviet complaints**: NA UK, FO 945 / 598 (Soviet Nationals: Repatriation of dissident displaced persons, 1945–6); **incomplete list of national organizations** (not including overtly political anti-communist and liberationist organizations; compiled from lobbying letters in UNRRA archives and secondary sources): **(Russian)** Committee of Stateless Russian Emigrants, Committee for Affairs of Orthodox refugees, Russian National Committee, Central Representation of Russian Emigration in Germany; **(Ukrainian)**: Ukrainian National Committee (aka Ukrainian Red Cross), Central Representation of the Ukrainian Emigration, Central Ukrainian Relief Committee; **(Belorussian)** Belorussian Council, White Ruthenian National Committee, Belorussia (Kryvian) Committee; Belorussian Central Administration; **(Latvian)** National Latvian Committee, Latvian Central Committee, Latvian Central Council, Latvian National Council; Office of Latvian Refugee Relief; *Privat*-living Latvian Committee in Munich; **(Lithuanian)** Lithuanian National Committee; Lithuanian Exile Committee; Lithuanian Central Executive Committee; **(Estonian)** Estonian National Committee; Estonian Central Council: Estonian Central Committee; Estonian Committee in Germany; **few activists with many hats**: see, for example, the case of a 1949 Latvian repatriate, an educated man in his thirties, said to have been active in his years in Germany in the Latvian Central Committee and the Latvian veterans' organization Daugavas Vanagi as well as up a YMCA in his camp and recruiting DPs for work in Britain, under *Westward Ho!* (GARF: 7317 / 20 / 146, 57–62: interviews with Valentin Gobniets, the case in point, and Janis Bruvinsh, July 19, 1949); **rare cooperation between nationalities**: UA: S-0411-0002-01 (Eligibility files, February–August 1946) contain only a few cases, notably some letters signed by chairmen of Baltic Committee, Committee of Stateless Russian emigrants, National Latvian Committee, Lithuanian National Committee, and Estonian National Committee to Sir Frederick Morgan, August 7, 1946, protesting a recent screening in the Memmingen camp that had removed four hundred out of about four thousand DPs, and a letter signed by several different Latvian groups protesting against screening in US zone in February 1947; **mutual spy denunciations**: e.g., story of man and daughter so accused in Ukrainian émigré organization, AN: AJ / 43 / 467 (case of Wsewolod Charnetskyj, before IRO Review Board in 1951); GARF: 7317 / 20 / 146, ll, 57–60, 61–62 (interviews with Gobnieks and Bruvinch, July 19, 1949).

16. **UNRRA deceived**: Antons, "Britischer Umgang," 64–65; **Ukrainian propaganda**: UA: S-1021-0081-0003 (pamphlet attached to letter of Paul B. Edwards, Zone Director, to Chief, Field Operations, American Zone, February 13, 1947, on his dealings with Dr. Walter Gallan, President, United American Ukrainian Relief Committee); **Ukrainian anti-communism and anti-Russianism**: Holian, "Between National Socialism and Soviet Communism," 105; **Anti-Bolshevik Bloc of Nations**: Holian, "Between National Socialism and Soviet Communism," 126; Jayne Persian, *Fascists in Exile: Post-War Displaced Persons in Australia* (London: Routledge, 2023), 92–94; **concern about Banderite activity in camps**: UA: S-1021-0081-0003 (Report of Ralph Price, May 24, 1947); Roman Smolorz, "Der Alltag der osteuropäischen Displaced Persons 1945–1949 unter dem Einfluss von ost- und westeuropäischen Geheimdiensten," in Defrance, Denis, and Maspero, *Personnes déplacées et guerre froide*, 202–3 (*Pravda* July 10, 1946); **Belorussians**: Smolorz, "Alltag," 202–3 (*Pravda* July 10, 1946); AN: AJ / 43 / 807 (Folder on Belorussian Central Administration).

17. **Latvian organizations**: Purs, "'How Those Brothers in Foreign Lands,'" 56–59; UA: S-1021-0081-0002 (petition on screening from Baltic DPs' representatives, including A. Kacens and K. Kalnins, Latvian Central Committee, to General McNarney, commanding US forces, February 4, 1947); **Daugavas Vanagi**: created by Latvian POWs (legionnaires) in Belgium in December 1945 to represent their interests and those of their families in Germany (Carpenter, "Folklore," 215); **Latvian Legion's status**: see chap. 6; **Latvian camp administrations**: Hilton, "Cultural Nationalism," 297; **ethnic homogeneity**: Purs, "'How Those Brothers in Foreign Lands,'" 62–63; **Baltic Central Council**: UA: S-0411-0002-01 (signatory to joint letter to Sir Frederick Morgan, August 17, 1946); **Lithuanian organizations**: Balkelis, "Living in the Displaced Persons Camp," 40; UA: S-1021-0081-0002 (petition on screening from Baltic DPs representatives, including Prof. G. Galvanauskas, Lithuanian Central Executive Committee, to General McNarney, commanding US forces, February 4, 1947); **Estonian organizations**: AN: AJ / 43 / 807 (Political Dissidents General, list of organizations as of August 31, 1951); UA: S-1021-0081-0002 (petition on screening from Baltic DPs' representatives, including Profs. Woldemar Päts and Oskar Tozäär [?], Estonian Central Committee, to General McNarney, commanding US forces, February 4, 1947); **Baltic representation in ABN**: Holian, "Between National Socialism and Soviet Communism," 126.

18. **Russians and ABN**: Holian, "Between National Socialism and Soviet Communism," 128; **Russian organizations**: Sigizmund Dichbalis, *Zigzagi sud'by: Vospominaniia* (Moscow: IPVA, 2003), 58 (note that Dichbalis seemed to see SAF as a Vlasovite organization, while Tromly, *Cold War Exiles*, xiv, characterizes it as far-right monarchist); **Vlasovites**: Fischer, "New Soviet Emigration"; Tromly, *Cold War Exiles*, 32–40; **relative popularity among DPs**: Holian, "Between National Socialism and Soviet Communism," 114, 125; **NTS**: Prianishnikov, *Novopokolentsy*, 242–49, 256 (quotation 248); Janco, "Soviet 'Displaced Persons,'" 206, n. 28.

19. **Allied censorship**: Prianishnikov, *Novopokolentsy*, 256; **US intelligence attitudes**: Holian, "Between National Socialism and Soviet Communism," 136; Tromly, *Cold War Exiles*, 102–20; Holian, "Between National Socialism and Soviet Communism," 103; **German funding for ABN**: Smolorz, "Alltag," 206; **DP protests against sentencing of Cardinal Mindszenty**: Holian, "Between National Socialism and Soviet Communism," 140–49 (participants included Belorussians, Lithuanians, Estonians, Slovaks, Cossacks, and Turks from the Caucasus as well as Ukrainians); **"concrete evidence of sympathy"**: Holian, "Between National Socialism and Soviet Communism," 138–39 (quoting US High Commissioner for Germany John J. McCloy).

Chapter 4. Occupations

1. **"Taking care of each other"**: quoted Inta Gāle Carpenter, "Memory-Theater as Cultural Generativity: *Eslingena*: A Musical in Toronto and Riga," *Journal of Baltic Studies* 38:3 (2007), 320; **barter with surrounding population**: Mark Wyman, *DPs: Europe's Displaced Persons, 1945–1951* (Ithaca, NY: Cornell University Press, 1989), 116; **cigarettes as currency**: Susan T. Pettiss and Lynne Taylor, *After the Shooting Stopped: The Story of an UNRRA Welfare Worker in Germany 1945–1947* (Victoria, BC: Trafford, 2004), 137; Wyman, *DPs*, 115; **police raids on camps**: Ben Shephard, *The Long Road Home: The Aftermath of the Second World War* (London: Vintage, 2010), 280; **cross-border black-marketeering**: GARF: 9526 / 6s / 675, ll. 134–37; GARF: 9526 / 6s / 669, ll. 287–90.

2. **UNRRA involvement in black market**: AN: AJ / 43 / 759 (January 1948 report); UA: S-0409-0014-20 (Administration of UNRRA Services, Schleswig-Holstein Region); Shephard, *Long Road Home*, 280; **British and US Army involvement**: Shephard, *Long Road Home*, 267 (quotation on British from Yugoslav DP); Sigizmund Dichbalis, *Zigzagi sud'by: Vospominaniia* (Moscow: IPVA, 2003), 58–59 (US Army driver story); **barter not illegal in British zone**: UA: S-0411-0002-10 (Jewish Survey Meeting, April 2, 1946—"Mr. *Nurock* [financial advisor to Control Commission Germany] pointed out that bartering is now legal in the British Zone"); **DP status could be lost**: Wyman, *DPs*, 116; **"Tally Ho!" Operation**: Kathryn Hulme, *The Wild Place* (Boston: Little, Brown, 1953), 109–19; **Jewish DP involvement**: Shephard, *Long Road*, 281–83 (his assessment of evidence suggests that, while there was racial stereotyping at play, there was indeed substantial Jewish involvement in the big end of the black market); **German police raids pogrom complaints**: AN: AJ / 43 / 140 (report of meeting held between Wilkinson, British FO, and Hacking et al. for IRO History Unit, February 16, 1952) (the camp raided was Hoehne, formerly the barracks of Bergen-Belsen's German guards); Hulme, *Wild Place*, 95–98; (Reinburgstrasse incident) UA: S-1021-0081-0003 (Jewish Infiltration Report by L. Doughty, Chief Program Analyst, July 1947); **UNRRA concern**: UA: S0425-0010-17 (Statement of the Executive Staff of UNRRA [April 1946] in "Report on General Situation and Living Conditions of Displaced Persons and UNRRA, 20.9.1945-10.4.1946," including comment that "German police are taking advantage of their restored authorities by persecuting DPs in true Nazi fashion"); **German indignation at "DP criminality"**: see Wolfgang Jacobmeyer, *Vom Zwangsarbeiter zum Heimatlosen Ausländer* (Göttingen: Vandenhoeck & Ruprecht, 1985), 46–50.

3. **Working for Germans: Soviet objections**: UA: S-0437-0022-15 ("Restricted" instruction from Brig.-Gen. R. B. Lovett, HQ US Forces, European Theater, summarizing orders of General Patton, November 17, 1945) (ban, at least temporarily, on employment of DPs in German-owned farms and factories in the US zone, at Soviet request); A. I. Briukhanov, *Vot kak eto bylo* (Moscow: Gospolitizdat, 1958), 132, 136; **DP work requirements**: George Woodbridge, *UNRRA* (New York: Columbia University Press, 1950), vol. 2, 519–21 (Work was made compulsory in the French zone by the military authorities in February 1946, but this was not rigorously enforced, and UNRRA was unhappy with the requirement; the US zone followed in June 1946, though exempting "persecuted groups"; in the British zone, a law requiring DPs to work was introduced toward the end of the year, over UNRRA objections that it failed to provide "safeguards for persecuted groups," that is, exemption for Jews); **exemptions "a cumulative defeat"**: University of Queensland, Fryer Library Collections 44, Cilento Papers, Box 18, Folder 107 (Cilento, "Escape from UN-Reality," 129).

4. **Jewish and Baltic DPs' resistance to taking available jobs**: Cilento Papers, Box 18, Folder 107 ("Escape from UN-Reality," 122); UA: S-1021-0081-0003 (A. V. Taraska, Field Operations Officer, "Jewish Community, Regensburg," March 1947); UA: S-0411-0002-10 ("Survey of conditions of Jews in the British Zone of Germany in March 1946" by A. G. Brotman, Jewish Committee for Relief Abroad, UK, and H Viteles, AJDC, US); **Latvian objections**: UA: S-1021-0081-0003 (Baltic Camp Bettenhausen, Kassel) (but note the contrary view of a German historian that Baltic, Ukrainian, and Hungarian DPs were willing to work for Germans, whereas Poles preferred to work for the occupation authorities: Roman Smolorz, "Der Alltag der osteuropäischen Displaced Persons 1945–1949 unter dem Einfluss von ost- und westeuropäischen Geheimdiensten," in Defrance,

Denis, and Maspero, *Personnes déplacées et guerre froide*, 209; **uneven distribution of work opportunities**: UA: S-1021-0081-0003 (Report on DP Assembly Center Ellwangen by director W. V. Buckhantz, March 1947); Woodbridge, *UNRRA*, vol. 2, 519.

5. **Employment statistics**: UA: S-1021-0082-0001 (Reports and Statistics by Mrs. E. M. Doig, Asst. Chief Reports and Statistics, UNRRA HQ Heidelberg, April 22, 1947: "Labor Monthly Reports," August 1946) (total of 87,828 DPs employed; **Scheinfeld and Seedorf camps**: Tomas Balkelis, "Living in the Displaced Persons Camp: Lithuanian War Refugees in the West, 1944–1954," in *Warlands: Population Resettlement and State Reconstruction in the Soviet-East European Borderlands 1945–50*, ed. Peter Gatrell and Nick Baron (New York: Palgrave Macmillan, 2009), 35; **Russian and Jewish work participation**: UA: S-1021-0082-0001 ("Labor monthly reports," August 1946) (The absolute number of employed DPs in each national group was 119,765 Poles, 55,229 Jews, 54,349 Ukrainians, 44,818 Latvians, 18,821 stateless, and 4,990 Russians).

6. **DP employment in Western zones**: Woodbridge, *UNRRA*, vol. 2, 519; Wyman, *DPs*, 114; **proportion of employed working for UNRRA / IRO: (US zone, August 1946)** UA: S-1021-0082-0001 ("Labor Monthly Reports"—the two relevant categories are "UNRRA Burgomeister" [32,686 out ot a total of 87,828 employed] and "UNRRA work projects" [34,731 out of 87,828]; **(three zones, mid-1947)** Woodbridge, *UNRRA*, vol. 2, 519; Wyman, *DPs*, 114; **(British zone, mid-1947)** Arieh J. Kochavi, "British Policy on Non-Repatriable Displaced Persons in Germany and Austria, 1945–7," *European History Quarterly* 21 (1999), 371; Balkelis, "Living in the Displaced Persons Camp," 35; **UNRRA jobs in camps**: Wyman, *DPs*, 113.

7. **Working for German employers: (US zone)** UA: S-1021-0081-0003 ("Labor monthly reports," April 1947 (6,000 out of a total of 87,828 total working); **(British zone)** Kochavi, "British Policy," 371 (21,000 out of a total of 76,000 working); **Jewish furrier case**: UA: S-0408-0043-07 ("Memo to director of UNRRA team 806 from Hoehne Camp," October 25, 1946); **obstacles to Jews registering businesses**: UA: S-0411-0002 / S-0411-0002-10 (Survey of conditions of Jews in the British Zone of Germany in March 1946 by Brotman and Viteles); **Olga Danos as DP business-woman**: University of Chicago Special Collections: Michael Danos Papers (letters from Olga to Michael on Geestacht and Flensburg workshop plans, March 1, 12, 24, and April 29, 1946; letters from Olga to Michael, January 1947, on her establishment of contact with an art dealer and completion of her first religious figurine; Fulda business card [in English] enclosed in letter from Olga to Michael, June 23, 1949); **"going on German economy"**: I have been unable to find any official statement outlining the circumstances in which a DP should "go on to the German economy," or the rules surrounding their retention of resettlement eligibility, although there are numerous passing references to the practice with regard to individual cases under IRO from 1947 on. IRO appears not to have collected statistics on numbers of DPs "going on the German economy."

8. **"Amis"**: DP terms for the Americans. Mischka Danos pronounced it with a short "a," like an anglicization of the French *amis* (friends), but another source says American soldiers were "known as 'Amis', pronounced ah-meez": Ella E. Schneider Hilton, *Displaced Person* (Baton Rouge: Louisiana State University, 2004), 84; **working for the Americans: (statistics)** UA: S-1021-0082-0001 ("Labor Monthly Reports," showing that in the US zone as of August 1946, less than 10 percent of working DPs were employed by the US military) (But note that other passing references to DP military employment are quite out of line with these figures: e.g., that

fifty thousand out of sixty thousand DPs in the British zone who were working in the summer of 1946 were employed by the British Army [Kochavi, "British Policy," 371], or that in the American zone "some 40,000 DPs" were employed in mid-1947 in "U.S. Army labor-service companies" [Wyman, *DPs*, 113–14]); (**individual reports**) : *Avstraliada* no. 21 (1999), 7 (Kisliakoff); GARF: 9526 / 6 / 890, l. 73 and GARF; 9236 / 6 / 669, ll. 92–99 and 240–41 (repatriates Shevelev and Barinov); Eugene Schlusser, *Escape from the Sun* (Melbourne: Australian Scholarly Publishing, 2017), 216–17 (Schlüsser); Sheila Fitzpatrick, *Mischka's War: A European Odyssey of the 1940s* (Melbourne: Melbourne University Press, 2017), 122 (Danos); **pay not always high**: Ivan Nikolajuk, *Deda's Memoirs for the Grandchildren*, trans. by Yura Nikolajuk (Melbourne: self-published, 2020), 330 ("the worst kind of job in the [DP] camp is better paid than the work I carried out as an Engineer in the employ of the Americans"), 324; **useful for resettlement selection**: see chap. 8.

9. **DPs used as guards by Allied military**: Cilento Papers, Box 4, Folder 4 (Cilento, July 23, 1945, personal and confidential to Dr. Andrew Topping, Health Section, ERO, UNRRA, London); David Nasaw, *The Last Million* (New York: Penguin Press, 2020), 190–94; **discussions in UN**: AN: AJ / 43 / 32 (Extract from Third Committee, n.d.; **Soviet allegations**: AN: AJ / 43 / 32 (statements from Soviet representatives Medvedev and Tepliakov; the British representative was Frank Beswick); **British thoughts on utility of DP forces**: David Cesarani, *Justice Delayed: How Britain Became a Refuge for Nazi War Criminals* (London: Phoenix Press, 2001), 103–4 (the proposal came in 1945 from Canadian-Ukrainian Gordon R. Bohdan, head of the Central Ukrainian Relief Bureau, who had seen service in the Royal Canadian Airforce in Britain during the war).

10. **Lodge on Volunteer Freedom Corps**: James Jay Carafano, "Mobilizing Europe's Stateless: America's Plan for a Cold War Army," *Journal of Cold War Studies* 1:2 (1999), 64–70; **support in US Department of War**: Carafano, "Mobilizing," 64, 67; **Clay's objections**: *The Papers of General Lucius D. Clay, Germany 1945–1949*, vol. 1, ed. Jean Edward Smith (Bloomington: Indiana University Press, 1974), 315–16; **military use of Polish DPs**: Nasaw, *Last Million*, 354–55, 358 (the P&A director was Maj.-Gen. W. S. Paul, writing on May 28, 1947); **US State Department's objections**: Nasaw, *Last Million*, 190–91; *New York Times* **objection to "armies of mercenaries"**: *New York Times*, February 4, 1946, cited Nasaw, *Last Million*, 192–93 (the author of the article was Raymond Daniell, head of the paper's Berlin bureau).

11. **Brukhanov's allegations**: Briukhanov, *Vot kak eto bylo*, 103–4; AN: AJ / 43 / 610 (report of meeting with DP Division, Soviet forces, Berlin on September 30, 1949); **repatriation interviews**: GARF: 9526 / 6 / 889, ll. 22–23 (Soviet repatriate Evgeny Shevelev described serving in a Polish unit under US command, wearing US Army uniform); **Volunteer Freedom Corps idea revisited**: Carafano, "Mobilizing," 70–84.

12. **Foreign Legion recruitment (Soviet repatriate testimony)**: GARF: 9526 / 6 / 676, ll. 33–35 (Seliverst Merzanov-Letskevich, October 1950); GARF: 7317 / 20 / 145, ll. 15–16 (Vladimir Poranko, February 4, 1949—note that while Poranko gave the legion's recruitment age as eighteen to thirty-five, Merzanov-Letskevich said nineteen to forty-seven); GARF: 9526 / 6 / 669, ll. 92–99 (Avgust Kukurus, September 1949); ibid., ll. 38–40 (Iakov Rokoshko, born 1930; September 1949); ibid., ll. 395–96 (Gennady Maevsky, December 1949).

13. **First British recruitment**: Diana Kay, "Westward Ho! The Recruitment of Displaced persons for British Industry," in Johannes-Dieter Steinert and Inge Weber-Newth, *European*

Immigration in Britain 1933–1950 (Berlin-Boston: K. G. Saur, 2019; reprint), 153: **Belgian mines**: Lieselotte Luyckx, "Soviet DPs for the Belgian Mining Industry: The Daily Struggle against Yalta of a Forgotten Minority?" (PhD diss., European University Institute, 2012), 106–7; Shephard, *Long Road Home*, 332; **IGCR**: see chap. 6; **recruitment at Wildflecken**: Hulme, *Wild Place*, 162, 178–83.

14. ***Westward Ho!***: Cesarani, *Justice Delayed*, 69–72; **UNRRA's and Soviet reactions**: Kim Salomon, *Refugees in the Cold War: Toward a New International Refugee Regime in the Early Postwar Era* (Lund: Lund University Press, 1991), 203–4; **IRO involvement**: Louise Holborn, *The International Refugee Organization* (London: Oxford University Press, 1956), 474–75; Salomon, *Refugees*, 206; **British selection criteria**: Kay, "Westward Ho!," 156–59; **nationalities preferences**: Shephard, *Long Road Home*, 332; AN: AJ / 43 / 612 (Charles H. Jordan, AJDC; European Emigration HQ, Paris, August 7, 1948, to Wing-Commander Robert Innes, PCIRO Geneva); Kay, "Westward Ho!," 153; Jacques Vernant, *The Refugee in the Post-War World: Preliminary Report of a Survey of the Refugee Problem* (Geneva: United Nations, 1951), 371 (table 1: "Operation Westward Ho!); ***Westward Ho!* becomes a resettlement scheme**: Kay, "Westward Ho!," 169; **unenthusiastic welcome**: Shephard, *Long Road Home*, 332; **IRO position**: Salomon, *Refugees*, 206; Holborn, *International Refugee Organization*, 474–75.

15. **Belgian employment scheme numbers**: Gerard Daniel Cohen, *In War's Wake* (Oxford: Oxford University Press, 2012), 104; **evaluation**: Janet Flanner, "Letter from Aschaffenburg," *New Yorker*, October 30, 1948, 101; **communist campaign against**: Luyckx, "Soviet DPs," 128–29; **Belgian authorities' economic focus**: Luyckx, "Soviet DPs," 134; **impact of work in Belgium on resettlement opportunities**: Luyckx, "Soviet DPs," 154; **subsequent repatriation to USSR (cases)**: GARF: 9526 / 6 / 676, ll. 2–4, 9–10 and 77–79, GARF: 9526 / 6 / 669, ll. 186–87, 190–93, 197–200, 202, 240–41, 236–39; **French employment scheme: (communist opposition)** Cesarani, *Justice Delayed*, 74–75; **(numbers)** Cohen, *In War's Wake*, 104, 107; Shephard, *Long Road*, 335 (his numbers are slightly different from Cohen's: thirty thousand DPs ultimately settled in France, plus a further five thousand in the French colonies of Morocco, Tunisia, and French Guiana); **overall European recruitment numbers**: Cohen, *In War's Wake*, 107; **European resettlement numbers**: V. N. Zemskov, "'Vtoraia emigratsiia' i otnoshenie k nei rukovodstva SSSR, 1927–1955," in *Istoriia rossiiskogo zarubzh'ia: Emigratsiia iz SSSR-Rossii 1941–2000 gg. Sbornik statei*, ed. Iu. Poliakov et al. (Moscow: RAN, 2007), 69–70: table 3: Geografii rassleeniia i natsional'nyi sostav "vtoroi emigratsii" (po dannym organov repariatsii na 1 ianvaria 1951 gg.).

16. **Education as a DP option**: Cilento Papers, Box 18, Folder 107 ("Escape from UN-Reality," 122); **camp schools in native languages**: UA: S-1450-0000-0244-00001 (memo on "Education," January 20, 1947) (the Polish government in Warsaw objected to the anticommunist / patriotic tone of instruction in schools in Polish DP camps, attributing it to the influence of London Poles); **Ukrainian schools**: Omelian Pritsak, "The Present State of Ukrainian Studies," *Canadian Slavonic Papers / Revue canadienne des slavistes* 14:2 (1972), 146; **study at German gymnasia**: individual cases reported in GARF: 9526 / 6s / 888, ll. 143–45 (Georgy Marfutenko) and *Avstraliada* no. 67 (2011) (Sergei Rebikov), 30; **adult vocational courses**: UA: S-1450-0000-0244-00001 (UNRRA Central HQ DP Operations Germany, Order no. 28 [revised]): "Policy on education for displaced persons in Germany," December 9, 1946; Holborn, *International Refugee Organization*, 282–84; **(Jewish)** Holborn, *International Refugee Organization*, 282; **(Ukrainian)** Pritsak, "Present State," 146.

17. **DPs at German universities**: Stefan Schroeder, *Displaced Persons im Landkreis und in der Stadt Münster 1945–1951* (Münster: Schoendorff Verlag, 2005), 278; Dailonis Stauvers, interview with author, April 10, 2007; UA: S-0408-0033-06 (letter of November 21, 1946, on arrangements for students, specifying a stipend of 25 RM per week and rations equal to those of an administrative worker); **fields of study**: UA: S-0409-0040-04 (memo of Helen Hrachovska, UNRRA HQ, BAOR, March 20, 1947: "Review of the Present Enrollment of DP University Students in Winter Semester 1946–7," appendix); **DP students a privileged group**: UA: S-0408-0033-06: Yngve Freykolm, "The DP Student's Dilemma," *Students' World*, October 29, 1946.

18. **Initial chaos**: UA: S-0409-0040-04 (Hrachovska memo, March 20, 1947); **UNRRA's lack of plan**: UA: S-0408-0033-06 (Freykolm, "DP Student's Dilemma"); **Mischka Danos's experiences**: Fitzpatrick, *Mischka's War*, 128–33; **UNRRA regulations violated**: UA: S-0409-0040-04 (memo on travel authorization for DP students, June 17, 1946; memo of August 6, 1946, informing military government branches of decisions of June Conference of University ECOs); **DP students not mixing with Germans**: UA: S-0408-0033-06 (quotation from Freykolm, "DP Student's Dilemma"; Bella Brodzki and Jeremy Varon, "The Munich Years. The Students of Post-War Germany," in Steinert and Weber-Newth, *Beyond Camps and Forced Labour*, ed. Johannes-Dieter Steinert and Inge Weber-Newth (Osnabrück: Secolo-Verlag, 2005), 154, 160–61; Fitzpatrick, *Mischka's War*, 166; interview with Andrejs Bicevskis, August 1, 2007; **enrollment statistics**: UA: S-1450-0000-0244-00001 ("Advanced educational training for DPs in the three zones" [July 1946]); **(by nationality)** UA: S-1450-0000-0244-00001 ("Advanced educational training for DPs in the three zones" and "Extracts from General Morgan's report for April 1946"); UA: S-0409-0040-04: "University Admissions Policy and Procedures 1946–7").

19. **National breakdown of DP students**: UA: S-0409-0040-04 ("University Admissions Policy and Procedures 1946–7"); UA: S-1450-0000-0244-00001: "Advanced educational training for DPs in the three zones" [July 1946]; **Polish and Soviet objections**: UA: S-1450-0000-0244-00001 ("Extracts from General Morgan's report for April 1946"); UA: S-0409-0040-04 ("Advanced educational training for DPs in the three zones"); Cilento Papers, Box 18, Folder 107 ("Escape from UN-Reality," 124); **Russian émigré students**: UA: S-0409-0040-04 ("University Admissions Policy and Procedures 1946–7") (the report says that the stateless group, allocated 10 percent of student places, numbered 218 out of a total of 2,064); **Soviet students**: UA: S-0402-0001-0008 ("Consultations with Government Representatives, 24 / 6 / 1945-9 / 10 / 1946"; AN: AJ / 43 / 873 Eligibility Appeals file, Declaration of Viktor Werbitsky, April 23, 1951; **Jewish students**: Brodzki and Varon, "Munich Years," 156, 159 (quotation); **(US study possibility)** UA: S-1450-0000-0244-00001 ("Extract from General Morgan's report, April 1946").

20. **UNRRA University**: UA: S-1450-0000-0244-00001 ("Extract from General Morgan's report, April 1946"); UA: S-1450-0000-0244-00001 ("Advanced educational training for DPs in the three zones" [July 1946]) (the full breakdown of students by nationality included 576 Lithuanians, 135 Latvians, and 160 Jews, as well as Poles and Yugoslavs); **Free Ukrainian University**: Wyman, *DPs*, 122–23; Dr. Roman S. Holiat, "Short History of the Ukrainian Free University," in Shevchenko Scientific Society, *Paper / Dopovidi*, 21–22; "Ukrainian Free University," Internet Encyclopedia of Ukraine, http://www.encyclopediaofukraine.com/display.asp?linkpath=pages%5CU%5CK%5CUkrainianFreeUniversity.htm, accessed June 7, 2022.

21. **Baltic University**: M. Vager, "Baltic Academic DPs in Germany," *Baltic Review*, 7–8 (1947), 396–97; UA: S-0409-0014-20 ("Confidential directive of 11 June 1946 on moving the Baltic Study Centre [earlier name for Baltic University] to the Allenby Barracks"; list of teachers with breakdown by nationality, May 20, 1946); Cilento Papers, Box 18, Folder 107 ("Escape from UN-Reality," 122); **"liberty-loving students"**: UA: S-0408-0033-08 ("Hamburg DP University"—comment by Robert C. Riggle, an American UNRRA Welfare Officer and admirer of the University's first rector, Fricis Gulbis); **"pathetically nationalistic"**: UA: S-0408-0033-06 (Freykolm, "DP Student's Dilemma"); **student numbers, 1947**: https://en.wikipedia.org /wiki/Baltic_University, accessed May 7, 2023; **dissatisfaction with pay and conditions**: Vager, "Baltic Academic DPs," 398; **unsuccessful attempts to save Baltic University**: *New York Times*, August 8, 1947, 19 ("Baltic University, Now in Germany, May Be Moved to Quoddy Village," quoting Joseph B. Laucka, executive director of United Lithuanian Relief Fund headquartered in Brooklyn); Wyman, *DPs*, 125–27.

22. **DPs' university study bad for repatriation**: UA: S-1450-0000-0244-00001 (ERO resolution cited by Helene Gifford, UNRRA's Displaced Persons Division, in letter to visiting British MP R. R. Stokes, February 13, 1947; **mounting criticism**: AN: AJ / 43 / 754 (British zone, monthly reports: Zone Director's monthly narrative report for June 1948, part IV: Employment and Vocational Training); **UNRRA withdraws student privileges**: UA: S-0409-0040-04 (Memo on "University Students" from Helen Hrachovska, March 18, 1947); **German universities' DP quota dropped**: UA: S-0409-0040-04 (Hrachovska, "University Students"); Schroeder, *Displaced Persons*, 287; **resettlement countries not interested in university graduates**: UA: S-1450-0000-0244-00001 ("Extract from General Morgan's report for April 1946"); AN: AJ / 43 / 613 (F. C. Blanchard, A / Dir office of planning and field service, to Mr Nostrand, February 16, 1949); **DPs should "get down to work"**: AN: AJ / 43 / 754 (British zone director's monthly narrative report for June 1948, part 4); **Mischka's Danos's PhD**: Fitzpatrick, *Mischka's War*, 222–41.

Chapter 5. Other DP Activities and Entertainments

1. **Age and gender of DPs**: UA: S-0425-0010-17 ("UNRRA-Administered D. P. Centres. Population Breakdown," US zone as of April 6, 1946); Louise Holborn, *The International Refugee Organization* (London: Oxford University Press, 1956), 190, 197 (annex 13: "Displaced Persons in Germany, Austria and Italy, 31 December 1946"); **Ostarbeiter pregnancies**: Ulrich Herbert, *Fremdarbeiter: Politik und Praxis des "Ausländer-Einsatzes" in der Kriegswirtschaft des dritten Reiches* (Berlin Bonn: Verlag J.H.W. Dietz, 1986), 247–50; Tara Zahra, *The Lost Children* (Cambridge, MA: Harvard University Press, 2011), 205 (Zahra writes that in the spring of 1943 the German authorities started forcing abortions on pregnant Ostarbeiter women, although if the father was a German, a local commission might deem the child "racially valuable" and take it from the mother for placement in Lebensborn homes; **women and children among Soviet repatriates:** A. Sheviakov, "Repatriatsiia sovetskogo mirnogo naseleniia i voennoplennykh, okazavshikhsia v okkupatsionnykh zonakh gosudarstv antigitlerovskoi koalitsii," in *Naselenie Rossii v 1920–1950 gg.: Chislennost', poteri, migratsii* (Moscow: Institute rossiiskoi istorii RAN, 1994), 213 (figures for February 1, 1946, USSR); V. N. Zemskov, *Vozvrashchenie sovetskikh peremeshchennykh lits v SSSR 1944–1952 gg.* (Moscow: Tsentr gumanitarnykh initsiativ, 2016), 176–77 (figures for August 1, 1946, RSFSR only).

2. **Sexual mores**: Sheila Fitzpatrick, "The Women's Side of the Story: Soviet Displaced Persons and Postwar Repatriation," *Russian Review* 81 (April 2022), 284–301; **"Sleeping with the enemy"**: Fitzpatrick, "Women's Side," and Seth Bernstein, *Return to the Motherland* (Ithaca, NY: Cornell University Press, 2023), 112–20; **reports of sexual promiscuity**: University of Queensland, Fryer Library Collections 233, Cilento Papers, Box 4, Folder 4, Report no. 2, July 19, 1945; Ben Shephard, *The Long Road Home* (London: Vintage, 2010), 295 (quoting French charity worker, 1945); Zahra, *Lost Children*, 112; UA: S-0409-0014-03 (memo from Anne Wood, I. O. Vol. Socs., to Sir Raphael Cilento, Zone Director, re PW and DP Div's memo on "Status and Treatment of DPs outside Assembly Centres"—quotations on "sexual irregularity" and "epidemic"); **baby boom**: Shephard, *Long Road Home*, 295; Mark Wyman, *DPs* (Ithaca, NY: Cornell University Press, 1989), 111–12; Adam R. Seipp, *Strangers in the Wild Place: Refugees, Americans and a German Town, 1945–52* (Bloomington: Indiana University Press, 2013), 70; Atina Grossmann, *Jews, Germans, and Allies: Close Encounters in Occupied Germany* (Princeton, NJ: Princeton University Press, 2007), 184–86; **Jewish child-bearing**: Grossman, *Jews, Germans, and Allies*, 184–235 (self-assertion argument); Muriel Knox Doherty, *Letters from Belsen 1945: An Australian Nurse's Experiences with the Survivors of War* (St. Leonard's, NSW: Allen & Unwin, 2000); **DP children by nationality**: UA: S-1021-0081-0001 ("Reports and Statistics" by Mrs. E. M. Doig, Asst. Chief Reports and Statistics, UNRRA HQ Heidelberg, April 22, 1947).

3. **Marriages**: Grossmann, *Jews, Germans, and Allies*, 184 (quoting J. Biber, *Risen from the Ashes*); Wyman, *DPs*, 111 ("neighbors" "strange marriages," and "are you married?" quotations); Ramona Koval, *Bloodhound: Searching for My Father* (Melbourne: Text Publishing, 2015), 34–35; **weddings**: Wyman, *DPs*, 111–12; **different degrees of commitment** (repatriating Soviet males, but not females, likely to dismiss DP cohabitation): GARF: 7317 / 20 / 128, ll. 38, 188; Fitzpatrick, "Women's Side," 293; **attitudes in camps to extramarital relationships**: Margaret McNeill, *By the Rivers of Babylon* (London: Bannisdale Press, 1950), 98 (quotation); AN: AJ / 43 / 806 (Ruth Reed, "Sociological effect of refugee life," 1951); GARF: 9526 / 6s / 675, ll. 254–58 (finger-pointing by middle-aged female Estonian repatriate in reentry interview); **"civil ceremony not real"**: Marvin Klemmé, *The Inside Story of UNRRA* (New York: Lifetime Editions, 1949), 252–3; **waiting to marry**: (Michael Danos) Sheila Fitzpatrick, *Mischka's War* (London: I. B. Tauris, 2017), 198–200; (Andrejs Bicevskis): "Bicevskis family history," email from Bicevskis to Sheila Fitzpatrick, May 6, 2008.

4. **Laws on marriage and citizenship**: Ruth Balint, *Destination Elsewhere* (Ithaca, NY: Cornell University Press, 2021), 63 (IRO was conflicted on this, since its constitution treated DPs of both sexes as individuals. But by the time resettlement was on the table, this had been in practice superseded by an emphasis on families that made the nationality of the head of the household that of all other family members); **marriages to foreigners**: these were forbidden by a Politburo resolution "On the Prohibition of Marriages between Soviet Citizens and Foreigners," February 15, 1947, which is best known for its impact on Western diplomats with Soviet fiancées, although the majority of such marriages in the postwar years were in fact made by Soviet DP women: see Fitzpatrick, "Women's Lives," 294–99; **German marriages to DPs**: Sheila Fitzpatrick, *White Russians, Red Peril: A Cold War History of Migration to Australia* (Melbourne: La Trobe University Press, 2021), 233–34 (1947 deportation of Egon Karl Lerch).

5. **Free meals for good-looking girls**: GARF: 7317 / 20 / 145, ll. 278–79 (quotation) and 118–24; GARF: 9526 / 6s / 669, l. 284; **Amis and DP women**: Ella E. Schneider Hilton, *Displaced*

Person (Baton Rouge: Louisiana State University, 2004), 123–24 (long quotation); **marriage not out of the question**: Hilton, *Displaced Person*, 125 (When one Ami left, "the girls picked up another Ami to continue their lifestyle and to learn more American until they found someone, maybe after a couple of children, who was willing to marry them." Black GIs, however, "could not always get permission to marry"); **Soviet DP women rebuff repatriation officers**: GARF: 7317 / 20 / 128, ll. 38, 188; **infanticide**: GARF: 7317 / 20 / 145, ll. 278–79; **Estonian nurse's story**: GARF: 9526 / 6 / 675, ll. 242–48 and 259–90.

6. **Marriages of Mischka's Riga girlfriends**: Fitzpatrick, *Mischka's War*, 75–77; interviews with Helen Machen, Downers Grove, IL, February 2, 2007, and February 23, 2008; **Soviet women DPs marrying Western foreigners**: Zemskov, *Vozvrashchenie*, 85; Fitzpatrick, "Women's Side," 294, 298; **Soviet DP women marrying East Europeans: (statistics)** Zemskov, *Vozvrashchenie*, 84; **(in Poland)** GARF: 9526 / 6 / 669, ll. 161–62, 275; GARF: 7317 / 20 / 145, ll. 405–7; **(in Yugoslavia)**: Fitzpatrick, "Women's Side," 297; **(emigrating with East European DP husbands)** GARF: 9526 / 6 / 888, l. 219 (Ianovich/Neuman); interview with Natalie Baitch, Plumpton, NSW, March 1, 2016 (Kashchenko-Baich); National Archives of Australia (NAA): A6119, 4715: MOKRAS, Lydia, vol. 2 (Jankovski/Mokras).

7. **DP tourism**: (Mischka Danos) Fitzpatrick, *Mischka's War*, 92; (Andrejs Bicevskis) Bicevskis, "Family History," email of May 1, 2008; (Ivan Popowski): Tamara Popowski, "'We Knew Things Would Get Better.' A Family Migration Story" (MA thesis, University of Sydney 2023), 133.

8. **Adventurers**: Sheila Fitzpatrick, "The Prodigals' Return: Voluntary Repatriation to the Soviet Union from Displaced Persons' Camps in Europe, 1949–50," *Cahiers du monde russe* 62:4 (2021), 529–51; **Rutkovsky's story**: GARF: 9526 / 6s / 669, ll. 41–44; **Kuntaras's story**: GARF: 9526 / 674, 232–33; **Kudinov's story**: GARF: 9526 / 6 / 675, ll. 134–37; **Gladyshev's story**: GARF: 9526 / 6 / 890, ll. 61–71 (neither of the two names he used shows up in Australian or Soviet lists of migrants departing from Australia); **Salnikov's story**: GARF: 9526 / 6 / 669, ll. 112–14.

9. **Women's adventures: Borman-Babaevo's story**: GARF: 9236 / 6 / 669, l. 261; **Egorova's story**: GARF: 9526 / 6 / 674, ll. 261–64; Sheila Fitzpatrick, "The Tramp's Tale," *Past and Present* 241:1 (2018), 59–60.

10. **DP sports**: David Nasaw, *The Last Million* (New York: Penguin, 2020), 146; Wyman, *DPs*, 118–19; **Jewish DP sports**: Shephard, *Long Road Home*, 145 (quotation; boxing); Nasaw, *Last Million*, 170; **Russian émigré team ineligible**: Denis Mitskevich, "Prelomleniia emigrantskogo opyta," in Liudmila Flam, ed., *Sud'by pokoleniia: 1920-1930-kh godov v emigratsii* (Moscow: Russkii put', 2006), 317.

11. **Mischka Danos: (Dresden)**: University of Chicago Special Collections, Michael Danos Papers (letter from Michael Danos to Olga Danos, June 16, 1944); Fitzpatrick, *Mischka's War*, 73–93; **(Flensburg)**: Danos Papers (letter from Michael Danos to Olga Danos, September 15, 1945); **Andrejs Bicevskis**: "Family History," email to Sheila Fitzpatrick, May 1, 2008; Interview with Andrejs Bicevskis, Brisbane, July 30, 2007; **Hanover competitions**: Danos Papers (postcard from Michael Danos to Olga Danos, July 5, 1946; letter from Michael Danos to Olga Danos, August 13, 1946); interview with Bicevskis, 2007; **zonal competitions in Cologne**: Danos Papers (letter from Michael Danos to Olga Danos, undated [before August 11, 1947]); **Paris**: Michael Danos Papers (letter from Michael to Olga, May 22, 1947); **Oxford disappointment**: Danos Papers (letter from Michael Danos to Olga Danos, undated [before August 11, 1947]); **Mischka**

eligible to compete in international competition as a German?: Danos Papers (letter from Michael Danos to Olga Danos, undated [1948?]).

12. **Scouts**: "Scouting in Displaced Persons Camps," https://en-academic.com/dic.nsf /enwiki/7456061#British_sector_camps," accessed February 22, 2024. In the American zone of Germany there were Latvian Scouts and/or Girl Guides groups in the Altötting, Amberg, Ansbach, Augsburg, Bayreuth, Berchtesgarten, Eichstätt, Erlangen, Esslingen, Fischbach, Fürth, Hanau, Ingolstadt, Karlsruhe, Kassel, Kleinkötz, Memmingen, Mühldorf, Munich, Neuötting, Nuremberg, Pegnitz, Schwäbish Gmünd, Traunstein, Ulm, Wetzlar, Würzburg, and Wiesbaden camps. Russian Scout groups were in Mainleus, Memmingen Airport, Mönchehof, München-Bogenhausen, München-Feldmoching, München-Freiman, Neiderraunau, Rotwesten, Schleis-sheim, Traunstein, and Zierenberg. In the British zone, there were Latvian Scouts and/or Girl Guide groups in Altgarge, Augustdorf, Blomberg, Börnsen, Dedelsdorf, Eutin, Flensburg, Geestacht, Giften, Granum, Greven, Hanover, Imbshausen, Lübeck, Neustadt, Oldenburg, Pinneberg, Sengwarden, Wedel, and Wolterdingen; **scouting and patriotism**: Laura Hilton, "Cultural Nationalism in Exile: The Case of Polish and Latvian Displaced Persons," *Historian*, 71:2 (2009), 309–10; **Russian émigré Scouts**: NA UK: FO 371 / 56844 (letter of V. Temnomeroff, Boy Scout Representative in US zone of Germany, to J. S. Wilson, Director, Boy Scouts International Bureau, London, January 17, 1946, with Wilson's commentary); **British wariness of DP scouting**: NA UK: FO 371 / 56844 (Pumphrey, for J. E. Galsworthy, to J. S. Wilson, February 1, 1946); **Russian DP Scout troops**: "Scouting in Displaced Persons Camps." The only purely Russian Scout group listed in the British zone was in Naternberg-Deggendorf, although Seedorf had a Scouts group that catered to a variety of nationalities including Latvian and Russian. In the American zone, there were Russian Scout groups in Mainleus, Memmingen Airport DP camp, Mönchehof, Munich-Bogenhausen, Munich-Feldmoching, Munich-Freiman, Pfaffenhofen, Purten, Regensburg, Rotwesten, Schleissheim, Traunstein, and Zierenberg. There was also a Russian Scouts troop in Ravensburg (Wangen) in the French sector, and, anomalously, one in the Soviet sector at Niedersachswerfen. **Mönchehof Scouts troop**: Irina Halafoff, *Svidetel' istorii* (Melbourne: University of Melbourne, 1988), 35 (quotation); Fitzpatrick, *White Russians, Red Peril*, 46–47, 184–85.

13. **DP churches**: Wyman, *DPs*, 109–11; **theological centers**: Wyman, *DPs*, 111; **nationalist connections**: Tomas Balkelis, "Living in the Displaced Persons Camp: Lithuanian War Refugees in the West, 1944–1954," in *Warlands: Population Resettlement and State Reconstruction in the Soviet-East European Borderlands 1945–50*, ed. Peter Gatrell and Nick Baron (New York: Palgrave Macmillan, 2009), 40; **factional conflicts**: AN: AJ / 43 / 807 (folder on Belorussian Central Administration, protest dated November 7, 1949).

14. **Russian Orthodox Church Abroad**: Ciprian Burlacioiu, "Russian Orthodox Diaspora as a Global Religion after 1918," *Studies in World Christianity* 24:1 (2018), 4–24; **Russian church in Mönchehof**: Halafoff, *Svidetel'*, 36; **Regensburg**: Roman Smolorz, "Der Alltag der osteuropäischen Displaced Persons 1945–1949 unter dem Einfluss von ost- und westeuropäischen Geheimdiensten," in Corine Defrance, Juliette Denis, and Julia Maspero, eds., *Personnes déplacées et guerre froide en Allemagne occupée* (Brussels: Peter Lang, 2015), 205; **DP priests**: (Martos) Michael Alex Protopopov, "The Russian Orthodox Presence in Australia," (PhD diss., Australian Catholic University, 2005, 244–45); G. I. Kanevskaia, *"'My eshche mechtaem o Rossii . . .' Istoriia russkoi diaspory v Avstralii* (Vladivostok: Izd. Dalnevostochnogo Universiteta, 2010), 120–23

(Martos emigrated as a DP to Australia in 1949, served as vicar bishop, later archbishop, under ROCA in Australia as well as bishop in Buenos Aires); (Deresa): Protopopov, "Russian Orthodox Presence," 147–48; *Edinenie* no. 23 (1953), 5; (Mogileff): Protopopov, "Russian Orthodox Presence," 399. For a detailed analysis of Russian Orthodox DP priests who ended up resettled with other DPs in Australia, see Fitzpatrick, *White Russians, Red Peril*, 47–48, 174–83.

15. **Jewish DPs' religious practice**: Nasaw, *Last Million*, 174–75; Wyman, *DPs*, 151 (Irish beef quotation); **Zionism**: Avinoam J. Patt, "Finding Home and Homeland: Jewish DP Youth and Zionism in the Aftermath of the Holocaust" (PhD diss., New York University, 2005), 5; **military training**: Susanne Rolinek, "Clandestine Operators: The *Bricha* and *Betar* Network in the Salzburg Area, 1945–1948," *Journal of Israeli History* 19:3 (2008), 41–61; **JDC doubts**: Grossman, *Jews, Germans and Allies*, 129; **DPs leaving camps for ad hoc kibbutzim**: Patt, "Finding Home and Homeland," 5.

16. **Latvian churches**: Aldis Purs, "'How Those Brothers in Foreign Lands Are Dividing the Fatherland': Latvian National Politics in Displaced Persons Camps after the Second World War," in Gatrell and Baron, *Warlands*, 54 (quotation); **Latvian Evangelical Lutheran Church**: UA: S-1021-0081-0002 (letter to McNarney from Prof. Dr. T. Grünbergs, Archbishop of Latvian Evangelical-Lutheran Church, Esslingen, September 18, 1946); **religious diversity in Latvia (statistics)**: "Religion in Latvia," https://en.wikipedia.org/wiki/Religion_in_Latvia#:~:text=Historically%2C%20the%20west%20and%20central,due%20to%20migration%20from%20Latgale, accessed April 21, 2023; **minorities in Latvia**: Purs, "'How Those Brothers in Foreign Lands Are Dividing the Fatherland'," 63 (quotation).

17. **Folk culture and national identity**: Inta Gāle Carpenter, "Folklore as a Source for Creating Exile Identity among Latvian Displaced Persons in Post-World War II Germany," *Journal of Baltic Studies* 48:2 (2017), 224; Irene Elsknis Geisler, "The Gendered Plight of Terror: Annexation and Exile in Latvia 1940–1950" (PhD diss., Western Michigan University, 2011), 243–44 (quotation); **weaving and the invention of tradition**: Karen Schamberger, "Weaving a Family and a Nation through Two Latvian Looms," *Immigrants and Minorities* 36:2 (2018), 178–98; and see Eric Hobsbawm and Terence Rangers, eds., *The Invention of Tradition* (Cambridge, UK: Cambridge University Press, 2014).

18. **"Show them we are cultured people"**: Carpenter, "Folklore," 223 (quoting Latvian DP newspaper, late 1945); **Latvian People's University**: UA: S-1021-0081-0003 (file on Baltic Camp Bettenhausen, Kassel: statement from University's director, Prof. Dr. E. Roze, circa 1947); **book production**: Modris Eksteins, *Walking since Daybreak* (Boston: Houghton Mifflin, 1999), 161; Carpenter, "Folklore," 224; **opera singer to folk singer**: (Olga Danos's sister Mary): Fitzpatrick, *Mischka's War*, 136; **performing nationalism**: (Latvians) Hilton, "Cultural Nationalism in Exile," 281–82; Carpenter, "Folklore," 210–11 (drawing on Erving Goffman's concept of "spoiled identity" in his *Stigma*) and 215–16 ("moral guardians"); (Lithuanians) Balkelis, "Living in the Displaced Persons Camp," 37–38; (Jews) Grossmann, *Jews, Germans and Allies*, 158.

Chapter 6. IRO and Its Mandate

1. **IRO's long gestation**: a draft constitution was submitted to the second session of the United Nation's Economic and Social Council in May 1946 and approved by the council in September and by the United Nations General Assembly on December 15, 1946, but it was more

NOTES TO PAGES 154–158 293

than six months before IRO's Preliminary Commission started work on July 1, 1947: Louise Holborn, *The International Refugee Organization* (London: Oxford University Press, 1956), 766–68 ("Chronology"); **funding and Cold War**: Ben Shephard, *The Long Road Home* (London: Vintage Books, 2010), 262; **Soviet Union stays out**: Gerard Daniel Cohen, *In War's Wake* (Oxford: Oxford University Press, 2012), 30 (other non-joiners included Eastern European states in the Soviet orbit); **IRO's relationship with UN**: Michael R. Marrus, *The Unwanted: European Refugees in the Twentieth Century* (New York: Oxford University Press, 1985), 342; **funding**: Shephard, *Long Road Home*, 262.

2. **"US must run this show"**: quoted Andrew Harder, "The Politics of Impartiality: The United Nations Relief and Rehabilitation Administration in the Soviet Union, 1946–7," *Journal of Contemporary History* 47:2 (2012), 365; **reducing pressure on US**: Shephard, *Long Road Home*, 262; **displacement and repatriation**: AN: AJ / 43 / 148, Manuels d'éligibilité. Manual for Eligibility Officers, no. 242, n.d., (1947?), 20, citing Section C of Part 1 of the Annex to the IRO Constitution (AN: AJ / 43 / 457). If the objections made did not mee IRO's standards, the displaced person would cease to be considered within IRO's mandate but would still be "free to choose his own mode of action," that is, not liable to forcible repatriation. **Extension of mandate to refugees**: AN: AJ / 43 / 148 (Preliminary Draft of Instructions on IRO Eligibility, Volume I. *Handbook* [Rome: Eligibility Office of PCIRO—Italy, October 1947]), 9; **different categories from UNRRA**: AN: AJ / 43 / 707 (World Council of Churches file; "United Nations Special Committee on Refugees and Displaced persons," May 9, 1946); **refugees and DPs defined**: AN: AJ / 43 / 148 (Preliminary Draft of Instructions on IRO Eligibility, 8).

3. **Soviet sensitivities on Russian émigrés**: Arieh J. Kochavi, "British Policy on Non-Repatriable Displaced Persons in Germany and Austria, 1945–7," *European History Quarterly* vol. 21 (1991), 373–74; **staffing of IRO**: AN: AJ / 43 / 707 (USA folder: Meeting with the Revercomb committee [Committee on the Judiciary] of the Senate, November 1, 1947); **handover to IRO from UNRRA and IGCR, July 1, 1947**: UA: S-1450-0000-0266-00001 ("Transfer to the IRO of the IGC [Intergovernmental Committee on Refugees]); Kathryn C. Hulme, *Undiscovered Country: A Spiritual Adventure* (London: Muller, 1967), 266–71; **disappointment at American director**: University of Queensland, Fryer Library Collections 233, Fedora Fisher Papers, Box 3 (note by Raphael Cilento, June 22, 1947); **William Hallam Tuck**: Register of the William Hallam Tuck papers, Online Archive of California, https://oac.cdlib.org/findaid/ark: /13030/kt809nf69h/entire_text/, accessed October 25, 2021; **Donald Kingsley**: AN: AJ / 43 / 461 (press release of August 5, 1949, on appointment of J. Donald Kingsley as director-general); obituary, *New York Times*, June 2, 1972; Cohen, *In War's Wake*, 100.

4. **Characterization of IRO resettlement program**: Cohen, *In War's Wake*, 11; **"M" project**: Cohen, *In War's Wake*, 100–102 (drawing on Henry Field, *"M" Project for FDR: Studies on Migration and Settlement*, 1962); **population movements**: Eugene M. Kulischer, *Europe on the Move: War and Population Changes, 1917–47* (New York: Columbia University Press, 1948); Joseph B. Schechtman, *Postwar Population Transfers in Europe, 1945–1955* (Philadelphia: University of Pennsylvania Press, 1962); Antonio Ferrara, "Eugene Kulischer, Joseph Schechtman and the Historiography of Migrations," *Journal of Contemporary History* 46:4 (2011), 717–19; **plans for resettlement in Palestine**: Avinoam Patt and Kierra Crago-Schneider, "Years of Survival: JDC in Postwar Germany, 1945–1947," in Avinoam Patt et al., *The JDC at 100* (Detroit: Wayne State University Press, 2019), 369–70; Atina Grossmann, *Jews, Germans and Allies: Close Encounters*

in Occupied Germany (Princeton, NJ: Princeton University Press, 2007), 158–59; **stateless Russian resettlement**: George Woodbridge, *UNRRA* (New York: Columbia University Press, 1950), vol. 3, 189, 197, 203.

5. **IGCR: few accomplishments**: David Nasaw, *The Last Million* (New York: Penguin Press, 2020), 183–84; **leadership and budget**: UA: S-1252-0000-0071-00001 (document on "apparently over-lapping responsibilities of international bodies dealing with displaced persons," signed G. L. Warren, February 11, 1943; Kochavi, "British Policy," 366; **division of responsibilities with UNRRA**: Nasaw, *Last Million*, 183; **Soviet resignation from IGCR**: UA: S-1252-0000-0071-00001 ("Intergovernmental Committee on Refugees," Washington, DC, November 1944); UA: S-1451-0000-0074-00002 (Keith Aickin to A. H. Feller: Memo on "Distinction between displaced persons who cannot and who do not desire to be repatriated," December 4, 1944; letter from Herbert H. Lehman, Dir. Gen. UNRRA, to Sir Herbert Emerson, IGCR, April 7, 1945); **unproductive negotiations on resettlement**: UA: S-1252-0000-0070-00001 (Plenary Meeting of December 16, 1946: "Brief Analysis of Resettlement Prospects in South America as of 19 February 1947"); **views of IGCR**: Shephard, *Long Road Home*, 260; **Truman Directive**: Leonard Dinnerstein, *America and the Survivors of the Holocaust* (New York: Columbia University Press, 1982), 163–64; **impact of Truman Directive on repatriation**: Cilento Papers, Box 18, Folder 107 ("Escape from UN-Reality," 130).

6. **British resistance to Jewish immigration to Palestine**: Nasaw, *Last Million*, 212–18, 359–60 (the British were under pressure in late 1945 to issue one hundred thousand certificates for Jewish DPs to enter Palestine, but were in fact issuing only fifteen hundred certificates a month); **Jewish smuggling network**: Susanne Rolinek, "Clandestine Operators: The *Bricha* and *Betar* Network in the Salzburg Area, 1945–1948," *Journal of Israeli History* 19:2 (2008), 41–61; **Exodus story**: Nasaw, *Last Million*, 368–79; **JDC and HIAS**: Yehuda Bauer, *Out of the Ashes: The Impact of American Jews on Post-Holocaust European Jewry* (Oxford: Pergamon Press, 1989), xvii–xix, 181–82; Sheila Fitzpatrick, "Migration of Jewish 'Displaced Persons' from Europe to Australia after the Second World War: Revisiting the Question of discrimination and Numbers," *Australian Journal of Politics and History* 67:2 (2021), 232–33 (Australian Immigration Minister Arthur Calwell on HIAS).

7. **IRO and repatriation**: Cohen, *In War's Wake*, 32; (Ukrainian negotiations) AN: AJ / 43 / 610 (Repatriement, 1947–50: cables of June 1947); **"Red scare" in US**: Daniel Yergin, *Shattered Peace: The Origins of the Cold War and the National Security State* (New York: Penguin Books, 1977), 285; **US assessment of Soviet capacities**: Melvyn P. Leffler, *A Preponderance of Power: National Security, the Truman Administration, and the Cold War* (Stanford: Stanford University Press, 1992).

8. **Soviet expectations of depression in US**: Alan Bullock, *Ernest Bevin, Foreign Secretary, 1945–1951* (Oxford: Oxford University Press, 1983), 423, and see chap. 1, n. 2; **Soviet perception of Bizonia as threat**: Vladimir O. Pechatnov, "The Soviet Union and the World 1944–53," in *The Cambridge History of the Cold War*, ed. Melvyn P. Leffler and Odd Arne Westad (Cambridge, UK: Cambridge University Press, 2010), 106 (quoting memo of A. Smirnov to V. Molotov, March 12, 1948); **Soviet analysis of US aims**: Kenneth M. Jensen, ed., *Origins of the Cold War: The Novikov, Kennan, and Roberts "Long Telegrams" of 1946* (Washington, DC: US Institute for Peace, 1991), 3–16 (Novikov Telegram, Washington, September 27, 1946); Pechatnov, "Soviet Union and the World," 102; **Marshall Plan**: Carole K. Fink, *Cold War: An International History* (Boulder, CO:

Westview Press, 2017), 89; Cohen, *In War's Wake*, 7 (Acheson quotation); **and Eastern Europe**: Pechatnov, "Soviet Union and the World," 105; Leffler, *Preponderance of Power*, 236.

9. **Stalin and the Allies**: Norman M. Naimark, *Stalin and the Fate of Europe: The Postwar Struggle for Sovereignty* (Cambridge, MA: Harvard University Press, 2019), 12 (quotation); **alarm at US covert operations**: Pechatnov, "Soviet Union and the World," 107; **Soviet prohibition of marriage to foreigners**: *Stalin i kozmopolitizm: Dokumenty agitpropa TsK KPSS, 1945–1953* (Moscow: Mezhdunarodnyi Fond "Demokratiia," Izd. "Materik," 2005), 107–8 (decree of February 15, 1947); **anti-cosmopolitan campaign**: Sheila Fitzpatrick, *On Stalin's Team* (Princeton, NJ: Princeton University Press, 2015), 215–19; Gennady Kostyrchenko, *Out of the Shadows: Anti-Semitism in Stalin's Russia* (Amherst, MA: Prometheus, 1995); **Molotov and Mikoian in danger**: Fitzpatrick, *On Stalin's Team*, 209–22; **Molotov on Marshall Plan**: Feliks Chuev, *Sto sorok besed s Molotovym: Iz dnevnika F. Chueva* (Moscow: Terra, 1991), 88.

10. **Soviet stubbornness on repatriation**: Cohen, *In War's Wake*, 8; Naimark, *Stalin and the Fate of Europe*, 109; **efforts to repatriate resettled Soviet DPs**: Sheila Fitzpatrick, "Soviet Repatriation Efforts among 'Displaced Persons' Resettled in Australia, 1950–1953," *Australian Journal of Politics and History* 63:1 (2017), 45–61, and see chap. 9; **IRO resettlement and repatriation**: AN: AJ / 43 / 707 (in the period July 1 to December 1, 1947, 77,493 DPs of all nationalities were resettled and 35,015 repatriated); GARF: 7317 / 20 / 43, ll.33 (Soviet Military Administration in Germany report of January 15, 1949, showed 6,674 Soviet citizens "taken away to other countries" and 663 repatriated); Holborn, *International Refugee Organization*, 437 (over a million DPs of all nationalities resettled, 1947–52); Kim Salomon, *Refugees in the Cold War: Toward a New International Refugee Regime in the Early Postwar Era* (Lund: Lund University Press, 1991), 125 (73,000 repatriated, 1947–52).

11. **DPs as cheap labor for West**: A. I. Briukhanov, *Vot kak eto bylo: O rabote missii po repatriatsii sovetskikh grazhdan (Vospominaniia sovetskogo ofitsera)* (Moscow: Gospolitizdat, 1958), 99; G. Mikhailov and G. Semenov, "Sovremennye amerikanskie rabotorgovtsy," *Izvestiia*, March 23, 1952, 3 ("slave traders" quotation); AN: AJ / 43 / 610: comments attributed to Soviet repatriation officials in protest to US authorities from Parsch DP camp, Salzburg, September 1948 ("looking in their mouths," "seated like slaves" quotation); **Soviet children at risk**: Briukhanov, *Vot kak eto bylo*, 171–73; AN: AJ / 43 / 610: "Repatriation to Soviet Russia" (cutting from *Washington Post* of September 14, 1948, "Reds Given Custody of Girl Cripple").

12. **Soviet repatriation missions hindered**: Briukhanov, *Vot kak eto bylo*, 188–89; V. N. Khaustov et al., eds., *Lubianka" Stalin i NKVD-NKGB-GUKR "Smersh'"* (Moscow: Mezhdunarodnyi fond "Demokratiia," 2006), 550–52 (memo from security chief S. N. Kruglov to Soviet Politburo, February 13, 1946); **need for missions questioned**: UA: S0409-0014-02: (minutes of a meeting between UNRRA officials and Soviet repatriation officers, Fürstenhof, February 24, 1947); AN: AJ / 43 / 6110 (draft letter following discussion of memo of W. H. Tuck and P. L. Boal, September 2, 1947; report of meeting with Soviet representatives in Berlin, September 30, 1949); **Soviet mission in British zone closed down**: AN: AJ / 43 / 610 (P. L. Boal to Tuck, September 2, 1947); **IRO Repatriation Department concerned**: AN: AJ / 43 / 610 (Radin to Blanchard, September 8, 1947; **restrictions in US zone**: AN: AJ / 43 / 610 (Col. Biddle to Tuck, September 2, 1947).

13. **Closure of Soviet mission in US zone: exchanges between General Clay and Marshal Sokolovsky**: GARF: 7317 / 20 / 143, l. 23 (Clay to Sokolovsky, January 11, 1949; Sokolovsky to

Clay, January 19, 1949); **"gangster-like behavior"**: GARF: 7317 / 20 / 143, l. 119 (statement of Marshal V. D. Sokolovsky, Berlin, March 2, 1949); **Soviet capitulation**: GARF: 7317 / 20 / 143, ll. 126 and 139 (statement from Soviet Military Administration Information Bureau, March 2, 1949; report by Iurkin of SVAG's repatriation department to K. D. Golubev, deputy head of the Repatriation Agency in Moscow, March 16, 1949). March 4 is the date of departure in the Soviet version; the official history of IRO gives the date of their departure as March 3 (Holborn, *International Refugee Organization*, 769); **"shameful operation"**: GARF: 7317 / 20 / 143, 117–18 (statement of Marshal V. D. Sokolovsky, Berlin, March 2, 1949); **Soviet hopes that mass repatriation might still be possible**: GARF: 7317 / 20 / 143, ll. 140, 144 report by Iurkin to Golubev, March 16, 1949 (noting assessment given in off-the-record conversation by IRO repatriation officer Elizabeth Braun that "if IRO did not exist, 80% of the DPs would repatriate," and pointing out that IRO was due to go out of business in the current year, and that at the recent Geneva conference of IRO, "many thought that as a result the number of those wanting to repatriate would grow a lot in the next six to eight months").

14. **Tolstoy Foundation**: "Origins," https://tolstoyfoundation.org/tolstoy.html, accessed May 12, 2023 (Alexandra Tolstoy biography); Vitalij Fastovskij, Justus-Liebig-Universität Giessen, "Humanitäre Hilfe im Kalten Krieg. Die Unterstützung von Displaced Persons and Flüchtlinge durch die Tolstoy Foundation (1949–1989)" [communication from author, 2020], 20; **Tolstoy's contacts with IGCR**: AN: AJ / 43 / 5 (folder on "The Tolstoy Foundation, Inc. New York": letter of representatives of Tolstoy Foundation in the United States to Martha Biele, February 21, 1945; letter of Deputy High commissioner of IGCR to Alexandra Tolstoy, March 28, 1945; letter of Alexandra Tolstoy to Dr. Leland Rex Robinson, Chair, Committee on Displaced Persons, American Council of Voluntary Agencies for Foreign Service, October 2, 1944); AN: AJ / 43 / 75 (letter of Deputy High Commissioner to Alexandra Tolstoy, October 11, 1944); **UNRRA's wariness**: UA: S-1267-0000-0328-00001 (letter from passport division of State Department to Mrs. Schaufuss, August 5, 1946; note from H. E. Coustin, December 7, 1945, on meeting of the Director-General [presumably UNRRA] with Miss Tolstoy—"because of the political status of these refugees the Administration's action would require careful consideration"); AN: AJ / 43 / 75 (Martha H. Biehle, American Resident Representative, to Sir Herbert W. Emerson, Director. Attn. Dr. Kullmann, July 11, 1946); **Soviet sensitivities**: UA: S-1267-0000-0328-00001 (memo from David Cobb to Leonard L. Henninger, UNRRA, Washington, DC, April 1, 1946).

15. **Tolstoy Foundation in Europe**: UA: S-1267-0000-0328-00001 (Schaufuss's revised application, submitted June 20, 1946); Paul B. Anderson, "The Tolstoy Foundation," *Russian Review* 17:1 (1958), 63–64; **Foundation on US DP Commission's list of voluntary organizations**: Nasaw, *Last Million*, 442; **depiction of stateless Russians as anticommunists, not pro-Nazis**: AN: AJ / 43 / 572 (confidential memo from Mrs. T. A. Schaufuss, European representative of the Tolstoy Foundation, to Mr. Ugo Carusi, Chair, US DP Commission, Washington, DC, September 25, 1950); Alexandra Tolstoy, "The Russian DPs," *Russian Review* 9:1 (January 1950), 58 (quotation); AN: AJ / 43 / 572 (memo from Schaufuss to Carusi, September 25, 1950 (quotation).

16. **Soviet DPs "a positive security asset"**: AN: AJ / 43 / 395 (testimony of president of Tolstoy Foundation Alexandra Tolstoy before Senate Subcommittee on Immigration and Naturalization March 9, 1951); **IRO shift**: Cohen, *In War's Wake*, 110–11 (quoting statement that "the

suffering [the DPs] have endured under totalitarian rule has reinforced their devotion to democratic ideals" from IRO's "Guide for Publicity on Displaced Persons," May 1948; such sentiments, however, remained comparatively rare in IRO materials); **earlier handling of collaborators**: Fitzpatrick, *White Russians, Red Peril*, 48; **1947 instructions on eligibility**: AN: AJ / 43 / 148 ("Preliminary draft of Instructions on IRO Eligibility," Volume I: "Handbook" [Rome: Eligibility Office of PCIRO—Italy, October 1947], 32); **need for "liberalization of eligibility"**: Holborn, *International Refugee Organization*, 210–11 (quotation); **"benefit of the doubt"**: AN: AJ / 43 / 303 ("Eligibility of certain categories of Baltic refugees" by T. J. Bartus, chief, Field Services, IRO, Hamburg, June 6, 1951); **Kingsley on liberalization**: AN: AJ / 43 / 193 (Kingsley, Dir. IRO, to the Foreign Office, London and other foreign offices, February 25, 1952); **UNHCR**: Set up in December 1950; its founding principles were enunciated in the 1951 Refugee Convention, which defined a refugee owed protection as someone who "owing to well-founded fear of being persecuted for reasons of race, religion, nationality, membership of a particular social group or political opinion, is outside the country of his nationality" (war criminals excepted): Convention and Protocol Relating to the Status of Refugees, available at UNHCR, https://www.unhcr.org/us/media/convention-and-protocol-relating-status-refugees, accessed November 5, 2023; **countervailing voices**: AN: AJ / 43 / 457 (letter from Simon Wiesenthal to Bedo, Salzburg, October 20, 1948); Ruth Balint, *Destination Elsewhere* (Ithaca, NY: Cornell University Press, 2021), 49–50.

17. **Mischka Danos's call-up**: Fitzpatrick, *Mischka's War*, 68–72; **UNRRA on Latvian Legion**: UA: S-0411-0002-01 ("Survey of the Army Screening on the 15th March 1947 in the moment of withdrawal of the UNRRA representatives," prepared by Mr. B. J. Deichman-Sörensen); ibid., S-0400-0004-02: F. E. Morgan to R. Liepins, Latvian Red Cross, May 1, 1947 (Morgan summarized the US military's practice, as to "assign Displaced Persons status to ex-Latvian soldiers identified not to be war criminals, traitors, collaborators or volunteers for military service"); **better treatment in British zone**: UA: S-0400-0003-02: PNC, legal adviser, to F. E. Morgan, March 13, 1946 (while "UNRRA should *not* be caring for these people, . . . they were getting more favourable treatment in the British Zone, perhaps wrongly"); **Valdmanis's screening**: UA: S-0400-0004-02 (Morgan to Liepins, May 1, 1947); **Nuremberg ruling**: *Nuremberg Trial Proceedings*, vol. 22, September 30, 1946, 512–15, available at https://avalon.law.yale.edu/imt /09-30-46.asp, accessed May 14, 2023; **new IRO position on Baltic Waffen-SS**: Gerhard P. Bassler, *Alfred Valdmanis and the Politics of Survival* (Toronto: University of Toronto Press, 2000), 209; **reconsiderations of eligibility**: AN: AJ / 43 / 808, Folder on Balts: e.g., cases of Roberts Garoza (interviewed by eligibility board March 24, 1948) and Janis Pruzinskis (declared eligible on second appeal in October 1950).

18. **US policy under 1948 Displaced Persons Act**: Dinnerstein, *America and the Survivors*, 196 (quotation); State Department ruling: Shephard, *Long Road Home*, 375; DPC recommendation: Christopher Simpson, *Blowback: America's Recruitment of Nazis and Its Effects on the Cold War* (New York: Weidenfeld & Nicolson, 1988), 207; Dinnerstein, *America and the Survivors*, 197; Harry Rosenfield oral history interview by James R. Fuchs, 1980: https://www.trumanlibrary .gov/library/oral-histories/rosenfld, accessed May 17, 2023.

19. **Ukrainian Galician Division**: David Cesarani, *Justice Delayed: How Britain became a Refuge for Nazi War Criminals* (London: Phoenix Press, 2001), 30, 102–115, 129; AN: AJ / 43 / 303: eligibility narrative report by R. J. Bilinski, dated August 16, 1951 (reports lobbying on their

behalf by the Ukrainian Voluntary Agency); **Marcel de Baer's protest**: Balint, *Destination Else-where*, 37, 165 n. 64.

20. **Rogozhin group**: NA UK: FO 1020–2507 (memo from Peter Gibson, September 21, 1948; memo from DP Branch, signed with initials DK, to Director, International Affairs Division, HMG, April 4, 1949 ["DK" is probably Donald Keegan of the DP branch, Internal Affairs, Allied Commission in Austria]). "Rogozhin" is the correct transliteration, but contemporary British documents often use "Rogoshin." The Germans called the Russkii Korpus (Russian Corps) the Russisches Schutzkorps in their employment, from whence the alternative English label of "Russian Protective Corps."

21. **Tolstoy Foundation**: AN: AJ / 43 / 149 (Folder "R.S.K": IRO interoffice memo on "Rogozhin Schutzcorps," of December 1950, including a Nominal Roll of the group compiled by Mrs. Schaufuss); NA UK: FO 371 / 87432 (Tatiana Schaufuss, European rep. of Tolstoy Foundation to mbrs. of Exec. Comm. of IRO on "Eligibility of members of the Russian Protective Corps," October 14, 1949 [quotation]); AN: AJ / 43 / 149 (Folder "R.S.K.": appeal of Kalitwenzew Theodor, July 15, 1950 ["no question" quotation]); **Alexandra Tolstoy's intercessions**: NA UK: FO 371 / 87432 (Schauffuss and Alexandra Tolstoy to Foreign Minister Bevin, January 10, 1950 [quotation]); D. Keegan to Boothby, Refugee Dept FO, January 20, 1948; **lobbying on individual cases by Foundation**: NA UK: FO 1020 / 2507 (Rogoshin group, vol.1, 1947–50: "notes on individual cases from Tatiana Schaufuss").

22. **Lyons's criticism of IRO**: AN: AJ / 43 / 73 (quoted in letter from Leo N. Kay, President, Executive Board, Humanity Calls, to Hallam Tuck, June 27, 1950); **Rogozhin question raised at General Council**: NA UK: FO 371 / 87432 (WR Refugee Department: Schaufuss and Alexandra Tolstoy, Tolstoy Foundation to Bevin, Sec. State for Foreign Affairs, January 10, 1950); **Bennigsen's suggestion**: NA UK: FO 371 / 87432 ("Problem of disposal of the Rogozhin Group (White Russians)—discussion between Arthur W. H. Wilkinson [Refugee Department of British Foreign Office] and Sir Arthur Rucker [deputy director, IRO], April 25, 1950; memo from Wilkinson on Bennigsen's visit, May 30, 1950).

23. **Bending the rules on Rogozhin group**: NA UK: FO 371 / 87432 (Edmunds, Geneva, to Foreign Office, March 11, 1950); **eligibility "in effect"**: NA UK: FO 1020 / 2507 (Balance [DP Branch, ACABE, Vienna] to Lee, October 27, 1950); **Thomas Cook to the rescue**: NA UK: FO 371–87432 (memo of May 24, 1950, on departure of Dorman family); **Vlasov Army members benefit**: Holborn, *International Refugee Organization*, 210; Eugenia Hanfmann and Helen Beier, *Six Russian Men—Lives in Turmoil* (North Quincy, MA: Christopher Publishing House, 1976), 85.

Chapter 7. Resettlement as Policy

1. **Resettlement not in UNRRA mandate**: George Woodbridge, *UNRRA* (New York: Columbia University Press, 1950), vol. 3, 23–32 ("Agreement for the United Nations Relief and Rehabilitation Administration, 9 November 1943," 189, 197, 203); agreements with military governments, late 1945–early 1946 (resettlement not UNRRA's task, though it might be organized on a small scale by IGCR or some other body); UA: S-0400-3-23: ERO Directive of Operations no. 2, October 1945 (quotation); **UNRRA should not hamper efforts of others**: UA: S-0400-0003-23 (UNRRA Policy Directive, unsigned, December 4, 1946); (Jewish resettlement in

Palestine): extract from ERO Directive of Operations, no. 2, October 1945—"limited assistance" quotation); **Harrison report**: UA: S-0400-0003-23: Pollack to Brig. Stawell, Arolsen, January 17, 1946; and see chap. 1.

2. **IRO and resettlement mandate**: Louise Holborn, *The International Refugee Organization* (New York: Columbia University Press), 366: **problems of immigration to Palestine**: David Nasaw, *The Last Million* (New York: Penguin Press, 2020), 365, 382; Holborn, *International Refugee Organization*, 415–16; IRO **resettlement of DPs in Israel**: Holborn, *International Refugee Organization*, 442, annex 43: "Resettlement," and see appendix to this book (Israel's intake was 132,109 out of a total of 1,038,730); **US Displaced Persons Act**: Holborn, *International Refugee Organization*, 367.

3. **Postwar assisted emigration from Europe**: Gerard Daniel Cohen, *In War's Wake* (Oxford: Oxford University Press, 2012), 100, 118–25 (the West European departures of 1952–57 were, however, not organized by IRO but by ICEM, the Intergovernmental Committee for European Migration set up under American control after IRO's demise. The outflow died down in the late 1950s because of European economic recovery, but by 1960 a million Europeans had departed under ICEM auspices); **Volksdeutsche**: Sheila Fitzpatrick, *White Russians, Red Peril* (Melbourne: Latrobe University Press, 2021), 236–67 (Australia); Myron Momryk, "Ukrainian DP Immigration and Government Policy in Canada, 1946–52," in *The Refugee Experience: Ukrainian Displaced Persons after World War II*, ed. Wsevolod W. Isajiw, Yury Boshyk, and Roman Senkus (Edmonton: University of Alberta, 1992), 423–25 (Canada); Nasaw, *Last Million*, 481–83 (US).

4. **Disinclination to accept Jews**: Cohen, *In War's Wake*, 116 (quotation); **Russians also unpopular**: AN: AJ / 43 / 612 (Charles H. Jordan, American Joint Distribution Committee, European Emigration HQ, Paris, August 7, 1948, to Wing-Commander Robert Innes, PCIRO Geneva, critically citing IRO circular stating that *Westward Ho!* was "open to all nationalities, except Jews, Russians, Russian-Ukrainians, White Russians and Stateless Russians"); **IRO's evasion of Jewish quotas**: Sheila Fitzpatrick, "Migration of Jewish 'Displaced Persons' from Europe to Australia after the Second World War," *Australian Journal of Politics and History* 67:2 (2021), 235–41; AN: AJ / 43 / 140 (Interviews de fonctionnaires de l'OIR par Michael Hacking, historien d l'OIR 1950–52: in interview, Donald Kingsley, IRO's second director, noted that while "IRO discriminated against Jewish Agencies" in its first years, this was a bias he had set out to correct).

5. **"Whiff of the slave market"**: Janet Flanner, "Letter from Aschaffenburg," *New Yorker*, October 30, 1948, 101 (first two quotations); Cohen, *In War's Wake*, 113 (Sears Roebuck quotation, from *Collier's*, July 17, 1948; **hard cases for resettlement**: GARF: 7317 / 20 / 143, l.42 (quotation in Soviet Military Administration in Germany files from speech of Ugo Carusi, head of US Displaced Persons Commission, Germany); **resettlement destination statistics**: see appendix to this volume.

6. **Opposition in US to admitting DPs**: Robert A. Divine, *American Immigration Policy, 1924–1952* (New Haven: Yale University Press, 1957), 118 (Gossett and American Legion quotations); Leonard Dinnerstein, *America and the Survivors of the Holocaust* (New York: Columbia University Press, 1982), 113 (*Newsweek* quotation), 140 (report in *Fortune* magazine of general view that "D.P.'s were mostly Jews or Communists or both"); **opposition to Jewish immigration**: Marvin Klemmé, *The Inside Story of UNRRA* (New York: Lifetime Editions, 1949), 291–92, 294, 295.

7. **Support for DP Bill**: Divine, *American Immigration Policy*, 119; **Latvian lobbying**: Laura Hilton, "Cultural Nationalism in Exile: The Case of Polish and Latvian Displaced Persons," *Historian* 71:2 (2009), 315–16; **Lithuanian lobbying**: *Foreign Relations of the United States, 1948, Eastern Europe; the Soviet Union*, vol. 4, document 272, https://history.state.gov /historicaldocuments/frus1948v04/d272, accessed April 9, 2022; Lithuanian-American Council, Lithuanian-American Information Center: Memorandum of Conversation, by the Assistant Secretary of State for Political Affairs ([Norman] Armour), Washington, DC, February 27, 1948, meeting with Mr Leonard Simutis, Pres. of Lithuanian-American Council and others; **lobbying from diaspora of annexed regions**: Divine, *American Immigration Policy*, 120–21; **Russian lobbying**: Alexandra Tolstoy, "The Russian DPs," *Russian Review* 9:1 (1950), 56–58; **Truman disappointed with DP Act**: Divine, *American Immigration Policy*, 120–21, 128–33; **Displaced Persons Commission**: Dinnerstein, *America and Survivors*, 184; Harry Rosenfield oral history interview by James R. Fuchs, 1980: https://www.trumanlibrary.gov/library/oral-histories /rosenfld, accessed May 17, 2023.

8. **Sponsorship system**: Dinnerstein, *America and Survivors*, 184–85, 204; security check and physical: Dinnerstein, *America and Survivors*, 189–91; **amended bill**: Divine, *American Immigration Policy*, 132; Rosenfield, oral history interview (quotation); Divine, *American Immigration Policy*, 137, 141–44 (the amended bill as passed also provided for the admission of 54,744 Volksdeutsche and 4,000 Europeans from China, mainly White Russians).

9. **1950 Amendment to Displaced Persons Act**: *Congressional Record*, June 16, 1950: Amendment to Displaced Persons Act of 1948; **later relaxation of restrictions on collaborators**: Divine, *American Immigration Policy*, 171 (the McCarran Act of 1952 eased up the restrictions on former party members, allowing the admission of immigrants who had renounced their former fascist or communist allegiance and had actively opposed this ideology for the past two years); **target "mostly the communists"**: Rosenfield, oral history interview, 90; **visiting US senators' concerns about communists**: AN: AJ / 43 / 707 (USA folder, 1947–50: 1947 briefing to staff from PCIRO on how to answer the senators' enquiries); **Internal Security Act of 1950**: Gil Loescher and John A. Scanlan, *Calculated Kindness: Refugees and America's Half-Open Door, 1945 to the Present* (New York: Simon & Schuster, 1986), 25, 29; **political reliability scale**: Nasaw, *Last Million*, 356 (Ukrainians and Yugoslavs came in at 90 percent, Poles, other than Polish Jews, at 80 percent; **suspicions of Russians**: E. L. Nitoburg, "Russkie 'peremeshchennye litsa' v SShA: Istoriia i sud'by," *Novaia i noveishaia istoriia* 4 (2001), 17 (citing 1951 comments); Loescher and Scanlon, *Calculated Kindness*, 28; **emerging view of Russian DPs as freedom fighters**: Tolstoy, "Russian DPs," 58 ("suffering" quotation); **"China" Russians**: Bernard John Maegi, "Dangerous Persons, Delayed Pilgrims: Baltic Displaced Persons and the Making of Cold War America, 1945–1952" (PhD diss., University of Minnesota, 2008), 106–7 (quotation from witness Prof. Nicholas Alexander, Dean of Holy Trinity Orthodox Seminary in Jordanville, New York). Note the irony that this group of Russians could potentially have been at risk from the ban on entry of members of Nazi and communist parties, had fascist parties been explicitly added to the list, since the Russian Fascist Party was strong in China in the 1940s (see Edwin Oberlander, "The All-Russian Fascist Party," *Journal of Contemporary History* 1:1 [1966], 158–73)—but nobody seemed to worry about fascist parties, as distinct from Nazis, and the question seems never to have been raised in connection with their immigration to the United States.

10. **Australia's agreement with IRO**: AN: AJ / 43 / 897 (press release, September 19, 1947); NAA: A6980–250104 ("Australian Resettlement Scheme," PCIRO, September 23, 1947); **migration process**: Jayne Persian, *Beautiful Balts: From Displaced Persons to New Australians* (Sydney: NewSouth, 2017); **Jewish community**: Suzanne D. Rutland, *Edge of the Diaspora: Two Centuries of Jewish Settlement in Australia* (Sydney: Brandl and Schlesinger, 2001); **stringent medical standards for entry**: AN: AJ / 43 / 645 (Galleghan to Miss Vermuelen, IRO, February 21, 1949 [quotation]); AN: AJ / 43 / 696 (memo from C.C.K. Grierson Rickford, IRO, to K.J.W. Lane, Australian Selection Mission March 18, 1948); AN: AJ / 43 / 619 ("Mass resettlement. Australia 1948–50"); NAA: A6980-S150106 (memo on "Medical Standards of DPs" by A. J. Metcalfe, Commonwealth Director-General, Health, February 1, 1949); **"horny-handed toilers"**: NAA: A6980 / S250104 (quotation from Australian News and Information Bureau report from Berlin, July 18, 1947: NAA: A6980-S250104 (Conference on Displaced Persons, Berlin, July 17–18, 1947).

11. **"No discrimination on race or religion"**: NAA: A6980, S250104 ("Agreement between the Government of the Commonwealth of Australia and the Preparatory Commission of the International Refugee Organization," Geneva, July 21, 1947); **Australia's nationality preferences**: Egon F. Kunz, *Displaced Persons. Calwell's New Australians* (Sydney: Australian National University Press, 1988), 43; **("white Russians")**: Fitzpatrick, *White Russians*, 62–63; **first shipload all Balts**: NAA: 6980 S250104 (PCIRO Lemgo / F. B. Buckingham, "Recruitment of D.P.s for emigration to Australia"); Persian, *Beautiful Balts*, 45–58; **restrictions on Jewish migration**: Fitzpatrick, "Migration of Jewish 'Displaced Persons,'" 235–41; **trade union worries about cheap labor**: Andrew Markus, "Labour and Immigration, 1946–9: The Displaced Persons Program," *Labour History* 13 (1983), 87; **anxieties about Nazi collaborators and communists**: Fitzpatrick, *White Russians*, 233–39.

12. **Canadian opening to DPs**: Irving Abella and Harold Troper, *None Is Too Many: Canada and the Jews of Europe 1933–1948* (New York: Random House, 1982), 242; Hugh L. Keenleyside, *Canadian Immigration Policy* (Vancouver: University of British Columbia, 1948), 10–12 (quotation 12) (based on lecture of April 5, 1948); **"Sponsored Labour Scheme"**: this was a codification of "Bulk Labour Movements" that began in April 1947: Henriette von Holleufer, *Zwischen Fremde und Fremde: Displaced persons in Australien, den USA und Kanada 1946–1952* (Osnabrück: Universitätsverlag Rasch, 2001), 85–86; **lack of enthusiasm for East European and Jewish migrants**: Abella and Troper, *None Is Too Many*, 224; **existing Ukrainian population**: "Canadian Population Origins," *Eighth Census of Canada*, vol. 3, 1941, https://publications.gc.ca/site/eng/9.833108/publication.htm, accessed February 22, 2024; von Holleufer, *Zwischen Fremde*, 85–86; Abella and Troper, *None Is Too Many*, 208–9.

13. **Canadian Sponsored Labor scheme**: Holleufer, *Zwischen Fremde*, 140, 144, 264–65; (false rumor) NAA: A446-57-67774 (Displaced Persons Policy Part 2: Canada, Dept. of Labor news release, November 14, 1947); **industry sponsors**: Holleufer, *Zwischen Fremde*, 143, 267; Holborn, *International Refugee Organization*, 397 (this must be the same request described by Kathryn C. Hulme in *The Wild Place* [Boston: Little Brown, 1953,] 173–78, as the affair of "the Flying Virgins"); **policy on dependents**: Holborn, *International Refugee Organization*, 373 (quotation), 375; **"no discrimination" agreement**: Holborn, *International Refugee Organization*, 396; Abella and Troper, *None Is Too Many*, 224–25; **Jewish selection**: Holleufer, *Zwischen Fremde*, 145; **furriers**: Holleufer, *Zwischen Fremde*, 145 (quotation); Abella and Troper, *None Is Too Many*, 268–70. With regard to special requests for "Jewish" trades like furrier and needlework,

Abella and Troper note elsewhere that "the hidden agenda was to secure the entry of Jews" (258) and that "the team members, all of whom were Jewish, understood that their hidden agenda was to bring as many Jews as possible into Canada under this scheme" (262).

14. **Ukrainian community's objections to "Nazi" DPs**: Lubomyr Y. Luciuk, "'This Should Never Be Spoken or Quoted Publicly': Canada's Ukrainians and Their Encounter with the DPs," in *Canada's Ukrainians: Negotiating an Identity*, ed. Lubomyr Y. Luciuk and Stella Hryniuk (Toronto: University of Toronto Press, 1991), 116–22; **Canadian security concerns**: Abella, *None Is Too Many*, 227–28; Holleufer, *Zwischen Fremde*, 184.

15. **Latin American resettlement prospects**: M. N. Moseikina, A. V. Antoshin, and E. S. Golousova, *Russkaia diaspora v Argentine: Istoriia i sovremennost'* (Moscow: Rossiiskii universitet druzhby narodov, 2022), 116–18; M. N. Moseikina, *"Rasseiany, no ne rastorgnuty": Russkaia emigratsiia v stranakh Latinskoi Ameriki v 1920–1960 gg.* (Moscow: RUDN, 2011), 225; **disappointing results**: Holborn, *International Refugee Organization*, 400–403, 437–40; **Argentina**: Moseikina, *"Rasseiany, no ne rastorgnuty,"* 60; **Orthodox Church in Argentina**: Moseikina et al., *Russkaia diaspora*, 121; **Perón**: Robert J. Alexander, *Juan Domingo Perón: A History* (New York: Routledge, 2018), 22–23 (Italy before the war); Gerald Steinacher, *Nazis on the Run* (New York: Oxford University Press, 2011), 213–15 (Perón's immigration policy of the 1940s); **Soviet disapproval**: Moseikina et al., *Russkaia diaspora*, 116–19, 123 (quotation); **British Foreign Office information**: NA UK: FO 1020–2507 (London-Vienna correspondence, March 23 and April 4, 1949; **visas procured for Russians**: Moseikina et al., *Russkaia diaspora*, 124, 121 (it appears from correspondence on their later invalidation that these may not actually have been visas but landing permits); **Argentinian doors closed**: NA UK: FO 1020–2507 (D. K., Vienna, to London, April 4, 1949—"I am told that the Argentine is off and that that country is taking no more refugees," no reason cited; probably referring only to Russians); Moseikina et al., *Russkaia diaspora*, 125–26 (Argentinian concern about relations with the Soviet Union could have been a factor); **Russians resettled in Argentina (statistics)**: Holborn, *International Refugee Organization*, annex 41,137–40; and see appendix to this volume.

16. **Venezuela**: Holborn, *International Refugee Organization*, 407–9, 437–40, and see appendix to this volume; **Paraguay**: Holborn, *International Refugee Organization*, 437–40; **Brazil**: AN: AJ / 43 / 698 (Brazil file: Alan Brady, Chief of Resettlement, World Council of Churches, reporting on trip through Latin America, July 12, 1949 [first quotation]; "Notes for Mr Tuck on the Brazilian situation," December 31, 1948 [second quotation]); **general resistance to taking Jews**: Kim Salomon, *Refugees in the Cold War: Toward a New International Refugee Regime in the Early Postwar Era* (Lund: Lund University Press, 1991), 212; AN: AJ / 43 / 566 ("Restrictions on Jewish Immigration in South America," June 24, 1947); AN: AJ / 43 / 613 (memo from Grierson Rickford to Col. Peters, January 2, 1949; Brazil, Argentina, Guatemala, Venezuela, Bolivia, and Peru are specifically named); **Paraguay's Jewish intake**: AN: AJ / 43 / 134 (report on Paraguay, from Arnauld H. de Soucy, Chef de Mission, May 30, 1951).

17. **Jewish DPs resettled in Palestine/Israel**: Holborn, *International Refugee Organization*, 437–40; **admissions under British Mandate**: Holborn, *International Refugee Organization*, 414–15; **IRO seen as facilitating British restrictions**: Dinnerstein, *America and Survivors*, 200; **IRO changes position**: Holborn, *International Refugee Organization*, 415–16; **countries of origin of resettled Jewish DPs**: Holborn, *International Refugee Organization*, annex 41, 437–40 (but note that that almost 40 percent of the 130,408 DPs going to Israel failed to report a country of origin).

18. **Morocco**: Holborn, *International Refugee Organization*, annex 41, 437–40 (1,446 DPs were resettled in French Morocco, including 505 identified as Nansen/stateless and 67 as Soviet); **Boldyrev's plan**: Ivan Nikolajuk, *Deda's Memoirs: For the Granchildren*, trans. Yura Nikolajuk (Melbourne: self-published, 2020), 489, quotation from K. B. Boldirev [*sic*], "In a Search for New Solutions"; Andrew Paul Janco, "Soviet 'Displaced Persons' in Europe, 1941–1951" (PhD diss., University of Chicago, 2012), 225; **Russian DPs in Morocco**: Boldirev, "In a Search," 495; Nikolajuk, *Deda's Memoirs*, 496; Janco, "Soviet 'Displaced Persons,'" 227; B. Prianishnikov, *Novopokolentsy* (Silver Spring, MD: self-published, 1986), 249; Liudmila Flam, ed., *Sud'by pokoleniia 1920-1930-kh godov v emigratsii* (Moscow: Russkii put', 2006), 63–140 (Moroccan memoirs); **why Morocco?**: Nikolajuk, *Deda's Memoirs*, 317 (first quotation), 385 (second quotation).

19. **"Mongol ancestors"**: Cilento Papers, 44, Box 18, Folder 107, "Escape from UN-Reality," 46, 63, 64; **Osttruppen**: Mark R. Elliott, *Pawns of Yalta* (Urbana: University of Illinois Press, 1982), 15 (as of December 1942, the 573,850 Osttruppen included 10,000 Crimean Tatars, 15,000 North Caucasians, 36,500 Azerbaijanis, and 20,550 "Turks," probably other Soviet Turkic groups); **UNRRA/IRO and Turkish issue**: AN: AJ / 43 / 502 (Folder 6: White Russians, Turkestan, etc.); UA: S-1479-0000-0115-00001 (minutes of meeting of UNRRA representatives with Soviet Consul-General, Italy, January 16, 1946); AN: AJ / 43 / 604 (Musulmans européens en Moyen-Orient 1947: P. A. de Maerel, memo on history of Moslem problem, September 30, 1947); NA UK: FO 1020 / 2846: "Soviet repatriation mission, vol. 2 (1946), Turkic" (quotation on languages of communication with Turks); UA: S-1479-0000-0115-00001 (letter from Maj. Titov, representative of Soviet Union to UNRRA in Italy, to the Dir-Gen of UNRRA, Fiorello La Guardia, Rome, July 23, 1946); AN: AJ / 32 / 573: report from US zone Germany, 1949 ("all Soviet citizens" quotation).

20. **Turkey agrees to accept DPs**: AN: AJ / 43 / 604 (Maerel memo, September 30, 1947); **offer**: AN: AJ / 43 / 604 (Brig. M. S. Lush, Chief of Mission, Middle East HQ, Cairo, to IRO Geneva, October 21, 1947); **DPs resettled in Turkey**: Hollen Vitale et al., "Refugees in Turkey 1945–1955", available at University of Georgia, https://digilab.libs.uga.edu/exhibits/exhibits/show/refugees/turkey, accessed May 24, 2023.

21. **Moslem DPs in Egypt**: AN: AJ / 43 / 572 (Refugiés folder: M. H. Thomas to M. L. Hacking, September 14, 1949); **Australia's policy**: NAA: A2169 1949 (ninth meeting of Commonwealth Immigration Advisory Council, January 1949, statement of P. R. Williams); NAA: A445 235 / 1 / 2 (Revised Policy—1947. Admin. Non-British Europeans); **IRO hope**: AN: AJ / 43 / 572 (Réfugiés folder: Paterson, IRO, Egypt Office, to Brig. Lush, September 21, 1949); cable from Cairo to Geneva, received November 5, 1949 (apparently Australia finally took thirteen out of a group of about one hundred after Egyptian philanthropic sources had contributed 500 Egyptian pounds).

22. **US preference for "European race"**: Maegi, "Dangerous Persons," 106–7; **Cilento on Buryats**: Cilento Papers, "Escape from UN-Reality," 64; **US doubts about Tatars, Armenians**: AN: AJ / 43 / 268 (Réinstallation aux États-Unies June 1950–January 1951, Division of Resettlement and Repatriation: quotation from case of Ufa-born Tatar, Mohamed Schamiloglu, new ruling on eligibility on basis of revised instruction that "Tartars of eastern Russia in the Ufa area are members of the white or so-called European race, in spite of their Asiatic origin" and are thus eligible along with other racial groups in Asia minor, notably Armenians ["common understanding of the racial characteristics of the group identifies them with Europeans"]).

23. **Kalmyks: history**: Michael Khodarkovsky, *Where Two Worlds Meet: The Russian State and the Kalmyk Nomads, 1600–1771* (Ithaca, NY: Cornell University Press, 2006), 5–9, 33, 76–79;

on White side in Russian Civil War: AN: AJ / 43 / 808 (4th Kalmyk folder: IRO Munich document of November 23, 1948); Elvira Churyumova and Edward C. Holland, "Kalmyk DPs and the Narration of Displacement in Post-World War II Europe, *Slavic Review* 80:2 (2021), 345; **retreat with Germans**: AN: AJ / 43 / 808 (4th Kalmyk folder: letter from Chamba Balinov, Switzerland, Kalmyk DP representative, to Dr. Wu Man-Ju, Minister-Plenipotentiary, Chinese Legation [1948?]); **surrender to Allies**: Elliott, *Pawns of Yalta*, 15; Churyumova and Holland, "Kalmyk DPs," 346; **IRO estimate of numbers**: AN: AJ / 43 / 808 (2nd Kalmyk folder); **Kalmyks' stories about themselves**: AN: AJ / 43 / 808 (3rd Kalmyk folder); Churyumova and Holland, "Kalmyk DPs," 343 (quotation); **divisions in community**: AN: AJ / 43 / 808 (3rd Kalmyk folder 9: [Memo on "The History of Efforts to Resettle the Kalmyks; Minutes of Conference between IRO and Voluntary Agencies re Kalmuk Resettlement, August 30, 1951]); AN: AJ / 43 / 808 (4th Kalmyk folder); **long effort to resettle Kalmyks**: AN: AJ / 43 / 808, 4th Kalmyk folder (Minutes of Conference, August 30, 1951); **considered "Asiatic"**: AN: AJ / 43 / 808, 4th Kalmyk folder (letter of Balinov to Wu Man-Ju; New York University, Tamiment Library Archives (hereafter TAM), TAM 029, Kalmyk Resettlement Committee Records, Box 1, Folder 1 [Clipping from Russian newspaper *Echo*, May 26, 1949]); **unsuccessful efforts at resettlement**: AN: AJ / 43 / 808 (3rd Kalmyk folder [minutes of conference, August 30, 1951]); AN: AJ / 43 / 808 (4th Kalmyk folder: letter from Balinov to Wu Man-Ju): **"the people nobody wants"**: AN: AJ / 43 / 571 (Kalmouks, 1950–1, Folder 1: Blake Ehrlich, "The People Nobody Wants," undated clipping from the *Reporter*).

24. **Individual Kalmyk applications**: AN: AJ / 43 / 866 (Réinstallation collectives aux Etats-Unis. Dossiers individuels de réfugiés montrant les efforts de reinstallation et les différents problems [Abremov and Andrejew files]); **"looks Mongol"**: AN: AJ / 43 / 571 (Kalmouks, 1950–1, Folder 1: Reports of American Vice-Consul James H. McFarland, November 2, 1949, and August 25, 1949); **US Nationality Act**: Churyumova and Holland, "Kalmyk DPs," 360; **US support for Kalmyks:** AN: AJ / 43 / 395 (Tolstoy Foundation: minutes of conference between IRO and Voluntary Agencies re Kalmuk Resettlement, August 30, 1951); Churyumova and Holland, "Kalmyk DPs," 343; TAM 029, Kalmyk Resettlement Committee Records, Box 1; Columbia University Libraries, Special Collections, Kapatsinskii, Dmitrii Konstantinovich (henceforth, Kapatsinskii Papers), Box 1 BA #0182 (Kapatsinskii chaired the United Committee to Aid Russians in Europe); Jessica Johnson, "The Labor of Refuge: Kalmyk Displaced Persons, the 1948 Displaced Persons Act, and the Origins of U.S. Refugee Resettlement" (PhD diss., Brown University), 2013; **Oliver Stone**: AN: AJ / 43 / 808 (1st Kalmyk folder: letter from Philip E. Ryan, chief of IRO mission in Washington, to Oliver Stone August 17, 1951); **Paraguay plan**: TAM 029, Box 1 (Roland Elliott, US Church World, to B. N. Oulanoff, Paris; letter to editor of *Novoe russkoye slovo*, September 30, 1950; David Martin, IRC, to Mr. Mark Citroen, IRO, Geneva, November 4, 1950). Paraguay seems a strange choice, as it was one of the countries that had indicated to IRO that it was not interested in taking Kalmyks because they were "Asiatic" (AN: AJ / 43 / 808, 4th Kalmyk folder). The US committee's hopes of Paraguay were probably based on the fact that one of the Kalmyks' most active supporters in the United States, Kurt Halle of the Flatbush Unitarian church, was a food broker with Arthur L. Pearson, a major importer of South American corned beef with extensive interests in Paraguay (TAM 029, Box 1 [letter of Halle to *Christian Science Monitor*, July 1, 1950, "Kalmuks Balked in Search of a Home"]).

25. **Remilev case**: Kapatsinskii Papers (undated letters from Remilev to Halle and Mr. Tripp, INS—quotations from letter to Tripp); **Stone's argument**: TAM 029, Box 1 (Exclusion Proceedings, Immigration Service v. IRO, April 20, 1951); **favorable decision**: Churyumova and Holland, "Kalmyk DPs," 360; TAM 029 (Exclusion Proceedings; memo from Roland Elliott to members of Kalmuk Resettlement Committee, August 9, 1951); AN: AJ / 43 / 808 (1st Kalmyk folder); **confirmation by Attorney General**: AN: AJ / 43 / 571 (Kalmouks, 1950–1, Folder 3 [James L. Carlin, Chief, US branch for Resettlement and Repatriation (IRO), Instruction to visa divisions, September 6, 1951]); **Kalmyk resettlement in US**: AN: AJ / 43 / 808 (2nd Kalmyk folder: letter from Public Information to Mr. Camillo Noel, Ansbach, November 8, 1951); AN: AJ / 43 / 571 (Kalmouks, 1950–1, Folder 3: cable from Tolstoy Foundation to Jacobsen, IRO, November 21, 1951); Churyumova and Holland, "Kalmyk DPs," 343. The Brethren Service Commission's Kalmook Resettlement Program, based at New Windsor, Maryland, was instrumental in placement of the DPs on the ground, mainly in Pennsylvania and New Jersey.

26. **Collaborators: complaints about UNRRA screening**: UA: S-1021-0081-0002 (P. Nielsen, "Eligibility and Screening," May 1947); **Fitzroy Maclean's efforts**: David Cesarani, *Justice Delayed: How Britain Became a Refuge for Nazi War Criminals* (London: Phoenix Press, 2001), 5–13, 132; *New York Post* **article**: Nasaw, *Last Million*, 456–65 (the paper was owned by Dorothy Schiff of the German-Jewish banking family, a New Deal supporter); **Calwell's riposte**: NAA: A446-57-67774, statement to press (December 1948); **Australian immigration interview**: Janco, "Soviet 'Displaced Persons' in Europe," 293; **DP migrants with SS tattoos**: AN: AJ / 43 / 611 (International Movement officer to Zone Director, British Zone, Lemgo, September 9, 1947, re sailing of SS *Lumberton*).

27. **Security rejections: (Australia)** David Horner, *The Spy Catchers: The Official History of ASIO, 1949–1962* (Sydney: Allen & Unwin, 2014), 256; **(US)** Salomon, *Refugees in the Cold War*, 193 (of 450 rejections in November 1948, 120 were for TB, 52 for syphilis, and the rest for "other reasons" or "no reason given"); **Norr's investigations**: Columbia University, Special Collections, B1 / Barr, N.G. / 23, Papers of Norbert George Barr; File 4 (L-N) from Special Investigation Reports (cases of Victors Krumins and Jakob and Chatische Adamowitsch); **loyalty oaths**: AN: AJ / 43 / 268: (Patricia Zegart, Port Liaison officer, New York, to Col. E. J. van Horne, Movements Officer IRO, Washington, n.d. [September 1950]; Kathryn Hulme to dir. UUARC Munich-Pasing, September 8, 1950; Susan Petties, Resettlement Officer, IRO New York, to Helen Wilson, Resettlement and Repatriation, Geneva, November 8, 1950); **Russian immigration "effectively stopped"**: AN: AJ / 43 / 395 (quotation from testimony of president of Tolstoy Foundation, Alexandra Tolstoy, before Senate Subcommittee on Immigration and Naturalization, March 9, 1951); AN: AJ / 43 / 572 (confidential memo from Mrs. T. A. Schaufuss, European representative, Tolstoy Foundation, to Mr. Ugo Carusi, Chair, US DP Commission, Washington, September 25, 1950); **British exclusions**: Cesarani, *Justice Delayed*, 132.

28. **DPs held at Ellis Island**: AN: AJ / 43 / 267 (INS, Jacket 1: incoming cable from Inorefug Washington to Inorefug Geneva, October 19, 1950); **IRO's attitude to communists**: AN: AJ / 43 / 612 (memo "Immigration of so-called 'politically undesirables' into Latin-American Countries under PCIRO auspices" from Deputy Executive Secretary PCIRO [Gustav] Kullmann [head of IRO's Office of Legal Advisor] to Executive Secretary, March 4, 1948); **should IRO circulate security rejections?**: AN: AJ / 43 / 457 (R. Innes, Director of Resettlement, to Mrs. Lane, November 16, 1948); AN: AJ / 43 / 457 (internal discussion of draft of "Letter to

Governments on Security Suspects," March 1949) ("Spanish refugees" are those from the Spanish Civil War of the late 1930s, responsibility for whom IRO had inherited from IGCR; Trotskyites were communists, but anti-Stalin and generally anti-Soviet; Victor Kravchenko was a high-ranking Soviet communist who defected to the West in 1944 and in 1946 published the memoir *I Chose Freedom*).

Chapter 8. DPs Weigh the Options

1. **"Baltic Pilgrims"**: My account follows Bernard John Maegi, "Dangerous Persons, Delayed Pilgrims: Baltic Displaced Persons and the Making of Cold War America, 1945–1952" (PhD diss., University of Minnesota, 2008), 9, 59–63; **President Truman:** quoted Maegi, "Dangerous Persons," 80; **President Kennedy:** Maegi, "Dangerous Persons," 72–75.

2. **Reasons for nonrepatriation**: Eugenia Hanfmann and Helen Beier, *Six Russian Men— Lives in Turmoil* (North Quincy, MA: Christopher Publishing House, 1976), 59, 63, 79 (based on interviews with Soviet DPs in Germany, Austria, and the United States conducted by the Harvard Project on the Soviet Social System, largely funded by US government agencies, in 1950–51); **Schlusser family**: Eugene Schlusser, *Escape from the Sun* (Melbourne: Australian Scholarly Publishing, 2017), 212–19; **Danos family**: Sheila Fitzpatrick, *Mischka's War* (London: I. B. Tauris, 2017); **late-applying DPs**: Louise Holborn, *The International Refugee Organization* (London: Oxford University Press, 1956), annex 17a: Summary of IRO statistics, 1 July 1947–31 December 1951, 202; AN: AJ / 43 / 303: (Jablonski, Hamburg, "Report on eligibility for January and February 1951," March 8, 1951); R. J. Bilinski, Chief, Office of Eligibility, "Eligibility narrative report," August 16, 1951; Mark Wyman, *DPs: Europe's Displaced Persons, 1945–51* (Ithaca, NY: Cornell University Press, 1989), 202 (quotation).

3. **Lure of America**: Susan Pettiss, *After the Shooting Stopped* (Victoria, BC: Trafford, 2004), 78 (quotation); Ruth Balint, "Hopscotch Australia: Displaced Persons Taking the Long Way around to the Rest of the World," in *When Migrants Fail to Stay: New Histories on Departure and Migration*, ed. Ruth Balint, Joy Damousi and Sheila Fitzpatrick (London: Bloomsbury Academic, 2023), 41; Agathe Nesaule, *A Woman in Amber* (New York: Soho Press, 1995), 136–37; **choosing a destination**: UA: S-0436-0030-06 ("DP journals" file); Janet Flanner, "Letter from Aschaffenburg," *New Yorker*, October 30, 1948, 101. On Sweden and its dealings with DPs, see Cecilia Notini Burch, *A Cold War Pursuit: Soviet Refugees in Sweden, 1945–54* (Stockholm: Santérus Academic Press, 2014).

4. **Playing the field**: AN: AJ / 43 / 447, vol. 17 ("Jews from Shanghai" file); AN: AJ / 43 / 476 (Iwan Epifanenkow case, January 11, 1950); **Belgian returnees**: AN: AJ / 43 / 303 (Bilinsky, "Eligibility narrative report," July 9, 1951); **Jewish choices**: Yehuda Bauer, *Out of the Ashes* (Oxford: Pergamon Press, 1989), 86 (Montevideo anecdote); Joseph Berger, *Displaced Persons* (New York: Washington Square Press, 2001), 310; **applications refused**: Schlusser, *Escape from the Sun*, 212–19; **application accepted**: Ella E. Schneider Hilton, *Displaced Person* (Baton Rouge: Louisiana University Press, 2006), 116, 159–62.

5. **Forged documents**: Ruth Balint, *Destination Elsewhere* (Ithaca, NY: Cornell University Press, 2021), 27 (de Baer quotation); AN: AJ / 43 / 698: Brazil (February 1948 report) (Ukrainian examples); **correction of false statements**: Anne Kuhlmann-Smirnov, "'Stiller als Wasser, tiefer als Gras': Zur Migrationsgeschichte der russischen Displaced Persons in Deutschland nach dem

Zweiten Weltkrieg (Bremen: Forschungsstelle-Osteuropa an der Universität Bremen, 2005), working paper of Forschungstelle Osteuropa, #68, 8 (block quotation), 9; AN: AJ / 43 / 572 (confidential memo from T. A. Schaufuss to Ugo Carusi, Chair, DP Commission, September 25, 1950); Berger, *Displaced Persons*, 279–80, 310–11.

6. **Marriage as an aid to resettlement**: AN: AJ / 43 / 759 (British zone, report by H. E. Greenfield, June 15, 1950—"Polish," Romanian, and Yugoslav cases); **shipboard transformations**: NAA: A446-57-67774 ("Displaced persons travelling on 'General Heintzelman,' due to arrive Fremantle 26 November 1947"); NAA: A446-57-67774 (memo from A. J. Nutt, Asst. Sec., Immigration, "Displaced Persons [Nurses, Waitresses and Domestics] SS General Stuart Heintzelman, Fremantle, 28 November 1947," December 1, 1947); Ann Tündern-Smith, *Bonegilla's Beginnings* (Wagga Wagga: Triple D Books, 2007) (further biographical information on individual passengers).

7. **Friends in UNRRA**: AN: AJ / 434 / 383 (letters from Miss Bertha Hohermuth, Chief, Individual Migration Section of IRO at US Zone HQ, to Mr. H. A. Citroen, IRO HQ, Geneva, June 1, 1949, and April 13, 1949); **US "assurances"**: Rudolf Heberle and Dudley S. Hall, *New Americans: A Study of Displaced Persons in Louisiana and Mississippi* (Baton Rouge: Displaced Persons Commission, 1951), 12; Kathryn Hulme, *The Wild Place* (Boston: Little, Brown, 1953), 118–19; **cheap labor for the American South**: Hilton, *Displaced Person*, 170–207 (firsthand account); Heberle and Hall, *New Americans*, 46–47; **brides wanted in Africa**: Holborn, *International Refugee Organization*, 421.

8. **"Shirt-tail relatives"**: Wyman, *DPs*, 199; **Posev's Guidebook**: Kuhlmann-Smirnov, "Resettlement," 4; **contacting United Committee**: Columbia University Libraries, Special Collections, Kapatsinskii papers, Box 1 (file of autobiographies with photos of applicants for immigration sponsorship (letters from Voldemar [Vladimir] Bergs dated February 2, 1949; Vasilii Minenkovskii, May 31, 1949); **contacting Tolstoy Foundation**: Vitalij Fastovskij, "Humanitäre Hilfe im Kalten Krieg: Die Unterstützung von Displaced Persons and Flüchtlinge durch die Tolstoy Foundation (1949–1989)" (2020 communication with author) (Ukrainian presenting as Russian); **Olga Danos's sponsor**: Fitzpatrick, *Mischka's War*, 63–64, 139–42.

9. **Resettlement of collaborators**: **Rogozhin group**: NA UK: FO 1020 / 2507 (Bruce Lowe reporting Mr Edmond's interview with Col. Rogoshin [*sic*] at Kellerberg camp, April 6, 1950; and see chap. 6; **Vlasovites**: Sheila Fitzpatrick, *White Russians, Red Peril* (Melbourne: Latrobe University Press, 2021), 48–49 (quotation from Bogut); **Poppe case**: David Cesarani, *Justice Delayed: How Britain Became a Refuge for Nazi War Criminals* (London: Phoenix Press, 2001), 149–54; Lebed case: David Nasaw, *The Last Million* (New York: Penguin Press, 2020), 475–78 (Lebed was soon naturalized, assumed a leadership role within the Ukrainian nationalist community, and worked for the CIA for three decades until retirement, despite accusations of war crimes being belatedly raised in the 1980s); **NTS**: B. Prianishnikov, *Novopokolentsy* (Silver Spring, MD: self-published, 1986), 250; **CIA involvement**: Christopher Simpson, *Blowback: America's Recruitment of Nazis and Its Effects on the Cold War* (New York: Weidenfeld & Nicolson, 1988), 202–3; **US Refugee Relief Act**: Carl J. Bon Tempo, *Americans at the Gate: The United States and Refugees during the Cold War* (Princeton, NJ: Princeton University Press, 2008), chap. 2; Roger Daniels, *Guarding the Golden Door* (New York: Hill & Wang, 2004); Benjamin Tromly, *Cold War Exiles and the CIA* (Oxford: Oxford University Press, 2019), 237; **text of act**: available at San Diego State University, loveman.sdsu.edu/docs.1953RefugeeReliefAct.pdf, accessed

June 18, 2020); **Russians entering under act**: E. L. Nitoburg, "Russkie 'peremeshchennye litsa' v SShA: Istoriia i sud'by," *Novaia i noveishaia istoriia* 4 (2001), 25; N. A. Troitskii, "Put' 'vtoroi volny' i budushchee Rossii," in A. V. Popov, ed., *V poiskakh istiny: Puti i sud'by vtoroi emigratsii* (Moscow: RGGU: 1997), 23; **CIA support**: Tromly, *Cold War Exiles*, 237.

10. **"Rightless and humiliated" in resettlement**: GARF: 7317 / 20 / 5 *Sbornik po istorii Otdela repatriatsii i rozyska sovetskikh grazhdan upravleniia delami sovetskoi kontrol'noi komissii v Germanii za period s 1-go iiulia 1948 goda po 1-e ianvaria 1950 goda, vol. 3, 80—"Don't let yourselves be deceived [*Ne davaite sebia obmanyvat'*]," propaganda leaflet addressed to "Russians, Latvians, Ukrainians, Lithuanians, Belorussians and Estonians living in West Germany"); **false promises**: GARF: 7317 / 20 / 5 Sbornik po istorii Otdela 1940–50, vol. 3, 84–85 (Propaganda leaflet, "Soviet citizens, the Motherland is waiting for you [*Sovetskie grazhdane, Rodina zhdet Vas*]," addressed to "Soviet citizens living in West Germany"); **voluntary repatriation statistics**: V. N. Zemskov, *Vozvrashchenie sovetskikh peremeshchennykh lits v SSSR 1944–1952 gg.* (Moscow: Tsentr gumanitarnykh initsiativ, 2016), table 7, 141 (over the period July 1947–June 1952, forty-one thousand persons were repatriated to the Soviet Union from Europe, the Middle East, and countries of resettlement, but most of these came from the Soviet occupation zones of Germany and Austria and the "fraternal" countries of Eastern Europe).

11. **Difficulties of repatriating**: GARF: 9526 / 6 / 669, ll. 41–44; 208–9; 287–90; 388–89; 9526 / 6 / 675, ll. 139–42; **stated reasons for return**: ("couldn't stand their democracy") GARF: 7317 / 20 / 145, ll. 373–75; (**"start a new life"**) GARF: 7317 / 20 / 145, ll. 99–101; (**Salnikov**) see this volume, chap. 5; (**forced emigration claim**) GARF: 9526 / 6 / 669, ll. 456–61 (the camp was Spakenburg in Geesthacht, British zone); (**living in tents**) GARF: 9236 / 6 / 669, l. 45 (August 1949), and see this volume, chap. 5; **"pull" factors**: GARF: 9526 / 6 / 669, ll. 172–76; (**family**) GARF: 9526 / 6 / 669, ll. 77–79, 273, 675; (**radio appeals and letters**) GARF: 9526 / 6 / 676, ll.77–79, 388–89, 397, 669, 675; GARF: 7317 / 20 / 145, ll. 342–43, and see this volume, chap. 2; (**skepticism about letters**) see this volume, chap. 2, for Danos family); (**"genuine" letter**) GARF: 9526 / 6 / 669, ll. 52–53; **"push" factors**: (**unemployment**) GARF: 9526 / 6 / 669; (**work in Belgian mines**): GARF 9526 / 6 / 676, ll. 2–4, 9–10 and 77–79, GARF 9526 / 6 / 669, ll. 172–76, 186–87, 190–93, 197–200, 202, 236–39, 240–41; **accused of being Soviet spies**: GARF: 9526 / 6 / 675, ll. 208–10, 211–14 (two cases of Soviet DP women married to Dutchmen who, when the marriage broke down, denounced them as spies); GARF: 9526 / 6 / 669, ll. 74–77 (interview with Erik Suurviali, October 22, 1949. His story of the generosity of the Soviet government throughout this ordeal, including financial support for his family, and his immediate employment after repatriation with the Finnish department of the Radio Committee of Estonia—both unique in the files of repatriating DPs—does suggest some sort of special relationship with the Soviet authorities); (**Jewish nurse**) GARF: 9526 / 6 / 675, ll. 139–42; **taunts from local population**: GARF: 7317 / 20 / 145, ll. 40–43; GARF: 9526 / 6 / 669, ll. 74–77.

12. **Decision to return**: (**happenstance**) GARF: 9526 / 6 / 674, l. 14; (**fears**) GARF: 9526 / 6 / 66, ll. 190–93; GARF 9526 / 6 / 669, ll. 190–93; GARF 9526 / 6 / 669, l. 276 (quotation on hair); **famine unmentioned by late 1940s repatriates**: but note that some arriving in the mass repatriation of 1945, evidently peasants taken as Ostarbeiter during the war, expressed fears of hunger back home and a naive appreciation of all the food in Germany: GARF 9526 / 6 / 50, ll. 148–50; **continuing worry after arrival**: GARF 9526 / 6 / 674, ll. 57–60; **rare buoyant mood**: GARF 9526 / 6 / 669, ll. 273–311 (interview with Moskaltsova, November 12, 1949).

13. **Women's failed marriages to foreigners**: (**Polish husbands**) GARF: 9526 / 6 / 669, ll. 77–79, 159–62, 242, 244–45, 273–74, 311, 675; (**Italians**) GARF: 9526 / 6 / 669, ll. 306, 308 (1949 cases); GARF: 9526 / 6 / 676, ll. 150–52, 160–61, 177–78 (1950 cases); (**British**): GARF: 9526 / 6 / 674, ll. 201–5 (1950 cases); (**Yugoslavs**) GARF: 9526 / 669, ll. 26–28, 84–86, 270–71, 284 (1949 cases); (**Belgians**) GARF: 9526 / 6 / 669, ll. 193–94, 303–4 (1949 cases); (**Dutch**) GARF: 9526 / 6 / 669, ll. 392 (1949 case); GARF: 9526 / 6 / 675, ll. 204, 208–14 (1950 cases); (**French**) GARF: 9526 / 6 / 675, ll. 55–57, 159–65 (1950 cases); (**Czech**) GARF: 9526 / 6 / 675, ll. 72–73, 236–39 (1950 cases); (**Armenian from Abyssinia**) GARF: 9526 / 6 / 675, ll. 16–17 (1950 case); **men with criminal records**: GARF: 7317 / 20 / 146, ll. 83–86 (Petr Prokhunov, July 19, 1949, quotation); GARF 9526 / 6 / 626, ll. 6–7 (Anton Gverzhdis, August 31, 1950); GARF 9526 / 6 / 676, ll. 163–64 (Ivan Masevich, October 24, 1950).

14. **Baltic repatriates**: Of the 1949 Soviet Military Administration in Germany interviews (GARF, *fond* 7317), thirty-seven (45 percent) are from the Baltic region. The percentage in the Repatriation Agency interviews in 1950 (GARF, *fond* 9526) is much smaller (thirty-two, or about 10 percent), making an overall figure of eighty-nine out of three hundred seventy-eight (24 percent); **educational level**: GARF: 9526 / 6 / 674, ll. 43–44, ll. 201–5; GARF: 9526 / 6 / 669, ll. 82–83, 115–16, 195–96; GARF: 7317 / 20 / 145, ll. 99–101 and 342–43 (of Baltic repatriates who provided data on education, the great majority, male and female alike, had secondary education, and just one—a Lithuanian man born in 1926—had only four years schooling, which was still fairly common among repatriates from other parts of the Soviet Union); **"withdrawn" returning student**: GARF: 7317 / 20 / 145, ll. 342–43 (Leonid Lapsa, May 1949 interview); **circumstances of departure**: Only two Baltic repatriates said they had been "taken to Germany" before 1944, presumably as forced labor (GARF: 9526 / 6 / 676, ll. 41–44; GARF: 9526 / 6 / 669, ll. 195–96), while a third said they went to Germany in 1943 without specifying how (GARF: 7317 / 20 / 145, ll. 342–43). But another eight whose paths to Germany were identified in their interviews said they were taken there in August–September 1944 (GARF: 9526 / 6 / 675, ll. 242–48; GARF: 9526 / 6 / 676, ll. 36–40; GARF: 9526 / 6 / 674, ll. 43–44, 369–72; GARF: 9526 / 6 / 669, ll. 82–83, 92–99, 163–64, 202); **admitting to voluntary departure**: GARF: 9526 / 6 / 669, ll. 82–83 (interview with Robert Klanners, November 2, 1949—there is no notation on the file suggesting that the case be brought to the MGB's attention, and its handling appears to have been normal).

15. **Process of resettlement departure: duration**: Wyman, *DPs*, 198; **obstacles: criminal convictions**: AN: AJ / 43 / 874 (S Zone: Reclamation pour or contre des refugiés, arrêtés d'expulsion, dossier of Lia Smidonis, March 21, 1950; (abortion case) Barr Papers (investigation report on Dr. Ernest Ansmits, June 7, 1951); **"moral turpitude"**: AN: AJ / 43 / 267, l. 35 (INS, Jacket 1:decision protested by IRO legal officer, 1950); Wyman, *DPs*, 200; **health problems**: Wyman, *DPs*, 198; Prianishnikov, *Novopokolentsy*, 265; (disabled children) AN: AJ / 43 / 331 (case of Spekters family [October 1949]); Balint, *Destination Elsewhere*, 99–112; (Olga Danos) Fitzpatrick, *Mischka's War*, 215–16.

16. **Departures** (Schneider family); Hilton, *Displaced Person*, 161–65; (Mishka Danos) Fitzpatrick, *Mischka's War*, 238–39; (Schlüsser family) Schlusser, *Escape from the Sun*, 210–17, 236–49, 257–58.

17. **Voyages**: (**to Australia**) Fitzpatrick, *White Russians*, 152–55; (**to Rio de Janeiro**); Columbia University Libraries, Special Collections, Papers of Valentin Iosifovich Lekhno (typescript

"Evropa—Iuzhnaia Amerika" by Lekhno, n. d.); **shipboard accusations**: Fitzpatrick, *White Russians*, 226–27; Nasaw, *Last Million*, 455–56, 502; **child's experience**: Hilton, *Displaced Person*, 166; **Danos family's experiences**: Fitzpatrick, *Mischka's War*, 219–20, 239–40; **emotions on repatriating**: GARF: 9526 / 6 / 669, ll. 116–17 (see this volume chap. 5, on Salnikov's story); **emotions on arrival in New York**: (Olga Danos) Fitzpatrick, *Mischka's War*, 220–21; (Schneider family) Hilton, *Displaced Person*, 168.

Chapter 9. Unfinished Business

1. **Resettlement statistics**: Louise Holborn, *The International Refugee Organization* (London: Oxford University Press, 1956), 202 (annex 17a: "Summary of IRO statistics, 1 July 1947–31 December 1951") and 437–40: annex 41: "Resettlement: Country of destination and country of citizenship"), and see appendix to this volume: table 1: "IRO Resettlement of Russian / Soviet / Baltic DPs, 1947–51, by Destination Country."

2. **Hard core categories**: AN: AJ / 43 / 888 (American zone, 1951, "Classes of the hard core"); **criminal record**: AN: AJ / 43 / 888 (American zone, 1951, "Hard core solutions"); **security risks:** Few individual cases of security rejections show up in IRO's archives, and there is also little discussion of this category of hard core. A rare mention comes in a note from a Lithuanian advocate for DPs in 1950, whose list of five thousand Lithuanians remaining in IRO's hard core included "a small group of persons who have been falsely accused by Soviet agents or their sympathizers." NAA: A6980–5150106 (Department of External Affairs London to Secretary of Department of External Affairs [Canberra], March 14, 1950, appended note).

3. **TB cases**: AN: AJ / 43 / 698 ("Visit of the Director-General, IRO, Mr. J. Donald Kingsley, to Ottawa, July 5–8, 1950); **Russians on Tubabao**: AN: AJ / 43 / 502 (Progress report of April 2, 1951, signed Mrs Johanna Boetz, Supervisor, LWF-LCC Counselling Service, Salzburg); **TB issue on Tubabao**: Sheila Fitzpatrick, "Russians in the Jungle: Tubabao as a Way Station for Refugees from China to Australia, 1949," *History Australia* 16:4 (2019), 708–9; **VD cases**: AN: AJ / 43 / 343: Brooke Chisolm, M.D., to New Zealand Director-Gen. Health and External Affairs, July 18, 1951; Dr. Charles H. Fish, Senior Surgeon, USPHS, to Dr. Frank Reynolds, Chief, VD Section, WHO Geneva (1951).

4. **"Mental cases"**: AN: AJ / 43 / 343 ("Repatriement des malades inc malades mentales 1948–51," Folder 4: P. Jacobsen, A / Dir-Gen for Repatriation and Resettlement, "Repatriation—legal and political aspects" [n. d., circulated August 1949]—in 1949, 650 DP mental cases were in IRO care in Germany and Austria); **care in location**: AN: AJ / 43 / 698 ("Visit of the Director-General, to Ottawa, July 5–8, 1950"): **repatriation "normal" solution**: AN: AJ / 43 / 343 (Folder 4: Marie D. Lane, Chief, Welfare Division, IRO to Red Cross Geneva 20.6.1950; "Repatriation of the insane," circular [August 1949] sent by P. Jacobsen, A / Dir.-Gen. for Repatriation and Resettlement, to F. B. Buckingham, A / Dir, Re-establishment [British zone], September 14, 1949); **Baltic and Ukrainian nationalist objections**: AN: AJ / 43 / 573 (Folder marked "Refugees—lunatics": opinion of October 13, 1948); UA: S-0437-0022-17 (memo on "Mental Patients of Russian and Ukrainian Nationality)"; AN: AJ43 / 610 (Baltic complaints discussed by Poignant, Chief of IRO in the French Zone, and Myer Cohen, acting head of IRO's DP operations, in October 1949; letter from IRO Washington, April 3, 1950, on Ukrainian protest from French occupation zone); **insanity on Tubabao**: AN: AJ43 / 1078 ("What is taking place on Samar Island?"—translation from Russian newspaper

New Life, May 30, 1949); AN: AJ / 43 / 107 (Samar. v. 7; Australie. v. 12. 1949–51; Folder 1, list of Samar mental cases; memo on "Deteriorated mental condition of Samar refugees" from Frederick Thompson, Chief of Operations in the Philippines, to Chief of Operations, IRO Geneva, June 20, 1951).

5. **Disabled admission to US**: AN: AJ / 43 / 387 (James L. Carlin, Chief US branch, Resettlement and Repatriation, IRO, to Mrs. A. Matson, International Rescue Committee, Munich, April 16, 1951); **disabled child abandoned**: Ruth Balint, *Destination Elsewhere* (Ithaca, NY: Cornell University Press, 2021), 97–98; **"over-age group"**: AN: AJ / 43 / 502: (progress report, April 2, 1951); **aged Lithuanian couple in Philippines**: AN: AJ / 43 / 502 (Mollie Rule, Resettlement officer, IRO-Tacloban, Leyte, letter to Rev Robert Plagens [representative of Lutheran Federation], Manila, February 8, 1952); **aged Lithuanians in Europe**: NAA: A6980–5150106 (Department of External Affairs London to Secretary of Department of External Affairs [Canberra], March 14, 1950 [Balutis's note appended]); **individual placements**: AN: AJ / 43 / 889 ("Institutional Hard-Core. Resettlement and repatriation statistics, Munich, January 19, 1951); **Australia unresponsive**: NAA: A6980–250108 (extract from minutes of House of Representatives, May 17, statement of PM Harold Holt—the only concession Australia made was to relax the requirements on age and fitness previously imposed on DPs sponsored by relatives who had already immigrated).

6. **DPs remaining in Germany (statistics)**: Holborn, *International Refugee Organization*, 202, gives a figure of 140,011; Wolfgang Jacobmeyer, *Vom Zwangsarbeiter zum Heimatlosen Ausländer* (Göttingen: Vandenhoeck & Ruprecht, 1985), 224, gives a minimum figure of 103,300, of whom 64,000 were in the British zone; Christian and Marianne Pletzing, eds., *Displaced persons: Flüchtlinge aus den baltischen Staaten in Deutschland* (Munich: Martin Meienbauer, 2007), 34; **DPs remaining in Austria**: Holborn, *International Refugee Organization*, 202 (gives a figure of 23,170); Robert Knight, "National Construction Work and Hierarchies of Empathy in Postwar Austria," *Journal of Contemporary History* 49:3 (2014), 509; **"Soviet" DPs remaining in Germany**: V. N. Zemskov, "'Vtoraia emigratsiia' i otnoshenie k nei rukovodstva SSSR, 1947–1955," in *Istoriia rossiiskogo zarubezh'ia: Emigratsiia iz SSSR-Rossii 1941–2001 gg. Sbornik statei*, ed. Iu. A. Poliakov, G. Ia. Tarle, and O. V. Budnitskii (Moscow: Institut rossiiskoi istorii, RAN, 2007), 71. (As of January 1, 1952, the Soviet estimate was that 84,825 Soviet citizens remained in West Germany, of whom 44,468 were from the Baltics and the rest mainly from Ukraine and Russia, and 18,891 in Austria, of whom 60 percent were Ukrainian and the rest mainly Russian and Belorussian). But these figures did not include late resettlers, especially to the United States, and is almost certainly too high. A later scholarly estimate based on diaspora sources of the number of Baltic DPs remaining in West Germany is "about 20,000": Tillman Tegeler, "Esten, Letten und Litauer in Nachkriegsdeutschland," in Pletzing and Pletzing, *Displaced persons*, 26; **earlier concern about adding to German manpower**: Kim Salomon, *Refugees in the Cold War: Toward a New International Refugee Regime in the Early Postwar Era* (Lund: Lund University Press, 1991), 205–6 (1945 statement by Gen. Morgan); **German law on "homeless foreigners"**: Jacobmeyer, *Vom Zwangsarbeiter*, 223, 226–31; **Austria and DPs**: Tara Zahra, "Prisoners of the Postwar: Expellees, Displaced Persons, and Jews in Austria after World War II," *Austrian History Yearbook* 41 (2010), 198–204; Knight, "National Construction Work," 491–513.

7. **Last camps closed**: Angelika Eder, "Displaced Persons / 'Heimatlose Ausländer' als Arbeitskräfte in Westdeuschland," *Archiv für Sozialgeschichte* 42 (2002), 13; **hard for DPs to find jobs**: Eder, "Displaced Persons," 15; **criticism of DP rights and benefits**: Jacobmeyer, *Vom*

Zwangsarbeiter, 226–31; **"half-hearted integration"**: Patrick Wagner, *Displaced Persons in Hamburg: Stationen einer halbherzigen Integration 1945–1948* (Hamburg: Dölling und Galitz, 1997); **Latvian sense of stigma**: Richards Plavnieks, "Nazi Collaborators on Trial during the Cold War: The Cases against Viktors Arājs and the Latvian Auxiliary Security Police" (PhD diss., University of North Carolina at Chapel Hill, 2013), 138–39; **lukewarm welcome in Austria**: Zahra, "Prisoners of the Postwar," 199–200, 204 (quotation); Knight, "National Construction Work," 506; **Lithuanian widow**: AN: AJ / 43 / 888 (Zone américaine, Cas difficiles / Hard core solutions, 1951); **pension eligibility**: AN: AJ / 43 / 303 (Z. J. Jablonski, IRO Hamburg, "Report on eligibility for May, 1951"); AN: AJ / 43 / 806 (comments by Dr. Maurer, April 10, 1951); **falling through cracks**: AN: AJ / 43 / 888 (American zone, Munich case, December 1951).

8. **Jewish DPs remaining**: (**Germany**) Gerard Daniel Cohen, *In War's Wake* (Oxford: Oxford University Press, 2012), 150; (**Austria**) Knight, "National Construction Work," 502 (citing US embassy report); **still in DP camps**: Avinoam Patt and Kierra Crago-Schneider, "Years of Survival: JDC in Postwar Germany, 1945–1947," in Avinoam Patt et al., *The JDC at 100* (Detroit: Wayne State University Press, 2019), 387; **Föhrenwald camp**: Patt and Crago-Schneider, "Years of Survival," 383, 386, 388–89, 403 (quotation); "Foehrenwald Displaced Persons Camp," Holocaust Museum, Holocaust Encyclopedia, https://encyclopedia.ushmm.org/content/en/article /foehrenwald-displaced-persons-camp, accessed February 25, 2023; **illegal returnees**: Patt and Crago-Schneider, "Years of Survival," 394–95; **DPs in Jewish community in FRG**: Michael Brenner, *After the Holocaust: Rebuilding Jewish Lives in Postwar Germany* (Princeton, NJ: Princeton University Press, 1997), 137, 159–60 (Bubis was not a DP *strictu sensu*, as he was in Dresden in the Soviet zone of Germany in the immediate postwar years before moving to West Germany).

9. **Canadian rejections of mentally ill**: AN: AJ / 43 / 331 (9th folder, "Rejections on medical grounds," February 24, 1948); AN: AJ / 43 / 698 ("Visit of the Director-General, IRO, Mr. J. Donald Kingsley, to Ottawa, July 5–8, 1950"); **Australian rejections**: NAA: A446 57–67774 (Department of Immigration. Displaced Persons Policy part 2; memo from T. H. Heyes to Officer in Charge, Defence Secretariat, to be cabled to Berlin, December 22, 1947); **Australian legal justification**: Jayne Persian, "'Far Right Security Risks?' Deportations and Extradition Requests of Displaced Persons, 1947–1952," in *When Migrants Fail to Stay: New Histories on Departure and Migration*, ed. Ruth Balint, Joy Damousi, and Sheila Fitzpatrick (London: Bloomsbury Academic, 2023), 56–57; **Australian DP deportations**: (**statistics**) NAA: A6980 S250240 (cuttings from newspapers of March 16 and 17, 1950, citing figures given by External Affairs Minister Harold Holt to Parliament on June 6, 1950); (**list of offences**) AN: AJ / 43 / 619 (Galleghan, head, Australian Military Mission in Berlin, to Director Resettlement PCIRO Geneva, June 25, 1948).

10. **IRO's early tolerance of returns**: AN: AJ / 43 / 457 (memo on "Deportation from Australia" sent by Hacking, Division of Mandates and Reparations, to Dr. V. Gross, Protection Division, July 14, 1949); **stance toughened**: AN: AJ / 43 / 862 (letter from R. J. McPherson for John F. Thomas, Chief, Resettlement & Repatriation Division, April 18, 1951, to Control Center Schweinfurt: "Subject: Australia—deportees"); AN: AJ / 43 / 457 ("Deportation and return for causes," memo from Mass Resettlement Geneva to offices abroad, May 24, 1949); AN: AJ / 43 / 613 (memo on legal and political protection, November 4, 1949); **Lach case**: Balint, *Destination Elsewhere*, 124–25, 131–33.

11. **1951 Statute of Refugees**: Persian, "'Far Right Security Risks'?" 57; obstacles to **deportation**: Persian, "'Far Right Security Risks'?" 59 ("attempted twice" quotation); Balint, "Hopscotch," 47 ("none existed" quotation), 48 ("iron curtain" quotation); **Akulshin case**: *Scope of Soviet Activity in the United States. Hearings, April 27 and May 17, 1956, Part 21* (Washington, DC: United States Government Printing Office, 1956): testimony of Alexandra Tolstoy, May 23, 1956, 1326 and ibid., 1327 (Exhibit 274: letter from Alexandra Tolstoy of Tolstoy Foundation to Attorney-General, September 27, 1954); **papers needed to leave Australia**: Balint, "Hopscotch," 44–46; **provoking deportation**: Balint, "Hopscotch," 46–48; Persian, "'Far Right Security Risks?" 58; **Chlopoff case**: International Tracing Service (ITS), Bad Arolsen #6501: Chlopoff, Mstislav; NAA: SP 1121 / 1 Chlopoff Mstislav; **successful attempts**: AN: AJ / 43 / 619 (Galleghan, Australian Military Mission in Berlin, to Dir. Resettlement PCIRO Geneva, June 25, 1948); **Talts case**: GARF: 9526 / 6 / 674, ll. 43–44, 397–402 (interviews, January 26 and June 13, 1950); **unsuccessful attempt**: NAA: A6980 S250240 (Deportation of Displaced Persons—Policy, 1949–55; case of Joseph Brydon).

12. **Chistokhodov case**: GARF: 9526 / 6 / 797, ll.372–79 (notes of three conversations between Chistokhodov and consul Kushnirov, August 30, 1951); **Maria Nelson case**: GARF 9526 / 6 / 674, ll. 202–5 (reentry interview with Maria Nelson, Viljandi, Estonia, April 10, 1950); Sheila Fitzpatrick, "The Women's Side of the Story," *Russian Review* 81 (2022), 298–99 (whether Sam Nelson was ever allowed into the Soviet Union is moot, given the 1947 ban on Soviet marriages to foreigners—see chap. 5, note 4; **Kasenkina affair**: Susan Carruthers, *Cold War Captives: Imprisonment, Escape and Brainwashing* (Berkeley: University of California Press, 2009), 23–32 (the Alsops' column appeared in the *Los Angeles Times* on August 18, 1948; *Leap to Freedom* was the title of the book that Kasenkina, who stayed in the United States and gained citizenship in 1956, published about her experiences).

13. **Embassies responsible for repatriation**: Iu. N. Arzamaskin, *Tainy sovetskoi repatriatsii* (Moscow: Veche, 2015), 204 (citing law of May 17, 1948); **difficulties of repatriating from US**: GARF: 9526 / 6 / 888 (Report of D. Solod, acting head of USA Department of Soviet Foreign Ministry, to Col. N. A. Filatov, Repatriation Agency under Soviet Council of Ministers, n.d. [1952]); **Canberra Legation's problems**: GARF: 9526 / 6 / 735, l. 12 (memo from F. Gubanov, June 27, 1950); the notice was published in the *Canberra Times*, May 7, 1948; in addition to local reactions, the international reverberation was loud enough for a garbled report to appear in a Ukrainian DP newspaper warning DPs against migrating to Australia: AN: AJ / 43 / 899 (cutting from *Ukrajinski Wisti*, July 24, 1948); **requests for extra personnel for repatriation**: GARF: 9526 / 6 / 836, ll. 19 and 96 (N. Filatov, Repatriation Agency, to deputy Foreign Minister Andrei Gromyko, February 10, 1951 [refers to earlier request made to the Foreign Ministry on December 24, 1949]; V. Zorin, deputy Foreign Minister, to Filatov, April 2, 1951); GARF: 9526 / 6 / 888, ll. 1–2: (D. Solod, USA Department of Foreign Ministry, to N. Filatov, Repatriation Agency [1952], approving request); **Soviet undercover agents**: Arzamaskin, *Tainy*, 206 (as of January 1, 1951, the Repatriation Agency had nineteen such special representatives working abroad: four each in Sweden, England, and Italy, two in Argentina, and one each in Denmark, Belgium, Canada, Finland, and Australia. Reports in GARF files (9526 / 6 / 797, l. 344; 9526 / 6 / 888, l.1; 9526 / 6 / 797, ll. 61–66) indicate that agents included D. Kholodenin in England, Col. Stasenko and later Lieut.-Col. Morozov in Venezuela, and G. Kushniruk and D. A. Mishin in Argentina, in addition to Gordeev and his later-arriving colleagues in Australia, Dmitri Pavlov and Janis

Platkais (Sheila Fitzpatrick, "Soviet Repatriation Efforts among 'Displaced Persons' Resettled in Australia, 1950–53," *Australian Journal of Politics and History* 63:1 [2017], 51).

14. **DP resistance to repatriation agents**: M. N. Moseikina, *"Rasseiany, no ne rastorgnuty": Russkaia emigratsiia v stranakh Latinskoi Ameriki v 1920–1960 gg.* (Moscow: RUDN, 2011), 256; **reciprocal hostility**: GARF: 9526 / 6 / 888, l. 1; **sympathetic responses:** (Canada) GARF: 9526 / 6 / 727, l. 250 (N. Poliakov, "Zapis' o poezdke v Toronto, 23–25 iiulia 1951 g.); **Russian Social Club in Sydney**: Ebony Nilsson, *Displaced Comrades: Politics and Surveillance in the Lives of Soviet Refugees in the West* (London: Bloomsbury Academic, 2023), 25–46; Fitzpatrick, *White Russians*, 174–98; **Gordeev's repatriation efforts**: Fitzpatrick, "Soviet Repatriation Efforts, 51–59; Fitzpatrick, *White Russians*, 211–22; **repatriates from Australia**: Fitzpatrick, "Soviet Repatriation Efforts," 54–60; Fitzpatrick, *White Russians*, 215–21; (Chlopoff's wife) on Chlopoff, see above, note 11; (Juris) Nilsson, *Displaced Comrades*, 99–120 (Nilsson uses first names only for her case studies); (Zelensky) Fitzpatrick, *White Russians*, 214, 219; **repatriation statistics**: V. N. Zemskov, "'Vtoraia emigratsiia' i otnoshenie k nei rukovodstva SSSR, 1947–1955," in *Istoriia rossiiskogo zarubezh'ia: emigratsiia iz SSSR-Rossii 1941–2001*, ed. Iu. Poliakov et al. (Moscow: Institute Rossiiskoi istorii RAN, 2007), 81; idem, *Vozvrashchenie sovetskikh peremeshchennykh lits v SSSR 1944–1952 gg.* (Moscow: Tsentr gumanitarnykh initiativ, 2016), 141. These data are obviously incomplete: Australia is credited with only four repatriates—half of the total claimed by Gordeev, and only a quarter of nineteen named repatriates from Australia recorded as arriving in the Soviet Union up to the end of 1952 in the Repatriation Agency's register: GARF: 9526 / 6 / 1101, ll. 33–34 (Kniga po personal'nomu uchetu sovetskikh peremeshchennykh grazhdan, repatriirovannykh iz za granitsy i ob ikh trudoustroistve ianvaria 1951–31 dekabria 1952).

15. **Serov's initiative**: *Istoricheskii arkhiv*, 1995 no. 2, 10–12 (memo of KGB chairman I. A. Serov to the Central Committee of the Soviet Communist Party, December 14, 1954); **1955 amnesty**: *Istoricheskii arkhiv*, 1995 no. 2, 12–13 (text of Decree of the Presidium of the Supreme Soviet of the USSR, September 17, 1955, "On Amnesty for Soviet Citizens, Working for the Occupiers during the Great Patriotic War 1941–1945"; Zemskov, "'Vtoraia emigratsiia,'" 87–88 (text of resolution of Council of Ministers of the USSR, September 17, 1955); **Soviet Repatriation Committee**: Simo Mikkonen, "Not By Force Alone: Soviet Return Migration in the 1950s," in *Coming Home?*, ed. Scott Soo et al., vol. 1, *Conflict and Return Migration in the Aftermath of Europe's Twentieth-Century Civil Wars* (Newcastle upon Tyne: Cambridge Scholars, 2013), 186, 190; **conflicts with anti-communists in Latin America**: M. N. Moseikina, A. V. Antoshin, and E. S. Golousova, *Russkaia diaspora v Argentine* (Moscow: Rossiiskii universitet druzhby narodov, 2022), 109–10; **Slepukhin's return**: Moseikina et al., *Russkaia diaspora*, 208–9; "Slepukhin, Iurii Grigorevich," Russian-language Vikipediia, accessed February 13, 2022; **Juris's return**: Nilsson, *Displaced Comrades*, 110–14.

16. **War crimes trials:** (1940s) Tanja Penter, "Local Collaborators on Trial: Soviet War Crimes Trials under Stalin (1945–1953), *Cahiers du monde russe* 49:2 / 3 (2008), 341–64; (Soviet message to West) David Nasaw, *The Last Million* (New York: Penguin Press, 2020), 512 (quotation), 514; **extradition requests**: (Australia) Mark Aarons, *War Criminals Welcome: Australia, a Sanctuary for Fugitive War Criminals since 1945* (Melbourne: Black, 2001), 449–54 (quotation from *Commonwealth Parliamentary Debates*, March 22, 1961); (UK) David Cesarani, *Justice Delayed: How Britain Became a Refuge for Nazi War Criminals* (London: Phoenix Press, 1962), 195–96; **strong rebuttals**: Nasaw, *Last Million*, 467–68 (citing Nussbaum, "Pro-

Nazis Entering US under DP Law That Keeps Out Jews," *New York Times*, November 19, 1948, 2); **weak protests**: Isi J. Leibler (President, Executive Council of Australian Jewry), "Preface" to Mark Aarons, *Sanctuary: Nazi Fugitives in Australia* (Melbourne: William Heinemann Australia, 1989), xiv.

17. **Daugavas Vanagi**: Ieva Zake, *American Latvians* (New Brunswick, NJ: Transaction Publishers, 2010), 94 (according to Latvian émigrés, the editor, Paul Ducmanis, a well-known sports journalist in Latvia before the war, had himself been a Nazi collaborator); *Return to Homeland*'s accusations: Alexandra Tolstoy made this claim testifying before a subcommittee of the US Senate in 1956, see *Scope of Soviet Activity in the United States. Hearings, April 27 and May 17, 1956*, part 21 (Washington, DC: United States Government Printing Office, 1956), 1328 (Testimony of Alexandra Tolstoy) and 1331–35 (Submission No. 272, Tolstoy Foundation, Inc. European Headquarters, Munich, Germany: "Soviet activity to encourage repatriation among Russian escapees"); **German war crimes unit**: Siobhán Hyland and Paul Jackson, "Campaigning for Justice: Anti-Fascist Campaigners, Nazi-Era Collaborator War Criminals and Britain's Failure to Prosecute 1945–1999," in *The Palgrave Handbook of Britain and the Holocaust*, ed. Tom Lawson and Andy Pearce (Cham, Switzerland: Palgrave-Macmillan, 2020), 207; **Latvian resentment**: Plavnieks, "Nazi Collaborators," 138–39; **Arājs's capture**: Nasaw, *Last Million*, 466; Ieva Zake, "The 'Secret Nazi Network:' Post World War II Latvian Immigrants and the Hunt for Nazis in the United States," *Baltic Studies* 41:2 (2010), 92; Plavnieks, "Nazi Collaborators," 143–47.

18. **Hāzners case**: *New York Times*, March 12, 1978 (report on Hāzners trial); "Vilis Hāzners. KGB targets Latvian Émigré Leadership, INS Obliges," https://latvianlegion.org/index.php?en /accused/hazners/evidence/level-030-origins.ssi, accessed June 14, 2023; **"any one of us"**: quoted Zake, *American Latvians*, 106; **OSI**: Nasaw, *Last Million*, 521; Allan A. Ryan, *Quiet Neighbors: Nazi War Criminals in America* (San Diego: Harcourt Brace Jovanovich, 1984), 68–93; **OSI convictions**: Plavnieks, "Nazi Collaborators," 260 (but note that the 134 prosecutions constituted only a small proportion of the total of 1,500 investigations); Nasaw, *Last Million*, 529 (gives a somewhat higher success rate of 108 convictions out of 137 court cases).

19. **Use of Soviet evidence**: Plavnieks, "Nazi Collaborators," 129; Ryan, *Quiet Neighbors*, 85; **evidence from Yad Vashem and Wiesenthal Center**: Efraim Zuroff, *Occupation: Nazi-Hunter: The Continuing Search for Perpetrators of the Holocaust* (Hoboken, NJ: KTAV, 1994); **nationality of defendants**: Ryan, *Quiet Neighbors*, 249; **arguments about validity of Soviet evidence**: Nasaw, *Last Million*, 523; **deportations to Soviet Union**: Plavnieks, "Nazi Collaborators," 295; Nasaw, *Last Million*, 524.

20. **Kalejs case**: Plavnieks, "Nazi Collaborators," 260, 192–309; Aarons, *War Criminals Welcome*, 10, 19–20, 482, 505; *Guardian*, November 12, 2001 (Kalejs obituary); **war crimes commissions**: (Canadian Commission of Inquiry into War Criminals, 1985) Nasaw, *Last Million*, 529; (Australian Special Investigations Unit into War Crimes, 1987); Aarons, *War Criminals Welcome*, 141–52; (British Official War Crimes Inquiry, 1988) Hyland and Jackson, "Campaigning for Justice," 214–15; **Soviet cooperation**: Cesarani, *Justice Delayed*, 197–98, 209–11; Hyland and Jackson, "Campaigning for Justice," 213; **reevaluation of postwar Soviet trials**: Plavnieks, "Nazi Collaborators," 165.

21. **Diaspora resistance to OSI**: Zake, *American Latvians*, 108; **rejection of Soviet evidence in court**: Plavnieks, "Nazi Collaborators," 16; (Polyukovich trial) Aarons, *War Criminals*,

11; David Fraser, *Daviborshch's Cart: Narrating the Holocaust in Australian War Crimes Trials* (Lincoln: University of Nebraska Press, 2010); **Kalejs extradition**: Aarons, *War Criminals*, 11; Sheila Fitzpatrick, "Justice across the Seas: War Crimes Accusations against Postwar Migrants from 'Displaced Persons' Camps in Europe," forthcoming in *Injustice, Survival and Memory in Twentieth-Century Australia*, ed. Christina Twomey and Seumas Spark.

BIBLIOGRAPHY

Archival Sources

Columbia University Libraries, Special Collections, New York (Robert A. Jackson Papers, Dmitrii Kapatsinskii Papers; Norbert George Barr Papers; Valentin Lekhno Papers)

Ivan Nikolajuk Papers (in possession of his family)

International Refugee Organization (IRO) archives in Archives Nationales (AN), Paris (AJ / 43)

International Tracking Service (ITS), ITS Tracking Records, Bad Arolsen (files of Olga Danos, Michael Danos, Mstislav Chlopoff)

National Archives of the United Kingdom (NA UK)

National Archives of Australia (NAA)

New York University, Tamiment Library Archives (TAM) (Kalmyk Resettlement Committee Records)

State Archive of the Russian Federation (GARF)

University of Chicago Special Collections (Michael Danos Papers)

University of Queensland, Fryer Library Manuscript Collections (Raphael Cilento Papers; Fedora Fisher Collection)

UNRRA Archives (UA), in United Nations Archives, New York

Official Records

Commonwealth Parliamentary Debates (Australia)

Congressional Record (US)

Foreign Relations of the United States, 1948, Eastern Europe; the Soviet Union

Scope of Soviet Activity in the United States. Hearings before the Subcommittee to Investigate the Administration of the Internal Security Act and Other Internal Security Laws of the Committee on the Judiciary, Eighty-Fourth Congress, Scope of Soviet Activity in the United States, April 27 and May 17, 1956, Part 21. Washington, DC: United States Government Printing Office, 1956.

Oral History Interviews and Emails

Ayerst, Wally. Telephone interview with Sheila Fitzpatrick, February 23, 2008.

Baitch, Natalie. Interview with Sheila Fitzpatrick, Plumpton, NSW, March 1, 2016.

Bicevskis, Andrejs. Interview with Sheila Fitzpatrick, Brisbane, July 30, 2007; "Family Memoir" in email to Sheila Fitzpatrick, May 6, 2008.

Hanfmann, Eugenia, and Helen Beier. *Six Russian Men—Lives in Turmoil*. North Quincy, MA: Christopher Publishing House, 1976.

Ireland, Kristian. Interview with Sheila Fitzpatrick, Berlin, November 3, 2015 (on Russian-Ukrainian grandparents).

Machen, Helen. Interviews with Sheila Fitzpatrick, Downers Grove, IL, February 2, 2007, and February 23, 2008.

Rosenfield, Harry. Oral history interview by James R. Fuchs, 1980. https://www.trumanlibrary .gov/library/oral-histories/rosenfld. Accessed May 17, 2023.

Stauvers, Dailonis. Telephone interview with Sheila Fitzpatrick, April 10, 2007.

Dissertations

Geisler, Irene Elsknis. "The Gendered Plight of Terror: Annexation and Exile in Latvia 1940–1950." PhD diss., Western Michigan University, 2011.

Holian, Anna Marta. "Between National Socialism and Soviet Communism: The Politics of Self-Representation among Displaced Persons in Munich, 1945–1951." PhD diss., University of Chicago, 2005.

Janco, Andrew Paul. "Soviet 'Displaced Persons' in Europe, 1941–1945." PhD diss., University of Chicago, 2012.

Johnson, Jessica. "The Labor of Refuge: Kalmyk Displaced Persons, the 1948 Displaced Persons Act, and the Origins of US Refugee Resettlement." PhD diss., Brown University, 2013.

Luyckx, Lieselotte. "Soviet DPs for the Belgian Mining Industry: The Daily Struggle against Yalta of a Forgotten Minority?" PhD diss., European University Institute, 2012.

Maegi, Bernard John. "Dangerous Persons, Delayed Pilgrims: Baltic Displaced Persons and the Making of Cold War America, 1945–1952." PhD diss., University of Minnesota, 2008.

Patt, Avinoam J. "Finding Home and Homeland: Jewish DP Youth and Zionism in the Aftermath of the Holocaust." PhD diss., New York University, 2005.

Plavnieks, Richards. "Nazi Collaborators on Trial during the Cold War: The Cases against Viktors Arājs and the Latvian Auxiliary Security Police." PhD diss., University of North Carolina at Chapel Hill, 2013.

Popowski, Tamara. "'We Knew Things Would Get Better.' A Family Migration Story." MA thesis, University of Sydney, 2023.

Protopopov, Michael Alex. "The Russian Orthodox Presence in Australia." PhD diss., Australian Catholic University, 2005.

Unpublished Documents

Fastovskij, Vitalij. "Humanitäre Hilfe im Kalten Krieg: Die Unterstützung von Displaced Persons and Flüchtlinge durch die Tolstoy Foundation (1949–1989)" [2020 communication with author].

Published Personal Papers

Clay, Lucius. *The Papers of General Lucius D. Clay, Germany 1945–1949*. Vol. 1, edited by Jean Edward Smith. Bloomington: Indiana University Press, 1974.

Roosevelt, Eleanor. *The Eleanor Roosevelt Papers*. Vol. 1, *The Human Rights Years, 1945–1948*. Detroit: Thomas Gale, 2007.

Stalin, I. V. *Sochineniia*. Vol. 16. Moscow: Izd. ITRK, 2011. (Eng.: Works)

Documentary Publications

Khaustov, V. N., et al., eds. *Lubianka: Stalin i NKVD-NKGB-GUKR "Smersh'"*, *1939–mart 1946*. Moscow: Rossiia XX vek, 2006. (Eng.: Lubianka: Stalin and the NKVD-NKGB and GUKHR's Smersh, 1939–March 1946)

Korotkov, A. V. et al., eds. "Posetiteli kremlevskogo kabineta Stalina." *Istoricheskii arkhiv*, beginning with the 1994 no. 6 issue and concluding with 1997, no. 1. (Eng.: Visitors to Stalin's Kremlin office)

Stalin i kozmopolitizm: Dokumenty agitpropa TsK KPSS, 1945–1953. Moscow: Mezhdunarodnyi Fond "Demokratiia," Izd. "Materik," 2005. (Eng.: Stalin and cosmopolitanism. Documents of the Agitprop Department of the Central Committee of the CPSU, 1945–1953)

Memoirs, Family Histories, and Literary Representations

Acheson, Dean. *Present at the Creation: My Years in the State Department*. London: Hamish Hamilton, 1970.

Balodis, Janis. *Too Young for Ghosts*. Sydney: Currency Press, 1991.

Barto, A. L. *Naiti cheloveka*. Moscow: Geroi otechestva, 2005. (Eng.: To find a person)

Berger, Joseph. *Displaced Persons*. New York: Washington Square Press, 2001.

Briukhanov, Aleksei Ivanovich. *Vot kak eto bylo: O rabote missii po repatriatsii sovetskikh grazhdan (Vospominaniia sovetskogo ofitsera)*. Moscow: Gospolitizdat, 1958. (Eng.: That's how it was: On the work of the mission to repatriate Soviet citizens [Memoirs of a Soviet officer])

Chuev, Felix. *Sto sorok besed s Molotovym: Iz dnevnika F. Chueva*. Moscow: "Terra," 1991 [1970s interviews with Molotov]. (Eng.: 140 conversations with Molotov)

Clay, Lucius. *Decision in Germany*. London: William Heinemann, 1950.

Dichbalis, Sigizmund. *Zigzagi sud'by: Vospominaniia*. Moscow: IPVA, 2003. (Eng.: Zigzags of fate: Memoirs)

Doherty, Muriel Knox. *Letters from Belsen 1945: An Australian Nurse's Experiences with the Survivors of War*. St. Leonard's, NSW: Allen & Unwin, 2000.

Eksteins, Modris. *Walking since Daybreak*. Boston: Houghton Mifflin, 1999.

Halafoff, Irina. *Svidetel' istorii*. Melbourne: University of Melbourne, 1988. (Eng.: Witness to history)

Hilton, Ella E. Schneider. *Displaced Person*. Baton Rouge: Louisiana State University, 2004.

Hulme, Kathryn C. *Undiscovered Country. A Spiritual Adventure*. London: Muller, 1967.

Hulme, Kathryn. *The Wild Place*. Boston: Little, Brown, 1953.

Klemmé, Marvin. *The Inside Story of UNRRA*. New York: Lifetime Editions, 1949.

Konstantinov, Protoierei D. "'Vtoraia volna'—vospominaniia i razdumi'ia o rossiiskoi emigratsii." In Popov, *V poiskakh istiny*, 57–85. (Eng.: The second wave—memories and reflections on the Russian emigration)

Koval, Ramona. *Bloodhound: Searching for My Father*. Melbourne: Text Publishing, 2015.

MacDuffie, Marshal. *The Red Carpet: 10,000 Miles through Russia on a Visa from Khrushchev*. London: Cassel, 1955.

McNeill, Margaret. *By the Rivers of Babylon: A Story of Relief Work among the Displaced Persons of Europe*. London: Bannisdale Press, 1950.

Mitskevich, Denis. "Prelomleniia emigrantskogo opyta." In Flam, *Sud'by pokoleniia*, 309–22. (Eng.: Refraction of emigrant experience)

Morgan, Frederick. *Peace and War: A Soldier's Life*. London: Hodder and Stoughton, 1961.

Nash, Gary. *The Tarasov Saga: From Russia through China to Australia*. Sydney: Rosenberg, 2002.

Nesaule, Agathe. *A Woman in Amber*. New York: Soho Press, 1995.

Nikolajuk, Ivan. *Deda's Memoirs for the Grandchildren*. Translated by Yura Nikolajuk. Melbourne: Self-published, 2020.

Pettiss, Susan T., with Lynne Taylor. *After the Shooting Stopped: The Memoir of an UNRRA Welfare Worker, Germany 1945–1947*. Victoria, BC: Trafford Publishing, 2004.

Popov, A. V., ed. *V poiskakh istiny: Puti i sud'by vtoroi emigratsii*. Moscow: RGGU, Istoriko-arkhivnyi institute, 1997. (Eng.: In search for the truth: Paths and fates of the second emigration)

Plume, Ventis, and John Plume, eds. *Insula Displaced Persons Assembly Center: A Latvian Memoir*. Minneapolis: Kirk House Publishers, 2004.

Priannishnikov, B. *Novopokolentsy*. Silver Spring, MD: Self-published, 1986. (Eng.: People of the new generation)

Schlusser, Eugene. *Escape from the Sun: Surviving the Tyrannies of Lenin, Hitler and Stalin*. Melbourne: Australian Scholarly Publishing, 2017.

Troitskii, N. A. "Put' 'vtoroi volny' i budushchee Rossii." In Popov, *V poiskakh istiny*, 25–55. (Eng.: The path of the "second wave" and the future of Russia)

Russian Newspapers and Journals

Avstraliada (Strathfield, NSW, Australia).

Edinenie (Melbourne, 1951–76; Sydney, 1977–)

Novoe russkoe slovo (New York)

Secondary Sources

Aarons, Mark. *Sanctuary: Nazi Fugitives in Australia*. Melbourne: William Heinemann, 1989.

Aarons, Mark. *War Criminals Welcome: Australia, a Sanctuary for Fugitive War Criminals since 1945*. Melbourne: Black, 2001.

Abella, Irving, and Harold Troper. *None Is Too Many: Canada and the Jews of Europe 1933–1948*. New York: Random House, 1982.

Alexander, Robert J. *Juan Domingo Perón: A History*. New York: Routledge, 2018.

Anderson, Paul B. "The Tolstoy Foundation." *Russian Review*, vol. 17, no. 1, 1958, pp. 60–66.

Antons, Jan-Hinnerk. "Britischer Umgang mit militanten Antikommunisten, Kollaborateuren and mutmasslichen Kriegsverbrechern unter osteuropäischen DPs." In Defrance, Denis, and Maspero, *Personnes déplacées et guerre froide en Allemagne occupée*, 61–75. (Eng.: British approach to militant anti-communists, collaborators and probable war criminals among East European DPs)

Armstrong-Reid, Susan, and David Murray. *Armies of Peace: Canada and the UNRRA Years.* Toronto: University of Toronto Press, 2008.

Arzamaskin, Iu. N. *Tainy sovetskoi repatriatsii.* Moscow: Veche, 2015. (Eng.: Secrets of Soviet repatriation)

Balint, Ruth. *Destination Elsewhere: Displaced Persons and Their Quest to Leave Postwar Europe.* Ithaca, NY: Cornell University Press, 2021.

Balint, Ruth. "Hopscotch Australia: Displaced Persons Taking the Long Way around to the Rest of the World." In Balint, Damousi, and Fitzpatrick, *When Migrants Fail to Stay,* 35–49.

Balint, Ruth, Joy Damousi, and Sheila Fitzpatrick, eds. *When Migrants Fail to Stay: New Histories on Departure and Migration.* London: Bloomsbury Academic, 2023.

Balkelis, Tomas. "Living in the Displaced Persons Camp: Lithuanian War Refugees in the West, 1944–54." In Gatrell and Baron, *Warlands,* 25–47.

Bassler, Gerhard P. *Alfred Valdmanis and the Politics of Survival.* Toronto: University of Toronto Press, 2000.

Bauer, Yehuda. *Out of the Ashes: The Impact of American Jews on Post-Holocaust European Jewry.* Oxford: Pergamon Press, 1989.

Bernstein, Seth. *Return to the Motherland: Displaced Soviet in World War II and the Cold War.* Ithaca, NY: Cornell University Press, 2023.

Best, Geoffrey. *War and Law since 1945.* Oxford: Oxford University Press, 1997.

Bethell, Nicholas. *The Last Secret: Forcible Repatriation to Russia 1944–7.* London: Deutsch, 1974.

Bleiere, Daina, et al. *History of Latvia in the 20th Century.* Riga: Jumava, 2006.

Bon Tempo, Carl J. *Americans at the Gate: The United States and Refugees during the Cold War.* Princeton, NJ: Princeton University Press, 2008.

Brenner, Michael. *After the Holocaust: Rebuilding Jewish Lives in Postwar Germany.* Princeton, NJ: Princeton University Press, 1997.

Brodzki, Bella, and Jeremy Varon. "The Munich Years: The Students of Post-War Germany." In Steinert and Weber-Newth, *Beyond Camps and Forced Labour,* 154–63.

Brubaker, Rogers. "Aftermaths of Empire and the Unmixing of People." *Ethnic and Racial Studies,* vol. 18, no. 2, 1995, pp. 189–218.

Bullock, Alan. *Ernest Bevin, Foreign Secretary, 1945–1951.* Oxford: Oxford University Press, 1983.

Burch, Cecilia Notini. *A Cold War Pursuit: Soviet Refugees in Sweden, 1945–54.* Stockholm: Santérus Academic Press, 2014.

Burlacioiu, Ciprian. "Russian Orthodox Diaspora as a Global Religion after 1918." *Studies in World Christianity,* vol. 24, no. 1, 2018, pp. 4–24.

Carafano, James Jay. "Mobilizing Europe's Stateless: America's Plan for a Cold War Army." *Journal of Cold War Studies,* vol. 1, no. 2, 1999, pp. 61–85.

Carpenter, Inta Gāle. "Folklore as a Source for Creating Exile Identity among Latvian Displaced Persons in Post-World War II Germany." *Journal of Baltic Studies,* vol. 48, no. 2, 2017, pp. 205–33.

Carpenter, Inta Gāle. "Memory-Theater as Cultural Generativity: *Eslingena*: A Musical in Toronto and Riga." *Journal of Baltic Studies,* vol. 38, no. 3, 2007, pp. 317–47.

Carruthers, Susan. *Cold War Captives: Imprisonment, Escape and Brainwashing.* Berkeley: University of California Press, 2009.

Cesarani, David. *Justice Delayed: How Britain Became a Refuge for Nazi War Criminals.* London: Phoenix Press, 2001.

Churyumova, Elvira, and Edward C. Holland. "Kalmyk DPs and the Narration of Displacement in Post-World War II Europe." *Slavic Review*, vol. 80, no. 2, 2021, pp. 341–62.

Cohen, G. Daniel. "Between Relief and Politics: Refugee Humanitarianism in Occupied Germany 1945–1946." *Journal of Contemporary History*, vol. 43, no. 3, 2008, pp. 437–49.

Cohen, Gerard Daniel. *In War's Wake: Jewish Displaced Persons in the Postwar Order*. New York: Oxford University Press, 2012.

Daniels, Roger. *Guarding the Golden Door*. New York: Hill & Wang, 2004.

Deery, Phillip, and Sheila Fitzpatrick, eds. *Russians in Cold War Australia*. London: Rowman and Littlefield, 2024.

Defrance, Corine, Juliette Denis, and Julia Maspero, eds. *Personnes déplacées et guerre froide en Allemagne occupée*. Brussels: Peter Lang, 2015. (Eng.: Displaced persons and Cold War in occupied Germany)

Dinnerstein, Leonard. *America and the Survivors of the Holocaust*. New York: Columbia University Press, 1982.

Divine, Robert A. *American Immigration Policy, 1924–1952*. New Haven: Yale University Press, 1957.

Edele, Mark. *Soviet Veterans of the Second World War*. Oxford: Oxford University Press, 2008.

Edele, Mark, Sheila Fitzpatrick, and Atina Grossmann, eds. *Shelter from the Holocaust: Rethinking Jewish Survival in the Soviet Union*. Detroit: Wayne State University Press, 2017.

Eder, Angelika. "Displaced Persons / 'Heimatlose Ausländer' als Arbeitskräfte in Westdeuschland." *Archiv für Sozialgeschichte*, vol. 42, 2002, pp. 1–17. (Eng.: Displaced persons / "homeless foreigners" as labor force in West Germany)

Elliott, Mark R. *Pawns of Yalta: Soviet Refugees and America's Role in Their Repatriation*. Urbana: University of Illinois Press, 1982.

Fastovskij, Vitalij. "Erzählte Migration: Die 'russische Sache' der Alexandra Tolstoy." In Felix Jeshke, Hannah Maischein and Anke Stephan, eds., *Das osteuropäische München in der Nachkriegszeit und im Kalten Krieg*. Munich: Allitera, forthcoming 2024.

Ferrara, Antonio. "Eugene Kulischer, Joseph Schechtman and the Historiography of Migrations." *Journal of Contemporary History*, vol. 46, no. 4, 2011, pp. 715–40.

Fink, Carole K. *Cold War: An International History*. Boulder, CO: Westview Press, 2017.

Fischer, George. "The New Soviet Emigration." *Russian Review*, vol. 8, no. 1, 1949, pp. 6–19.

Fisher, Fedora Gould. *Raphael Cilento: A Biography*. St. Lucia, Queensland: University of Queensland Press, 1994.

Fitzpatrick, Sheila. "'Determined to Get On': Some Displaced Persons on the Way to a Future." *History Australia*, vol. 12, no. 2, 2015, pp. 102–23.

Fitzpatrick, Sheila. "Justice across the Seas: War Crimes Accusations against Postwar Migrants from 'Displaced Persons' Camps in Europe." In Christina Twomey and Seumas Spark, eds., *Injustice, Survival and Memory in Twentieth-Century Australia*, forthcoming.

Fitzpatrick, Sheila. "Migration of Jewish 'Displaced Persons' from Europe to Australia after the Second World War: Revisiting the Question of Discrimination and Numbers." *Australian Journal of Politics and History*, vol. 67, no. 2, 2021, pp. 226–45.

Fitzpatrick, Sheila. *Mischka's War: A European Odyssey of the 1940s*. Melbourne: Melbourne University Press, 2017.

Fitzpatrick, Sheila. "The Motherland Calls: 'Soft' Repatriation of Soviet Citizens from Europe, 1945–1953." *Journal of Modern History*, vol. 90, no. 2, 2018, pp. 323–50.

Fitzpatrick, Sheila. *On Stalin's Team: The Years of Living Dangerously in Soviet Politics.* Princeton, NJ: Princeton University Press, 2015.

Fitzpatrick, Sheila. "The Prodigals' Return: Voluntary Repatriation to the Soviet Union from Displaced Persons' Camps in Europe, 1949–50." *Cahiers du monde russe,* vol. 62, no. 4, 2021, pp. 529–51.

Fitzpatrick, Sheila. "Russians in the Jungle: Tubabao as a Way Station for Refugees from China to Australia, 1949." *History Australia,* vol. 16, no. 4, 2019, pp. 695–713.

Fitzpatrick, Sheila. "Soviet Repatriation Efforts among 'Displaced Persons' Resettled in Australia, 1950–1953." *Australian Journal of Politics and History,* vol. 63, no. 1, 2017, pp. 45–61.

Fitzpatrick, Sheila. *Tear off the Masks! Identity and Imposture in Twentieth-Century Russia.* Princeton, NJ: Princeton University Press, 2005.

Fitzpatrick, Sheila. "The Tramp's Tale." *Past and Present,* vol. 241, no. 1, 2018, pp. 259–90.

Fitzpatrick, Sheila. *White Russians, Red Peril: A Cold War History of Migration to Australia.* Melbourne: Latrobe University Press, 2021.

Fitzpatrick, Sheila. "The Women's Side of the Story: Soviet 'Displaced Persons' and Postwar Repatriation." *Russian Review,* vol. 81, no. 2, 2022, pp. 284–301.

Flam, Liudmila, ed. *Sud'by pokoleniia, 1920–1930-kh godov v emigratsii.* Moscow: Russkii put', 2006. (Eng.: Fates of a generation, the 1920s and 1930s in emigration)

Flanner, Janet. "Letter from Aschaffenburg." *New Yorker,* October 30, 1948.

Fraser, David. *Daviborshch's Cart: Narrating the Holocaust in Australian War Crimes Trials.* Lincoln: University of Nebraska Press, 2010.

Garland, Libby. *After They Closed the Gates: Jewish Illegal Immigration to the United States, 1921–1965.* Chicago: University of Chicago Press, 2014.

Gatrell, Peter. *The Making of the Modern Refugee.* Oxford: Oxford University Press, 2013.

Gatrell, Peter. *A Whole Empire Walking: Refugees in Russia during World War I.* Bloomington: Indiana University Press, 1999.

Gatrell, Peter, and Nick Baron, eds. *Warlands: Population Resettlement and State Reconstruction in the Soviet-East European Borderlands 1945–50.* New York: Palgrave Macmillan, 2009.

Goffman, Erving. *Asylums.* New York: Anchor Books, 1961.

Goffman, Erving. *Stigma: Notes on the Management of Spoiled Identity.* New York: Simon & Schuster, 1963.

Goldman, Wendy, and Donald Filtzer. *Fortress Dark and Stern: The Soviet Home Front during World War II.* Oxford: Oxford University Press, 2021.

Govorov, Igor Vasilevich. "Fil'tratsiia sovetskikh repatriantov v 40-e gg." *Cahiers du monde russe,* vol. 49, no. 2 / 3, 2008, pp. 365–82. (Eng.: Filtration of Soviet repatriates in the 1940s)

Grossmann, Atina. *Jews, Germans, and Allies: Close Encounters in Occupied Germany.* Princeton, NJ: Princeton University Press, 2007.

Harder, Andrew. "The Politics of Impartiality: The United Nations Relief and Rehabilitation Administration in the Soviet Union, 1946–7." *Journal of Contemporary History,* vol. 47, no. 2, 2012, pp. 347–69.

Heberle, Rudolf, and Dudley S. Hall. *New Americans: A Study of Displaced Persons in Louisiana and Mississippi.* Baton Rouge: Displaced Persons Commission, 1951.

Herbert, Ulrich. *Fremdarbeiter: Politik und Praxis des "Ausländer-Einsatzes" in der Kriegswirtschaft des dritten Reiches.* Berlin: Verlag J. H. W. Dietz, 1986. (Eng.: Foreign workers: Policy and practice of the "Foreigner Units" in the war economy of the Third Reich)

Hilton, Laura. "Cultural Nationalism in Exile: The Case of Polish and Latvian Displaced Persons." *Historian*, vol. 71, no. 2, 2009, pp. 280–317.

Hilton, Laura. "Pawns on a Chessboard? Polish DPs and Repatriation from the US Zone of Occupation of Germany, 1945–1949." In Steinert and Weber-Newth, *Beyond Camps and Forced Labour*, 90–102.

Hirsch, Francine. *Soviet Judgement at Nuremberg*. New York: Oxford University Press, 2020.

Hobsbawm, Eric, and Terence Ranger, eds. *The Invention of Tradition*. Cambridge, UK: Cambridge University Press, 2014.

Holborn, Louise W. *The International Refugee Organization: Its History and Work*. London: Oxford University Press, 1956.

Holian, Anna. *Between National Socialism and Soviet Communism: Displaced Persons in Postwar Germany*. Ann Arbor: University of Michigan Press, 2011.

Holiat, Dr. Roman S. "Short History of the Ukrainian Free University." In Shevchenko Scientific Society, *Papers / Dopovidi*, no. 21, 1964, pp. 9–32.

Horner, David. *The Spy Catchers: The Official History of ASIO, 1949–1962*. Sydney: Allen & Unwin, 2014.

Hyland, Siobhán, and Paul Jackson. "Campaigning for Justice: Anti-Fascist Campaigners, Nazi-Era Collaborator War Criminals and Britain's Failure to Prosecute 1945–1999." In Tom Lawson and Andy Pearce, eds., *The Palgrave Handbook of Britain and the Holocaust*, 201–18. Cham, Switzerland: Palgrave-Macmillan, 2020.

Isajiw, Wsevolod W. "The Ukrainian Diaspora." In Allon Gai et al., eds., *The Call of the Homeland: Diaspora Nationalism, Past and Present*, 289–319. Leiden: Brill, 2010.

Isajiw, Wsevolod W., Yury Boshyk, and Roman Senkus, eds. *The Refugee Experience: Ukrainian Displaced Persons after World War II*. Edmonton: University of Alberta, 1992.

Jacobmeyer, Wolfgang. *Vom Zwangsarbeiter zum heimatlosen Ausländer: Die Displaced Persons in Westdeutschland 1945–1951*. Göttingen: Vandenhoeck & Ruprecht, 1985. (Eng.: From forced laborer to homeless foreigner. The displaced persons in West Germany, 1945–1951)

Janco, Andrew Paul. "'Unwilling': The One-Word Revolution in Refugee Status, 1940–51." *Contemporary European History*, vol. 23, no. 3, 2014, 429–46.

Jensen, Kenneth M., ed. *Origins of the Cold War: The Novikov, Kennan, and Roberts "Long Telegrams" of 1946*. Washington, DC: US Institute for Peace, 1991.

Jones, Heather. "A Missing Paradigm: Military Captivity and the Prisoner of War, 1914–18." *Immigrants & Minorities*, vol. 26, no. 1 / 2, 2008, 19–48.

Kanevskaia, G. I. *"My eshche mechtaem o Rossii . . ." Istoriia russkoi diaspory v Avstralii*. Vladivostok: Izd. Dalnevostochnogo Universiteta, 2010. (Eng.: "We still dream of Russia . . ." The history of the Russian diaspora in Australia)

Kasenkina, Oksana. *Leap to Freedom*. Philadelphia: J. B. Lippincott, 1949.

Kay, Diana. "Westward Ho! The Recruitment of Displaced Persons for British Industry." In Johannes-Dieter Steinert and Inge Weber-Newth, eds., *European Immigration in Britain 1933–1950*, 151–70. Berlin-Boston: K. G. Saur, 2019 reprint [2003].

Keenleyside, Hugh L. *Canadian Immigration Policy*. Vancouver: University of British Columbia, 1948.

Khodarkovsky, Michael. *Where Two Worlds Meet: The Russian State and the Kalmyk Nomads, 1600–1771*. Ithaca, NY: Cornell University Press, 2006.

Knight, Robert. "National Construction Work and Hierarchies of Empathy in Postwar Austria." *Journal of Contemporary History*, vol. 49, no. 3, 2014, pp. 491–513.

Kochavi, Arieh J. "British Policy on Non-Repatriable Displaced Persons in Germany and Austria, 1946–1947." *European History Quarterly*, no. 21, 1991, pp. 205–382.

Kochavi, Arieh J. *Prelude to Nuremberg: Allied War Crimes Policy and the Question of Punishment.* Chapel Hill: University of North Carolina Press, 1998.

Kostyrchenko, Gennady. *Out of the Shadows: Anti-Semitism in Stalin's Russia.* Amherst, MA: Prometheus, 1995.

Kuhlmann-Smirnov, Anne. *"Stiller als Wasser, tiefer als Gras": Zur Migrationsgeschichte der russischen Displaced Persons in Deutschland nach dem Zweiten Weltkrieg.* Working paper of Forschungstelle Osteuropa, an der Universität Bremen, no. 68, 2005. (Eng.: Quieter than the water, deeper than the grass: Toward a migration history of Russian displaced persons in Germany after the Second World War)

Kulischer, Eugene. *The Displacement of Population in Europe.* Montreal: International Labour Office, 1943.

Kulischer, Eugene M. *Europe on the Move: War and Population Changes, 1917–47.* New York: Columbia University Press, 1948.

Kunz, Egon F. *Displaced Persons: Calwell's New Australians.* Sydney: Australian National University Press, 1988.

Leffler, Melvyn P. A. *Preponderance of Power: National Security, the Truman Administration, and the Cold War.* Stanford: Stanford University Press, 1992.

Leffler, Melvyn P., and Odd Arne Westad, eds. *The Cambridge History of the Cold War.* Cambridge, UK: Cambridge University Press, 2010.

Litvak, Yosef. "Jewish Refugees from Poland in the USSR, 1939–1946." In Zvi Gitelman, ed., *Bitter Legacy: Confronting the Holocaust in the USSR*, 123–50. Bloomington: Indiana University Press, 1997.

Loescher, Gil, and John A. Scanlan. *Calculated Kindness: Refugees and America's Half-Open Door, 1945 to the Present.* New York: Simon & Schuster, 1986.

Luciuk, Lubomyr Y. "'This Should Never Be Spoken or Quoted Publicly': Canada's Ukrainians and Their Encounter with the DPs." In Lubomyr Y. Luciuk and Stella Hryniuk, eds., *Canada's Ukrainians: Negotiating an Identity*, 103–22. Toronto: University of Toronto Press, 1991.

Maiksins, Gregory. *The Baltic Riddle.* New York: L. B. Fischer, 1943.

Markus, Andrew. "Labour and Immigration, 1946–9: The Displaced Persons Program." *Labour History*, no. 13, 1983, pp. 73–90.

Marrus, Michael R. *The Unwanted: European Refugees in the Twentieth Century.* New York: Oxford University Press, 1985.

Mikkonen, Simo. "Not By Force Alone: Soviet Return Migration in the 1950s." In Scott Soo et al., eds., *Coming Home? Vol. 1, Conflict and Return Migration in the Aftermath of Europe's Twentieth-Century Civil Wars*, 183–200. Newcastle upon Tyne: Cambridge Scholars, 2013.

Momryk, Myron. "Ukrainian DP Immigration and Government Policy in Canada, 1946–52." In Isajiw, Boshyk, and Senkus, *Refugee Experience*, pp. 413–34.

Moseikina, M. N. *"Rasseiany, no ne rastorgnuty": Russkaia emigratsiia v stranakh Latinskoi Ameriki v 1920–1960 gg.* Moscow: RUDN, 2011. (Eng.: Scattered but not torn apart: The Russian emigration in the countries of Latin America, 1920s to 1960s)

Moseikina, M. N., A. V. Antoshin, and E. S. Golousova. *Russkaia diaspora v Argentine: Istoriia i sovremennost'*. Moscow: Rossiiskii universitet druzhby narodov, 2022. (Eng.: Russian diaspora in Argentina)

Nachtigall, Reinhard. "The Repatriation and Reception of Returning Prisoners of War, 1918–22." *Immigrants & Minorities*, vol. 26, no. 1–2, 2008, pp. 157–84.

Naimark, Norman. *The Russians in Germany: A History of the Soviet Zone of Occupation, 1945–1949*. Cambridge, MA: Belknap Press, 1995.

Naimark, Norman. *Stalin and the Fate of Europe: The Postwar Struggle for Sovereignty*. Cambridge, MA: Harvard University Press, 2019.

Nasaw, David. *The Last Million: Europe's Displaced Persons from World War to Cold War*. New York: Penguin Press, 2020.

Nilsson, Ebony. *Displaced Comrades: Politics and Surveillance in the Lives of Soviet Refugees in the West*. London: Bloomsbury Academic, 2023.

Nitoburg, E. L. "Russkie 'peremeshchennye litsa' v SShA: Istoriia i sud'by." *Novaia i noveishaia istoriia*, no. 4, 2001, pp. 11–26 (Eng.: Russian "displaced persons" in the USA: History and fates)

Oberlander, Edwin. "The All-Russian Fascist Party." *Journal of Contemporary History*, vol. 1, no. 1, 1966, pp. 158–73.

Overy, Richard. *Russia's War*. London: Penguin, 1998.

Patt, Avinoam, and Kierra Crago-Schneider. "Years of Survival: JDC in Postwar Germany, 1945–1947." In Avinoam Patt et al., *The JDC at 100*, 361–420. Detroit: Wayne State University Press, 2019.

Pechatnov, Vladimir O. "The Soviet Union and the World 1944–53." In Melvyn P. Leffler and Odd Arne Westad, eds., *The Cambridge History of the Cold War*, 99–111. Cambridge, UK: Cambridge University Press, 2010.

Penter, Tanja. "Local Collaborators on Trial: Soviet War Crimes Trials under Stalin (1945–1953)." *Cahiers du monde russe*, vol. 49, no. 2 / 3, 2008, pp. 341–64.

Persian, Jayne. *Beautiful Balts: From Displaced Persons to New Australians*. Sydney: NewSouth, 2017.

Persian, Jayne. "Cossack Identities: From Russian Émigrés and Anti-Soviet Collaborators to Displaced Persons." *Immigrants and Minorities*, vol. 3, no. 26, 2018, pp. 125–42.

Persian, Jayne. "'Far Right Security Risks?' Deportations and Extradition Requests of Displaced Persons, 1947–1952." In Balint, Damousi, and Fitzpatrick, *When Migrants Fail to Stay*, pp. 51–66.

Persian, Jayne. *Fascists in Exile: Post-War Displaced Persons in Australia*. London: Routledge, 2023.

Pletzing, Christian, and Marianne, eds. *Displaced Persons: Flüchtlinge aus den baltischen Staaten in Deutschland*. Munich: Martin Meienbauer, 2007 (Eng.: Displaced Persons: refugees from the Baltic states in Germany)

Pritsak, Omelian. "The Present State of Ukrainian Studies." *Canadian Slavonic Papers / Revue canadienne des slavistes*, vol. 14, no. 2, 1972, pp. 139–52.

Popenhagen, Luda. *Australian Lithuanians*. Sydney: UNSW Press, 2012.

Purs, Aldis. "'How Those Brothers in Foreign Lands Are Dividing the Fatherland': Latvian National Politics in Displaced Persons Camps after the Second World War." In Gatrell and Baron, *Warlands*, 48–65.

Reinisch, Jessica. "'Auntie UNRRA' at the Crossroads." *Past & Present*, no. 218, 2013, pp. 70–97.

Riabova, A. V. "Organizatsionno-normativnaia baza 'fil'tratsii' sovetskikh grazhdan v 1940-e-nachale 1950-kh gg." In *Marginaly v sovetskom obshchestve: Mekhanizmy i praktika statusnogo regulirovaniia v 1930-1950-e gody. Sbornik nauch. statei.* Novosibirsk: Novosibirskii gosudarstvennyi universitet, 2006, 134–65. (Eng.: Organizational and normative basis of "filtration" of Soviet citizens in the 1940s and the beginning of the 1950s)

Roh, Kyung Deok. *Stalin's Economic Advisors: The Varga Institute and the Making of Soviet Foreign Policy.* London: I. B. Tauris, 2018.

Rolinek, Susanne. "Clandestine Operators: The *Bricha* and *Betar* Network in the Salzburg Area, 1945–1948." *Journal of Israeli History*, vol. 19, no. 3, 2008, pp. 41–61.

Rutland, Suzanne D. *Edge of the Diaspora: Two Centuries of Jewish Settlement in Australia.* Sydney: Brandl and Schlesinger, 2001.

Ryan, Allan A. *Quiet Neighbors: Nazi War Criminals in America.* San Diego: Harcourt Brace Jovanovich, 1984.

Salomon, Kim. *Refugees in the Cold War: Toward a New International Refugee Regime in the Early Postwar Era.* Lund: Lund University Press, 1991.

Schamberger, Karen. "Weaving a Family and a Nation through Two Latvian Looms." *Immigrants and Minorities*, vol. 36, no. 2, 2018, pp. 178–98.

Schechtman, Joseph B. *Postwar Population Transfers in Europe, 1945–1955.* Philadelphia: University of Pennsylvania Press, 1962.

Schroeder, Stefan. *Displaced Persons im Landkreis und in der Stadt Münster 1945–1951.* Münster: Schoendorff Verlag, 2005. (Eng. Displaced persons in the region and city of Munster, 1945–1951)

Seipp, Adam R. *Strangers in the Wild Place: Refugees, Americans and a German Town, 1945–52.* Bloomington: Indiana University Press, 2013.

Shephard, Ben. "'Becoming Planning Minded': The Theory and Practice of Relief 1940–1945." *Journal of Contemporary History*, vol. 43, no. 3, 2008, pp. 405–19.

Shephard, Ben. *The Long Road Home: The Aftermath of the Second World War.* New York: Vintage Books, 2012.

Sheviakov, A. "Repatriatsiia sovetskogo mirnogo naseleniia i voennoplennykh, okazavshikhsia v okkupatsionnykh zonakh gosudarstv antigitlerovskoi koalitsii" In *Naselenie Rossii v 1920–1950 gg.: Chislennost', poteri, migratsii.* Moscow: Institute rossiiskoi istorii RAN, 1994, 195–222. (Eng.: Repatriation of Soviet civilians and prisoners of war who found themselves in the occupied zones of states of the anti-Hitler coalition)

Simpson, Christopher. *Blowback: America's Recruitment of Nazis and Its Effects on the Cold War.* New York: Weidenfeld & Nicolson, 1988,

Slaveski, F. *Remaking Ukraine after WWII: The Clash of Central and Local Soviet Power, 1944–1953.* Cambridge, UK: Cambridge University Press.

Smolorz, Roman. "Der Alltag der osteuropäischen Displaced Persons 1945–1949 unter dem Einfluss von ost- und westeuropäischen Geheimdiensten." In Defrance, Denis, and Maspero, *Personnes déplacées et guerre froide en Allemagne occupée*, 199–211.

Speed, Richard B, III. *Prisoners, Diplomats and the Great War.* New York: Greenwood Press, 1990.

Steinert, Johannes-Dieter, and Inge Weber-Newth, eds. *Beyond Camps and Forced Labour: Current International Research on Survivors of Nazi Persecution. Proceedings of the First International*

Multidisciplinary Conference at the Imperial War Museum, London, January 29–31. Osnabrück: Secolo-Verlag, 2005.

Steinacher, Gerald. *Nazis on the Run.* New York: Oxford University Press, 2011.

Stoessinger, John G., with the assistance of Robert G. McKelvey. *The United Nations and the Superpowers: United States-Soviet Interaction at the United Nations.* New York: Random House, 1967.

Taylor, Lynne. "'Please Report Only *True* Nationalities': The Classification of Displaced Persons in Post-Second World War Germany and Its Implications." In David Cesarani et al., eds., *Survivors of Nazi Persecution in Europe after the Second World War.* London: Vallentine Mitchell, 2010, 3553.

Tegeler, Tillman. "Esten, Letten und Litauer in Nachkriegsdeutschland." In Pletzing and Pletzing, *Displaced Persons*, 13–27. (Eng. Latvians and Lithuanians in Postwar Germany)

Tolstoy, Alexandra. "The Russian DPs." *Russian Review*, vol. 9, no. 1, 1950, pp. 53–58.

Tolstoy, Nikolai. *Victims of Yalta.* London: Hodder & Stoughton, 1977.

Tromly, Benjamin. *Cold War Exiles and the CIA.* Oxford: Oxford University Press, 2019.

Tündern-Smith, Ann. *Bonegilla's Beginnings.* Wagga Wagga, New South Wales: Triple D Books, 2007.

Vager, M. "Baltic Academic DPs in Germany." *Baltic Review*, no. 7–8, 1947, 395–99.

Vernant, Jacques. *The Refugee in the Post-War World: Preliminary Report of a Survey of the Refugee Problem.* Geneva: United Nations, 1951.

von Holleufer, Henriette. *Zwischen Fremde und Fremde: Displaced Persons in Australien, den USA und Kanada 1946–1952.* Osnabrück: Universitätsverlag Rasch, 2001. (Eng: Among strangers and strangers. Displaced persons in Australia, USA and Canada, 1946–1952)

Wagner, Patrick. *Displaced Persons in Hamburg: Stationen einer halbherzigen Integration 1945–1948.* Hamburg: Dölling und Galitz, 1997 (Eng.: Displaced Persons in Hamburg. Way stations of a half-hearted integration)

Woodbridge, George. *UNRRA: The History of the United Nations Relief and Rehabilitation Administration.* 3 vols. New York: Columbia University Press, 1950.

Wyman, Mark. *DPs: Europe's Displaced Persons, 1945–51.* Ithaca, NY: Cornell University Press, 1998.

Yergin, Daniel. *Shattered Peace: The Origins of the Cold War and the National Security State.* New York: Penguin Books, 1977.

Zahra, Tara. *The Great Departure: Mass Migration from Eastern Europe and the Making of the Free World.* New York: Norton, 2016.

Zahra, Tara. *The Lost Children: Reconstructing Europe's Families after World War II* Cambridge, MA: Harvard University Press, 2011.

Zahra, Tara. "Prisoners of the Postwar: Expellees, Displaced Persons, and Jews in Austria after World War II." *Austrian History Yearbook*, vol. 41, 201, pp. 191–215.

Zake, Ieva. *American Latvians.* New Brunswick, NJ: Transaction Publishers, 2010.

Zake, Ieva. "The 'Secret Nazi Network:' Post World War II Latvian Immigrants and the Hunt for Nazis in the United States." *Baltic Studies*, vol. 41, no. 2, 2010, pp. 91–117.

Zemskov, V. N. *Vozvrashchenie sovetskikh peremeshchennykh lits v SSSR 1944–1952 gg.* Moscow: Tsentr gumanitarnykh initiativ, 2016. (Eng.: The return of Soviet displaced persons to the USSR, 1944–1952)

Zemskov, V. N. "'Vtoraia emigratsiia' i otnoshenie k nei rukovodstva SSSR, 1947–1955." In Iu. Poliakov et al., eds., *Istoriia rossiiskogo zarubezh'ia: Emigratsiia iz SSSR-Rossii 1941–2001*, 63–91. Moscow: Institute Rossiiskoi istorii RAN, 2007. (Eng.: The "second emigration" and the Soviet Union's attitude to it, 1947–1955)

Zuroff, Efraim. *Occupation: Nazi-Hunter: The Continuing Search for Perpetrators of the Holocaust.* Hoboken, NJ: KTAV, 1994.

INDEX

Acheson, Dean, 17, 37

acts: Displaced Persons Act 1948, 117, 179, 181–85, 252; Internal Security Act 1950, 185, 201; Lodge-Philbin Act 1950, 112; Refugee Relief Act 1953, 216–17

adventure, displaced status as: traveling men, 132–36; traveling women, 136–38

Africa, ix, 114–15

agency, 2–4, 73–76, 87, 253–55; voluntary repatriation, 6, 46, 217–22

Akulshin, Rodion, 239

Amis, 110–11, 130–31, 284n8. *See also* army

Amr Ibrahim, Prince, 195

Anders Army, 133–34, 191

Anti-Bolshevik Bloc of Nations (ABN), 98, 100

antisemitism, 22, 27, 35, 164

anti-Sovietism, 51, 67–69, 76, 95–96, 255; ABN, 98, 100; and CIA, 164; NTS, 82–85, 101, 193, 214, 216. *See also* communism

Arājs, Viktors, 247

archives, 8

Argentina, 191

army, Allied: Amis, 110–11, 130–31, 284n8; DP employment in, 110–15; and DP marriages, 130–31, 290n5; and Jews, 26; and repatriation, 42, 48; and UNRRA, 20–21, 24–25, 29–30. *See also* Anders Army; French Foreign Legion; Vlasov Army

Asia, ix

Atlee, Clement, 14

atomic bomb, 14, 163

Australia, ix, 185–88, 219; *Avstraliada*, 8; Catholics in, 186; and collaborators, 188;

200, 215; and DP labor, 160, 186–88; and Jewish DPs, 186–88, 195; Orthodox Church in, 186; and race, 187–88, 195; resettlement numbers in, 229, 259; and returnees, 237–40, 242–45; and war criminals, 249–50

Austria, 42, 233–35, 262n2

Avstraliada, 8

babies, 126–28. *See also* children

Baidalakov, Viktor, 216

Balkelis, Tomas, 78

Balmelle, Philippe, 84–85

Baltic DPs, 4–5, 39, 75, 181, 229, 252; agency of, 75, 255; and anti-Sovietism, 68, 76, 96, 255; and Australia, 188; Baltic University, 122–23; and collaboration, 32, 47 (*see also* Baltic Waffen-SS; Latvian Legion; Vald-manis, Alfred); education level of, 309n14; and labor, 108–9, 211–12; nationalism, 99–100; and nationality, 31–32, 88, 267n18; refugees on *Emma*, 204–5; repatriates, 222–23. *See also* Estonian DPs; Latvian DPs; Lithuanian DPs

Baltic University, 122–23

Baltic Waffen-SS, 171–74, 227, 247

Bandera, Stepan, 98

Banderites, 65, 98, 215

Barto, Agniya, 60

Barwick, Garfield, 245

Bauer, Yehuda, 26

Bavaria, 122

Bedo, Alexander, 171

Belgium, 103, 115, 117–18, 179, 219

Polish DPs, 35–36; adventurers among, 133–34, 136–37; Anders Army, 133–34, 191; births among, 128; and education, 286n16; and labor, 108, 113; Polish Jews, 5, 27, 41, 94; as students, 120; in Wildflecken camp, 35–36, 77, 81, 108, 127, 156, 213
politics, 94–101; anti-Soviet (*see* anti-Sovietism)
Pollack, Hansi, 178
Poppe, Nikolai, 215
Posev, 101, 214
Potsdam, 14, 162
POWs (prisoners of war), 1–2; repatriation of, 23–24, 29, 41–45, 57; Soviet, 100–101; and UNRRA DP mandate, 29; and Waffen-SS, 172; war criminals, 67
Prande, Rasma, 88
Price, Ralph, 47
Prince Amr Ibrahim, 195
prisoners of war. *See* POWs
PX stores, 90, 130

Quakers, 24, 156, 213

race, 252; and Australia, 187–88, 195; and Canada, 190; and Jews, 183; and Kalmyks, 196–99, 304n24; and Mongols, 194, 196–99, 252; and Tartars, 196, 303n22; and Turks, 194–95
Radin, Rhea, 166
radio, 55
Red Cross, 24
Red scare, 161
Refugee Relief Act 1953, 216–17
refugees: Baltic, 204–5; definition of, 155, 297n16; IGCR, 48, 115, 156, 158; Refugee Relief Act 1953, 216–17; Spanish, 202, 305n28. *See also* DPs
rehabilitation, 21
religion. *See* churches; Zionism
remainers, 6
repatriates. *See* returnees
repatriation, 6, 14; and anti-Sovietism, 51, 67–69, 76, 95–96, 255; of children, 60–63,

165–66, 275n18; closure of Soviet Repatriation Mission, 166–67; and Cold War, 1–2; of Cossacks, 42, 145; and DP letters, 55–56; and DP lists, 51–53, 57; and education, 123; and false identities, 4, 169; filtration during, 44–45; forced, 23–24, 39–43; of forced laborers (Ostarbeiter), 23–24, 41, 43–45; and human rights, 59; and IRO mandate, 154, 161, 296n13; and Jews, 5, 23, 41; and Poland, 35–36, 41; of POWs, 23–24, 29, 41–45, 57; Repatriation Agency (Moscow), 46, 271n6; *vs.* resettlement, 48, 164–65, 167; and Soviet liaison officers, 47, 51–57, 166, 273n12; and Soviet nationality, 31–32, 40; Soviet repatriation agents, 242–44; of Soviet war criminals, 45–46, 58–59, 64–67; statistics on, 308n10; and UNRRA, 23–25, 40, 45, 47–49; voluntary, 6, 46, 217–22. *See also* UNRRA
Repatriation Agency (Moscow), 46, 271n6
resettlement, 6; agency of DPs in, 76–77; and Amis, 110–11; in Australia, 160, 185–88, 219, 229, 259; in Belgium, 103, 117–18, 179, 219, 259; in Britain, 58, 116–17, 179, 229, 259; in Canada, 160, 188–90, 229, 259; and Cold War, 2, 7, 153–54, 160–61, 252–56; and collaborators, 169–77, 180, 184–85, 188, 191, 199–201, 215–17; and communists, 180, 184–85, 190, 201–3, 205; in France, 103, 118, 259, 286n15; of hard core (*see* hard core); impediments to, 223–26; and Kalmyks, 196–99, 304n24; in Latin America, 191–92, 229, 259; and marriage, 129–32, 211, 213, 290n5; in Morocco, 85, 193; and nationality, 88–90; numbers measuring, 229, 259; in Palestine/Israel, 26–27, 157–59, 165, 179, 192–93, 208, 229, 259; projects of, 157; *vs.* repatriation, 48, 164–65, 167; and returnees (*see* returnees); and ship travel, 226–28; in Soviet Union, 217–23, 240–45; and sponsorship, 183–84, 212–14; in